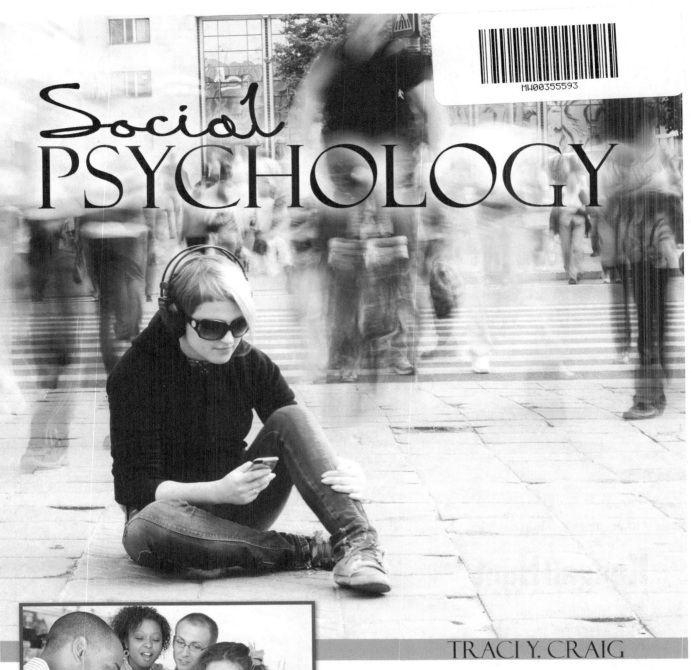

Social
PSYCHOLOGY

TRACI Y. CRAIG

University of Idaho

Kendall Hunt
publishing company

www.kendallhunt.com
Send all inquiries to:
4050 Westmark Drive
Dubuque, IA 52004-1840

Contents

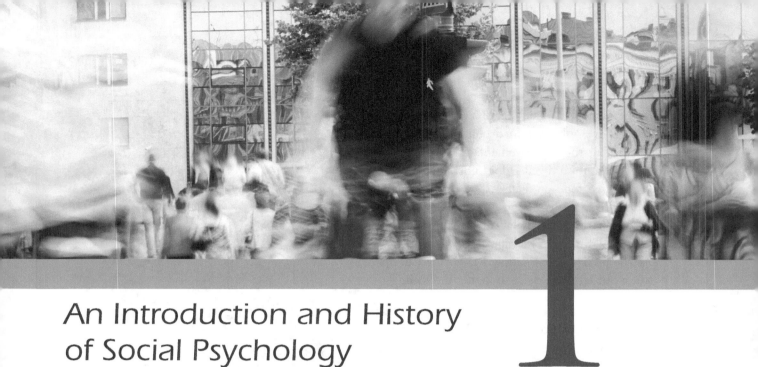

An Introduction and History of Social Psychology

1

What Is Social Psychology?

Social psychology is the study of person–situation interactions. Social psychology is a social scientific approach to understanding and explaining how thoughts, feelings, and behaviors of individuals are influenced by the actual, imagined, or implied presence of other human beings.

First, social psychologists are not concerned solely with behavior, but rather the ABC triad of **A**ffect (i.e., feelings), **B**ehavior, and **C**ognitions (i.e., thoughts). Examining only the behavior of a person does not provide much insight into cognitions that may lead to a future behavior. For example, a person living in a

Image © Juergen Faelchle, 2014. Used under license from Shutterstock, Inc.

rural area may routinely be exposed to commercial advertisements for restaurants that are not available locally. If we only examined behavior, we might conclude that the advertisements are not very effective as the rural dweller does not ever purchase the advertised food products. However, if we also examine the cognitive and affective experiences after watching the commercial we may find that this person is highly interested and motivated to purchase the products, but simply has not had an opportunity to act upon these thoughts and feelings.

There are a number of interesting concepts in this definition. Let us now consider the actual, imagined, or implied presence of others. It is relatively straightforward that the actual presence of someone else would change your behavior. Not cursing in front of your grandmother or children, demonstrates this well. However, when considering the role of imagination or implication we can also understand that even when we are "actually" alone we behave in ways that belie our social nature. Consider shopping in a convenience store, when you notice the security cameras or surveillance mirrors, there is an implied other. Even if you have no intention of stealing, people often behave differently with this awareness.

If you have a roommate, you likely behave in a particularly polite and modest way in their presence, employing social etiquette. However, if you arrive home and see that your roommate is gone, you might take up more of the shared living space with a project, or turn your music up loud. Now consider arriving home after work to find your roommate hanging out in the shared living space. You decide to retire to your room and turn on some music or watch a movie on your laptop. You might intentionally wear headphones to do this and refrain from laughing out loud too much during funny portions of the movie. After a bit you decide to take a break and venture out into the shared living space, where you find that your roommate is no longer home. There is a sense that you might have behaved differently had you known you were alone, but your roommate's implied presence changed your behavior.

The basic premise of social psychology is that the complexity of human experience lies not only within the person but is also reliant on situational factors. Ideas about peer pressure, groupthink, stereotyping, discrimination, and marketing are not solely about individuals but about individuals embedded in a rich social context. Psychology is literally the study of the mind. Psychologists primarily focus on understanding how individuals perceive, think about, and interact with the world. Social psychologists are certainly interested in understanding people, but are particularly interested in understanding how situations impact individuals.

Social Psychology: A Distinct Social Science

The primary distinction between social psychology and other fields is best understood by exploring the level of analysis. For example, students often mistake a social psychology course for a sociology course, but the level of analysis and the fields operate relatively independent of one another.

Social psychology is a social science, distinct from other social sciences, although sociologists and social psychologists do have some similar topical interests. For example, both sociologists and social psychologists study prejudice and discrimination. The primary distinction concerns the level of analysis. Sociologists are interested in the study of social systems or societal level concerns. However, social psychologists are concerned with the impact of situations on individuals. Consider a case of discrimination in a large, federally funded corporation. A sociologist might discuss the topic as one of institutionalized oppression or societal levels of bias and systems of oppression. A social psychologist is going to ask questions about what situational factors led to a particular act of discrimination. In addition, social psychologists are interested in understanding the specific impact on the individual(s) against whom the discrimination occurred and on the individuals who carried out the discriminatory act.

There are also branches of psychology that share common interests (e.g., aggression, helping behavior, cognition) that still differ in their level of analysis. For example, a clinical approach to aggression focuses on individual mental health as a cause or consequence of aggression. A developmental psychologist might be interested in how aggressive responses change as a person ages through developmental stages. A cognitive psychologist might be more interested in how easily words are remembered that have affective meanings (i.e., aggression, fight, anger, hate). Personality psychologists might focus on individuals who have a predisposition toward aggression. Social psychologists are interested in how others and situations impact individual responses to aggression or elicit aggressive responses in individuals.

Historical Contexts

Plato is often credited as being the first person to discuss the idea of the "crowd mind." It is clear that Plato understood that there was a significant impact of other people on our own behavior but also an impact on an individual's thoughts. However, as a philosopher there was little experimental evidence to substantiate his claim beyond that it

resonated with people who hear the idea. Indeed, when you first consider how you behave when in a crowd or with others compared to your behaviors when alone, you can intuitively understand the attractiveness of this idea.

Norman Triplett conducted a study in 1898 in which children were asked to use a fishing reel apparatus to move a flag along a silk cord. Participants did this either alone or while competing with another participant. Triplett concluded from his experiment that the presence of another person improved performance. It was not until 2005 that Strube conducted statistical analyses on these results to determine whether there was support for Triplett's conclusion. The results indicate that the effect of facilitation seems largely driven by two left-handed participants who had carried out the task using their right hands (Stroebe, 2012).

Thus, this often-noted study remains popular in textbooks because it was cited in Allport's 1924 textbook. However, there were other experiments exploring the idea of social facilitation conducted prior to Triplett's experiment. Stroebe (2012) reports the first experiment may have been Féré's 1887 experiment, in which participants engaged in a hand grip task and their efforts exerted were found to be greater when another person also engaged in that task with them. While these early experiments have some relation to social psychology, the questions the researchers sought to answer had little to do with the power of the situation upon the individual and were often designed to answer questions about human performance (Stroebe, 2012). Stroebe also suggests that 1924 might be the year in which social psychological experimentation began in earnest with the publication of Allport's 1924 textbook which provides the definition of social psychology.

Where does that leave *social facilitation*? Social facilitation is an effect that occurs when the presence of others improves our performance on task. However, social facilitation does not occur when a task is difficult. For difficult tasks, performance may actually suffer when others are present. Consider what tasks you do well or find simple to complete. It is likely that you are even better or quicker at completing these tasks when other people are present than if you are alone. Routine runners, who frequently go on solitary runs, find that having a running partner greatly enhances their speed and the other person helps to set and maintain the pace and the pace remains consistent. Why is this?

One early explanation was that the presence of other individuals enhances competition. However, even the mere presence of others observing was sufficient to produce social facilitation (Cottrell, Wack, Sekerak, & Rittle, 1968). Perhaps we do better at the task because we are concerned that we are being evaluated by others.

Robert Zajonc (1965) forwarded an alternative explanation. The presence of other people increases physiological arousal (heart rate, blood pressure, breath rate) and this in turn enhances our ability to perform simple or routine behaviors more quickly. Physiological arousal increases dominant responses or responses that are most common in a particular situation.

On the other hand if the tasks you must do are novel, complex, or challenging you might do better at them if you were left on your own to sort it out. Congruent with the evaluation apprehension explanation above, that if we are able to work without evaluation on a complex task then we may be willing to try a wider variety of approaches and learn from trial and error approaches to the task rather than failing to act for fear of making an error. In addition, the increase in physiological arousal that leads to a dominant or common response will also lead people to reproduce common errors when doing a more challenging task.

One example of dominant responding leading to poor performance on difficult tasks is that novel errors are less likely than common errors. Ted has been practicing a speech for a number of days to give in his public speaking course. Each time he comes to the part of the speech where he must explain a complex idea, he reverses two key concepts. When he gives this speech in front of other people and physiological arousal increases, the chances are that he will repeat this common error. It is unlikely that he will make an entirely new error in the speech.

In the early 1900s, psychologists were predominantly focused on behaviorist perspectives. In order to fit with other natural and empirical sciences, psychologists felt it was necessary to rely on what could be seen in order to understand behavior. This philosophical approach to knowledge is *logical positivism*, namely knowledge should be verified through direct observation. Psychologists John Watson and B.F. Skinner were predominantly running experiments that relied on behavioral responses to stimuli, without forwarding any hypotheses or speculation about what might be going on in the mind. However, some psychologists understood that the same stimulus presented to two different individuals might result in two different behaviors due to differences in the individuals' perception or beliefs about the stimulus. Social psychologists realized that it was imperative to not only understand how a person behaves toward a stimulus, but that the behavior is predicted in some part due to the stimulus itself and in some part due to the perception a person has of that stimulus and situation.

In 1908, William McDougall, an English psychologist, published the first textbook on social psychology. The same year an American sociologist, Edward Ross, also published a social psychology text. The distinction between these texts reflects the distinction between sociological and psychological approaches today. The McDougall text focused predominantly on the individual and situation, whereas the Ross text focused on societal structure. The third social psychology text authored by Floyd Allport in 1924 proposed that social psychologists should move beyond philosophical approaches to social psychological ideas and employ rigorous experimental methodology to understand the ways in which individuals perceive and subsequently respond to a variety of situations and stimuli.

Kelley (1950) told students in a course that a guest speaker would be giving the day's lecture. The students were given some short instructions indicating that a study was being conducted in which reactions to having a different instructor were to be gathered. The students were also given a brief biographical sketch of the guest speaker. For some of the students the description indicated that the guest speaker was "rather cold" and for others that the speaker was "very warm." Everything else in the biographical sketch was the same. He was described as a graduate student with three semesters of teaching experience. He was 26 years old, a veteran and married. After the guest speaker the students were asked to evaluate the speaker. The results were clear. The students who were told the guest speaker was "warm" indicated he was more considerate of others, informal, sociable, popular, and humorous than the students who read the same description that included the descriptor "rather cold." Remember the key is that everyone saw the same lecture, the same person giving it, but their interpretation of the lecture was quite different depending upon this adjective that framed their perceptions.

Social psychologists also realized that our perceptions are shaped by others and this social influence has a large impact on our perceptions and behavior. In the warm/cold lecturer study above, imagine that instead of reading the description of the lecturer you were sitting in the hallway waiting for the class doors to open. While sitting there you hear five or six other students discuss the same traits that were presented in the description. Hearing other people discuss the lecturer's style will likely have a similar influence on your evaluations of the speaker after the class, just as reading the description would.

The Great Depression and World War II led social psychologists to turn their attention to social problems and to apply their knowledge to the emerging concerns brought on by an economic crisis and a need to ration and work for the U.S. war efforts. Kurt Lewin arrived in the United States after fleeing Nazi Germany. He arrived at MIT, founded the Group Dynamics lab, and began working on issues of group decision making and social influence. Shortly after his arrival he was called upon to help the U.S. government persuade citizens to consume organ meats in order to promote rationing during the war. Dr. Lewin made persuasive appeals to housewives. The merits of eating organ meat for the war effort— nutritional value and financial conservation—were routinely delivered to a group of women who were primarily responsible for cooking meals. This lecturing and persuasive appeal was hardly convincing and only a very few of these women changed their household menus. Lewin found it was far more effective to have the women engage in a group discussion about the same material. At the conclusion of this group discussion more women made a final public commitment by show of hands to serve these meats in their homes. The presence of others committing to serving the organ meats was evidenced by their own discussion of doing so and a final public commitment by show of hands. The impact of the group discussion demonstrated the impact of others on the individual's thoughts, feelings, and behaviors.

History of Social Psychology

Recall Plato is credited with referring to a "crowd mind." The intent behind those words is simple. People are impacted by others. What a person does or thinks in isolation can be drastically shifted when others are also present. The concept of an angry mob rarely centers on a singular individual experience, but rather that the experience of being around other people changes each person's experience. In the case of rioting we see an amplification or even emotional contagion in which a group of people become violent in ways that would be unlikely if they were alone.

We interpret our own outcomes in comparison to others via a process of social comparison. Other people define how we understand our own experiences. Consider the cost and value of a college education. Everyone is charged the same tuition rate (though residency might matter) to attend the same lectures or seminars and each person's grade is determined by his or her effort in the course. Degree cheapening occurs when cultures of grade inflation take over and all students are receiving A's and B's irrespective of their effort or demonstrated skills. When you receive an "A" on a paper or exam you are likely to feel proud of your accomplishment and that you are deserving of that grade. Later you are comparing grades with classmates; you note that everyone got an "A". Individually you may feel a bit undervalued, but if you then find out that everyone in the course was given an "A" you may not only feel that your work was not necessary but that the degree that is to distinguish you from others is relatively meaningless. Conversely, if you receive a "D" on a paper you may feel horrible about your performance and that you did not meet the professor's expectations. However, if you find out that almost everyone else also received low scores, you may actually feel better about your quite poor performance. In the latter case you decide that the grade reflects something about the professor or the course or the material, but certainly not about your lack of knowledge or skill. Somehow the possibility that the large portion of the class could possibly not be very knowledgeable does not enter into your self-assessment. This is in part, because we want to feel good about ourselves and we also want to feel we are accurate in those assessments. Situations often drive our perceptions as we attempt to balance accuracy with positive views of ourselves.

POWERFUL SITUATIONS

I always imagined that if given an opportunity to travel somewhere I have never been I would go. After all, I enjoy a good adventure. A few years ago I had the opportunity to travel to China, a country I had not visited. Yet, I did not pursue the opportunity. Why would an adventurous person who enjoys travel decline such a trip? There are a number of reasons. Having parents of a certain age may mean you prefer not to leave without the opportunity to quickly and easily return. Or political unrest in the travel destination may make the opportunity more costly. Ultimately, there are a number of situational factors that undermine our ability to accurately forecast our future choices.

To better understand the power of the situation let us consider play behavior. Board games sell because they create a variety of novel situations which players must negotiate in order to achieve a goal. At the beginning of the game, particularly when playing with new people, there is likely to be some declaration of the seriousness with which play should be undertaken. Players may remind one another that "it's only a game." People often actively engage to make it clear that attributions about how well one plays the game can be balanced with social harmony and an attempt to have fun. Adults going to Las Vegas for a weekend of fun often repeat, "What happens in Vegas, stays in Vegas." This phrase is yet another example of how people are acknowledging the power of the situation and helping others to make attributions that are more about Las Vegas than about them as a person.

A classic game of charades, which requires a person to act out a particular idea or character and have others guess, is quite a unique situation in which we may do any number of things in order to communicate the correct response to our team members. A person who is quite comfortable doing this with a group of friends and family might even become known in the social group for being a particularly entertaining player or good team member. Playing the same game of charades in front of an audience of strangers significantly changes the situation. Even playing the game for fun versus for a monetary prize or reward is enough to change a team member's ability to do well at the task.

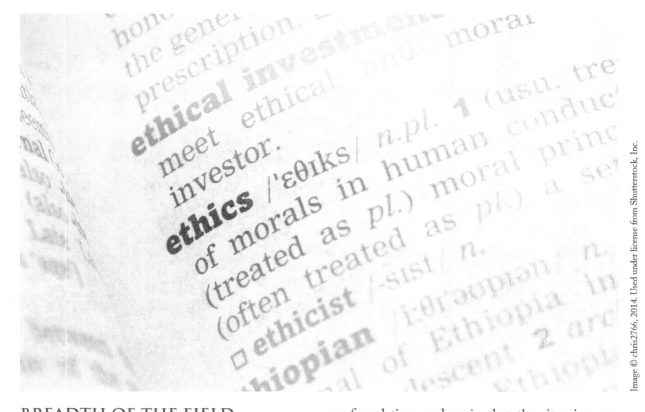

BREADTH OF THE FIELD

In 2003, researchers Richard, Bond, and Stokes-Zoota examined the state of research in social psychology. Through examination of meta-analysis papers they found that across 25,000 studies and 8 million participants that there were approximately 474 unique effects across 18 primary topics in the field. Those topics roughly line up with the chapters of this text and span from the study of social cognition and attribution to group processes and intergroup relations. In the 1900s, Triplett's 1898 study made up the total experimentation in social psychology. It's clear that the field of social psychology is growing and with this growth comes not only a greater understanding but a greater appreciation of the complexity of human experience.

ETHICS PAST AND PRESENT

Psychology has been at the center of ethical debate about involving human participants in experiments. Often in an attempt to demonstrate that people could overcome the situation, experiment-

ers found time and again that the situation was often too powerful for the average person to take a stand. Stanley Milgram invited participants to a learning experiment in the early 1960s (Milgram, 1963). Upon arrival a participant and a confederate were randomly assigned to be the teacher and the learner. However, the assignment was fixed (not random) and the confederate was always the learner. The participant, who was always in the role of teacher, was asked to follow a simple set of instructions to help the learner memorize a series of words. Each time the learner/confederate answered an item incorrectly the teacher/participant was to deliver an ever-increasing level of electrical shock to the learner. The experiment was set up so that the participant was often faced with delivering very high levels of shock even when the participant was complaining about the pain and a heart condition. While not all participants willingly flipped the switch to deliver the highest levels of shock to the learner, a number of participants did proceed to do so. The only encouragement they needed was the experimenter in a white lab coat saying, "The experiment must continue."

Image © Gennadii Borodin, 2014. Used under license from Shutterstock, Inc.

How do you think it might feel to live out your life in a cell this size?

Phil Zimbardo, a Stanford University professor, designed a clever experiment in which participants were recruited to participate in an experiment (Haney, Banks, & Zimbardo, 1973). All of the male participants were randomly assigned to be either prisoners or guards in a mock prison located in the basement of the psychology building at Stanford. The experiment was originally planned to last for two weeks, but was brought to an end after only six days. Guards began to treat the prisoners quite badly within the first full 24 hours of the experiment. Humiliating the prisoners became routine, even though both prisoners and guards *knew* they had been randomly assigned to these roles. Remember this is a mock prison; the "prisoners" had not committed any crime and the "guards" had no real authority. However, the situation of a mock prison was so powerful that not only did the guards quickly become abusive, but the prisoners also took on their role as prisoners.

These two classic experiments have become the primary focus of ethics in the field and indeed across many social scientific discussions on the ethical treatment of human participants. Today, there are federal regulations in place and institutional review boards (IRBs) tasked with ensuring that participant rights are protected and that ethical guidelines are followed. There were IRBs when Zimbardo undertook the prison experiment, but of course at that point, no one could have anticipated the experimental situation could be so powerful. Remember Zimbardo did have approval of Stanford University's IRB and the participants did sign a consent form which indicated they were volunteering for the study and could stop at any time. Institutional review boards examine each study carefully to ensure that participants are protected. However, there are a number of ethical issues that do not directly involve treatment of participants, but nonetheless have a huge impact on science.

Diederik Stapel has returned his 1997 PhD from the University of Amsterdam due to behavior that is "inconsistent with the duties associated with the doctorate" (Jump, 2011). He began a career as a social psychology professor/researcher at the University of Groningen in 2000 and later worked at Tilburg University beginning in 2006. He was the founder of the Tilburg Institution for Behavior Economics Research and even served as dean of the social and behavioral sciences faculty in 2010. Rather than treating participants in his studies poorly, he did not use participants at all. Stapel fabricated the data for over 50 studies that were later published in social psychology journals. Stapel did not always just create data, but rather manipulated his data to fit the story that would best support a theory. As time went on, Stapel spent time designing experimental methodology that was never carried out and fabricated all of the data he would then send to colleagues or students for analysis (Vogel, 2011). Historically, discussion of ethics in social psychology has focused predominantly on treatment of human participants, but it is also necessary to emphasize the importance of clear and proper data collection, analysis, and transparency of method and analysis.

Stapel and his students (who knew nothing of his fraudulent behavior) became well published; and once the fraudulent behavior was highlighted over 50 articles were retracted from academic journals. Included among the retractions are findings such as celebrities activating norms, but only when successful (Lindenberg, Joly, & Stapel, 2011); exposure to litter or even an abandoned bicycle can increase stereotyping and discrimination (Stapel & Lindenberg, 2011); women's body dissatisfaction being linked to not only human images but also exposure to vases of particular dimensions (Trampe, Stapel, & Siero, 2007); and powerful people more likely to be moral thinkers than people in positions of less power (Lammers & Stapel, 2009). However, another researcher was carefully examining his work and realized that the data were impossibly "perfect." It is worth noting that the ideas and methods remain quite interesting, but because they have not been properly tested, we cannot in fact draw the causal conclusions Stapel's papers implied. Indeed, the faking of the data undermined what could have been quite interesting

investigations into the questions he and his colleagues set out to explore.

You may now be wondering what you should trust and what you should dismiss as you read about experimental findings. There are several recommendations that can help you become a smart consumer of social psychological research. First, be certain you understand basic methodological concepts (covered in Chapter 2). Second, learn now how to write and understand methodology. Third, whether it is in conjunction with, before, or after this course, have a firm grasp of basic statistical analyses. This should also serve you well as you strive to understand data and conclusions not only in social psychology but across many domains of research. As you work in research labs as part of your undergraduate experience, you will see firsthand how data are collected and how a real experiment is rarely perfect. One of the first signs that something has gone awry is when the variance is quite small, when there are no outliers, or when effect sizes exceed what would be expected. You should take advantage of the many opportunities your college career provides to educate yourself about the research process. Finally, finding studies by different researchers that point in the same direction, uncover the same effects, and provide solid replications can provide some assurance that the research findings were legitimately obtained. Meta-analysis can also help to identify the ways in which many different studies and methodologies can be leveraged to address the same social psychological finding.

Social psychology is an experimental social science, with the goal of explaining human behavior across an array of situations. However, it is impossible to fully account for all of human behavior. Consider a time when you were younger and stayed out past curfew. When you arrived home late, a parent may have asked why you committed this transgression. You likely fumbled for a reason that would be both palatable to your parent and keep you out of trouble. However, even if you had been completely truthful, there are a number of factors that impacted your late arrival. You may not even be aware of the many factors that influenced your decisions.

In this text, we will explore effects that help us to understand why people think, feel, and behave the way they do. Our focus will be on situations and their power, as well as understanding how we might balance the pressure of the situation and individual motivations to be accurate, feel good about ourselves, and maintain our social relationships. The first part of the text focuses on research methodology and phenomena that provide a foundation within social psychology. Later chapters focus on topics such as stereotypes and prejudice, persuasion, and group dynamics. The final chapters focus on particular ways in which social psychology can help us to understand pro-social actions, aggression, relationships, group dynamics, and how the field of social psychology informs law, consumer behavior, environmental concerns, and healthcare.

Research Methods

2

What do we know? How did we come to know? These two questions are at the core of what scientists in many disciplines spend their lives asking. The scientific method provides one way of knowing that is widely accepted and is driven by **empiricism**. Of course, there are many ways of knowing that also inform our basic understanding of the social world.

Ways of Knowing

Image © Alena Hovorkova, 2014. Used under license from Shutterstock, Inc.

Think of something you know to be true. Now carefully think about how you know. Perhaps you know something through your ability to sense or perceive. Maybe you can ascertain truth because of past experience and logical connections that you also know to be true. Other times you may know something to be true because someone you trust has told you so.

For example, let's think of what you know about your social world. Consider your response to the following question: How many friends do you have? Your answer is likely to reflect many ways of knowing. You may know through *sense perception*. You can see people around you that are behaving in a friendly manner and ascertain they can be included in the number. *Language* provides another way of knowing. People may have linguistically expressed friendship to you by stating outright that they are your friend. *Emotion* or *intuition* may provide another way of knowing, so you feel as though certain people generally regard you as a friend and your emotional response to them matches the emotions you associate with friendship. Finally, *reason* or *logic* may allow you to logically ascertain the answer. For example, you may consider how many people attended your recent birthday party, subtract those that attended as friends of friends, add in the people who sent regrets that they couldn't attend but assured you of their friendship and well wishes for the coming year.

There are other ways of knowing as well. *Authority* may be another way of knowing, often knowledge delivered through language—that is, when someone gives you information and you take it on authority. For example, a police officer informing you of the speed limit may be a source of knowledge that you take on authority. A related way of knowing is common knowledge. Common knowledge is when something is known because many others agree that something is true. However, this may be problematic as it is also possible for many others to be incorrect even while agreeing with one another.

Others have attempted to address cultural differences in ways of knowing. Eastern and Western ways of knowing are distinct in that each values a different way of knowing. Eastern ways of knowing may rely on emotion or intuition, authority, and knowledge gained through self-understanding. Western ways of knowing reflect the individualistic culture and point to reason, logic, and science as primary sources of knowledge. Another cultural way of knowing is to draw a distinction between indigenous ways of knowing versus Western ways of knowing. Again, the Western ways of knowing are reliant on scientific method

and empiricism, while indigenous ways of knowing may emphasize intuition and language as important sources of knowledge.

Cultural differences in ways of knowing are also related to perceptions of the world as interconnected (collectivist) or as separate knowable parts that can be understood best as isolated from one another (individualist). The questions that arise from these different approaches to knowledge are also much deeper than can be presented here. Consider, for example, how knowledge that seeks to understand only one part of the human experience in isolation through the experimental method informs (or does not inform) a worldview that is fundamentally based on the interconnectedness of life. Importantly for social psychology, there are instances in which understanding a person's worldview can also help in predicting how a particular person will perceive that social world.

Sometimes these ways of knowing may lead us to have conflicting information or knowledge. However, there are also instances when different ways of knowing all lead to the same knowledge. For social psychologists, the scientific method provides the primary way of knowing that can be easily communicated and substantiated by others. Through empirical testing, knowledge about the social world is derived by eliminating alternative explanations for a particular cause-effect relationship. It is this way of knowing that will be the focus of this chapter and the information presented in the text will be derived from scientific or empirical ways of knowing.

Philosophy of Science

Positivism is a philosophy of science that relies on empiricism to develop scientific knowledge. Information from sensory experiences or mathematical logic is considered empirical evidence leading to scientific knowledge. Auguste Comte was a sociologist who argued that the physical world operates according to absolute laws and that society

© Bettmann/CORBIS

could be similarly predicted by determining the laws that guide a society. Emile Durkheim moved this particular brand of sociological positivism forward and this way of knowing has provided a widely accepted approach to social research. However, Durkheim's approach was focused on sociology rather than psychology and his text reflects this societal level of analysis.

Within psychology two primary approaches emerged in the late 1800s. **Structuralism** was embraced by William Wundt, who founded the first psychological laboratory in 1879 (Rieber & Robinson, 2001) and **functionalism** was forwarded by William James in his text *Principles of Psychology* (1890). Wundt was interested in understanding the underlying mental processes by investigating the basic components of thought. James by contrast felt that psychology should ultimately work to benefit people. In today's psychological laboratories, it is clear that psychologists are often engaged in basic research in order to improve the human condition, embracing both structuralism and functionalism through experimentation.

Positivism relies upon quantitative approaches and it is from this philosophy of science that behaviorism gained ground. Behaviorists relied on the behavior of an organism to provide the empirical evidence necessary to derive causal conclusions

or proof of a particular hypothesis. As psychology moved beyond behaviorism and psychologist became interested in understanding cognitive changes that occurred during experiments, it became necessary to find ways to measure or manipulate variables that could not be seen. Self-report of inner cognitive processes and reaction times provide two quantifiable methods that allow psychologists to quantify and analyze information about how cognitive processes might work. These methodological advances provided ways to measure or manipulate broader abstract constructs (e.g. love) and continue to embrace positivism as a way of knowing.

From Theory to Hypothesis

A key to a successful research project is to base the hypothesis on a solid **theory**. The scholarly literature provides a rich array of theories with many hypotheses remaining to be experimentally examined. Theories are concise logical statements that attempt to explain a particular causal relationship between factors. A theory is written in broad general terms and also provides a clear and parsimonious way to generate hypotheses. For example, stating that "love impacts lives" is not sufficient to be considered a theory. The theory should be clearer about what kind of love (e.g., romantic, familial?) and how lives are impacted. What part of life is being impacted specifically? Theories that have generated a great deal of research do so in part because they provide a compelling way to understand a particular phenomenon.

Theory should lead to a clear set of hypotheses that are easily tested and can confirm or disconfirm the tenets of the theory. Hypotheses are distinct from research questions. Research questions might be posed even prior to finding a theory that would help provide a framework for the research question. Hypotheses are statements or sets of statements derived from a theory that specify a particular relationship between two (or more) phenomenon.

Research Question: "How does Facebook impact developing close friendships?"

Theory: Social penetration theory states that as close relationships develop, interpersonal communication moves from shallow levels to more intimate or deeper levels of communication (Altman & Taylor, 1973).

Hypothesis: Facebook accelerates social penetration as self-disclosure between "friends" is facilitated by the disclosure of personal information on a Facebook profile (Pennington, 2008).

Constructs and Operations

Constructs are large abstract ideas that tend to broadly refer to an array of experiences or concepts. Some examples are love, hate, joy, evil, and peace. We use these words frequently to communicate about our own lives and the human condition. All of these words are theoretical and communicate a broad array of possible meanings. These concepts are considered constructs. Operations refer to the ways in which we might measure or manipulate or operationally define constructs.

Happiness is a construct that people often want to know more about. There are numerous books and self-help programs that focus on finding happiness, seeking happiness, being happy, and happy living. While we have a general understanding of happiness and could easily find the definition of the word, defining the construct for experimental purposes is a bit more complex. For example, if a particular place seems to make people happy we would need to find an empirical way to understand happiness and compare happiness in this place to happiness in other places. We might begin by simply determining whether people really were happy when they were in particular places.

Simply asking people to rate how happy they are on a 1–10 scale might be one such measure or operationalization. The construct is happiness and the operation is a 10-point scale in which a 10 would mean people were extremely happy and a 1 would mean that people were not at all happy. However, there may be other ways to measure happiness. For example, we could count the duration and intensity of smiling behavior using nonverbal coding of videos of people while they walk through a garden or park. There are numerous ways to operationalize a construct. What other operational measures can you generate?

Descriptive Methods

When first encouraged to consider doing research in social psychology, students often at once begin designing questionnaires. The popular press and social media have become inundated with opinion polls and most of the "findings" that are reported use descriptive findings rather than causal relationships. Consider this headline: "Facebook use related to social isolation." This type of headline is often the result of a descriptive survey rather than an experiment. People may be asked to complete scales that measure social isolation and asked how often they log in to Facebook or how many hours they spend on Facebook each week. Then a correlational analysis is conducted to determine whether hours spent logged in to Facebook are related to scores on social isolation measures.

In this example, the construct social isolation is being operationalized through scale measures of social isolation and the construct "Facebook use" is being operationalized as number of times a person logs in to Facebook and how many hours they spend "on Facebook." As any Facebook user is aware there may be certain Facebook user behaviors that would be more or less likely to be linked to the construct social isolation. For example, spending time reading friend's posts, generating interactive social media (e.g., polls and petitions), and sending messages, invites, or chatting might

Image © PromesaArtStudio, 2014. Used under license from Shutterstock, Inc.

Image © miya227, 2014. Used under license from Shutterstock, Inc.

all be related to LESS social isolation than other Facebook activities such as playing Facebook games that do not require friend cooperation, visiting commercial pages for favorite products, or lurking on public pages. In order to understand what is really meant by this type of headline, we should first consider not only these possible operations, but also the statistical analysis behind it.

A correlation is a statistical calculation represented by the correlation coefficient and noted by r. The correlation can be in simple terms thought of as the relationship between two continuous variables. The correlation coefficient has both valence (direction) and magnitude (strength). A positive correlation (e.g., $r = .75$) would indicate that as one variable increased the other also increased. Using the previous Facebook example a positive correlation would mean the more time spent on Facebook the more socially isolated a person was likely to be. A negative correlation ($r = -.98$) would mean that the more time someone spent on Facebook the *less* socially isolated that person was likely to be. Note, however, that correlations do not allow for causal conclusions and the order in which the findings are stated does not imply causation. Given the correlation coefficients the headline could lead to any of the following statements:

1. The more socially isolated people were the more time they spent on Facebook ($r = .75$).

2. The more time people spend on Facebook the more socially isolated they are ($r = .75$).

3. The more socially isolated people were the less time they spent on Facebook ($r = -.98$).

4. The less time people spend on Facebook the more social isolated they are ($r = -.98$).

The correlation coefficient can range from -1 to $+1$. Conceptually, you should be able to estimate a correlation coefficient even without the formula, given a set of data. A perfect correlation ($+1$ or -1) means that if you knew how much time a person spent on Facebook you could perfectly predict how they would score on a social isolation measure. A zero correlation ($r = 0$) means that the two variables are not related and would be illustrated by a perfectly horizontal or vertical line. Cohen (1992) indicates that a strong correlation in social science is about .50 or greater, moderate correlations would be about .30, and a small or weak correlation would be .10.

In all cases, correlations cannot be used to infer causation. For any correlational relationship a variety of causal links are plausible. It could be the case that A→B, B→A, or a third variable that was not measured "C" causes A and B to co-occur. In terms of the Facebook example above let's consider ONLY the positive correlation.

When $r = .75$:

A→ B: It *may* be the case that being on Facebook causes social isolation,

or

B➔A: It *may* be that social isolation increases Facebook use,

or

C➔ A&B: It may be that those who lack the social skills do not enjoy Facebook and are socially isolated.

A correlational design simply does not allow us to determine which of the above is true. The correlation only describes a relationship. We cannot ascertain the direction of causality, nor can we rule out alternative explanations for the relationship between these two variables.

The scatterplot in Figure 2.1 represents a correlation coefficient, $r = -.20$. If these data represent the confidence students reported going into an exam and their resulting exam score, what might be concluded?

The scatterplot in Figure 2.2 represents an $r = .35$. If these data represent the confidence students reported going into an exam and their resulting exam score, what might be concluded?

Practice

1. Using the Facebook example, provide the three possible explanations for the negative correlation in terms of A➔ B, B➔ A, and C➔ A&B.

2. Visit www.correlated.org and review some of the correlations derived from polls. Can you think of reasonable third variables that could cause the two variables of interest to co-occur? Do you think people infer causation for these correlations? If so, what could be some consequences of these erroneous causal conclusions?

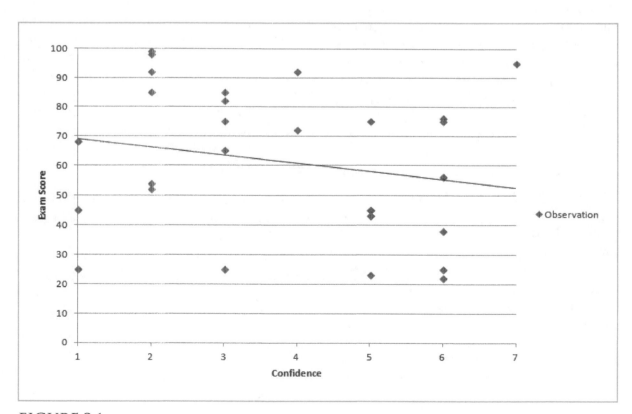

FIGURE 2.1

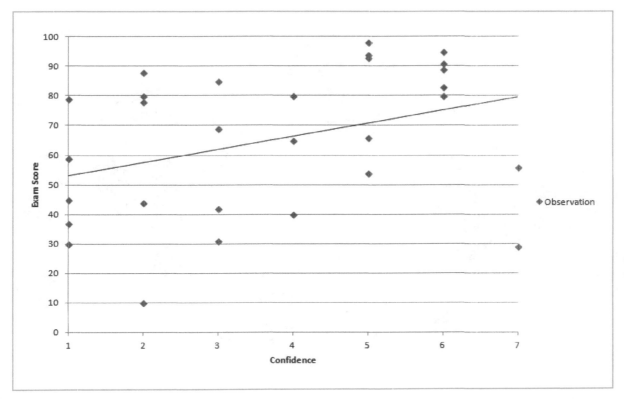

FIGURE 2.2

Experimental Method

RANDOM ASSIGNMENT AND RANDOM SAMPLING

Random sampling may be quite important for generalization of findings. Random sampling attempts to eliminate biases in an experiment by making sure that a large cross section of the population is included in the study. This is incredibly important for survey research that attempts to describe how people feel, act, or think. Random sampling is impractical and expensive for many experiments. However, there are other ways to address these issues when using the experimental method.

Random assignment is a distinct concept from random sampling. Random assignment refers to the method used to assign participants to one level of an independent variable. To assign participants to conditions randomly, we might flip a coin as each student enters the experiment. If the coin is heads they listen to funeral dirges and if it is tails they listen to upbeat music. What other methods can you derive that would ensure assignment is random?

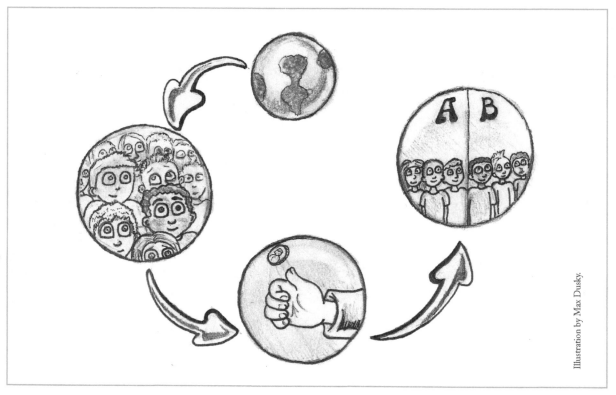

Illustration by Max Dusky.

FIGURE 2.3

Random assignment and random sampling are different from one another and serve two very different purposes. Random sampling is the practice of taking a random sample of people from the entire population of interest. For example, let's say you were interested in knowing how many college students actually read their textbooks. For random sampling you would begin by taking the entire sample of college students in the world and then randomly select a sample of these students to ask them whether they read their textbooks. This question that you can answer using a descriptive method would greatly benefit from random sampling. Random sampling requires that every member of the population of interest is equally likely to be included in the survey. There are a number of factors that could systematically exclude someone from taking a survey and lead to unintended bias in your research.

If you distributed a survey through your social network rather than to a random sample of col-

lege students, you would increase the chances that your results would reflect your own textbook reading habits. That is, your friends and their friends are more likely to be similar to your own textbook reading habits than people who travel in different social circles. By randomly selecting college students from directories and asking them about their reading of textbooks, you can eliminate some bias. It may be tempting to avoid random sampling and simply distribute the survey in textbooks themselves. However, even this method which would literally include every member of the textbook owning college student population would be biased. Students who would voluntarily complete such a survey are likely to be more conscientious, more intelligent, more sociable, and have a higher need for social approval (Rosenthal & Rosnow, 1975) and therefore more likely to read the text than the average college student. Indeed the students who are least likely to read the textbook are also least likely to open the book to even find the survey you distributed. However, for most social psychological *experiments* random assignment is more important than random sampling to reach valid conclusions.

Random assignment is critical. The experimental method requires that participants be randomly assigned to experimental conditions in order to reach causal conclusions. In this case, we can rely on volunteers even though they have a number of biases compared to the non-volunteer. For any experiment there must be at least two experimental conditions. In some cases this will be a treatment and control condition, in other cases the conditions might involve two or more treatments without a particular control condition. Random assignment to conditions means that each participant in the experiment has an equal chance of being placed in either condition A or condition B of an experiment. One way to randomly assign individual participants to conditions would be to flip a coin where all people receiving heads are in condition A and all coin-flips resulting in tails result in assigning the participant to condition B (Figure 2.3).

Why not let people choose their condition? Let's say that we are interested in whether taking an easy or a hard exam motivates people to study for the next exam. In order to test our hypothesis we would give participants either a hard or an easy exam and then measure how much time they spent studying over the next two weeks. If we allowed participants to choose which condition they would prefer, those who choose the hard exam are likely to

be people who routinely study and enjoy challenging themselves. People who would choose the easy exam may be more likely to not study very often and prefer to not try difficult academic work. Thus, if we found that the hard exam did result in more studying, we really have not learned anything about the impact of the exam itself, only about what types of people choose the exam and how they study. In order to test our hypothesis about the impact of difficult and easy exams we would need to randomly assign individuals to take either the difficult or the easy exam and then measure time spent studying over the next two weeks. We could do this by using a random number generator in which each participant is given a random number—and evens take the easy exam and odds take the difficult exam. What other approaches could we use to randomly assign participants? Can you use Microsoft Excel or another software program to generate random numbers?

INDEPENDENT AND DEPENDENT VARIABLES

The independent variable in an experiment is the variable that the experimenter manipulates. Independent variables are the manipulations in an experiment. In some cases this might include a control group and an experimental group. There can be many levels of an independent variable, but there must always be at least two levels of an independent variable. For example, if we are interested in the impact of mood on exam performance, our independent variable would be mood and our

dependent variable would be exam performance. First, mood as a construct must be operationalized. We would want to limit our experiment to explore perhaps a positive vs. negative mood. In this case we might operationalize our manipulation of mood by having students listen to music that would likely put them in a negative mood state (funeral dirges) or having students listen to music that would likely put them in a positive mood (upbeat music). It would be imperative that we randomly assign our participants to one of these two mood conditions.

Next we must operationalize our dependent variable construct, exam performance. First, we would have to decide what type of exam and think critically about how the type of exam might benefit from certain mood states. For example, we might decide to use a mathematical test which has clear and objective right and wrong answers.

FACTORIAL MODELS

There may also be more than one independent variable. Continuing our music and exam performance study, we might for example want to also manipulate the type of exam. For example, people may actually do better on the math test when in a negative mood, but do better on a psychology test when in a positive mood. So we would add "exam content" as a second independent variable. This experimental design would be described as a 2 x 2 between subjects design. We have two levels of mood (positive vs. negative) and two levels of exam (psychology vs. math). The term "between subjects" means that each participant in the study receives only one mood manipulation and takes

only one exam. As a simple illustration consider Tables 2.1 and 2.2. The first represents a "between subjects" design in which all participants were randomly assigned to receive only one combination of treatments (mood and exam type).

Table 2.2 represents a "within subjects" design in which all participants receive all possible combinations of treatments. The within-subjects design requires additional methodological controls be added. This means that for half of the participants, they will receive the positive mood induction while taking the math test then the psychology test, and for the other half they will receive the negative mood induction first. We would counterbalance the order of the exams and the order of the mood inductions. This helps to eliminate (somewhat) the effect of one mood manipulation on the other and controls for order of exams. It would also be advisable to have a mood neutralizing period between the mood inductions to avoid contamination between these conditions. The group that includes Raj, Juan, Kim, and Mary would begin by listening to the upbeat music and taking the psychology exam and then the math exam. After a mood neutralizing period they would then listen to the funeral dirges and take another version of the psychology exam followed by another version of the math exam.

Confounding variables must also be taken into account. For example, our operation of funeral dirges and upbeat music may in fact be manipulating something besides mood. Upbeat music may be manipulating mood, but may also be distracting compared to funeral dirges which tend to provide predictable rhythms. In our study, mood may be confounded with distraction. One way to

TABLE 2.1

Mood/Exam	Math	Psychology
Positive (upbeat music)	Sam, Tom, Ursula, Viola	Walter, Xena, Yohan, Zelda
Negative (funeral dirges)	Raj, Juan, Kim, Mary	Phil, Greg, Rosie, Nancy

TABLE 2.2

Mood/Exam	Math	Psychology
Positive (upbeat music)	1. Sam, Tom, Ursula, Viola 2. Raj, Juan, Kim, Mary 3. Walter, Xena, Yohan, Zelda 4. Phil, Greg, Rosie, Nancy	2. Sam, Tom, Ursula, Viola 1. Raj, Juan, Kim, Mary 4. Walter, Xena, Yohan, Zelda 3. Phil, Greg, Rosie, Nancy
Negative (funeral dirges)	3. Sam, Tom, Ursula, Viola 4. Raj, Juan, Kim, Mary 1. Walter, Xena, Yohan, Zelda 2. Phil, Greg, Rosie, Nancy	4. Sam, Tom, Ursula, Viola 3. Raj, Juan, Kim, Mary 2. Walter, Xena, Yohan, Zelda 1. Phil, Greg, Rosie, Nancy

eliminate this possibility is to conduct a manipulation check in which participants are provided a brief questionnaire assessing not only mood but also how distracted participants found the music. If both types of music are equally distracting but lead to different mood states we can be less concerned about possible confounds.

Another example of a confounding variable would be if the participants were led to a bright, sunny room following the positive mood induction to take their exams, but led to a dark, windowless room following the negative mood induction. In this case an extraneous variable, testing room, is interfering with our ability to infer that mood as induced by music causes exam performance. It could be that the testing room leads to exam performance and overwhelms any effect of our mood induction. How can we control for this confounding variable? Well, we could make sure that all testing rooms are the same or make sure that half of the participants in each testing room received the positive mood induction and half received the negative mood induction. What are some other solutions?

Understanding Results

In this section we are going to discuss some basic results from factorial designs and how you can interpret results from experiments. Vrij, Edward, Roberts, and Bull (2000) conducted a study exploring nonverbal distinctions between telling lies and telling the truth. Nursing students were recruited to be participants in a study entitled, "Telling Lies." In order to induce the nursing students to see the study as important, they were told that lying was an important skill for good nurses. The nursing students were then interviewed about a short video. In the video a patient's bag was stolen by a visitor. In the video, a woman enters the hospital, walks to the first floor, and takes a patient's handbag. The patient asks that the handbag be returned and a nurse arrives to see what the trouble is. The patient tells the nurse she doesn't know the visitor and the visitor indicates that the patient is confused and that the visitor is a neighbor. The nurse leaves the room and the visitor smiles as the purse is opened and the visitor sees money in the purse. After watching the video half of the participants were asked to answer three questions truthfully and the other half were asked to answer the same three questions deceptively.

Consider the results of this experiment. Simply put, a main effect indicates that the mean responses in one condition are significantly different than another condition. In this case, the liar condition yielded longer responses than the truth-telling condition. The results indicate that truth tellers ($M = 89$ s, $SD = 46$) gave longer answers than liars ($M = 42$ s, $SD = 19$), $F(1,71) = 34.06$, $p < .01$. **Main effect** is a term that indicates an overall effect of one independent variable on a dependent variable ignoring all other independent variables. This design is a simple one-factor study and the difference in means can be discussed as a simple difference in means or as a main effect of truth-telling instructions.

Now let's explore the results of a more complex case. Madey and Gilovich (1993) conducted a study in which participants read a diary of a student who had been required to predict seemingly unpredictable events each week for several weeks. The diary included the student's prediction and events from the week about which prediction was made. Participants were randomly assigned to a temporally unfocused condition wherein the predictions that were read had no temporal frame or to a temporally focused condition in which a specific time frame was mentioned in the prediction (e.g., Friday). A second factor was added in that for half of the prophecies the prediction was confirmed by the events that later took place and half were disconfirmed as noted in the event description following the prediction. After reading the diary, participants completed a filler task, and then were asked to recall as many prophecies and events as they could. The results indicate that confirmed prophecies were recalled more frequently regardless of temporal condition. This would be considered a main effect of confirmation. However, for disconfirmed events, those in the temporally focused condition were more likely to recall these predictions than those in the temporally unfocused condition. An **interaction** effect occurs when an independent variable's impact on a dependent variable depends on the level of a second independent variable. This indicates that there is an interaction between temporal focus and confirmation. Temporal focus improved memory for unconfirmed predictions, but had no effect on confirmed predictions.

Craig and Kelly (1999) randomly assigned groups of participants to different levels of interpersonal cohesiveness (liking for the group) and task cohesiveness (liking or attraction to the task). Groups who were assigned to the high interpersonal co-

hesiveness task were asked to spend 15 minutes sitting in very close proximity and getting to know one another and were then asked to generate a team name. Groups who were assigned to the low interpersonal cohesiveness were not given time to get to know one another or generate a team name. Groups in the high task cohesiveness groups were told the task was very important as the ability to work in a team was highly regarded in the workplace and they were also told that the group with the "best effort" would receive a $30 prize. Those in the low task cohesiveness condition were not told about the award or importance of the task until the end of the experiment. Groups were then assigned to collaboratively draw pictures of either mansions or bridges and these pictures were then judged for creativity. The results for groups who drew pictures of mansions are depicted in Figure 2.4. High interpersonal cohesiveness improved creative performance only when task cohesiveness was also high. When viewing the graph you can clearly see that the high interpersonal cohesiveness / high task cohesiveness condition is higher than the high interpersonal cohesiveness / low task cohesiveness condition. The difference between task cohesiveness conditions goes away when interpersonal cohesiveness was low. The bars are slightly different, but this difference is not statistically significant. This result is an interaction; the impact of interpersonal cohesiveness on creativity is dependent upon whether task cohesiveness was high or low.

In viewing bar charts such as the one in Figure 2.4, you can deduce that there is an interaction by drawing lines between the two brick bars and the two black bars. If the lines would intersect, then most likely there is going to be a reported interaction. If the lines are parallel to one another, then the graph may depict a main effect (or even two!), but there is no possibility of an interaction.

The case of two main effects, no interactions occurs when both independent variables have an effect on the dependent variable but these effects are independent or additive. Let us say that we

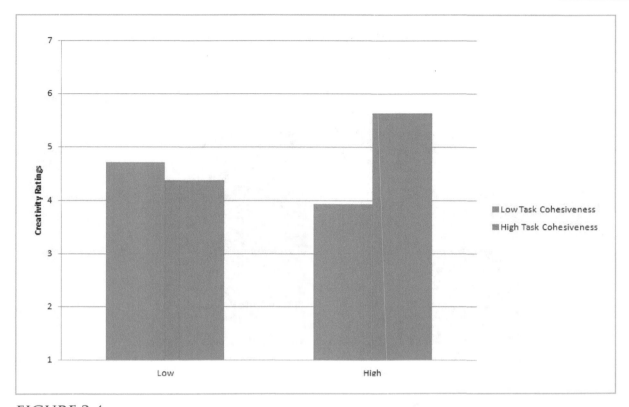

FIGURE 2.4

are interested in stress management. In this study we might manipulate time spent outside and minutes engaged in a deep breathing exercise prior to a stressful test. Some participants will spend 5 minutes outside and others will spend 15 minutes outside. Likewise some participants will spend 5 minutes engaged in a guided deep breathing exercise and others will spend 15 minutes engaged in the deep breathing exercise. All participants will be randomly assigned to conditions. If we then use test scores to measure how effective these relaxation techniques were at improving test scores and we expected two main effects and no interactions, we might have a graph like the one in Figure 2.5.

In this case you can see that if you spend 10 extra minutes outside there is a 10-point increase in the test score and if you spend an extra 10 minutes in guided deep breathing you will also receive 10 more points than you would without the extra

minutes. Figure 2.5 depicts an example of two main effects with additive effects on test scores. There is a main effect of guided deep breathing and a main effect of time spent outside. If you draw two lines, one connecting the patterned bars and one connecting the black bars you would see that the lines are parallel and there is no interaction effect.

QUASI-EXPERIMENTS

We have covered factorial designs in which participants can be randomly assigned to conditions that we manipulate (e.g., type of exam, time spent in deep breathing exercise). However, there are other questions that researchers often want to find answers to that do not lend themselves to random assignment. For example, questions about whether men or women or transgendered individuals are more or less likely to be hired or questions about

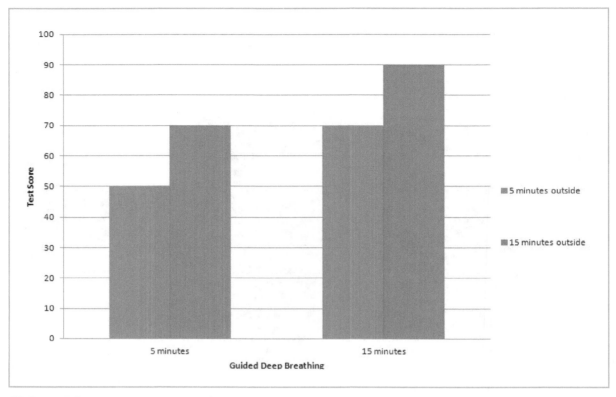

FIGURE 2.5

whether racial/ethnic background would change responses in certain contexts. In these cases the category of interest cannot be randomly assigned, but rather participants arrive as members of these groups. In this case, sex, race, sexual orientation, age, socioeconomic class, political affiliation, religious affiliation, and even personality characteristics can be used as independent variables even though participants are not randomly assigned to have those characteristics. This lack of random assignment to independent variables is frequently referred to as a quasi-experiment. Some experiments will use both random assignment and quasi-experimental methods. For example, if you randomly assign participants to read a long or short persuasive essay and are also interested in the quasi-independent variable of participant sex this would be considered a quasi-experimental design.

STATISTICAL VS. PRACTICAL SIGNIFICANCE

Statistical significance refers to a p value calculation indicating the probability of obtaining the same results (rejecting the null hypothesis) even if the hypothesis of interest is not true. The value of p can be thought of as the likelihood that the same differences among conditions could be derived even if there is not a true effect of the independent variable. However, the p value is also impacted by the number of participants in the study, so that the more participants a study includes the more likely it is that any difference between groups might be statistically significant. For most social scientific inquiry, the acceptable level of p is set at .05, meaning that if there is a 5% (or less) chance of a study reaching the wrong conclusion, then that would be acceptable. By contrast research in medical fields where life and death decisions are often made based on the results of a study, the accepted p value might be held to less than .01 or .001.

Practical significance is a term used to critically examine findings to determine if a statistically significant difference ($p < .05$) has any practical application outside of the laboratory or in real-world settings. For some findings, the answer may at first seem quite clear that statistically significant differences do not necessarily have any real-world implications. However, interpreting results and considering possible real-world applications should take into consideration how small differences might have major consequences for people. For example, a standardized test may show that there is a statistically significant difference between male and female scores, but the size of the difference is small (10 points out of 600). It may seem that this difference has no practical implication, unless you are in the disadvantaged group and the cut-off score for funding is within 10 points of your score. Understanding not only the size of the difference, but how the numbers are used can also shape our understanding of practical versus statistical significance.

VALIDITY AND THREATS TO EXPERIMENTAL DESIGNS

There are three types of validity that should be considered in experimental and descriptive research: construct validity, internal validity, and external validity. Understanding both the ways in which experimental design accounts and controls for threats to these types of validity is critical to being a responsible consumer of research.

Constructs are broad abstract concepts about which we might form theories or hypotheses. Pride, thinking, decisions, moods, stereotypes, justice, and love are just a few examples of constructs. We can consider many ideas or questions that involve these broad ideas. For example, are similar people more likely than dissimilar people to fall in love with one another? In order to experimental-

ly test this idea we must first think carefully about what we mean by similarity and what we mean by love? We might first narrow down similarity by indicating we mean similar values or interests. Then we need to be more specific in order to measure or manipulate similarity. Perhaps we decide that our question might incorporate measures of shared religious values, political stances, and interests. This process is the first step to identifying our operations. **Operations** are the specific ways in which we measure or manipulate a construct. Perhaps we develop a measure of values, stances, and interests and have participants who are in relationships complete these scales. This seems pretty straightforward. Now let's turn to the second construct of interest: love. How should we measure whether people fall in love? We could ask them to rate how much they love one another on a 10-point scale or measure how physically affectionate they are with one another when they come in to the lab to complete our survey. Perhaps we might ask their close friends whether they think the couple is in love. When making decisions about how to operationalize constructs it is imperative to remain aware of threats to construct validity and ways to increase the construct validity in our study.

Construct validity is the extent to which an operation is a good measure of a construct. One possible operation for "love" might be physical affection, but this may also be problematic. For example, two people who have similar attitudes and are against public displays of affection would show high similarity on our scales, but then be rated quite low on our "in love" behavioral measure, which would undermine our hypothesis. This would be an example of poor construct validity. We can increase construct validity by using measures that are likely to reflect feelings of "being in love" across many couples. Construct validity can also be improved by choosing multiple measures or operations of constructs. In this example, we might want to ask the couple several questions to assess how "in love" they are with their partners. We might also want to have their best friends rate how in love each member of the couple is with the other.

When I first began running experiments examining creativity, there was some early evidence that positive moods might lead to more creativity. I was not particularly interested in moods at that point and set about designing experiments looking at other factors that might impact creativity. After a few weeks of running an experiment in which I had undergraduate research assistants help run participants through the protocol, I noticed a trend in the data. It appeared that I had an experimenter effect. An **experimenter effect** occurs when the dependent variable is impacted by which experimenter runs the protocol. It seemed that for one experimenter, the participants were exceedingly more creative. I held a lab meeting and asked each research assistant to discuss any anomalies or differences in how they ran the protocol. There did not seem to be any differences in their explanations or methods for handling participants. All of the experiments to that point had been videotaped, so I began watching the videotaped sessions and that is where I found the experimenter effect. I had one research assistant who wore a t-shirt during their second shift of the week (every week) that had a very big yellow smiley face on the front. It seemed that the participants in these sessions in particular were far more creative than those run by the same experimenter during their first shift of the week. After changing the protocol and enforcing a dress code, the experiment continued without further complication.

Demand characteristics refer to cues in the experimental context that leads participants to feel they are expected to respond in a particular way. In this case, participants may feel that there is an expected or preferred response in the experiment, so rather than acting of their own free will, participants may try to please the experimenter or in some way provide the preferred response. There are always those students who upon learning this do precisely the opposite and try to "ruin" experiments by doing precisely the opposite. However, Nichols and Maner (2008) found that most participants if given information about the study

"No, I'm not familiar with the dress code ... but I'm pretty darn sure that jammies aren't on it!"

focus more energy on providing evidence to confirm the hypothesis, so long as they also liked the experiment and experimenter. While these two groups of participants may well balance one another out, experimental design must take into account how participants will perceive the experiment. In some cases, participants engage in **hypothesis guessing**, whereby the bulk of the participants' energy is spent trying to sort out what the experiment is testing and then either going along to help provide evidence to support the hypothesis or attempting to sabotage the experiment once the participants believe they know the hypothesis. Deception about the true nature of an experiment or the specific hypothesis can also decrease hypothesis guessing and demand characteristics. For example, if you are asked to participate in an opinion survey, you may be less concerned about giving "right" answers. If you were asked to participant in an economic exercise, on the other hand, you might be more concerned about being correct or logical in your responding.

Experimenter expectancy can also shape experimental results. For example, if a participant is providing verbal responses to a questionnaire, the participant may pick up on nonverbal behavior or even explicit behavior that the experimenter provides to encourage or discourage a particular response. There are a number of solutions and methodological techniques that can decrease this threat to construct validity. First, computer-mediated data collection does not provide an opportunity for the experimenter to inadvertently influence participant responses. Second, having research assistants who are unaware of the particular hypotheses being tested or at least who are unaware of which participants are in which experimental and control conditions can also ameliorate the impact of experimenter expectancy. The solution is when neither the participants nor the researcher who interacts with the participants are aware of their experimental condition.

Internal validity refers to the ability to be certain that the independent variable is causally linked to

the dependent variable. In the previous study, we have no such control as it is a purely descriptive study resulting only in correlational data. However, we could design an experiment that would allow us to address our original hypothesis and infer causation. We could have participants read dating profiles of possible romantic partners and vary whether the profile describes someone who is similar or dissimilar to the participant in terms of values and interests. Then participants might answer a series of questions regarding how likely it is they would fall in love with someone like this person described in the personal ad. In this study our independent variable is whether the dating profile describes someone similar or dissimilar. We can insure internal validity by randomly assigning our participants to our two conditions (similar profiles or dissimilar profiles).

Internal validity is only one way to increase confidence that differences in the independent variable caused a change in the dependent variable. Statistical analysis attempts to control for this by using significance testing. The probability value or p value is the chance that the results are not a product of our experiment. Social psychologists (as well as many in the social sciences) limit the acceptable level of probability of this type of error to 5%. That is, the p value must be less than .05 to indicate that there is less than a 5% chance that the results could be due to chance rather than the experimental design. Research studies that do not result in statistically significant differences often have reported p values that exceed the 5% standard ($p > .05$).

External validity is determined by how well the results of a study can generalize to other populations or situations. For example, if we conducted this study on college-aged students, would the same hold true for people in their 70s? One way to ensure external validity is to employ random sampling. However, this is often not feasible and can be costly. **Psychological realism** is high when participants in a laboratory setting are having a psychologically similar experience to the experience they might have in the real world. For example, viewing online dating profiles in the lab is not very different than viewing such profiles at home. **Mundane realism** occurs when a study is conducted in a field setting or outside of the laboratory. For example, by partnering with an online dating site researchers could show each person who logged in profiles that were similar or dissimilar to their own and measure how long they spent reading the profile and then ask follow-up questions inquiring if they could see themselves falling in love with this person. **Replication** is conducting the same study in a new setting or with a new population. If our initial study of U.S. college students were to support our hypothesis then a replication might be done to determine if the same findings would occur for older people or people in other cultures. However, replications are notoriously difficult to publish (Spellman, 2012) as journals in the field are often interested in publishing new and interesting findings, rather than "re-runs" of effects.

Meta-analysis is a statistical technique that allows multiple studies by many researchers to be analyzed to determine what the "average" finding is for studies of a particular effect over the entire field. In a typical meta-analysis a researcher will begin by identifying a particular effect (e.g., social facilitation). Then all articles published on social facilitation would be retrieved from the library and online. However, there is one other set of studies that can be crucial to determining support for an effect—that is, data and results setting in file drawers in professor offices around the world. This problem stems in part from the lack of replications that get published in journals and from a backlog of data that simply does not meet the standards for publication because the study is small or because it is a failed replication! How can these studies inform the science of social psychology if no one knows they exist? Field-specific list servs often become places to post requests for data or studies that address an effect but were not published; and networking among colleagues to identify who was doing what has become crucial in finding these unpublished data sets. In 2011, Barbara Spellman and Hal Pashler (among others) began creating website repositories for replication work (www.psychfiledrawer.org) (Spellman, 2012).

Once researchers are confident that they have compiled an exhaustive set of studies, they would begin by reading through each paper and determining how the study was conducted, who the participants were, what manipulations were used, and what the statistical findings were. The statistical technique is dependent upon the nature of the effect, but in most experimental cases a d statistic is used to represent the size of the effect compared to a control condition. This statistic when used in meta-analysis takes into account the means and standard deviations from each study and also the sample size for each study so that a study involving 1,000 participants receives relatively more "weight" than a similar study involving only 20 participants.

Other Research Approaches

Archival analysis refers to an analysis of existing records, books, or other material that can be analyzed at a later time. For example, if someone were interested in understanding how depictions of boys and men have changed over the years, it would be appropriate to look at back issues of magazines that cater to male populations. These magazines could be coded for images or topics covered by articles. Another example would be to review movie footage from specific time periods and genres to determine if certain political attitudes seemed more or less favorable over time. Archival analysis is most useful when there is an interest in understanding how something has changed over time.

Field studies or field experiments are research protocols that involve observation or experimental manipulation and observation as it occurs in the real world. Rather than bringing people into the lab, experimenters can go directly to the situation of interest and conduct their observations and experiments in the field. Some of these studies involve unobtrusive observation while others are considered participant-observation research. An unobtrusive observational study that is a favorite of many social psychology students is Ruback

and Juieng's (1997) study of parking behavior. In a crowded mall parking lot, a series of 200 drivers were timed as they got into their parked cars and drove away. Observers noted both how long it took the driver to leave the space after entering the car and whether another car was waiting for the space. Most of us have been on both sides of this situation. When waiting for a parking spot to open up, it seems that the driver takes a very long time to vacate the space. However, when you are the one being pressured to back out quickly, you may feel as though you are doing so quickly. Results from the observational study indicate that drivers took around 7 seconds longer to vacate a parking space when someone else was waiting for the spot than when there was no one waiting.

One example of a participant-observation research study is Milgram's subway experiment. Students approached passengers on a subway if they would give up their seats so that the students might sit (Milgram & Sabini, 1978). What ensued was that even when provided no reason for doing it, 68% of the people stood or slid over and allowed the

student to sit in their place. Other passengers were randomly assigned to be approached and asked to give up their subway seat because "I can't read my book standing up." In this case, people were less likely to help with only 41.9% surrendering their seat. In this case the students conducted their study in the field, by making a request in a subway. Consider how different this situation might be from asking people on a survey if they would surrender their subway seat if asked or even if they were asked to give up their seat in a waiting room for an experiment. Would the results be the same in another setting?

COMPUTER- AND INTERNET-MEDIATED RESEARCH

One of the newest and most inexpensive tools that social psychologists can employ is the internet. Not only can many survey materials be delivered online, but an increased reliance on computer-mediated experiments has also allowed for the collection of experimental data online. The internet has been particularly useful for reaching beyond the department participant pool to reach participants with more diverse ages, occupations, interests, and backgrounds. However, there remain some selection biases in this research. For example, internet access does require some resources to access, thus many individuals in the lowest socio-economic class may have neither the time, energy, or internet access to complete an hour-long survey; of course, this is true for any lab experiment as well! The other primary disadvantage is that it is impossible to control the environment in which the internet experiment is being conducted.

Perhaps the most recent advance has been the use of applications on cell phones that allow participants to enter data as they go about their daily lives without having to take time to come into a laboratory setting. Some effects in social psychology are easily measured in online contexts, while other paradigms require face-to-face interaction to produce the same effects. External validity has become a key consideration. Now social

psychologists must determine which effects will generalize to online interactions. For example, social psychologists who are interested in group dynamics and who run face-to-face groups may find that some effects that rely on nonverbal cues among group members or seating position may not translate to online group discussion via Skype. Increased online interactions have also provided a broad array of situational contexts for social psychologists to explore.

Communicating Results

The topics of interest in social psychology often lend themselves to both interesting discussion and the probability of overgeneralization of findings in ways that may not always be appropriate. In any science it is crucial that the variables of interest and results are clearly defined (operationalized) and communicated. In this section, we will consider some common sources of confusion in writing about social scientific research and ways in which even everyday language use shapes perceptions of research.

First, it is critical that you specify the age of participants in a way that is both respectful and, more importantly, accurate. For example, you read about a study that asked boys and girls to read a particular story and then report how much they liked characters in the story. How old do you believe these participants were? Most people believe the participants were children and rightly so. The terms "girl" and "boy" refer to people under 18 with a particular gender that is likely based (though not necessarily) on their biological characteristics. Likewise the terms "women" and "men" refer to adult individuals who again have a particular gender assignment. If you are interested in study sex effects, then you should refer to participants as males and females, and to be particularly inclusive you might provide participants the opportunity to otherwise identify their biological sex (e.g., transsexual, intersexed). Similarly, if you are studying romantic relationships or sexual attraction, you should not presume that everyone is heterosexual and if collecting demographic information it would be appropriate to provide a list of possible sexual orientations from which participants might choose (e.g., lesbian, bisexual, gay, or asexual). What would be an appropriate demographic set of indicators for people to identify their race or ethnicity?

Gender and sex are two distinct terms and concepts. Sex refers directly to the biological features of a person that indicate whether that person is male, female, or intersexed. Sex has a wide variety of indicators from chromosomal sex to external genitalia. For the purposes of social psychology, we are most frequently concerned with how sex impacts social interactions or perceptions. The majority of the time having participants self-report sex and providing an alternative for those individuals who are either intersexed or transsexual will be sufficient to provide demographic data and answer our research questions. Gender is a social construction and might be thought of as how masculine or feminine a person is. Here people might respond to a demographic question asking whether they are masculine, feminine, or androgynous. Remember, gender is not always congruent with someone's sex. Although the majority of people identify their gender and sex as congruent, transgendered individuals may not identify as men and women in ways that match their biological sex. Also, sex and gender are completely separate constructs from sexual orientation. That is, a person can be transgendered and identify with any sexual orientation. Therefore, if you are doing research on relationships, sexuality, or even political attitudes, you should be clear about what demographics are most relevant to your topic and measure them accordingly.

Another problem that students often have when discussing the wide array of diversity in participant populations or even in understanding diverse population is using adjectives as nouns. Remember that one of the primary ethical principles in human participant research is respect for persons and that all participants are people and should be referred to as people. (See Table 2.3 for examples.)

Parallelism is another concern that should be considered. For example, if you are preparing stimulus materials describing faculty teaching styles and then having students rate how much they would like to be in each course, you should be mindful that the descriptions differ only in teaching style.

TABLE 2.3 *Which of the following statements illustrate respect for people?*

Write/Say this...	Not this...
Participants included 15 people who identified as gay men.	Participants included 15 people who identified as gays.
Participants included 52 people who racially identified as white.	Participants included 52 whites.
Participants included 60 people who indicated they were currently homeless.	Participants included 60 homeless.
Students at risk for early school dropout	At-risk students
Participants were randomly selected from members of the Nez Perce tribe.	Participants were randomly selected from a pool of Native Americans.
Forty-three participants reported below poverty-level incomes.	Forty-three poor people responded to the survey.

If one professor is provided a title, then all professors should be described with their appropriate title (e.g., Professor or Dr.). This is also good to practice in your professional communication. If you were to send an email to two PhD-holding faculty members and wrote the following, "Dr. Jones and Mr. Phelt," you would be communicating something about Mr. Phelt's lack of expertise or degree by not using the same form of address. Consider a male student over 21 who turns in the following: "I went out last night with some of the men in my house and met a girl that I really hope to ask out again." While you may infer that the "girl" is actually a woman, it would be much clearer if this was simply written to reflect her adult status rather than raise even the hint of pedophilia. Finally, generic masculine language in referring to a mixed-sex group of people is almost always inappropriate as it implies that there were no women present (Gastil, 1990; Miller & James, 2009). You might also want to revisit the APA guidelines for plural pronouns and alternative pronoun use (hir and zie).

Homophones provide particular challenges and can greatly impact the interpretation of your work. Proofread for these types of errors as most word processing programs will not catch or correct them for you. A list of particularly problematic homophones can be found in Table 2.4. For example, indicating that 83% of people definitely disagree with a new policy is a bit different than stating that 83% of people defiantly disagree with a new policy. Also, be certain that you use appropriate plural nouns (e.g., one woman, twenty women).

SUMMARY

Social psychology is a social scientific field of inquiry. As a social scientific discipline a positivist approach to knowledge often entails operationalizing constructs that allow for quantitative analysis. Descriptive research often involves correlational analysis which can be quite useful in determining if there is an association between variables of interest. Causation can only be inferred by undertaking theoretically sound experiments. The experimental method is the most frequently used method in social psychological research. The experimental method involves randomly assigning participants to specific conditions of an independent variable and accurately measuring a dependent variable. The results of many of these studies are discussed in terms of main effects and interactions. Archival analysis and observational methods are also useful in gaining a comprehensive understanding of a research topic. In all cases, external validity, construct validity, and, in the case of the experimental method, internal validity should be taken into consideration when designing a study. Finally, even a well-designed research undertaking must be communicated clearly and effectively. Being cognizant of language use and the ethical considerations of working with human participants are paramount to forwarding our understanding of social psychology.

TABLE 2.4 Proofread your work for these homophones and other misused words.

two vs. to vs. too	affect vs. effect	whether vs. weather
definite vs. defiant	their vs. they're vs. there	your vs. you're
its vs. it's	please vs. pleas	sail vs. sale
right vs. write	hear vs. here	heard vs. herd
principle vs. principal	lose vs. loose	desert vs. dessert
who's vs. hose	stair vs. stare	break vs. brake

NAME _____ DATE _____

Chapter Questions

1. What is the difference between random assignment and random sampling?

2. What is an independent variable?

3. What is a dependent variable?

4. Define internal validity. How do you increase internal validity?

5. Define construct validity. How do you increase construct validity?

For each fictitious factorial study below presume that all differences are statistically different from one another. Then write a brief results statement (one to two sentences) in APA format, using the appropriate main effects and interaction effect terms to describe the findings.

6. In this study, groups of either three or six people had a conversation online or in-person. The conversation was recorded and the number of positive statements counted. What is the impact of group size and conversation type (online or in-person) on positive statements? Do these results reflect main effects or interactions?

Conversation Type | Group Size	3-person group	6-person group
Online	20	40
In Person	40	60

7. In this study, participants were assigned to read either a long essay or a short essay and rate the author's competence. Half of the participants were told the essay was written by a woman and the other half were told that the author was a man. What is the impact of source sex and essay length on competency ratings? Do these results reflect main effects or interactions?

Essay | Group Size	Male Author	Female Author
Short	40	20
Long	40	60

8. Participants were asked to rate how much they liked a series of abstract art pieces. They were randomly assigned to do so while listening to classical music or to make ratings in silence. In addition, the abstract art pieces were presented in black and white or in color photographs. What is the impact of photo color/black and white and music on liking? Do these results reflect main effects or interactions?

Photos | Music	Classical	Control (silence)
Black and White	20	40
Color	40	60

Social Cognition

Social cognition is how people think (cognate) about people and social situations. This includes how we perceive people and how we perceive interactions with others. Keep in mind that "others" can be real, inferred, or imagined. The area of social cognition was historically referred to as person perception and research was focused predominantly on how we perceive others. However, social cognition research today encompasses a broad array of topics that examine when and how people think about social situations and interactions. Sometimes people devote a great deal of cognitive effort or energy to better understand a social situation or to make a decision; other times people use mental shortcuts to navigate

their social world. For most situations, people are inherently cognitive misers. Spending the least amount of energy thinking is often the default. Expending more than the minimum amount of thinking is reserved for complicated situations or decisions. In this chapter we will begin by examining low-effort thinking and then move to social cognitive effects that require more effort.

Thinking about Others: Forming Impressions

Social cognition researchers have examined the ways in which low-effort thinking leads to impressions of others. Often we do make snap judgments about people in large part because we have very little information to use when forming first impressions. Some research has found that these snap judgments are often not very different from first impressions formed when allowed considerable time to form them. Janine Willis and Alex Todorov (2006) provided participants with multiple photographs of people (head and shoulder photos) and asked them to rate each person on a variety of characteristics (e.g., competence, likability, and attractiveness). One-fourth of the participants were randomly assigned to take as long as they wanted to contemplate their ratings. Other participants were randomly assigned to one of three conditions in which they were only allowed to view each photo for a short period of time (100 ms, 30 ms, 1 second). Surprisingly the ratings across conditions were significantly correlated providing some evidence that quickly formed impressions are not so different from impressions formed without time constraint.

FIRST IMPRESSIONS

We have all been told that first impressions are important. In this section we will consider how first impressions are formed and why they are critical to understanding future social interaction. We not only form first impressions when we en-

counter a person, but also from the first moment that someone begins to tell us about someone else. Think about the first time a friend referred to their parents: "My parents are coming down next weekend." This does not at first seem very descriptive, but you have already begun making a number of assumptions. Did you assume the parents were heterosexual? Did you infer that the parents are going to be the same age as your own parents? Are they going to be the same race/ethnicity as your friend? Are they biological parents, adoptive parents, an interracial couple, divorced, a biological parent and stepparent? All of the options that you did not consider let you know what your "default" impression is for people who are parents.

Why are these first impressions so critical? One reason is the primacy effect. Information that we obtain first has a greater impact than information we learn later. Our first impressions influence all of the information we receive after those first few moments. However, mood can also play a role. People in positive moods tend to form more positive impressions of others, while those in negative moods form more negative impressions. In a study examining both mood and primacy effects on impressions, Forgas (2011) manipulated participants' moods to be positive, negative, or neutral (control condition). Forgas then asked participants to form impressions about Jim. Jim was either first described as an introvert, but later as an extrovert or vice versa. Results show that participants in good moods felt the information they heard first was most likely the correct impression of Jim. However, participants in bad moods did not show the primacy effect and took both introvert and extrovert information into account regardless of order. Although positive mood participants formed more positive impressions and negative mood participants formed more negative impressions than those in the control group.

First impressions are often based on visible information, physical appearance, and behavior. Physical appearance is used to infer a number of additional traits. "What Is Beautiful Is Good" or the WIBIG effect has found that a beautiful face is often assumed to indicate a person is interesting, warm, outgoing, and socially skilled (Eagly, Ashmore, Makhijani, & Longo, 1991). What exactly does beauty imply? This meta-analysis by Eagly and colleagues found that beauty was used particularly to infer social competence. In addition, beauty was also related to perceptions of adjustment and intellectual competence, but was not used to infer integrity or concern for others. However, are these impressions based on beauty accurate?

Lorenzo, Biesanz, and Human (2010) asked participants to have three-minute interactions with another participant. After each three-minute interaction, both participants were asked to rate the other person's personality, attractiveness, and intelligence. Then at the conclusion of the study, the participants completed the same ratings for themselves. Would their self-ratings match the rating their interaction partners made? Were those first impressions accurate? The study found that more attractive individuals were viewed more positively and perceived more accurately. Perhaps people pay more attention to attractive others or perhaps attractive others provide more information in interactions that would lead to accurate impressions. Not only do people judge books by their covers, but perhaps they read beautiful books more carefully (Lorenzo et al., 2010).

Men who were taller have been found to receive higher salaries than men who are relatively shorter (Judge & Cable, 2004). Blaker and colleagues (2013) had participants view photos of men and women who were depicted as being either tall or short and then rate these men and women on whether they looked intelligent, dominant, vital, and a leader. Their results illustrate that both tall men and women were rated as more leader-like than short men and women. In addition, men were reported to be more leader-like than women. What do you think this means for women? What about people who are shorter and seeking leadership positions? Superiors asked to rate female employees' suitability for management provided more favorable ratings for tall women than for short women (Lindeman & Sundvik, 1994). The WIBIG effect and favoring of tall individuals are just two examples of implicit theories of personality. Certainly, the supervisors rating their employees above would likely argue that height played absolutely no role in their ratings of managerial ability. Likewise most tall and short people would likely argue that their managerial abilities are not at all related to their height.

Implicit theories of personality are sets of traits or attributes that are thought to apply to a person based on very minimal information about the person. These theories are implicit in that people do not explicitly learn or even show a great awareness that they are using these associations when forming their impressions of others. We also have associations between personality traits and occupations, physical traits, demographics, and social roles. For example, consider what music you think professors like, what hobbies accountants enjoy, or what grandmothers are good at doing. You probably had a few ideas come to mind quickly; and these are just a few examples of how we form impressions about others.

Behavior also plays a role in how we perceive others. Without much cognitive effort we come to some conclusions about why a person behaved in a particular way. That is, we make attributions about the cause of a person's actions. When we assume that the reasons people play soccer are because they are athletic, enjoy playing soccer, or have a talent for the game, we are making internal attributions. The reasons they play the game have to do with reasons internal to each person. However, if we are playing soccer we may more quickly identify some external reasons for doing so. Perhaps a parent or coach has encouraged us to play and we do not want to disappoint them, or perhaps we have friends who also play on the team and playing soccer gives us more opportunities to socialize. It could even be that the motivation is to appear well-rounded on college applications or to stay in shape. The **fundamental attribution**

error occurs when we make a pattern of attributions for others that differs from the pattern we derive for ourselves. The fundamental attribution error occurs when the behavior of others is assumed to be due to internal factors (something about the person) and external factors (the situation) is presumed to not have much impact on their behavior. Conversely, when we are engaged in a behavior we may be more aware of both internal and external factors that are influencing our behavior.

Correspondence bias is another name for the fundamental attribution error and again is the idea that we assume that people are what they do. If people engage in a behavior, then that is because of the type of person they are (not due to situational factors). The classic study involves having participants read essays that were either pro- or anti-Castro (Jones & Harris, 1967). Half of the participants were told that the writer was assigned to write an essay with a particular position, the other half were told the writer could choose the stance of their essay. The results show the basic bias in the freely chosen condition. Participants believed the writers who freely chose the position of their essay in fact wrote an essay that corresponded to their attitudes. However, even when participants were told that the writer did not get to choose the position expressed in the essay, participants continued to believe that the essay reflected the writer's truly held opinion.

A more recent study by Bauman and Skitka (2010) had participants read essays supposedly written by members of a debate team on affirmative action. It was made clear to the participants that the debate team coach had assigned the position the debater had to defend based on a coin toss. Participants then read either an essay that was pro- or anti-affirmative action. Participants were then asked what they believed the essay author's true attitude toward affirmative action was. They found that over 50% of the people in their sample showed the correspondence bias effect, 27% reported no bias, and almost 20% indicated that they thought the essay author actually held the opposite position.

The authors introduce the idea that people who say the author holds the opposite view of the one espoused in the essay might be particularly aware of situational constraints. What other explanations might explain the 20% of people who indicated that the author actually was opposed to the position they wrote about?

Why do we make the fundamental attribution error? One explanation makes use of the **actor-observer effect**. The actor-observer effect is best explained by understanding the visual field of a person interpreting a situation. Imagine that you are walking across a room, when you trip. From your vantage point, you will see the floor (and perhaps the ceiling). Most people will then examine the floor for a wrinkled rug or an object that impeded their progress. However, someone across the room saw you trip; their visual field would likely be focused on you. If we ask the person across the room, he or she might infer you are clumsy or inebriated, while you are likely to focus on the flooring as the root cause of your stumble.

SCHEMAS: PURPOSE, DEVELOPMENT, AND USE

Social cognition research also tells us that low-effort thinking occurs when we are thinking about people in particular, but also when we use shortcuts to navigate everyday situations. **Schemas** are mental representations of our understanding of social (and some nonsocial) interactions. Schemas can include information about people, places, events, social roles, or even general situations. When we encounter a situation, often we have been in similar situations in the past and attempt to use our schemas to understand and determine how we should behave. The particular schema that will be activated is determined by cues in the environment. Cues or primes may make a schema more accessible and lead us to use a more accessible schema rather than a less accessible schema.

Consider two types of eating establishments. The first is one in which you stand in line at a counter, place an order, pay for your food, pick up the order at the counter, and seat yourself at table. When done you are expected to throw away your trash and place the tray in a stack of trays to be washed. The second requires you to wait to be seated and once seated a server will take your order and bring your food. When you are finished you then pay for the food and leave. It is pretty easy to identify the first option as a fast-food restaurant compared to a sit-down restaurant. However, a restaurant that uses some mix of these strategies may find customers are frequently confused about what they should or shouldn't do. When this happens people may rely on what actions other people take.

At one local restaurant there is a counter at which you place your order, pay for your food, and receive your beverage. You are then seated and a server will bring you your food. When the meal is over, some people bus their own tables, others leave their tables a mess and a server buses the table later. There are no obvious cues or norms about what precisely is required and there are no signs to provide guidance. Over time it is easy to see the influence of social cues as when one table cleans up their own table and delivers their dishes back to the counter, this seems to activate the fast-food schema and other tables follow suit. However, when one or two tables leave their dishes sitting on the table people may be primed to follow a sit-down restaurant schema and other people will also leave without busing their table.

Try to think of a time in which you encountered an entirely novel situation. It may have taken quite a bit of effort to figure out what you should do. When we encounter unfamiliar situations we may attempt several schemas, none of which may fit well, until we can ascertain what the appropriate actions might be. What would happen if we were not able to use schemas to understand our social world?

Individuals who cannot make new memories due to Korsakoff's syndrome cannot rely on schemas and encounter each situation as though they have never been in such a situation before (Sacks, 1998).

Individuals who have neurological conditions that do not allow them to form or retain schemas often have difficulty with very simple tasks, even remembering who they are. One of Sacks's patients must recreate both others and himself each moment as he cannot retain a memory of who he is or who others might be. However, in the case of a patient known as Dr. P, as described by Sacks, some schemata remained (e.g., chess boards and the game) while others were absent (e.g., people, gloves, shoes). For example, when Dr. Sacks asked a patient to put on his shoe, he did not seem to be able to differentiate his foot from his shoe and could not complete the task. The patient had no specific shoe-goes-on-foot schema. However, when asked to imagine a game of chess Dr. P was quite adept at using schemas about pieces, their moves, and ultimately winning the match. Perceiving each object, person, or situation by breaking down the details and describing the details but unable to use a stored schema or recollection to determine what it is, would be most troubling. For most of us, our schemas provide time-saving shortcuts that allow us to make meaning of our worlds and our lives.

Do schemas serve a larger purpose in our lives beyond simple tasks? How do we then go about developing schemas? How do we choose from many available schemas which should apply in a particular situation?

Schemas allow us to easily and quickly make sense of the world. Schemas allow us to differentiate between situations that will provide some reward and those that will prove dangerous or costly. We also use schemas to make the world a more predictable place. Developing a schema about who will fulfill your basic needs as a child is crucial to surviving. These types of schemas develop through simple associations. If one parent is a person who provides food, then when you are hungry you will seek out that parent to feed you. Another example occurred to a four-year-old of a friend. Michelle had a play date with Candice and quickly learns that Candice fits the schema for "mean child" and avoids playing with her as the play date continues. Several weeks later during day care, the four-year-old witnesses her friend Chloe having her crayons broken by another child. The four-year-old approached Chloe after the incident and applies her pre-learned schema, "Don't play with him, he's mean." Of course food and harm are only two of a multitude of purposes. People also have a strong need to belong to be accepted and schemas also allow us to develop friendships through learned associations about who is going to be friendly and who is not. We also develop schemas about ourselves. We use labels or schemas to understand who we are, where we belong, and how we should behave.

Associations are often at the core of how we develop schemas. Two concepts can become linked to one another or associated. When an association is developed, then whenever one of those ideas comes to mind, so does the other. In a recent conversation with my mother about body modification (e.g., piercings, tattoos), she noted she had a strong association between piercings and infection which made her then see people with multiple facial piercings as unclean in some way. I, on the other hand, associate this type of body modification with the concept of subculture or "alternative" and am quick to form impressions of people with tattoos or piercings as people who are more likely to dismiss conforming to mainstream cultural norms. Another faculty member associates tattoos and piercings with concepts such as unemployable and irresponsible and makes a point of warning students of how others might see them if they modify their bodies in these ways. Of course, none of us are necessarily accurate about our assumptions: Indeed there are many pierced and tattooed people on the faculty (gainfully employed), who are about as mainstream as they come, and no more prone to infection or "uncleanliness" than the next person. Thus, while associations may shape how we form impressions of others, the inaccuracy of these impressions should be acknowledged.

Priming provides one mechanism by which we determine which of our many schemas will fit a situation. One way to think of priming is to view associations between concepts as linked and when one concept becomes activated, that activation spread to other concepts that are closely linked to the original concept. When you think of the word "bread" this may also activate related concepts such as butter, yeast, food, and baking by spreading activation to related concepts. In classic priming studies, you might be given a lexical decision task. A lexical decision task shows a series of letter strings, some of which are words and others not, and the task is to indicate (usually by pressing a key on a keyboard) whether a word is or is not a word. The speed with which you respond provides some measure of how related two concepts are. The slower you are to recognize a word is a word, the less related that word is to the previous word. For example, it will take you less time to indicate that *butter* is a word if you have just seen the word *bread*. It will take you longer to indicate that *nurse* is a word after you have just seen the word *bread*. Priming also has important implications for how we perceive people and social situations.

Recall the "warm/cold" study conducted by Harold Kelley (1950) who invited a guest lecturer to speak to an economics class. Prior to the lecturer's arrival students were given a brief description of the lecturer. All students were told the instructor's age, experience, and some information about his personality. The personality information was preceded by one of two phrases. Half of the students were told the lecturer was a "very warm person" while the other half were informed that the lecturer was a "rather cold person." The guest speaker gave a 20-minute lecture and then students were asked to give ratings of the speaker. Students who were told the guest speaker was a warm person gave higher ratings than those who were told he was a cold person. The students who were primed with the idea that the speaker was warm were also more likely to participate in class discussion and ask questions.

Priming may have worked in this instance to lead students to interpret the lecturer's remarks to be congruent with their preexisting belief that the speaker was warm or cold. However, another study illustrates that making a particular idea accessible even after the event has occurred can lead to biased recollection. In 1981, Claudia Cohen conducted a study in which participants watched a video of a woman having a birthday dinner. Half of the participants were randomly assigned to a condition in which they were told the woman in the video was a librarian; the other half were told the woman was a waitress. The video contained information that was stereotypically congruent with both occupations. When they were done watching the video they were asked to recall as many items as they could from the video. As you would predict, the participants correctly recognized more items that were congruent with the occupation that was mentioned before they watched the video rather than items incongruent with the occupation. This implies that the participants were primed and therefore paid more attention and correctly recognized items that fit their schema for waitress or for librarian.

A similar study was conducted by Brewer and Treyens (1981) in which participants were asked to wait in a graduate student's office. After they had waited in the room for a bit, they were taken to another room and asked to recall what was in the office. Many participants reported that there had been books in the study—after all books are highly consistent with the schema of a "study." However, no books were actually present in the room. In this case the schema did not just guide attention to focus on schema-consistent information, but in fact caused participants to mistakenly recall that an item consistent with the schema was present when it was not.

However, there is also evidence that when we encounter information that is incongruent with our existing schema we are more likely to remember this inconsistency. Inconsistencies draw our attention and we spend more time and energy trying to make sense of this unexpected information. Social cognition researchers have also found that if participants are provided with an opportunity to free recall information about a particular person or situation (rather than a recognition task) they are more likely to recall information that is inconsistent with an existing schema (Srull, 1981).

Consider for a moment a schema that has real-world application and matters far more than the simple presence of absence of objects. Medical doctors are called upon to diagnose particular ailments and illnesses. Diagnosis of a particular illness often requires a doctor to take into account the pattern of complaints and symptoms the patient relays or that can be ascertained from a physical examination. There are several things that come into play as a doctor attempts to diagnose a patient. First, the doctor is likely to pursue a particular diagnostic possibility until it is sufficiently accounting for the presenting symptoms or is ruled out by a symptom that is inconsistent with the schema for that diagnosis. The majority of time this is likely a sound method for diagnosis. However, even schemas held by well-educated practitioners are not always accurate and the consequences can be life threatening.

It was winter when a friend of mine with a remarkably robust immune system had been experiencing shortness of breath and fatigue for a number of days. The symptoms did not seem to ever manifest as a cold virus, though it was the season for such illnesses to spread. Her symptoms did not seem to be improving so she went to the doctor's office. The doctor performed some rudimentary physical examinations (e.g., felt for lymph node swelling, examined nose and throat) and sent her home with a flu diagnosis and instructions to rest. Two days later while at home she experienced an odd feeling in her leg and was concerned enough to go to the emergency room. At the ER she was diagnosed with a deep vein thrombosis (i.e., blood clot in the leg) and put on blood thinners. Her oxygen levels were quite low and likely had been for some time. This explained the shortness of breath, fatigue, and weird feeling in her leg. The first physician's schema was shaped by having treated far more cases of flu than blood clots and it was not part of his typical diagnostic schema to even check oxygen levels for the presenting symptoms. In the months that followed, the clinic for which the physician worked changed their practice and implemented an oxygen measurement as part of routine diagnostic measurements if patients reported shortness of breath.

Schemas which are easily accessible are more likely to be used in interpreting situations and forming impressions of others. Cognitive accessibility refers to a particular idea, concept, schema, or trait being at the front of our mind. Accessibility helps us to retain our cognitive miserliness, while still allowing us to quickly categorize situations and people. When you are walking around campus, your understanding about others is guided by the accessible schemas for college students or faculty. When you encounter a person who is in their 30s, you may quickly categorize them as either faculty or nontraditional college student; but when you encounter someone in their early 20s you readily assume they must be a fellow student and those in their 40s are likely to be faculty or staff. Encountering the very same people at an amusement park, you may quickly interpret older adults as parents or grandparents visiting with children and not think much about their occupation.

Accessibility can also guide our thinking about topics that require more effort. For example, if you have ever been in the position to consider purchasing a new car, cars may very well be accessible. You will find yourself noting what car makes and models your friends drive and driving by a car lot will take on new significance. The concept of purchasing a car is now accessible and you are attempting to gather information about cars in order to make an informed decision.

Chronic accessibility refers to the traits or categories that are frequently used when forming impressions. Using the same concept over and over can lead to chronic accessibility of that concept. Consider traits that you think are important in

others. For some, especially academics, intelligence is chronically accessible. For other people, niceness or accepting might be more chronically accessible. When meeting someone for the first time or forming an impression of a professor for a new course, you might pay particular attention to behaviors that support forming an impression of your professor's intelligence. On the other hand, if you are the sort of student who must rely on professorial generosity to get through a semester, you may pay more attention to cues that help you determine whether they will be generous or understanding.

CAUSAL ATTRIBUTIONS. When we think about why a person behaves in a particular way, we are often looking for a reason or cause for the behavior. Based on our accessible schemas we then make an attribution to a particular reason or a causal attribution. Once a schema is accessible, it is then used to interpret events and while we may form impressions of others from visual cues (e.g., physical appearance), we also form impressions based on watching others in action. When trying to determine if someone has a romantic interest in us, we often think about all of their behaviors and then make a series of attributions about those behaviors. For example, if people smile at us when they walk by, did they smile because they like us, because they were just having a good day, because they smile at everyone? It is through a series of these types of attributions that we determine the reasons behind their behavior.

Salient causes may also be seen as the reason some behavior takes place. For example, whatever is in your visual range may be perceived as more likely to be the cause of a behavior. Remember the actor-observer effect; what you see becomes the cause of the event. Taylor and Fiske (1975) had participants view a conversation from different vantage points. Students tended to attribute more of the causal responsibility to the person that was at the center of their view. Lassiter, Geers, Handley, Weiland, and Munhall (2002) had participants watch a videotaped confession as part of a mock trial. When the camera angle focused on the suspect, participants believed the suspect freely confessed, but when the camera faced the interrogator, they were more likely to believe the confession was coerced. Salient information does not have to be visual.

Rempala and Geers (2009) provided participants with one of four scenarios about a date rape trial. The scenarios varied in how much nondiagnostic information was provided about the defendant and the alleged victim. Their results indicate that providing more information about the defendant increased the participants' ratings of defendant guilt (88%), but only when the information about the defendant was kept to a minimum. When the scenario included more information about the victim and relatively less about the defendant, the defendant was much less likely to be viewed as guilty of rape (63%). The added information increased the salience of that person in the vignette and resulted in more cause for the incident to be placed upon the person about whom there was the most information. When additional information was present (67%) or absent (82.8%) for both victim and defendant, the salience effect was not operating (neither party was more or less salient).

Kelley's covariation theory indicates that we consider three types of information when making attributions (Kelley, 1973).

1. *Consensus information:* Does everyone smile at you? If everyone smiles at you (high consensus), then you may be the sort of friendly person that makes people smile. If most people do not smile at you, but this person does (low consensus), then we might infer a unique interest.

2. *Distinctiveness information:* Does this person smile only at you (high distinctiveness)? If this person smiles at everyone (low distinctiveness), then perhaps the person is just being friendly. However, if this person infrequently smiles at people, but smiles at you then you may infer this person likes you in particular.

3. *Consistency information:* Does this person always smile at you (high consistency)? If your crush smiles at you one day, but the next day doesn't, then it may just have been the funny joke you were telling rather than a deeper interest. On the other hand, if this person smiles at you consistently (high consistency), every time (or almost every time) you see him or her, the smile might in fact communicate this person likes you.

All three of these factors must be considered together in order to understand how attributions are made. For example, if both consistency and consensus are high and distinctiveness is low, then the smiling might be attributed to the situation rather than a unique liking for one another.

APPLICATION SECTION ABOUT POLITICS AND LAW

Understanding the way in which certain primes lead us to attend to or recall information differently has important applications to our legal system. Concepts that are made accessible or primed can influence not only how we perceive the events that follow the prime, but also how we recollect past events. Eyewitness testimony can be impacted by certain phrases or words used in questioning. The classic study by Loftus and Palmer was conducted in 1974. Participants viewed slides of a car accident that involved a number of cars and were asked to describe the accident from an eyewitness point of view. After they provided an initial description, they were asked specifically, "About how fast were the cars going when the contacted each other?" Some participants were randomly assigned to be asked the same question but the verb for "contacted" was changed to either *hit, smashed, collided,* or *bumped.*

The speed estimates were significantly shifted depending on what verb was used in the question about speed. The verb *smashed* resulted in speed estimates over 40 miles per hour, whereas the verb *contacted* resulted in estimates just over 30 mph. A week later participants were brought back in and asked to recall whether there was any broken glass at the scene. Those participants who were asked about speed in the "smashed" condition recalled that there was in fact broken glass. In reality, there was no broken glass in the slides participants were shown.

In May 2010, slate.com readers were asked to participate in a survey in which they were prompted to recall four political events after viewing a photo and brief caption. One of the four events never occurred and was created for the purposes of an experiment (Frenda, Knowles, Saletan, & Loftus, 2013). Over 5,000 people completed the survey asking about three events that occurred: the Terri Schiavo controversy, Bush's Florida victory, and Powell's Iraq speech. In addition, the experimenters created five false events (participants were randomly assigned to provide a response to only one of the five): Lieberman's impeachment vote, Cheney/Edwards argument, Hillary Clinton's attack ad, Bush's Katrina vacation, and Obama's handshake. After viewing four (three true and one false) photos and captions, participants were asked whether they remembered the event and how they felt about the event at the time. After providing their responses, they were told that one of the events was in fact false and were asked to guess which of the incidents they were shown was not true. More than half of the participants reported they remembered the false event happening and half of those who reported they remembered the event indicated they had actually seen the event on the news.

To make matters more interesting, the researchers also found that political ideology increased the chances of remembering a false event that fit with your schema of the opposing party. For example, of the 50% who falsely remembered Bush's Katrina vacation almost 35% self-identified as liberal while the other 15% were conservative. Likewise a bit more than 35% of conservatives reported they remembered the false event of Obama's handshake compared to 25% of liberals. Remember these events never happened, but when they fit a person's schema for what someone from the other party might do, there was an increased willingness to report remembering something that easily fit the schema that was already in place. There were not political ideology differences in recall for the false events that did not pit one side against the other (i.e., Clinton's anti-Obama advertisement).

EMBODIED COGNITION

Our body can also prime schemas or thoughts and our thoughts can prime bodily responses. Some of these embodiments are embedded in our language. Giving someone the cold shoulder means to ostracize or snub someone. Zhong and Leonardelli (2008) found that participants actually thought the room temperature was colder when they were treated coldly and warmer when they were treated warmly. A more recent study by Ijzerman and colleagues (2012) found that after being excluded from a video game called Cyberball, participants actually had lower skin temperatures than when they were included.

Sheldon Cooper on the TV show "Big Bang Theory" may lack some social skills, but there are certain social rules that he follows such as offering a hot beverage to someone who is feeling sad. Ijzerman and colleagues (2012) found support for

Sheldon's inclination. Again participants played a game of Cyberball, in which they were randomly assigned to be included or excluded by other team members. Three minutes into this game the computer would malfunction and a confederate would come into the room to fix the error so the participants could continue playing the game. While fixing the error, the confederate handed a warm tea (or cold tea) to a participant to hold for the 30 seconds it took to fix the system. After they completed the game, the participants were asked to complete some questionnaires about how they were feeling. While everyone who was in the excluded condition reported more negative emotions than those who were included, those given the warm tea to hold did not report as much negative affect as those who were asked to hold the cold tea.

Fay and Maner (2012) extended findings regarding warmth to show that attachment avoidance influenced how far away participants believed a warm cup of water was to them. People who are low in attachment avoidance estimated that the warm cup of water was closer to them than those who are higher in attachment avoidance.

Epley and Gilovich (2004) asked people to estimate the number of states in the United States in 1940. In a separate study, participants were again asked to estimate the number of states in 1840, except they added a manipulation. Participants were asked to either push down on the table in front of them, while the other half were asked to pull up on the table in front of them while providing their estimates. Pushing down on the table is an avoidance posture, while pulling up on the table is an approach posture (Cacioppo, Priester, & Berntson, 1993). Participants asked to take on an approach posture (pulling up on the table) would indicate that participants felt favorably toward the values that occurred to them first (or early adjustments). However, those who are pushing down or asked to take an avoidant posture would reject

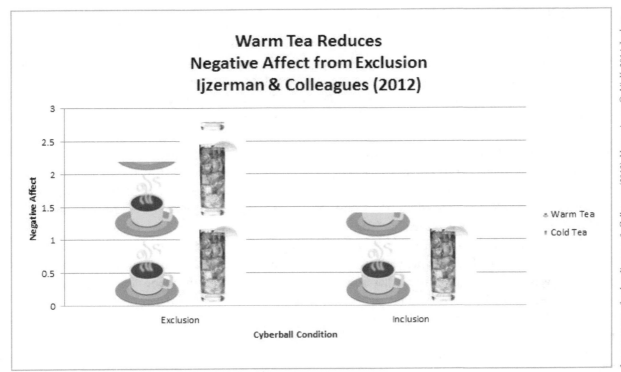

Image courtesy of author. Ijzerman & Colleagues (2012). Hot tea image © AijaK, 2014. Iced tea image © Nitr, 2014. Used under license from Shutterstock, Inc.

FIGURE 3.1 Graph of results from study 2 (Ijzerman and colleagues 2012).

early adjustments and continue to make adjustments over time. Participants in fact showed just this pattern; those who were engaged in approach postures showed the same pattern as before. However, those in the avoidant posture kept adjusting and on average responded with the correct number (26) of states for 1840! Anchoring and adjustment can lead to bias, but if people are persistent in their adjustments, the bias can be corrected.

CONFIRMATION BIAS

Once we form a first impression, how does that impression evolve overtime as we get to know someone? There are several biases that make a first impression difficult to change. Confirmation bias is the tendency to seek evidence that supports an initial belief. If we believe that someone is intelligent we may then seek out confirmation for our impression by asking them about their accomplishments or successes in the classroom. Generally, we are less likely to ask questions that would disconfirm our initial impression. Not asking them about their failures or weakest areas academically allows us to maintain our initial impression of the person as intelligent.

Michael Marks and Chris Fraley (2006) explored how confirmation bias perpetuates the sexual double standard in Western societies. Most people report there is in fact a sexual double standard in which men are judged positively for engaging in sexual behavior and women are judged negatively for doing so (Marks, 2002). However, when people are asked to form impressions of people and given some information about their sexual behavior, there are not significant differences in how men and women are viewed (see Gentry, 1998 for an example). Participants read a journal entry that was attributed to either a heterosexual male or female author. In the journal entries, authors indicate they met a person they knew from school and they attempted to study together, eventually they start dating and were having sex. Then after they break up they continue to have a sexual relationship. The author also writes that

one friend rewards this behavior, "Wow, you keep her(him) coming back, huh?" and another friend tells the author they should not have sex unless they are in a relationship. Participants were then asked how many positive or negative comments by others were included in the journal entry. In a second study, participants were asked to write down as many of the comments as they could remember from the journal entry. Remember everyone read the same journal entry (the sex of the partner and author were manipulated to always be heterosexual). When the author was male, participants thought that there was an even number of positive and negative comments. However, when the author was female, participants thought there were fewer positive comments and more negative comments about her sexual behavior. When asked to recall the comments, participants recalled more negative comments about the female author than any other types of comments. Confirmation bias helps explain these results. Participants are looking to confirm the sexual double standard and recall more positive comments about male sexual behavior.

Can we overcome confirmation bias? Research by Hernandez and Preston (2013) found that when people found a bias difficult to confirm because the information presented lacked fluency they were less likely to show the bias. In this case the manipulation was quite simple. Some participants read an article supporting capital punishment that in a legible (fluent) font, 12-point Times New Roman. The other half of the participants read the same article printed in italicized light gray Haettenschweiler font. Those reading the article in the fluent font were able to easily confirm their preconceived ideas about pro-capital punishment articles and retained their prior stance either for or against capital punishment. Those who read the dis-fluent passage moved to a more neutral position on the issue. However, it takes cognitive resources to effectively correct for the bias; participants in a second study under cognitive load continued to show the confirmation bias even under dis-fluent conditions.

HEURISTICS

Schemas and priming are just two of many heuristics or shortcuts we use when making sense of the social world. Remember that much of the time heuristics and shortcuts help us to cope with the massive amount of information we process as we move through our day and often they are accurate or at least good enough to allow us to navigate situations without causing too much harm to ourselves or others. However, heuristics are not foolproof and may lead to errors and misperceptions.

REPRESENTATIVENESS HEURISTIC. The representativeness heuristic relies on the matching of features or characteristics with a known schema or perception. For example, if you see an older man on campus carrying books you may see this as matching your schema for professor. On the other hand an older woman may not fit the schema for professor and you may decide that an older woman is a nontraditional student or perhaps a staff member in a campus office. However, if you see a younger woman going for a run near campus, your representativeness heuristic may lead you to overestimate the likelihood she is on the track team. This error is referred to as the base rate fallacy (or the failure to take into account base rates). There are likely far more young women on a college campus who go running for exercise than there are women on the track team.

AVAILABILITY HEURISTIC. The availability heuristic relies on how readily we can bring a particular idea to mind and presume the easier it is to generate examples the more relevant those examples must be. However, we also take into account how much information we can generate in determining what information might be relevant. Consider, for example, the teenager who is arguing with parents for access to the family car. He says, "Give me one reason why I can't go." Parents can often very readily come up with one reason right away and so the argument continues. However, if instead the teen asked for ten reasons why he was not allowed to borrow the car, parents may have had more difficulty coming up with so many and the argument may take quite a different turn.

ANCHORING AND ADJUSTMENT. This is another heuristic in which a particular number or standard may impact judgments of experiences after the initial anchor. For example, when you're buying a car, the salesperson often tries to makes sure the first price you hear is high, to provide an anchor from which it is easy to offer you a "deal" at a much lower price. The floor models of cars in the showroom often feature all the bells and whistles and come with prices higher to the cars parked outside in the lot that may lack some of these features. Thus, you get to walk away feeling as though you received quite the deal—after all you paid far less than the original anchor. Epley and Gilovich (2004) conducted a study in which they included a few questions to better understand anchoring and adjustment effects. Some read, "The United States declared its independence on July 4, 1776." Others read, "The United States celebrated its 225th anniversary on July 4, 2001." Then both groups were asked to estimate the number of U.S. states in 1840. Those who were anchored in 1776 may start with the original 13 colonies and work forwards (e.g., there were more states by 1840 than there were colonies). The second group is anchored in 2001 and begin with current numbers and work backwards (e.g., there are 50 states now so there must have been fewer then). The results show that people starting at 50 guess there were more states in 1880 than there actually were and those starting at 13 guess there were fewer states in 1880 than there actually were (see Figure 3.2). In 1840, there were 26 states comprising the United States. Thus, even without someone providing an explicit number, it appears that people in making these types of estimates use recently activated information and then adjust their estimates accordingly.

Anchoring and adjustment effects can also be found when thinking about how we form impressions of others. When we first encounter other people, if we believe they are similar to us, we

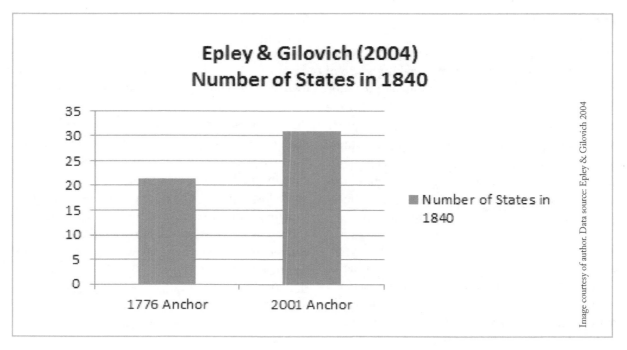

Epley & Gilovich (2004)
Number of States in 1840

Image courtesy of author. Data source: Epley & Gilovich 2004

FIGURE 3.2

often infer that they will also have similar attitudes and values. When we think others are less similar, we may believe their attitudes are slightly different than our own. We use our own attitudes as an anchor and then adjust our perceptions of others' attitudes away from our attitudes in proportion to how similar they are to us.

The **false consensus effect** is one effect that uses anchoring and adjustment and often leads us to overestimate the extent to which others share our opinions (Krueger & Zieger, 1993), or engage in the same activities (Nickerson, 1999). The false consensus effect occurs when we overestimate how many people have congruent attitudes, thoughts, or feelings or engage in behaviors. However, people also realize that others are not exactly the same as they are and adjust their perceptions of others accordingly. Therefore, people may believe that other people are generally as concerned about the economy as they are, but continue to see themselves as more (or less) concerned than other specific individuals. Ngoc Bui (2012) asked participants about their attitudes toward their favorite celebrities. Then participants were asked how

they thought others felt about their favorite celebrities. People tend to overestimate how much others will like their favorite celebrities. However, there are limits to this effect. The tendency to overestimate how many others share our positive attitudes does not extend to undesirable emotions or to certain traits. For example, people who believe they would be embarrassed in a particular situation are actually fairly accurate at predicting how many other people would be embarrassed in the same situation (Sabini, Cosmas, Siepmann, & Stein, 1999).

On the other hand, people who hold particular prejudicial feelings toward a group continue to overestimate how much prejudice others have toward that group (Watt & Larkin, 2010). It appears that many of these biases allow us to maintain a positive view of ourselves, while simultaneously feeling that we are accurate in our assumptions. Carol Sigelman (1991) found that participants who were relatively intolerant of certain groups also overestimated how many others shared their prejudiced feelings. On the other hand, participants who were relatively tolerant of others demonstrated the **false uniqueness effect**. When there is a particularly positive trait that we possess we tend to underestimate the number of others who share this trait in some instances. We are particularly likely to believe that our talents are unique to us, rather than widely shared. These two effects can be generally captured by the idea that we believe our vices are common to many and our virtues are unique to us alone.

SOCIAL COGNITIVE NEUROSCIENCE

Social cognitive neuroscience uses neuroscience technology and methods to explore what happens in our brains as we experience our social world (Lieberman, 2010). Positive emission tomography (PET) scans, functional magnetic resonance imaging (fMRI), event-related potentials (ERPs), and electroencephalographs (EEGs) are all methods used not only in medicine but also by social psychologists who study social cognition. Through these technologies and others the brain areas that are used in social perception have been identified and allowed for studies involving a particular type of social perception to be explored by examining a particular area of the brain.

Interestingly, we do not use the same area of the brain to process all stimuli about people, but rather seem to have particular areas in the brain that are used for processing different parts of people. For example, fusiform area (FFA) has been found to be used in the processing of faces. The FFA area also shows activity when experts perceive the object of expertise (Gauthier et al., 2000). However, the extrastriate body area (EBA) shows more activity when people are shown bodies (Downing, Yuhong, Shuman, & Kanwisher, 2001). The EBA is particularly active when bodies are shown and faces are not clearly visible, but even when both a person's body and face are shown both the FFA and EBA show activation. Further, this area is more active when looking at other bodies rather than looking at one's own body directly (Chan, Peelen, & Downing, 2004).

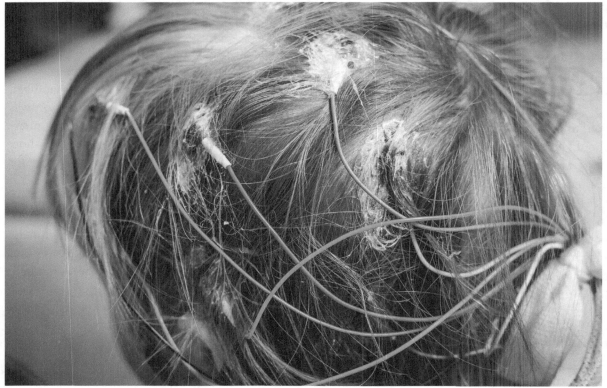

Image © Steve Buckley, 2014. Used under license from Shutterstock, Inc.

In animation and virtual reality design one of the ways in which animals or humans seem to come alive or really move the way a biological animal would move is by using computer programming that mimics the motion of a person or animal walking. Placing markers on the joints of a person while they move and recording that movement allows computer programmers to animate and mimic motion in ways that match the gait of a person. Showing people only the markers on joints and not an actual body is referred to as lightwalkers, where only a few joint locations are shown as a target moves. Fox and McDaniel (1982) found that infants could distinguish biological movement using lightwalker technology. The posterior superior temporal sulcus (posterior STS) shows activation in fMRI studies when lightwalker images are viewed rather than control images that are mechanically produced. Saarela and Hari (2008) found that even the sounds of people walking activated the posterior STS. It is clear that we seem to have particular parts of the brain involved in detecting faces, bodies, and human/animal movement. However, how does this translate into impression formation or other social information that is at the heart of social psychology?

Detecting emotions in others is also a key component of perceiving people and has clear evolutionary survival relevance. Understanding that another person is fearful of something can cue you to look around to determine whether you should also be afraid. The amygdala provides an important key to understanding how people process emotional information. Most of the work in affective neuroscience has focused on activation in the amygdala. Amygdala activation occurs for both positive and negative stimuli (Hamann, Ely, Hoffman, & Kilts, 2002). In addition, the amygdala also shows activation in response to novelty (Schwartz et al., 2003).

Now that we have some information about what parts of the brain are activated during person perception, how can we extend that information to help further social psychology theory? Wimmer and Perner (1983) used a task to test how children developed an ability to understand what it is that others know and what others do not know.

One method used is called the false belief test; it works something like this. Participants are told that John puts his marble in the bottom drawer. John leaves the room and Emily moves the marble to the top drawer. Where does John think his marble is? Clearly the answer is that John will still believe the marble is in the bottom drawer and will look there first. This seems simple, but children develop this theory of other minds around age 3 or 4. There are many other methods that require participants to take another person's perspective or understand their intent (see Lieberman, 2010 for a review). Across these studies the dorsomedial prefrontal cortex shows involvement in 91% of these mentalizing tasks (Lieberman, 2010).

EMPATHY

Lamm, Nussbaum, and colleagues (2007) presented participants (who were being scanned) with pictures showing needles piercing the skin of a person's hand. Half of the participants were randomly assigned to be told that the person's hand had been numbed prior to the procedure. Thus, all participants saw the same images, but participants who believed the hand was numbed could infer that the experience of the person was not painful. Would the participants show mentalizing or perspective taking or would they show mirror neuron activation? Providing support for the mirror system the pain regions of the brain (dorsal ACC, anterior insula, and somatosensory cortex) were strongly activated across conditions. However, the areas of the brain involved in mentalizing or perspective taking were more active in participants told that the hand had been numbed.

Thinking about the Self

You know yourself better than you know anyone else and better than anyone else knows you. Understanding how we perceive ourselves requires us to consider the ABCs (affect, behavior, cognition) of social psychology. The affective component of the self is how we feel about ourselves or our positive or negative evaluation of the self. **Self-esteem** is how we evaluate the content of our self-knowledge or self-concept. **Self-concept** is the cognitive component of the self and includes all of the information that we believe to be true about ourselves. The self-concept does not necessarily include evaluative information. When we evaluate our self-knowledge and decide that we like or do not like something about the self, this contributes to our self-esteem. The behavioral component of the self is best understood by looking at how we engage in **self-presentation**. Self-presentation refers to the ways in which we control our behaviors, appearance, and overall impression management. Self-presentation shapes not only how we attempt to make a good impression on others, but also how our self-presentation shapes our own understanding of who we are. In the next section we will take each of these in turn and explore the research that helps us understand how we perceive the self. We will begin with the cognitive component as the self-concept provides the foundation for the affective and behavioral components of the self.

SELF-CONCEPT

A person's self-concept is comprised of all of the knowledge a person has learned about who they are, what they do, how others see them, and what they do. **Self-knowledge** is learned by not only witnessing our lives as they unfold, but also by how others and society react to us. Socialization is a process through which other people shape our behavior and perceptions to allow us to understand how we fit (or do not fit) within a larger social context. The self also helps us to organize our worlds more generally. The self-reference effect has shown that if you relate something to your own life or yourself you have a better memory for that information than if you try to remember the information without finding a way to link it to yourself. Rogers, Kuiper, and Kirker (1977) asked people to view a list of words and then were either asked about the properties of the word itself or whether the word described the participant in some way. Participants were then asked to recall the words and showed significantly higher recall when they had been asked if the word was related to the self. Note this was true even if the word did NOT relate to the self, simply considering the word in relation to the self was enough to enhance recall of the word at a later time.

A similar effect is the **endowment effect**. Kahneman, Knetsch, and Thaler (1991) found that people put higher values on items if they felt they owned the item rather than valuing the same item that did not belong to them. Consider two identical shopping baskets, neither contains any items. If you had chosen one of those baskets and someone offered you another identical basket there would be some hesitation about trading "your" basket for another (even when you do not really own the basket at all)!

Self-knowledge is organized in part by self-schemas. You probably experience some shift in "who you are" as you engage in different aspects of your life. For example, you as an athlete may have a different set of traits that become accessible when you are playing sports. These traits may take a back seat when a self-schema of daughter is activated. For example, your athletic self may be competitive yet when in the role of daughter you may be far more cooperative.

EXERCISE 3.1

Begin with the sentence stem "I am" and complete this sentence 10 times, listing 10 things that you "are." Do this *before* you read the questions below. The list is likely to be varied and people differ in how easy it is to complete this task. Some will quickly come up with 10 and could easily jot down 20 or more. Others may have difficulty coming up with more than 5 ways to complete the sentence. Once you have your list, think about the ways in which you finished the sentence and answer the questions about this exercise at the end of the chapter.

We often have a multifaceted view of ourselves as we move through situations and take on new jobs, form new relationships, or develop new hobbies or skills. **Self-complexity** refers to the extent to which a person perceives the self as complex with many ways to see the self. A person who is highly self-complex is likely to see the self as fulfilling many roles or having many distinct ways of seeing oneself, whereas a person who is low in self-complexity may have only a few roles or ways or defining oneself. Self-complexity shapes how resilient we are when confronted with failure.

Linville (1985) measured how self-complex participants were and then gave them false feedback about their performance on a task. Individuals with low self-complexity showed greater drops in self-esteem after failure feedback and greater increases in self-esteem after success feedback. Individuals who were more self-complex had only modest positive changes in response to success and modest negative changes in self-esteem when given failure feedback. Self-complexity can provide a buffer against major changes in self-evaluation. Consider an example of two people, one with high and one with low self-complexity. The first person has been extremely successful in business and is primarily known to friends and colleagues as being a brilliant leader. This person spends most days in the office and down-time is typically between business trips spent in hotels and airports. There is little time for hobbies or relationships outside of work. A second individual is a chef at one of the busiest restaurants in a large city. While work days are long and arduous in the restaurant, life at home revolves around family. Cooking is this person's passion, but there is also a community orchestra, wood shop, and a novel in progress that fill days away from the restaurant. Now let's imagine that both women suffer job losses after a significant recession and work is hard to come by. While both women are likely to feel distressed and continue to look for work, the chef is less likely to suffer the severe negative moods that the business leader does. The ways in which the chef defines herself are varied and if one aspect of life is not going so well, there are other things to focus on. For the business leader, there is not much else to fall back on to boost her self-esteem.

The above case is quite simple and focuses mostly on roles, skills, and relationships rather than traits. However, let's consider one other case. Persons who see themselves primarily as a generous person and the list they might generate in the "I am…" exercise includes the following: a philanthropist, charitable, nice, kind, generous, sacrificing, on the advisory board for three nonprofits, a volunteer, giving, and religious. This may at first seem like someone who is very self-complex, but imagine that this person was accused of being greedy, what would happen to this person's mood? The self-complexity that is shown here really shows 10 different things that all overlap with one another and have a common theme of generosity. In order for self-complexity to truly provide a buffer against negative experiences, the self-complexity must highlight domains that do not have significant overlap with one another. From our earlier example, being a good cook does not make one an excellent viola player and failing at one would not detract from one's ability to continue to be successful at the other. However, the generous person accused of being greedy might experience failure that seeps into all 10 of the listed aspects of this person's self-concept.

Of course, the story is also a bit more complex than simply seeing the self as multifaceted. This type of self-complexity is only beneficial and buffering if all of the varied aspects of the self are authentically lived (Ryan, LaGuardia, & Rawsthorne, 2005). If one moves easily through their diverse roles and self-aspects then a singular failure does not undermine self-esteem, mood, or well-being. However, if persons feel as though the many hats they wear are challenging and perhaps not who they really are, these multiple self-aspects become chronic stressors and do not improve well-being. We all have people in our lives who we know to be more or less authentic in their various roles. Organization and informal policies such as "don't ask, don't tell" related to sexual orientation add stress to the lives of nonheterosexual people predominantly because they require individuals to take on roles that are inauthentic.

SELF-ESTEEM

Self-esteem has received a great deal of attention in popular culture, the media, and societal dialogue. It seems that any time someone is having a difficult time finding a job, partner, or has a bad day, self-esteem is thought to be at the root of the problem. If a person only had higher self-esteem, more self-confidence, more self-respect, everything would turn out just fine. It would seem that if everyone had a positive view of themselves, perhaps the world would be a better place. That is certainly the thinking behind self-esteem initiatives funded by states and schools in an attempt to boost self-esteem and reduce drug use, teen pregnancy, and antisocial behavior. There is some evidence that people with low self-esteem do not deal well with failure (Brockner, 1979) and are more depressed (Crocker & Wolf, 2001). However, Baumeister (1998) found that high self-esteem is simply a resource used in the face of failure that allows someone to persevere. Yet, there is very little evidence that low self-esteem leads to social problems directly (Crocker & Wolf, 2001).

Social psychologists define self-esteem as the evaluation of the self-concept. That is, a person may have a self-concept that includes self-knowledge that others may evaluate, but self-esteem is dependent upon the individual's *own* evaluation of the self-concept. While we cannot help but be influenced by what society indicates is a good or bad thing to be, it is naïve to assume that because society thinks that being short, fat, or bald is negative, it certainly isn't always the case. There are plenty of people who possess traits that society does not value, who see them as a core, valued, and positive part of their identity.

The media and some research have discussed self-esteem as a relative simple construct. Recall that self-esteem is the evaluation of the self-concept. Think back to the "I am..." exercise. This is only a partial reflection of your self-concept, but you can see that the types of things you list vary and how you feel about yourself is similarly diverse. The way in which we have discussed self-esteem to this point focuses on a construct referred to as global self-esteem. Global self-esteem is an overall evaluation of the entire self-concept and might be measured by asking whether you agree with statements such as, "I am a person of worth." However, the ways in which you determine whether you should agree or not agree, may depend on the basis for your self-worth. Some people may embrace a religious view and base their self-worth on whether they are loved by God or other spiritual beliefs about building good karma (Crocker & Wolf, 2001). Others may have self-esteem that is contingent upon physical appearance, wellness, or how skilled they are at a particular task. Most people will have multiple contingencies for determining their self-worth.

By contrast, state self-esteem refers to your self-esteem at any given point. For example, if you base your self-worth on being a good student, you will likely report a low self-esteem after failing an exam, even if you have only failed one exam in your entire academic career. While in that moment you are experiencing a state of self-esteem that is low, your global self-esteem is buoyed by all of the tests that you did not fail and other contingencies on which you based your self-esteem. In addition, failures in domains on which you do not base your self-esteem are not likely to have much impact on your self-esteem. If you have never bowled much in your life, but go out on the weekend to bowl a few rounds with friends, your five gutter balls in a row are not likely to lead to low self-esteem. State self-esteem shifts over time; trait self-esteem persists well into the future.

What does this research tell us about social problems? There are some limits to what can be blamed on low self-esteem. Indeed some research has demonstrated that people with very high self-esteem react violently when their self-esteem is threatened (Baumeister, Smart, & Boden, 1996). However, other research has found that adolescents with high self-esteem have better outcomes in adulthood (employed, less criminal behavior, better health, good economic prospects) (Trzesniewski et al., 2006). How do we make sense of these conflicting findings? The answer seems to return to the idea of contingencies. Self-esteem that is grounded in domains in which a person is legitimately competent shows that high self-esteem is related to resilience in the face of failure and generally positive outcomes. However, individuals who have baseless high self-esteem are going to show those violent tendencies when threatened. It is easy to imagine a bully who believes he is better than everyone else, but it's not clear exactly what he is better at doing, other than intimidating people. When the bully's self-esteem is threatened, rather than show resilience and dedication to improving in a particular domain, he lashes out toward those he finds threatening.

SELF-ENHANCEMENT

People have two primary motivations when perceiving the social world. The first is to be accurate

in our perceptions of our social world. An accurate understanding of how dangerous a situation might be or whether another person is going to be helpful is critical to survival. This often also means we need to be accurate in our perceptions of ourselves. Consider a playground conflict: The decision about whether to engage in a conflict with others is based not only on an assessment of their skills, but also an assessment of our own skills. A miscalculation on either side could result in losing face or even suffering physical harm. However, we have a second competing motivation to maintain a positive view of ourselves. People who view themselves (and their partners) as better than they really are show less depression. Indeed, a person who has a very accurate self-assessment is likely to be experiencing depression. People who are depressed show accuracy in predicting how other people feel about them (Lewinsohn, Mischel, Chaplin, & Barton, 1980) and how much control they exert over events in their lives (Alloy & Abramson, 1979). People who are not depressed tend to engage in a series of strategies to maintain positive illusions about the self.

Threats to self-esteem increase self-enhancement. Beer, Chester, and Hughes (2013) provided participants with false feedback about how likeable 10 strangers rated them based on a photo. Participants were either told that more than half (6, 7, or 8) of raters said they were unlikeable or in the control condition no one thought they were unlikeable. When participants were told that others perceived them as unlikable they rated themselves as possessing more favorable personality traits than their peers compared to participants in the control group. All participants engaged in self-enhancement indicating they had fewer undesirable traits than their average peer; but when self-esteem was threatened their self-ratings became even more positive. Does this bias happen relatively quickly or do people devote a great deal of effort when engaged in self-enhancement? In later experiments, Beer and colleagues (2013) had participants engage in the same task, but they were asked to remember a five-digit number (high cognitive

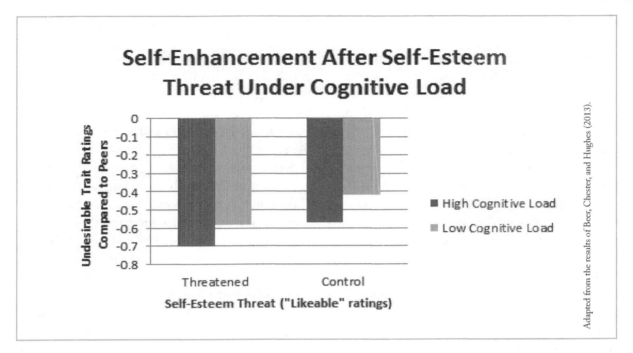

FIGURE 3.3

load) or one-digit number (low cognitive load) while making their trait ratings. Remembering a five-digit number requires significant effort and may make attending to trait ratings difficult. The results indicate that when cognitive resources were low (high cognitive load condition) and participants and their self-esteem were threatened, they were even more likely to indicate they had fewer undesirable traits than their average peer (see Figure 3.3).

Self-enhancement increases not only when self-esteem is threatened, but also when cognitive resources are limited. "A 2 (threat, no threat) × 2 (load, no load) between-subjects ANOVA predicting social comparisons of personality traits showed significant main effects of threat ($F(1,132) = 4.72$, $p = .03$, $\eta_p^2 = .04$) and load ($F(1,132) = 3.93$, $p = .05$, $\eta_p^2 = .03$) and a non-significant interaction term ($F(1,132) = .05$, $p = .82$, $\eta_p^2 = 0.00$)" (Beer, Chester, & Hughes, 2013, pp. 708-709). Can you interpret the main effects here? What conclusions can you draw given that the two-way interaction is not significant?

Self-serving bias is a strategy in which interpretation of events is skewed such that people take credit for their success and blame external factors for their failures. Do we always make attributions that are self-serving? Some research indicates that self-serving bias is more likely to occur when we are in good moods than in bad moods. Coleman (2011) induced participants to experience guilt, revulsion, or neutral affect. Then participants received false feedback or no feedback about their performance on an earlier knowledge test. Participants were randomly assigned to mood conditions and then again randomly assigned to receive positive, negative, or no false feedback. Participants were then asked whether their performance was due to their abilities on the exam. What would participants do? Would guilty participants take more responsibility for their performance? Would the feedback matter? Participants in the guilt and revulsion condition showed a smaller self-serving bias than those in the control condition; they made fewer internal attributions when given success feedback and fewer external attributions when given failure feedback.

What are the real-world applications for self-serving bias? Kriss, Loewenstein, Wang, and Weber (2011) found that when attempting to negotiate responsibility for changing policy to mitigate climate change, participants showed self-serving biases. Participants were given one of three scenarios: China vs. USA; Country A vs. B; or Farmer A vs. B. In each scenario there was some economic cost to enacting a particular plan and the participant was asked to use a sliding scale to indicate how much of the burden should be taken by each side. U.S. citizens reported that China should shoulder 41.69% of the burden, while Chinese citizens reported that China should take only 26.33% of the burden. However, in conditions where the countries in question are named only A and B, both citizens of the United States and China indicated that Country B should have a one-third of the burden. One implication of these findings is that self-serving bias significantly shapes perceptions of fairness and common ground can be reached in debates, but self-serving bias must be mitigated to do so. Can you think of examples from your own life when self-serving bias has been reduced?

Is self-serving bias an automatic response? Results from EEG work by Krusemark, Campbell, and Clementz (2008) indicate such attributions. When participants make non-self-serving attributions there is more activation in the dorsomedial frontal cortex indicating that self-control and effort are required to avoid self-enhancing bias. Participants in their study were asked to remember a series of faces and then provided false feedback about their recall performance. Participants provided self-serving attributions overall, but on the occasions when they did not, the part of the brain associated with cognitive control and deliberation showed more activity. For most people, the automatic tendency to engage in self-serving bias or other self-enhancing thoughts is automatic and it takes significant effort to question rather than accept our successes and consider rather than dismiss our shortcomings.

Self-handicapping is when persons themselves up so that if they fail they will have a good ex-

ternal factor on which to lay the blame. McCrea, Hirt, and Milner (2008) had participants come into the lab and complete a short verbal test on which they were all told they did well (top 10% of college students). Participants were also told that their score on this test indicates they should also do well on a second test to be given later in the experiment. During the delay before the second test, participants were given the opportunity to practice their skills for as long as they liked. Half were told that the practice would likely help them do well on the second test and the other half were told practice was not likely to matter. Results show that men were less likely to practice (e.g., more likely to self-handicap) than women when told that practice would help them perform well. Further, 25% of men compared to 4% of women spent less than 30 seconds on the practice task. This allowed men who did poorly on the second test to simply point to their lack of practice to explain their poor performance. The question remains, why did women actually practice? Women tend to score higher on a scale that measures the importance of effort compared to men and people who score high on valuing effort are less likely to engage in self-handicapping behaviors.

Self-handicapping allows a person to attribute their performance to a lack of effort. However, the sex difference paints a more complex picture. Certainly as McCrea and colleagues (2008) find, women do not seem to actually self-handicap, they practice and put in effort when provided the opportunity to do so. However, when asked to make verbal attributions for failure experiences, both women and men make excuses that point to external factors (not their own effort or ability). For example, two students, one male and one female, who are encouraged to go out the night before a big exam are both likely to go. However, the female student is likely to return home fairly early and put in some study time before the exam. The male student is likely to stay out later and not put in any study time before the exam. If they both do poorly on the exam, they both have an excuse, "I went out last night and didn't study as much as

I should have." However, the female student has reduced the likelihood she will need the excuse, but has set up the situation so that she can use it if needed.

BETTER THAN AVERAGE: UNIQUELY VIRTUOUS WITH COMMON VICES. In order to see ourselves in a positive light we tend to perceive that we are better than other people on average. Illusory superiority is a bias that people have in which they overestimate their good qualities and underestimate their bad qualities. Another term for this effect is the Wobegon effect, taken from Garison Keillor's novels about Lake Wobegon, a fictional town where "all the women are strong, all the men are good looking, and all the children are above average." For example, Armor and Sackett (2006) found that people predict that they will do much better on a hypothetical task and that their predictions are not aligned with their true performance.

Williams and Gilovich (2008) set out to determine whether people report they are better than average in laboratory settings, but in fact do not sincerely believe their overestimates. In a clever study, participants were asked to complete a bogus personality test of yes/no items. They were then asked how they thought they had scored compared to other students at the same university. All participants in the study estimated themselves to be above average on all four traits that were measured (intelligent, creative, mature, and positive). As a last phase of the experiment, participants were given the opportunity to make four bets for $1 each. Participants could either bet on whether they would score higher than a randomly selected anonymous peer on a particular trait or on the probability of drawing a token from the jar that had a particular number on it. The probability of the token drawing was yoked to their self-ranking, meaning that if they said they were more creative than 60% of their peers, the probability that they would win the token drawing was set at 60%. This means that if they were aware they were overestimating their ranking in the first part of the task, they should bet on the jar and if they were under-

estimating their ranking they should bet on the comparison with a peer. However, the findings revealed that participants saw the probabilities as entirely equal and therefore believed their self-ratings to be a true reflection of the self.

SELF-AWARENESS

When we are self-aware, all of the self-schema we have may have heightened activation. When this self-awareness becomes uncomfortable it is referred to as the spotlight effect. Many students in classrooms are experiencing the spotlight effect when they indicate they do not speak up in class because they are afraid they will say something that is incorrect and everyone will remember this error. Because we are so focused on our own experiences we may find it difficult to accurately assess how others are going to perceive our behavior. The reality is that students often have difficulty even recalling information they are there to learn so it is unlikely that a typical student question or comment is going to garner much more attention. However, the spotlight effect goes beyond negative experiences; we also believe that when we have a great success everyone will also see how great it was. Again, we overestimate how much attention others are paying to us and may be disappointed when no one seems to notice our recent exposition of brilliance.

Gilovich, Medvec, and Savitsky (2000) conducted a series of studies demonstrating that people overestimate how much attention others are paying to them. They asked participants to wear a t-shirt that depicted Barry Manilow (which had been pretested to be embarrassing). Once they had put the shirt on they were led to another room and seated facing several observers (who were also participants in the experiment but had been given a slightly earlier arrival time). After seating the Manilow-wearing participant, the second experimenter waits a few moments and then indicates that the experiment is too far along to allow for a late start participant and asks the participant to wait outside. Once in the hallway, the experimenter who had given the t-shirt

positive image, as did Bob Marley and Dr. King). The procedure was the same as before. Again, the findings revealed that the participants wearing the t-shirt estimated that 48% of the observers would accurately recall the t-shirt image. In this experiment only 8% recalled the image on the t-shirt. Did you notice that the observers were much less accurate in the positive shirt condition than in the embarrassing shirt condition? The authors of the study indicate it is likely due to how engaging the pretest questionnaire was in the second study (i.e., participants were involved in completing the questionnaire and did not pay as much attention to the late arrival of the t-shirt-wearing participant). Can you think of other explanations and how you might test your hypotheses?

SELF-REGULATION: THE SELF IN ACTION

How do thoughts and feelings about the self influence behavior? What role does motivation play

FIGURE 3.4 When self-awareness is low, we may be able to ignore a stain on our shirt and not consider what other people think. However, when self-awareness is high we may take extra care with our appearance and table manners.

Illustration by Max Dusky.

to the participant to wear asked the person how many of the people in the room would recall that the participant was wearing a Barry Manilow t-shirt. The participants who had arrived earlier and served as observers in the experiment were asked if they noticed who was pictured on the t-shirt the other participant was wearing. The person wearing the t-shirt estimated that about 50% of the participants would recall the t-shirt depiction, but only 25% identified the t-shirt as depicting Barry Manilow. Is the spotlight effect limited to only situations that might be embarrassing? To find out Gilovich, Medvec, and Savitsky (2000) ran a second study in which the t-shirts depicted Martin Luther King, Jr., Bob Marley, or Jerry Seinfeld (the study took place in the late 1990s and Seinfeld pretested as a

Image © Helga Esteb, 2014. Used under license from Shutterstock, Inc.

in determining self-regulation? Self-regulation refers to a person's ability to exercise control over his or her own behaviors. When people are relatively autonomous they are internally motivated to regulate their behavior. Legault and Inzlicht (2013) conducted a study in which participants were randomly assigned to either a choice condition, control condition, or baseline condition. In the choice condition, participants were told they could choose which of four tasks they would like to complete. The experimenter in the control condition would strongly encourage the participants to choose the fourth task. Finally, in the baseline condition, participants were simply given the task without pressure and without choice. The task in every case was the Stroop task which requires significant cognitive resources and self-regulation. While participants were completing this task they were also undergoing EEG recordings of their brain activity. Participants in the choice condition performed much better on the stroop task than those individuals who had less autonomy in the experiment (see Figure 3.5). This provides some evidence that self-regulation is highest when people are operating independently, rather than when

they are influenced by external factors. The advice that a person who is going to quit smoking or lose weight needs to "do it for themselves" is congruent with this finding. When people are internally motivated, they are more successful at regulating their own behavior.

Legault and Inzlicht (2013) also found that there was more brain activity in an area of the brain associated with negative affect for those individuals in the choice condition. However, this difference in brain activity only occurred when errors were made. There were no differences in brain activity when participants were responding correctly. When it comes to regulating your behavior, it is your ability to respond to failure that is more important than how you experience your successes.

Note: The Stroop task involves naming the color of words, all of which name a color. For example the word "RED" would be printed in blue ink. Your task is to say aloud the color of the word rather than read the word. So the appropriate response in this example would be to say, "blue." As you might imagine this requires significant focus.

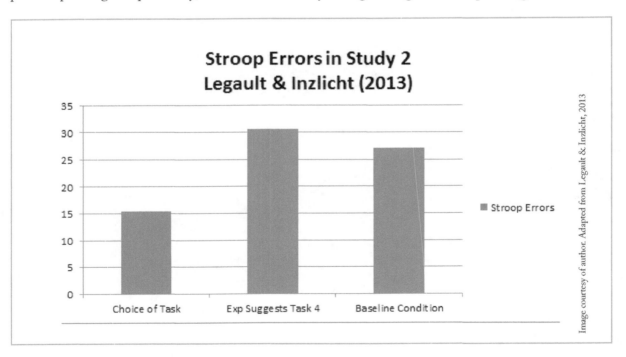

FIGURE 3.5

You can try it for yourself here: http://cognitive-fun.net/test/2.

Self-discrepancy occurs when a person's current view of the self does not match an ideal view of the self or an ought view of the self. Your ideal self is the person that you believe you possess the potential to become; an aspirational self. Your ought self is the person you believe you should be. Failure to live up to the expectations of the ideal and ought self lead to self-discrepancy. However, a barrier that prevents you from being your ideal self may lead you to be depressed or sad. When your actual self deviates from your ought self, you may feel anxious rather than depressed. This self-discrepancy is often motivating and encourages people to change their actual self to be more in alignment with the ought and ideal self.

In 2009, Brown and McConnell examined the role of self-complexity and affective responses on behavior. Participant's completed a measure of self-complexity and a measure of affect (positive and negative feelings). Then participants performed a task of verbal ability and were provided feedback indicating they had not done well. A second measure of affect was taken and then participants were provided an opportunity to practice the task under conditions of heightened self-awareness (in front of a mirror). How do you think people who are high and low in self-complexity responded? Who chose to practice? Who avoided the task? Some participants were told that the opportunity to practice would likely improve their performance and others were told that the practice was not very helpful in improving performance. Individuals low in self-complexity use their mood to regulate their behavior, by practicing only when their mood is negative and only if the practice would be effective. Participants high in self-complexity rely more heavily on external situations to guide their behavior rather than their internal state and typically put some effort into the practice regardless of mood, exerting the most effort when their mood was positive on the effective task.

NAME _____ DATE _____

Chapter Questions

1. Did you use traits describing your physical appearance (brunette, tall, muscular)?

2. Were there more temporary states on your list (e.g., hungry, tired, alive)?

3. How many social roles did you list (e.g., brother, partner, friend, student)?

4. Did you list skills or talents (e.g., pianist, accountant)?

5. Did you list demographics or social identities (e.g., American, straight, white, transgendered)?

6. Did you list things that you would have in common or make you unique from others?

7. What cultural influences do think influenced your list?

8. Why do you think you listed some items and not others?

9. What situations could you imagine that would lead you to generate a completely different list?

Social Influence

4

The Power of Others

In this chapter we will consider how others impact our own perceptions, behaviors, thoughts, and feelings. However, as you are reading about how other people influence us, we must at the same time recognize when this type of influence is mutual. What impact are you having on others as you move through your day?

In 1968, Bibb Latane and John Darley published the findings of a study about how people use other people as cues even in emergency circumstances. Participants were asked to sit in a small waiting room and complete a questionnaire. While the participants are completing the questionnaire the room is filled with smoke through air vents. Half of the participants were alone in the room completing the questionnaire, while the other half were filling out the questionnaire with two other individuals also

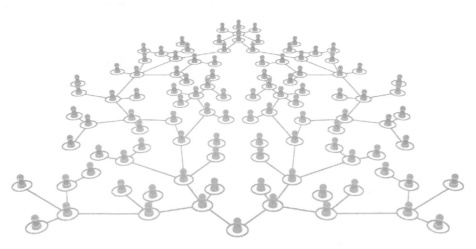

in the room. All participants were surreptitiously watched through a one-way mirror. When people were alone in the room, it only took about two minutes before they left the room to seek help. However, when participants were in the room with others, they continued to complete the questionnaire as the room filled with smoke. Indeed only three people (out of 24 participants) reported the smoke prior to completing the questionnaire. Latane and Darley (1968) concluded that having other individuals in the room who did not seem to be concerned about the smoke seeping into the room led other participants to decide that they should not worry about the smoke either. In this case, the power of others led people to endure rather unpleasant smoky conditions, but also to ignore signs of a potential emergency.

During a long layover in an airport, I noticed approximately 10 people (note how you immediately presume I mean adults rather than children, people = adults), pacing in circles that would widen until they encroached on someone else's circle and they would retreat back to their own pacing territory. They were all talking, but not to each other. They did not seem to know one another, but they were clearly behaving in a synchronous way. What do you think they were doing? They were talking on cell phones in a part of the airport that provided particularly good cell reception. There has not been a clear manual or even years of socialization that would shape why this should occur. Why were these people not sitting to have their conversation or simply standing still instead of risking collision with others?

One reason might be something referred to as reflexive mimicry. Chartrand and Bargh (1999) had participants complete a task in the presence of a confederate. The confederate would regularly rub their face or shake their foot while carrying out a task describing a series of photographs. The participants were doing the same tasks and the entire session was videotaped. The videotapes were then coded by independent raters for how often the participants either shook their foot or rubbed their face. The results show that participants were more likely to mimic the

behavior of the confederate than to engage in the behavior that they did not witness. However, this type of mimicry does not have any particular meaning in the social world, at least not much meaning. Although someone waiting for an anxiety-provoking event may find that another person exhibiting nervous foot tapping or shaking seems to heighten their own anxiety. However, other types of mimicry may serve a larger social function.

Another type of mimicry is emotional mimicry in which people imitate the emotional expressions of others. Consider how readily we smile when someone else is smiling at us, and how it can be a challenge to refrain from doing so. Laugh tracks in sitcoms provide a social cue to laugh and emotional contagion often means that even if you are alone watching the show you will laugh along when the laugh track is playing. There is not a social reward for doing so, but certain emotions seem to be contagious. Crying may work similarly; some people express this by saying, "don't cry or you'll make me cry." We seem to have some awareness of the contagion of emotions and yet we realize it takes some effort to not mimic the emotions of others. In order to effectively predict the behavior of others, we infer that people who are happy are likely to have affiliative intentions and people showing anger or disgust may not be friendly and could be a source of violence (Hess et al., 2000).

When do we engage in emotional mimicry? When we have a positive attitude toward a person we are more likely to mimic their emotions. However, when we have a negative attitude toward another person we rarely mimic their emotional expressions (Hess & Fischer, 2013). We are also more likely to mimic those with whom we are cooperative and less likely to mimic those with whom we compete (Weyers et al., 2009). We are more likely to emotionally mimic people we perceive as part of our in-groups compared to those we think of as being from out-groups. Van der Schalk (Schalk et al 2011) found that participants seeing fear in out-group member faces displayed contempt. We are also less likely to mimic angry faces if those faces seem to be directed at us, but if we see anger being directed elsewhere we may mimic anger expressions. Finally, while we do not mimic the smiling behavior of out-group members, smiling at strangers is often a low-cost behavior that can elicit or send affiliative cues to others (Hinsz & Tomhave, 1991). However, we are far less likely to mimic strangers who are frowning, as mimicry of a frown implies that we understand the sad situation and might be willing to offer help (Herrera, Bourgeois, & Hess, 1998).

Likowski and others (2011) had participants watch happy movie clips (from *When Harry Met Sally*) or sad clips (from *The Champ*) as part of a mood induction. Participants were then presented with a series of avatar facial expressions: happy, sad, neutral, and angry. The experimenters measured EMG (electromyograph) responses. Results show that individuals who watched *When Harry Met Sally* clips also showed more zygomaticus major activity (smiling: elevates the lips) when presented with the happy avatar. The corrugator supercilii muscle (frowning: knitted eyebrows) demonstrated most activity again when happy people viewed the sad faces or the angry faces. Finally, the frontalis medialis (angry expression muscles: wrinkled forehead) was also most active when happy people saw the sad or angry faces. Individuals who were sad did not seem to mimic expressions of avatars very readily, other than frowning in response to the happy avatar.

Why do we mimic others? Sims, Reekum, Johnstone, and Chakrabarti (2012) measured electromyographic activity in the zygomaticus major (smiling muscle) while participants viewed a series of faces. In the first part of the experiment, participants were conditioned to associate certain faces with positive rewards. Participants played a simple card game in which they were presented with a photo of the neutral face and two cards face down. They were asked to guess (by pressing a key) which would be higher. If participants guessed correctly they received a few points and if they guessed incorrectly they lost points. There were four targets: one paired with 90% of wins, one paired with 60% of

wins, one paired with 60% of losses, and one paired with 90% of losses. Thus, one of these four faces was associated with high positivity. It is important to note that the faces were described to participants as part of a memory task they would complete later in the experiment. In the second part of the experiment, participants were again presented the four faces expressing happiness or anger. Results show that participants exhibited more zygomaticus major activity in response to the high-reward happy face than to the low-reward happy face. Participants also completed the autism spectrum quotient, which measures the extent to which someone has autistic traits. Individuals who had higher scores (indicating more autistic traits) did not show a difference in smiling behavior in response to faces based on reward conditioning. The authors suggest that having difficulty linking empathy (as measured by emotional mimicry) and reward may explain in part why some autistic individuals do not respond to social rewards.

In a real-world setting, Fischer-Lokou, Martin, GuéGuen, and Lamy (2011) demonstrated the impact of mimicry on helping behavior. Passersby were asked for directions to a nearby location by a confederate. The confederate mimicked either the passersby's verbal behavior or both the verbal and nonverbal behaviors. In a control condition, the confederates did not mimic the participant when asking for directions. Further down the street the same participant encountered a second confederate who asked for some money to ride the bus. The dependent variable was if any bus fare was provided or not. Here the experiment's results provide some evidence that mimicry during a prior helping act provides some social reward that is then paid forward to a second request for assistance. Remember the second requestor did not mimic and did not have any clear connection to the first requestor.

Some have proposed that we mimic others as preparation for interaction with them. This fits nicely with the idea that we do not mimic people we hope to avoid (e.g., angry people). Cesario, Plaks, and Higgins (2006) asked participants to

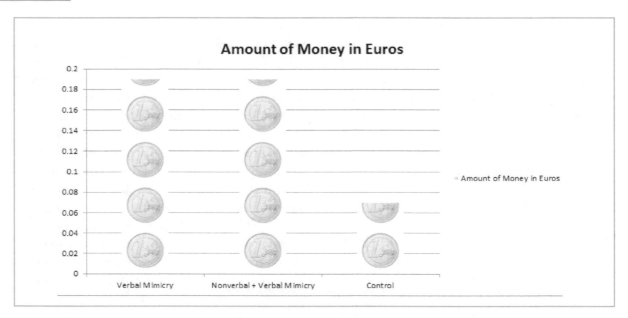

FIGURE 4.1A

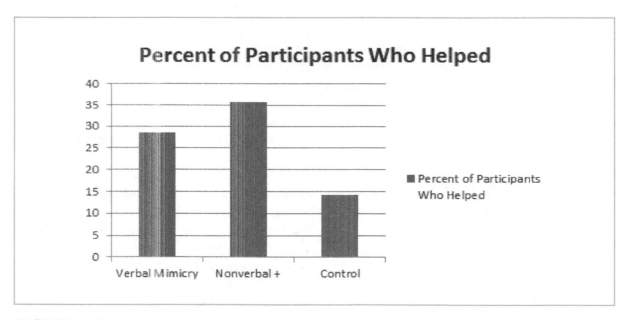

FIGURE 4.1B

think about older adults and found that after they had spent time doing so they took longer to walk down the hallway to the elevator to leave the experiment. Thus, the idea that older people move more slowly seemed to be primed and mimicked even though there were no interactions or even older people present as part of the study. Of more interest, participants who had more positive attitudes were more likely to take up this slower pace than those with negative attitudes toward the elderly.

CONSENSUS BUILDING VS. PEER PRESSURE

Whenever there is a social problem, particularly involving young people, most people point to peer pressure as the root cause. However, peer pressure operates well beyond our teenage years and with mixed effects that are not always evidence from media coverage. However, peer pressure is not limited to teens. Pre-school children also exhibit peer pressure effects.

In a pre-school version of the Asch line study, four-year-olds were provided picture books consisting of two pages (Haun & Tomasello, 2011). On the first page a small (baby), medium (mother), and large (father) animal were pictured. On the second page only one of the animals was pictured. The children were asked to indicate which animal ran to the other page. Children participated in groups of four and in each group one child was given a book that differed from the other three so that the animal on the second page

was a different size. When children were asked to respond by pointing to the image on the first page that matched the image on the second page, children performed correctly on about 97% of the trials. However, when asked to say the answer out loud, the child who was given the different book would respond along with the majority and give a response that was incorrect based on the different book. In only 61% of trials did they give a correct response aloud; while pointing to the correct response privately in their own book. Children as young as four years give in to peer pressure and provide wrong responses in the face of conflict with other children's perceptions.

In another study college-aged students were asked to complete a decision-making task in which they had to make a series of decisions about whether they would prefer a smaller amount of money now or a larger sum at a future date (O'Brien, Albert, Chein, & Steinberg, 2011). For example, would you rather have $500 today or $1,000 one year from now? Some participants made these decisions while their friends were present and making similar decisions, others made these decisions alone. Participants working with their peers often took a lower and more immediate award; those working alone were more willing to wait longer for a higher reward. It seems that one way in which peers influence us is by increasing the value of a short-term reward or at least making the short-term reward more salient than a longer term reward.

Reyniers and Bhalla (2013) conducted a study showing that adult participants were also susceptible to peer pressure. Participants were first paid 10 pounds for completing a short survey and then asked whether they wished to donate any of their earnings to charity. Some participants were asked to make their donations on their own, while others were paired with another person and given the opportunity to discuss their initial donations and then adjust their donations after discussion. After they made their donations, the participants completed a final questionnaire asking them how happy they were with their decision. They found that partner donations influenced one another. Paired participants donated more overall than control group subjects, perhaps because they knew they would be discussing this with someone else. The peer pressure of others knowing how much was donated may have increased donations. However, the final questionnaire found that people were less happy with their donation if they had been in pairs. While adolescents who give in to peer pressure may reap the high social reward, it appears that adults are more begrudging in their conformity.

PERCEPTION VS. REALITY OF OTHERS

Not only do people that we care about or know personally influence our behavior, but our perception of others also plays a role. Consider how many times you have heard someone do or not do something and make statements such as, "They will make fun of me" or "They will think I'm crazy." Who are "they"? Are there actual people who would do this or simply the impressions that society would disapprove? On the other hand, sometimes we are impacted by others who we know quite well: "My mom would be so upset if she knew."

The perceptions we have of other people (even other people we know) may not always be accurate and certainly when we use our impressions to take another step and infer how they would perceive us, we are likely to be even less accurate. Consider the middle-aged man who engages in a deep intellectual debate about the meaning of life with an anonymous person online. The man makes inferences about this anonymous individual based upon their exchanges and concludes that this person is very educated and likely his age or older. Imagine his surprise when it turns out to be a 14-year-old boy. What other examples can you think of where a person's perception of someone is quite different from the reality?

In some cases, we believe that others must be very knowledgeable and perhaps know more than we

do in a particular situation. Consider a professor who has just explained a concept to the class and you really did not quite understand the example that was provided. When the professor asks if anyone has any questions, you think about raising your hand to ask a question. However, you quickly note that no one else is raising a hand and so maybe you were the only person who did not understand, and choose not to inquire further about the example. In reality, everyone else is also going through the very same process. When this occurs it is called **pluralistic ignorance** and clearly has a negative impact on learning.

Normative vs. Informational Influence

Normative influence occurs when people behave in particular ways in order to be accepted by others in the group. Informational influence refers to conformity with a group not simply because everyone else is engaged in the behavior, but because the behavior itself is perceived to be based on some factual or correct information. A person who goes with a group of friends to the local tattoo parlor and is encouraged by friends to get a tattoo with the rest of them is experiencing normative influence. However, a person who believes the right or appropriate way to show respect for someone is to get a tattoo commemorating that person is likely experiencing information influence.

Claidiere and Whiten (2012) have expanded our understanding of conformity beyond social psychology to include non-human animals who also display some level of normative or informational influence. Chou and Richerson (1992) trained two groups of rats to prefer either cinnamon- or cocoa-flavored food. Then placed a naïve rat in with a group that included a mix of cocoa and cinnamon liking rats and watched which food the naïve rat would prefer. Their results found that the more rats in the group that liked one food over the other significantly influenced which food type the naïve rat would choose in a food choice test 24 hours after being in the group. This would see most congruent with the concept of information influence. The naïve rat learns this food is "right" and complies even when not in the group. However, there is much less evidence for normative influence among non-human animals.

The key question in making this distinction is often to explore what is risked if one does not conform. If you ignore informational influence, then you may well miss your plane, not evacuate a building in danger, or find yourself in some other predicament that would have been avoided had you gone along with the group. On the other hand, resisting normative influence may result in social rejection or standing out in the crowd, but may not necessarily result in having missed out on correct information due to lack of conformity.

Consider a clever study by Salganik, Dodds, and Watts (2006) that provided free music downloads of unknown bands via the internet. They set the number of previous downloads to be either relatively high or low, indicating that many (or few) others had already downloaded one of the particular songs. Note that the download counter was not dynamic, but the findings demonstrate that songs that were made popular by the higher number of reported downloads, did in fact result in more downloads. Was this informational or normative influence? Taste in music or art cannot necessarily be deemed "correct" information, so were the songs downloaded to "fit in" with the masses of people on the internet?

Another study found that when people already felt that they fit in and had plenty of social support, normative influence had less impact (Cullum et al., 2013). When college students felt that they had good social support their drinking behavior was less influenced by how much they believed their peers were drinking alcohol. However, when participants did not believe they had good social support, their drinking behavior was more likely to be influenced by their perceptions of their peers'

drinking behavior. It is clear that normative influence does have more impact when we want to fit in with others or desire social approval. However, the power of normative influence is diminished when we feel we already have good social support.

Informative influence is most likely to have an influence when you cannot rely on your own perceptions and others provide information that you believe will enhance your own accuracy. The classic demonstration of this uses the **autokinetic effect**. Our eyes engage in saccadic eye movements; as we scan our environment our eyes move very slightly left to right to take in visual input. Sherif (1935) had groups of people view a single point of light on a wall in a dark room. The autokinetic effect makes this light appear to move and every person perceives this movement differently. In reality the pinpoint of light is not moving at all. Participants were first asked to privately report how far the light moved, and each participant provided a different response ranging from one to eight inches. The next day participants were asked to come back and make the same estimate again by stating the distance aloud to the group. After four days of reporting their estimates in the group, they all began to report the light was moving the same distance.

Informational influence is most powerful when situations are ambiguous or when there is an emergency requiring a quick response and people lack time to consider their actions. This is in part why it is illegal to scream "Fire!" in a crowded theater. Theaters are dark and make the situation ambiguous and fire is clearly an emergency situation. As soon as a few people begin to panic and rush the exits, other people will follow suit assuming that this is the correct action and basing their own behavior on the information they are gathering from the actions of others.

CONFORMITY AND COMPLIANCE

Conformity and compliance are distinct concepts. People conform or behave in ways that are consistent with what others are doing for a variety of reasons. Some people conform in order to be accepted into a particular group or to fit in. Other people may conform because they believe that what everyone else is doing is correct. When you believe that the group is engaging in behavior that is right or correct, we call this private conformity. For example, if you are waiting for an airplane in a crowded terminal, you may see other people start queuing up to board the plane. When you see other people lining up you may believe that they have information about the arrival of the aircraft and get in line with them. This illustrates both private conformity and informational influence. We might also conform due to normative influence, as when you wear a particular shirt to a football game to fit in with other fans like you. Compliance or public conformity occurs when you go along with something not necessarily because you want to fit in or because you think others are right, but to avoid the negative reactions if you did not go along.

Speed limits provide a nice example here. You may conform to the speed of others around you and "go with the flow of traffic" and exceed the speed limit. This could be private conformity due to informational influence; everyone else believes this is a safe and appropriate speed so it must be okay. And certainly when traffic on a busy highway slows down suddenly there is an air of informational influence, as the drivers ahead know something important about what is up ahead and we should conform to their speed choices. Or perhaps you speed along due to normative influence; you do not want others to think you are a slow driver or lack driving skills. On the other hand, if you see a police officer you may quickly comply with the posted speed limit in order to avoid getting a ticket. When you comply only in the presence of a reminder of authority, it is likely that you are not conforming because you believe this is a good or correct speed, but rather only complying or publicly conforming when the probability of a negative consequence is high.

In 1951, Solomon Asch invited individuals to participate in a very simple experiment on con-

formity. Participants were told they would take a "vision test" and would be asked to make some judgments about the length of lines that would appear on a board at the front of the room. Even though there were several other people in the room all posing as participants, there was in fact only one participant who was being studied. The other individuals were all confederates who had received instructions prior to the study about how they should respond. On the display board there was a line on the left and three comparison lines on the right, each marked with a letter A, B, or C. It was clear to everyone that C would be the correct response when asked which line was the same length as the one on the left. However, the confederates all gave the same incorrect answer and then when it was the participants' turn to provide an answer 32% of the respondents went along with the group and provided an incorrect response. Why would they go along with the group, when the correct answer was so blatantly obvious? What about the 67% of respondents who did not go along with the group? Why were they willing to give the correct answer?

To better understand what occurred in the experiment, Asch conducted additional versions of the experiment. If only one of the confederates provided a correct answer, then the participant was substantially more likely to provide the correct answer as well. Also, if the group was small, only one or two people besides the confederate, conformity was not nearly as likely (only 13% of participants give the wrong answer in a group of three persons). In addition, if the lines depicted made the correct answer more difficult to discern, conformity increased. If participants were allowed to write down their responses rather than say them aloud after everyone else in the group said their answers aloud group conformity decreased.

To this point we have discussed ways in which other people impact our own perceptions of the world and our behavior. In the next section we will take this a bit further to understand how these perceptions are a two-way street.

NORM OF RECIPROCITY

While the norm of reciprocity operates at some level for the majority of people, there are interesting cultural differences about when the norm of reciprocity guides behavior. When we engage in gift giving in the United States, we may value the selflessness of the gift—particularly that people should not give a gift if they are doing so only because they expect something in return. However, Shen, Wan, and Wyer (2011) conducted a cross-cultural study to understand how Asians and North Americans refuse small gifts and why.

In Shen and colleagues' (2011) first experiment they had Chinese and European-American Canadians consider a vignette. They were asked to imagine they had shared a cab to the airport and when you arrive your friend offers to pay the fare. Participants were asked whether they would let the friend pay and say thank you, offer to pay the fare themselves, or insist on paying their half. More Canadian participants (26%) let the friend pay and said thank you compared to only 9% of the Asian participants. Equally interesting, none of the Chinese participants chose to pay the entire fare, as they would not visit the felt obligation on their friend any more than they would want to have the obligation of reciprocation resting on their shoulders.

In the second experiment by Shen and colleagues (2011), participants sat up a table in a common area at a university and asked participants to complete a survey about how they rated several products. There were two conditions: One was a short questionnaire where they made simple scale ratings and took less than a minute; the second was a long questionnaire that took almost 10 minutes and asked participants to write out examples of how they might use the products. Once they finished they were told to help themselves to some chocolate candy and they could take as many chocolate bars as they wished. European Canadian participants took the same number of chocolate bars regardless of condition, but the Chinese participants took fewer chocolate bars when they completed the short questionnaire and more when they had finished the longer questionnaire. For some cultures, the value of the gift is weighted by the cost of reciprocating.

If you receive a gift, then you may feel you must also give a gift to that person to reciprocate. The authors conclude that North Americans are not particularly likely to feel obligated to repay or reciprocate the gift, while Asians do feel that if you give a gift then there should be a reciprocal gift in return. This creates a circumstance in which few North Americans would ever refuse a gift, they gratefully accept the gift and do not feel the burden of reciprocation with the same level of intensity as Asian individuals. However, in order to avoid this indebtedness Asian persons may refuse a gift they could not easily reciprocate. When these interactions occur cross-culturally, there is plenty of room for misunderstanding. The North American who was giving the gift freely feels rejected when the gift is declined and yet the Asian person is essentially refusing the obligation of reciprocity even when reciprocity is often not expected.

However, this discomfort with the obligation is not quite as culturally specific as noted above. Most people are hesitant to accept a gift they feel they could not reciprocate. Indeed when we feel we cannot pay someone back for the generosity they have shown to us, we may decide to pay it forward by being generous to someone else. Gray, Ward, and Norton (2012) conducted five experiments to explore when participants would choose to pay it forward. In the control condition, participants were given $6 and asked to play a game in which they should anonymously split the $6 between themselves and another person. They were instructed to place the portion of money they wished to give to the other person in an envelope. In other conditions, participants receive an envelope that they were told was left to them by the previous splitter. The envelopes in these conditions contained no money (greedy splitters), $3 (equal splitters), or $6 (generous splitters).

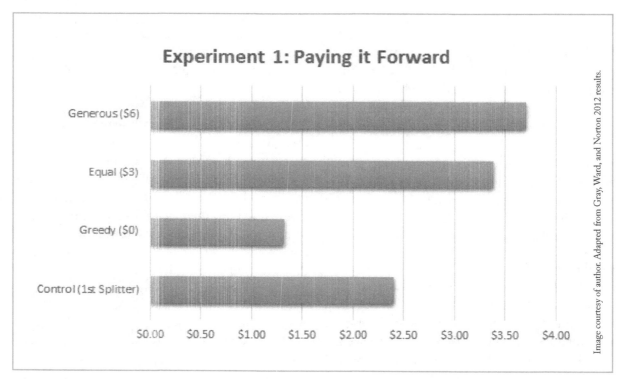

Experiment 1: Paying it Forward

Image courtesy of author. Adapted from Gray, Ward, and Norton 2012 results.

FIGURE 4.2

Then the participants were asked to play the role of splitters themselves and were given $6 to split between themselves and the next person. Who would "pay forward" the most money? The results show that an equal split or a generous split led to a more generous pay it forward decision.

DOOR-IN-THE-FACE. This is a persuasion technique that relies heavily on the norm of reciprocity. First, an outrageous request is made with some certainty that it will be declined. Then a second more reasonable request is made and people are more likely to comply with this second request. How is this related to reciprocity? Reciprocal concessions may be at the root of this effect. Essentially, you perceive that the requestor had done you a favor by reducing their request to something reasonable and now you feel the need to pay them back for this concession by agreeing to their second request. In one study participants are asked if they would volunteer for two hours per week for two years and no one agreed to do so. After they said no, they were asked if they would consider volunteering for two hours at an upcoming event and 76% agreed and 85% of those people actually showed up for their volunteer shift. On the other hand, when people were only asked for the two-hour commitment (no previous request) only 29% said they would volunteer and of those only half actually attended the event to volunteer (Miller, Seligman, Clark, & Bush, 1976).

Feeley, Anker, and Aloe (2012) conducted a meta-analysis of door-in-the-face studies and concluded that overall the technique is effective for verbal behavior and volunteer behavior. However, they also found that the technique was not as effective if there was a request for money or resources involved. Some have suggested that door-in-the-face works in part due to guilt about saying "no" to the initial request (O'Keefe & Figge, 1997). Social responsibility may also play an important role in the door-in-the-face effect. Specifically, having to say no to a request for help violates a norm that we should try to help others. Violation of the norm also activates the norm of responsibility which then impacts our next behavior when the second request is made.

THAT'S-NOT-ALL. This technique also relies on commitment. In this technique an initial request is made, but before a person can respond to the request, there are some added bonuses or concessions made to the initial offer. Most infomercials make use of this technique, so they show you the product and an initial price, which is almost immediately dropped and then the amount of product you get doubles, providing such a good deal (compared to the initial request) that you feel you should also make a concession and buy the item. A sale is much more effective if people know that they are saving money compared to a previous price. Consider advertising something that costs $5 in a store. People see the price and assume that is and may have always been the price. Advertising the same item with an original price of $10 with 50% off will surely increase your sales of that item.

Obedience

One of the more fascinating and widely discussed experiments in social psychology is the "shock experiment" conducted by Stanley Milgram in the 1960s and 1970s. More specifically it is Experiment 5 in Milgram's demonstrations that has gained widespread media attention (Milgram, 1974). Participants arrive at the lab with a confederate who the participants believes is another participant in the study. There is a drawing which is designed to always have the participant fulfill the role of teacher and the confederate the role of the learner. The learner is strapped into a chair with a number of electrodes attached to his arm. The teacher is then led into an adjacent room and is told to use an intercom system to test whether the learner could correctly learn paired associations. Each time the learner responds incorrectly the teacher must deliver a shock to the learner by flipping a switch on a machine that indicates the shock ranges go from 15 to 450 volts at 15-volt increments. For each error, the learner will receive

a shock that is one step higher than the last error and the first error was always met with the 15-volt shock per experimenter instructions.

Of course the learner who is a confederate is actually not receiving any shocks, but convincing verbal responses and grunts are transmitted over the intercom to the teacher who is flipping the switches. In fact at 150-volts, the learner begins to protest loudly and indicates he would like to stop the experiment and that he thinks his heart is bothering him. Once the 300-volt shock is delivered the learner goes silent and refuses to respond when prompted to the test. At this point the experimenter encourages the teacher to continue when they hesitate to do so. There were four requests from the experimenter when a participant showed concern or seemed to be about to disengage. The experiment ends when the participant either delivered the full range of shocks, delivering the last level three times, or when the participant refused to go on at all. The media attention was riveted on the finding that 65% of the participants finished the experiment by delivering the highest possible level of shock three times. Indeed prior to the study Milgram had asked students and psychiatrists what they believed would happen in such an experiment and no one thought a person would ever go all the way to the highest voltage. Of course, the main reason that these people proceeded was because they were obeying the experimenter, a perceived expert who would ultimately be responsible should anything go wrong and who they believed they could trust. Milgram openly acknowledges this rationale in 1983, but reminds us that most "real world" situations would likely involve a similar authority giving orders.

Of course there were 35% of participants who stood up to the experiment, refused to continue, and stopped the experiment before the last switch, but it was the majority that had people concerned. What did this finding might mean about obedience, free will, and human nature? In addition, people were concerned about the ethics of this type of experiment, even though the learner was never actually shocked; the distraught participants thought they may have really harmed someone. In addition, many people today after learning about the experiment, report they would never do what these obedient participants did in the 1970s.

Burger (2009) decided to find out what, if anything, might have changed since 1974. Milgram (1974) had asked experts and others how far they thought the teachers might go in the experiment and most guessed no one would surpass the 150-volt mark. However, those who went past the 150-volt mark after the learner's complaints were likely to continue to the very end of the volt switches; and the majority of those among the 35% who stopped before reaching the end did so at the 150-volt mark. Using this information Burger (2009) proposed a replication that would only go to the 150-volt mark. In addition, to address ethical concerns he also had participants read or hear, at least three times, that they could withdraw at any time and that they would still be paid the $50 for participating. Burger greatly reduced the pressure on teachers to continue compared to Milgram's study. However, the findings were remarkably similar. In Burger's study 70% of participants continued past the 150-volt mark, a number not significantly different than Milgram's results revealed.

There are multiple reasons why we may obey. Fear of punishment, not wanting to engage in any conflict, strong belief in respect for those in authority—all may play a role in when and why people obey others. Someone who is an expert or who has some perceived power over another person may overestimate how much control those with less power believe they have in a situation. Given the power of social influence, when might we decide to disobey? What conditions would lead us to stop conforming or obeying?

Perhaps seeing someone else model disobedience would help. Burger (2009) found that if a first teacher (another confederate) disobeyed after the second voltage switch, then the second teacher (the participant) was slightly less likely to contin-

ue through to the end. However, there are many situations in which power differentials overwhelm this modeling. Gibson (2013) provides an account of the Milgram studies that highlights the level of power that was exerted in other experiments carried out by Milgram and how participants disobeyed. Gibson reviews transcripts of the recorded Milgram sessions which were not necessarily included in the final reports and which demonstrates that some participants sought consent not only from the experimenter but from the learner as well. As reported by Gibson (2013) one participant states, "…well will you please ask him, when I'm there, if he wants to get out or not…" This sort of disruption was managed within the experiment by refusing to seek re-consent from the confederate. Even when the participants were willing to obey, they raised questions about whether the learner could also be given a choice. Can you think of other situations where consent and obedience are crucial? What role does power play? What circumstances beyond research contexts have serious implications for consent, power, and obedience?

Commitment

Commitment is a norm that is taken to be quite difficult to resist. We have a need to be consistent. It is more pleasant to feel authentic and trustworthy, than for others to believe you are unpredictable or that you are not reliable. One way we create an authentic and trustworthy self is by keeping our commitments. In this section, there are several techniques routinely used to influence people by relying on the norm of commitment.

Foot-in-the-door technique occurs when a person first makes a small commitment when asked for a small favor. The second step is to then ask for something larger that is congruent with the small commitment. The basic technique is to get a person to make a small commitment, so that when asked to make the larger commitment they feel they must do so in order to be consistent with

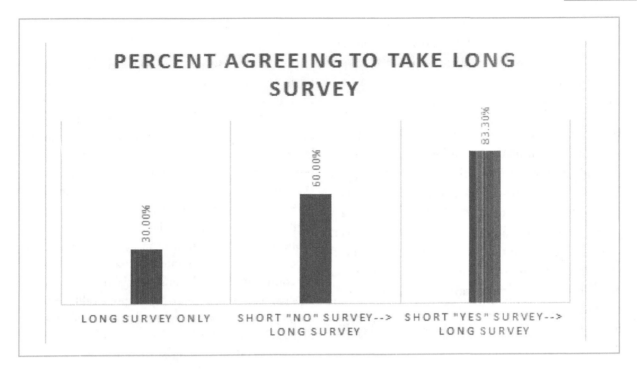

FIGURE 4.3

their prior commitment. Most of the research demonstrating this effect has involved a face-to-face interaction between the requester and the participant.

Gueguen and colleagues (2013) demonstrated the foot-in-the-door technique by showing that participants who agreed to complete a short verbal survey, and did so, were more likely to take home a longer survey to be mailed back than those participants who were only asked to complete the longer survey. However, the study went a step further as well, to explore another technique based upon commitment and consistency.

Consistent verbal behavior may also have an impact that can provide some important information for how to frame initial requests in the foot-in-the-door technique. The **four walls** technique is also based on consistency and predicts that people who are answering questions to which they say "yes" are also more likely to say "yes" to a subsequent request. Gueguen and colleagues (2013) conducted a study in which participants were

asked several questions that were framed so that the participant would either answer all with "no" or all with "yes." Following these initial responses, participants were asked if they would be willing to take a paper and pencil survey home with them and return it in a pre-addressed postage paid envelope that was provided. Results show that participants who had responded in the affirmative on the previous questions were also more likely to take the survey home compared to those who answer the questions with a "no" response.

Another persuasion technique that relies heavily on commitment is called the **low-ball** technique. The simplest demonstration of this technique was conducted by Cialdini, Cacioppo, Bassett, and Miller (1978). Participants were asked to participate in an experiment. Half of the participants were asked if they would be interested in the study and after they agreed were told the experiment would require them to report to the lab at 7 o'clock in the morning. Students were given the opportunity to back out after learning of the time, but over half (56%) agreed to keep their initial commitment. The other half of the participants were asked if they would be interested in participating in a study that would take place at 7 o'clock in the morning, and only 27% agreed to participate in the full-disclosure condition.

Bait and switch is also a technique that relies on your initial commitment to influence you to follow through even when the initial agreement changes. First, this technique is illegal and considered to be fraud. You may go to a store because they have a great sale on your favorite soft drink. However, when you get there they no longer have the brand you came for, but since you are already there you do a bit of shopping anyway. The advertisement created an initial commitment to buy, now you fulfill your commitment by buying something else you did not intend.

SUMMARY

It is clear that we rely on other people to help us navigate a variety of situations, from emergencies to purchase decisions. Almost all of our decisions involve some level of social influence. In some cases we go along with a group to feel as though we belong, in other cases we believe that others have more information than we do and must be doing the right thing. In some cases, others have an influence because we perceive them in a particular way, while in the case of obedience others may play a more active role in ensuring we comply. There are a host of persuasion strategies that rely on norms of commitment and consistency, norms of reciprocity, and norms of social responsibility—all of which focus on our need to live with other people without causing ourselves or others any undue harm. It is possible to resist these influences, by reminding ourselves we have a strong social support network and do not need to go along to fit in. Or perhaps by remembering that these techniques are in some cases used with intentions for which our social norms were not originally intended we can successfully avoid making purchases or committing to decisions without the added pressure of others.

NAME _____ DATE _____

Chapter Questions

1. What are the persuasion techniques that you have experienced?

2. Peer pressure is often blamed for many of our bad behaviors. What good behaviors are also the result of social influence?

3. Describe the distinction between informational and normative influence.

4. If you were hoping to persuade someone to help you with a task, what techniques might you employ?

5. What is the difference between door in the face and foot in the door?

6. Have you noticed how having someone mimic you makes you feel? Once you notice it is occurring is it still as persuasive?

7. Which of these techniques would be most effective in persuading someone to purchase an expensive item?

8. How can you resist being influenced by these techniques?

9. Sometimes people are intentionally implementing a social influence technique. However, we are also influenced by others who may not have any intention to persuade. Can you think of a time when you were persuaded by someone, even though this person was not actively attempting to influence you?

10. Explain the norm of reciprocity. How does this norm impact interactions with others?

Attitudes and Persuasion

Attitudes are the ways in which you think or feel about a particular person, object, event, or other attitude object. An attitude object is a term used in social psychology to indicate anything about which a person might possess an attitude. Colloquially people may say, "She has a bad attitude." However, in this case they are using a different meaning and are really not meaning that she has a malfunctioning attitude toward a particular attitude object. Rather the implication is that she has a negative perspective on life in general or toward authority. In this chapter we are going to be discussing the social psychological understanding of attitude, rather than the colloquial putdown.

Image © Alena Hovorkova, 2014. Used under license from Shutterstock, Inc.

The Properties of Attitudes

Attitudes have a valence. Attitudes can be either positive or negative. Indeed one of the core components of an attitude is some evaluation which may be affective in nature, an initial positive or negative feeling toward the attitude object. Something you like or feel favorably about will likely mean that you have a positive attitude toward that attitude object. Attitudes also have strength—that is, attitudes can be weak (easily changed) or strong (resistant to change). It is possible to have a weak negative attitude toward something. This would mean that you do not like something all that much, but you do not feel particularly strong about this attitude object. Consider a new curbside in the park lined with flowers. You do not particularly like the color of the flowers and think it looked better before they put in the new landscaping. However, if this is a relatively weak attitude, you are not going to do anything about it. You probably would not necessarily even mention it to anyone, unless it came up in a conversation directly. On the other hand, you might have a strong positive attitude toward the new landscaping and might go out of your way to tell others how good it looks now and compliment the city council on their efforts to invest in the park.

WHERE DO ATTITUDES COME FROM?

Now that we know what an attitude is we need to understand where attitudes originate. Certainly, we are not born with particular attitudes. Attitudes are developed over time as we have a variety of experiences. In some cases, we learn an attitude through direct experience and other times we learn by watching others. Other attitudes we cognitively generate by using our attitudes toward similar other objects. For example, you decide you do not like green vegetables based on a particular attitude about green peas.

Direct experience is just one of many ways we might form an attitude. If you have never encountered a particular type of cell phone before but go into a store and start experimenting with the model on the shelf, you are having a direct experience with the attitude object. Your attitude toward the phone will be strongly shaped by your experience with this demonstration model. If it does not function the way you expect or if it is not intuitive to use, you

may become frustrated, and you are likely to form a negative attitude toward the phone. Indeed, it will be very difficult to change your attitude toward the phone if this initial direct experience is negative. This is one reason why sales staff almost immediately ask if they can help when they see you are trying out a demonstration model.

More interestingly, direct experience leads you to form stronger attitudes than indirect experience. Seeing your friend use his or her new phone and demonstrate the features may lead to a positive attitude, but it will be weaker than if your friend lets you use the phone and explains to you how to get the most out of the device.

In some cases, our attitudes are learned. We may be rewarded for having a particular attitude or experience negative consequences for another. For example, if you notice that all of your friends seem to really like listening to a particular song, then you are likely to find it rewarding to go along with the group and your friends will provide affirmation of your attitude. On the other hand, if you really detest their new favorite, it is quite possible that you could find yourself in a heated debate, excluded from a fun trip to a future concert, or in other ways experience negative outcomes for expressing your negative attitude.

BEHAVIOR: SELF-PERCEPTION

We have already discussed that attitudes can be either strong or weak, positive or negative. However, attitudes can also be relatively ambiguous. You may not be sure how you feel about a particular policy. Perhaps you do not have much information about a new school policy that is being passed. When asked what you think about it, you are not really sure. So you may think of the last time there was a school policy and extrapolate your attitude toward the current policy by thinking about how you felt or reacted to the previous policy change. This is called self-perception theory. You think about your past behavior and use that behavior to infer your attitude.

For example, I had not formed a strong attitude toward a new model of car but was in a conversation where someone asked me how I felt about it. I thought about the last time I drove a car that was similar to the one being discussed and that I had enjoyed it, so told the person asking that I thought it seemed like a pretty good choice of vehicle. However, later in the conversation someone asked about another type of car toward which I had a strong negative attitude having owned one and spent significant time and money repairing it over the years. I did not have to think about my history with that car and could immediately respond that I did not like that type of car at all.

ATTITUDES: PURPOSE AND FUNCTION

Other than communicating with people about what we like or don't like, what purpose do our attitudes serve? First, and perhaps most importantly, attitudes may predict how we behave. We are likely to approach attitude objects and repeat behaviors we have positive attitudes toward, while we are likely to avoid situations and behaviors associated with our negative attitudes.

Attitudes also serve a variety of functions. There are three that we will discuss in this text: knowledge/mastery function, self-esteem function, and the value-expressive function. Some attitudes help us understand the world and provide some mastery over our environment. Having a negative attitude about foods that have made you ill or situations that might lead to danger help you navigate the world without experiencing poor health or taking unnecessary risks. You may also have attitudes that help you feel good about yourself. These attitudes fulfill the self-esteem function. If you are a particularly talented pianist, you probably have positive attitudes about music and musicians that make you feel good about yourself. Finally, attitudes can be value-expressive. Political attitudes or attitude toward particular religions, environmental issues, or food choices may be one way that you are using your attitudes to express an entire set of values. For example, vegetarians may have attitudes that help to express their beliefs about how animals should be treated and shape their purchasing behavior.

IMPLICIT VS. EXPLICIT ATTITUDES

Attitudes can be implicit or explicit. Implicit attitudes are attitudes that we may not be aware we have, but shape our behavior and perceptions. Explicit attitudes are those attitudes that you could readily express on a survey or report to others. Some of our explicit attitudes may not be socially acceptable so we may not express them, but that does not make them implicit. Implicit attitudes on the other hand are those that we do not have awareness about. Even if we were asked, we would not be able to report accurately our implicit attitudes.

Rydell and McConnell (2006) demonstrated that implicit and explicit attitudes change in different ways. Explicit attitudes seem relatively quick to change, while implicit attitudes seemed to change at a slower pace. Perhaps more interestingly is that implicit attitudes are more predictive of spontaneous behaviors and show evidence of being influenced by information that might not be considered explicitly. Implicit attitudes are more likely to predict subtle, less deliberate behavior and explicit attitudes more predictive of thoughtful actions (McConnell & Leibold, 2001). Implicit attitudes might also be more susceptible to primes that you might not consider explicitly. For example, your implicit attitude toward a student attending a rival school might predict how far you sit away from her on a bus. This might occur even when your explicit attitude differentiates between school rivalry and individual students.

ATTITUDE CONSISTENCY

Cognitive consistency was initially described by Festinger in 1957 as a key factor in understanding psychological need. More recently Gawronski (2012) has revived this idea but forwarding the idea that cognitive consistency is a core motive. Perhaps the essential nature of consistency is brought to light, by understanding how we react when we experience inconsistency. For example, many people are uncomfortable when they find inconsistencies in strongly held attitudes. A person often experiences some inconsistency or discomfort when it is pointed out that they have stated they believe that for some crimes capital punishment is appropriate and also believe in the biblical commandment, "Thou shall not kill." It takes significant cognitive effort to overcome or think through this cognitive inconsistency. Cognitive dissonance is another term for this type of inconsistency. These inconsistencies serve as a cue that there may be an error in the way in which these beliefs are framed.

Festinger and Carlsmith (1959) conducted the now classic study demonstrating the cognitive dissonance effect. Here the key is to understand how cognitive dissonance can be resolved by making external attributions. Participants arrived at the laboratory to participate in an experiment dealing with "measures of performance." At the beginning of the semester the students in the participant pool were told that the department of psychology was doing a study to better understand and evaluate the current experiments and so after being in experiments they may be interviewed about their experiences serving as participants. When the participant arrived for the measure of performance study they were told that the experiment would take just over an hour, but was scheduled for two hours and so they may be asked to participate in one of the interviews being conducted by the department about their experiences.

Participants were seated at a table. On the table were 12 spools and the participants were to use one hand to move the spools on and off of the tray repeatedly. This went on for almost half an hour. The next task was to manipulate the pegs on a peg board. Participants were instructed to turn each peg a quarter of a turn one way, and then turn the pegs again and again. This too went on for a bit more than half an hour. This task was designed to be monotonous and tedious and after the participant had been at these tasks for just over an hour the experimenter indicated the experiment was over. However, it was only then that the experiment began in earnest.

The participants were told that there were two groups in the experiment and the participant had just participated in the group that would come in and do the tasks without much of an introduction to the experiment. However, the other group is greeted by another student who is hired to work on the experiment, a confederate. The confederate's job is to pretend to be a participant in the study who has just finished the experiment. Usually the confederate was introduced to the waiting participant and told to explain a bit about the experiment. The confederate always gave the same explanation. Namely that the experiment was very enjoyable, fun, intriguing, exciting, and so on. Remember this is all being explained to a participant who just finished a rather boring and tedious task.

Now participants who had just heard about the missing confederate are randomly assigned to one of three conditions. One-third was assigned to a control condition in which participants were led to the waiting room to see if they would need to be interviewed as part of the department's study. The other two-thirds were told that the confederate is not going to be able to make the next session and of course the experimenter could not serve as the confederate and have the story be believable. The experimenter then asked participants if they were willing to fill in for the missing confederate and since they already knew how the experiment and confederate role were played out, perhaps they would be willing to serve in this capacity again in the future if the confederate cannot make it to the experiment. Now of these participants, half were offered $1 for doing this work and the other half, $20. Participants who agreed then proceeded to fill in for the confederate by explaining how fun and exciting the task was to the next participant.

After a few minutes of being in the waiting room (control condition) and after talking to the participant (experimental conditions) the department did indeed conduct an interview about the quality of the experiment. Here the participants are asked how enjoyable the experiment was they completed today on a -5 to +5 scale. The findings were congruent with a cognitive dissonance explanation. As you might expect participants in the control condition rated the experiment a -.45 on the enjoyableness item. In addition, the participants paid $20 to tell the next person how fun it was also gave a rating indicating it was not in fact very enjoyable (-.05). Here, participants lied, but resolved dissonance about what they told the subject and what they actually experienced by attributing their lying behavior to the $20 payment. However, the participants in the $1 condition could not bring themselves to admit they had lied for $1, and they seemed to have changed their opinion of the experiment by giving a higher enjoyable rating (1.35).

Cognitive dissonance indicates that a person who has two inconsistent beliefs must reconcile those. In the $20 condition they do so by making an external attribution; in the $1 condition they change their belief and decide that perhaps the task was in fact enjoyable. However, some participants resolved their dissonance by refusing to be hired for this purpose (three participants), taking the money but refusing to carry out the lie by telling participants they had been paid to say it was enjoyable but in fact it was pretty boring (two participants), or in one case lying but then wanting to wait for the participant to finish the experiment so he could tell the truth (one participant).

POX THEORY

POX theory or balance theory is one way we can understand our strong need to have consistent attitudes (Heider, 1946). When we experience imbalance or inconsistency we are often uncomfortable and will likely change our behaviors or attitudes to bring them back into alignment. In POX theory, the P refers to a person who has a particular attitude. The O refers to the attitude object (which could be a person, thing, entity, idea, or anything else). The X can be another person, a policy, another attitude object, so long as it is clear that there are reasonable and logical ways to understand the relationships between these attitude objects.

Illustration by Max Dusky.

FIGURE 5.1 *Mary has a pet snake and Ryan needs a roommate. What would balance theory say needs to happen for this situation to be balanced?*

Let's say that Marianna really enjoys playing a particular computer game online. She plays every chance she gets. Marianna is also an advocate for equality and believes that sexism and racism are wrong and she takes every opportunity to eliminate this unfairness from her life and the lives of others. However, she finds out that the computer game company that produces her favorite game has begun supporting a gaming policy that clearly discriminates against women and minorities. This is going to create significant imbalance for Marianna. She is now going to have to take some action to resolve this dissonance. What are her options?

People remember balanced triads better and are more favorable toward consistent or balanced triads (Gawronsky, Walther, & Blank, 2005). In a study by Langer, Walther, Gawronski, and Blank (2009), participants were asked to imagine that they had just started working at a new company and were learning about their new colleagues. They saw photos of eight individuals and were given some brief information about each person (e.g., insults the secretary; helps colleagues). Then after participants had formed these first impressions, they were asked to imagine they now knew the first group, but there were other colleagues left to meet. In the second part, photos of unknown colleagues were then presented with neutral information about them, but also information about the unknown person's relationships with some of the known colleagues from the first part of the experiment. In the third part of the experiment, participants were asked to imagine they had been at the job for several weeks and were learning more about their colleagues. Participants were now presented with information about the first set of colleagues that was inconsistent with their first impression or neutral information. Of course, the expectation is that if you now have some conflicting information you might change your impression of the person. However, what would happen to your impression of the colleagues from the second part of the experiment who liked (or disliked) the targets? Would your evaluation of these individuals change as well?

The results of the Langer et al. (2009) study found that people not only reevaluated their first impressions of the initial targets, but also changed their attitude toward the people from the second round based on whether the two like each other.

You may have similar experiences you can think of in your own life. For example, say that you first move into an apartment with a roommate and you get along with your new roommate, Linda. Linda is responsible, clean, and nice to be around. In the first weeks of your new housing situation you meet Linda's friends briefly, but have very little information other than that you like Linda and Linda likes them so they must be a nice group of people. However, as the months go on you find out that Linda can be moody and disrupts your sleep by staying up late listening to loud music. Think about how you would feel about her group of friends now? Would you still view them as positively? If you are like the participants in the Langer et al. (2009) study, you probably would have a slightly more negative impression of them.

JUSTIFICATION OF EFFORT

In some cases, our behaviors shape our attitudes. In some cases self-perception theory focuses our attention on our behavior and more importantly on how much effort we have exerted. If we have gone through a lot of trouble to buy a product then we may value that product more. Parents who encourage teenagers to buy their own computers, cell phones, and cars are aware that if you earned the money to make the purchase you will value the purchase more than if it was given to you without any real effort. Consider for a moment how you might feel if you worked really hard on a new idea and then did all of the work to market your idea and as a consequence you become an instant success and had made several million dollars. Now imagine that you bought a lottery ticket and won several million dollars. Even though this is a great deal of money you might spend this money quite differently.

The classic research by Aronson and Mills (1959) asked women whether they were interested in participating in group discussion that involved sexual topics. Participants were randomly assigned to a control condition with no pre-screening, a mild screening condition, or a severe screening condition. In the screening conditions, the women were told they first had to be screened prior to being allowed to enter the group to make sure they would not be too shy to participate. A male experimenter carried out the pre-screening test and told the women he would be determining their fitness for the group by observing their levels of discomfort and embarrassment during the screening test. Half of the women read words from index cards that were obscene (and would be bleeped out in primetime TV shows even today!). The women in this high effort condition were also asked to read two passages from contemporary novels that described sexual activity. Women in the mild condition were asked to read words that were sexual in nature but not obscene (e.g., prostitute, virgin, petting). Following this task, the women listened to an audio tape of the group having a relative-

ly boring discussion about the details of animal reproduction. The original article describes the discussion the participants heard as "...one of the most worthless and uninteresting discussions imaginable." The women who had to read the more embarrassing words as part of the pre-screen felt they needed to justify their effort (embarrassment) and reported they liked the group discussion more than those who read only mildly suggestive words (see Figure 5.2).

CHOICES

One of the more remarkable things about the typical United States supermarket is the sheer number of options for a single product. At first a wide array of options may be appealing, but can there be too many options? The concept that too many choices can have negative consequences is referred to as the **excess choice effect**. According to research by Iyengar and Lepper (2000), when people have too many options to choose from their satisfaction with their selection is diminished. In one study participants were presented with either

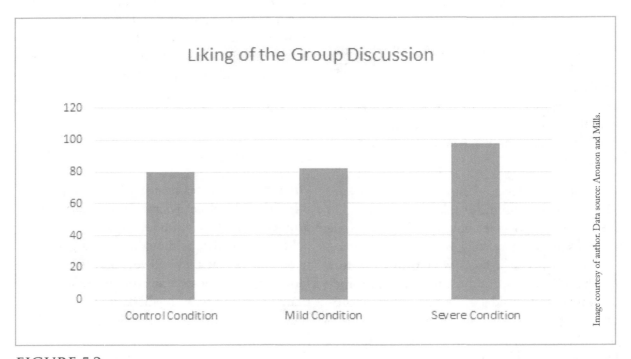

FIGURE 5.2

Image © 06photo, 2014. Used under license from Shutterstock, Inc.

How many choices do we need?

24 chocolates or only 6 chocolates. Participants were told they could choose whichever one they liked. Once they had chosen their preferred chocolate, they were asked to rate their satisfaction with the chocolate. Those who had more choices liked their selections less than those who had fewer choices.

Dar-Nimrod, Rawn, Lehman, and Schwartz (2009) found that some people were motivated to make the best possible choice, while others were more likely to be seeking a satisfactory choice. Consider a person who is willing to drive to a number of stores, spend time researching a product online, and spend a great deal of time identifying all the possible choices available and from that large set of options attempts to select the best possible choice. This person would be considered a "maximizer." Another person invests consider-ably less time and energy into finding the ideal and rather only looks long enough to find a product that is satisfactory. This person is considered a "satisficer." The **maximization paradox** occurs because the maximizers tend to be less satisfied with their selections than the satisficers.

Hafner, White, and Handley (2012) took this finding a step further by providing participants with either a small set of choices of drawing implements or a large set. However, in a second study half of the participants were told they could change their mind and select a different drawing implement, while the other half were only allowed to make a single, nonreversible selection of drawing implements.

Predicting Behavior

Opinion polls during election years are import-ant measures of attitudes toward candidates. One reason that people are very interested in the atti-tudes of the public is, these attitudes tend to pre-dict voting behaviors and election outcomes. Our attitudes do not always match our behavior, but there are times in which our attitudes are more consistent with our behaviors. There are several factors that increase the likelihood that knowing people's attitude will allow you to predict their fu-ture behavior.

LEVEL OF SPECIFICITY

Often the goal of measuring an attitude is predict-ing some related behavior. For example, asking people about their attitudes toward a particular policy or candidate is thought to be a good way to determine how they will vote on Election Day. However, if you measure an attitude toward some-thing broad and try to predict a specific behavior, your prediction may be off the mark. You can im-prove the predictive value of attitudinal informa-tion by measuring an attitude at the same level of specificity as the behavior you hope to predict.

For example, let's say you are trying to predict interest in how many people might be interested in going on a spring break trip this year to Lake Tahoe. If you ask people how they feel about going on a spring break trip you may be disappointed in how many people actually end up going. However, if you ask people something more specific your initial count of people who are interested will be closer to the actual number of people who go on the trip. How would you like to go on a trip to Lake Tahoe for spring break? This more specific question will be a better predictor of behavior. However, people who are excited about the prospect may lack the resources or be interested in going for a future spring break, so even if they indicate yes they would like to go on such a trip, in reality they may not ultimately make the trip.

SELF-AWARENESS

If an attitude serves a value-expressive or a social identify function then making people self-aware will increase the chances that their behavior will conform to their attitudes. For example, when there is a mirror placed in front of someone this increases their self-awareness and they may behave in ways that are more consistent with their attitudes related to the self.

Beaman, Klentz, Diener, and Svanum (1979) observed children trick or treating. The trick-or-treaters were greeted by an experimenter who told them to take only one of the candies from the candy bowl. For children randomly assigned to the individuation manipulation they were asked what their names were and where they lived, the experimenter then repeated the information back to the children to make sure it was clear that she knew their names and information. For children who were also assigned to the high self-awareness condition they approached a house with a mirror placed right next to the candy bowl that induced self-awareness. The experimenter then left the children to select their candy. An unobtrusive observer recorded the amount of candy each child took. Of the children who were anonymous (experimenter

did not ask their name), about 20% took more than the one piece of candy as instructed; however, for those who were individuated and faced a mirror, only 9% took more than one piece of candy. Interestingly, of those who were individuated but then left to their own devices without a mirror, almost 38% took more than one piece of candy.

Self-awareness may also increase the accessibility of attitudes that are closely tied to our self-concept. When we have low self-awareness or get lost in the crowd the accessibility of our attitudes related to our individuality may also decrease. Consider how fans behave during soccer games. The de-individuation or decrease in self-awareness seems to decrease the accessibility of attitudes they might otherwise endorse (e.g., politeness, concern for others).

ATTITUDE ACCESSIBILITY

Implicit attitudes are often measured by examining response latencies. Response latency is the time that passes between exposure to a stimulus and response to a particular item. Participants are asked to make their responses as quickly as possible without sacrificing accuracy by random responses. When an attitude is accessible, behavior is more likely to be shaped by that particular attitude. A person might have a strong positive attitude toward environmentalism and want to avoid driving when alternative transportation is available. A person might also have a strong positive attitude toward having a polished physical appearance at work. Upon waking up on a rainy day, which attitude is going to determine whether a person bikes or drives to work? It likely depends upon whichever attitude is more accessible that morning. If a person just watched a documentary about the harm of pollution, the work wardrobe might take a backseat as he bikes to work. On the other hand, if an article about the importance of looking professional in the workplace was on the coffee table, it is more likely he will drive to work and avoid muddying up his shoes.

Another example would be having people vote in an election at a polling location in a church basement. It is likely that votes cast in the church basement will result in votes that are more congruent with their religious values compared to having them vote in a government building which may lead them to cast ballots based on their political attitudes which may or may not be congruent with the religious values.

THEORY OF REASONED ACTION

The theory of reasoned action was proposed by Ajzen and Fishbein (1972) to incorporate not only attitudinal information but also information about subjective norms to allow for better prediction of behavior. There are four components to this theory. The attitude is the sum of one's beliefs and evaluations of those beliefs about engaging in a particular action. A subjective norm in this theory is measured by asking what you think others who are important to you think you should do. Both the attitude and subjective norm impact the intention to perform the behavior. And finally, the intention to perform the behavior impacts the behavior itself. Attitudes and subjective norms do not directly predict behavior, only the intention to perform the behavior. We often have intentions that do not result in the intended behavior even when predicted by a positive attitude toward enacting the behavior and believing that others who are important to us also think we should behave in a particular way. For example, your dentist believes you should floss every day. You probably do intend to floss every day, but the reality of your flossing behavior likely falls short of this intention.

The theory of reasoned action is a good model for understanding when and if people will engage in behaviors that are relatively independent. Behaviors over which a person has singular discretion are better predicted by this model than behaviors that require the cooperation of others. Flossing, voting, many health behaviors, and purchase decisions can be well explained with the theory of reasoned action. However, you must also remember that level of specificity matters. Note that we did not discuss intentions to have good dental hygiene

but rather daily flossing behavior. The model would likely do even better if we framed the behavior as flossing at a particular time of day. The goal of these models is not necessarily to encourage a behavior, but rather to predict when people will (or will not) engage in a particular behavior.

THEORY OF PLANNED BEHAVIOR

The theory of planned behavior (Ajzen & Madden, 1986) is an extension of the theory of reasoned action discussed previously. In this case, the model has been changed to account for behaviors that are more interdependent or that require the cooperation of other people. A fifth component is added to the theory of reasoned action to form the theory of planned behavior. Perceived behavioral control is the extent to which a person has control over engaging in the behavior. Perceived behavioral control has two links in this model, one directly to the formation of a behavioral intention and one to the behavior itself.

In the original Ajzen and Madden (1986) study students were asked to complete a survey measuring their attitudes, subjective norms, perceived behavioral control, and behavioral intentions to attend class or to earn an "A" in the course. These measures occurred either halfway through a course or at two different times during the term. The results indicate that perceptions of perceived behavioral control allowed for more accurate prediction of actual attendance and grades. Consider another example. A teenager may have a positive attitude toward going to a party and many of her friends (important others) believe she should attend. The theory of reasoned action would predict that the intention to attend will be high and predict that the behavior is therefore likely to occur. However, for teenagers, attending a party may require borrowing the family car and getting permission to go to a particular place. Therefore, the perceived behavioral control might be lower for the teenager than for someone in their 30s and the teen may be less likely to follow through with her intention to attend.

THE ROLE OF EXPECTATIONS

One critique of these two theories is that if you ask persons about their intentions you might receive quite a different response than if you asked them about their expectations. We have been socialized to have good intentions and we are rewarded if our intentions are stated positively. Asking others if they intend to brush their teeth twice a day and floss every day is likely to result in overwhelmingly positive affirmations indicating that they will in fact brush twice and floss once a day. However, if asked to state one's expectations a more tempered answer might be provided; "I certainly intend to brush twice a day, but in reality I do not expect to be very successful over the long term." If we really wanted to be able to predict behavior with a high degree of accuracy we would want people to be honest about the likelihood they would engage in the behavior and rule out concerns about social desirability and the need to have good intentions.

A common approach to the social desirability concern is to have participants complete a scale that measures how likely they are to respond to a questionnaire in a socially desirable way. The Mar-

lowe-Crowne scale (Crowne & Marlowe 1960) is just one example of such a scale. Items are all asked in a true or false format. Some items are: "Before voting I thoroughly investigate the qualifications of all the candidates" and "When I don't know something I don't mind at all admitting it." Others even more would have trouble responding positively and honestly: "I have never deliberately said something that hurt someone's feelings." Obviously, someone who answers all the questions in the socially desirable way is more likely to have answered other questions in the same experiment with less candor as well. This allows a researcher to either statistically account for variance that might be attributed to social desirability or to determine if there is a correlation between responses on the social desirability scale and on the measures of reported behavioral intentions.

Warshaw and Davis (1985) found that behavioral expectation is a more accurate predictor than behavioral intentions. This is in part because an expectation may take into account a wide variety of behavioral determinants that are not captured in a well-reasoned attitude or perception of subjective norms. Individuals have information about their past behavior, habits, and other idiosyncratic information that is added to their formulation of an expectation. Indeed they found that behavioral expectations were better predictors of performance of 18 common behaviors than behavioral intentions.

Attitude Change, Persistence, and Resistance

People often change their mind about some decisions, but are stalwart in their support of other ideas. When are you going to change your attitudes? When will attitudes persist? How can you resist persuasion attempts? A great deal of attitude changes can be explained by knowing how much cognitive effort people have exerted in the formation of their attitudes and in listening to persuasive attempts. In other words, how much information-processing behavior has occurred will often give some insight into the stability of a person's attitudes.

INFORMATION PROCESSING

Information processing refers to the ways in which people consider and use information that is presented to them. In some cases, people may be very motivated to think deeply about a decision, while at other times people may not be inclined to spend much energy thinking about a topic. There are two models that have gained popularity among researchers that explore how and when people will cognitively invest in a decision or topic.

The Elaboration Likelihood Model (ELM) proposed by Petty and Cacioppo (1981) posits that individuals who process information deeply can be viewed as having a high elaboration likelihood, while those less willing to invest cognitive energy might be more likely to have a low elaboration likelihood. Someone who is likely to spend time and energy elaborating on or thinking about a topic or decision would be considered to have a high likelihood of elaboration and vice versa. People who have a low likelihood of elaboration are using peripheral thinking, paying attention to cues in the environment or prior decisions to allow them to expend the least amount of effort to arrive at the most accurate conclusion. However, those who are high in elaboration likelihood are more likely to engage in the central route of processing and put significantly more effort into critically considering as much information as they are able in order to arrive at an accurate conclusion. The visual representation of this model is a continuum with low and high elaboration likelihood anchoring a single horizontal line at each end. Clearly, most decisions are not necessarily at either extreme and are likely to fall somewhere along the continuum between high and low elaboration likelihood. In addition, a person's ability and motivation to process are sometimes heavily influenced by environmental or situational con-

"Here's where you give me non-comprehending nods of approval."

straints (e.g., time pressure). In some cases, the information we are presented is simply too complex and we may simply agree because it "seems" like it must make sense.

A person who is high in elaboration likelihood will be more likely to resist counterarguments, have a stronger and longer lasting attitude, and be more difficult to persuade. A person who is low in elaboration likelihood will be relatively easier to persuade. Although most people at one time or another engage in thinking across the spectrum from low to high elaboration likelihood depending on the type of decision they are making. However, individual differences may also impact how people process information. One such individual difference is need for cognition. People who are high in need for cognition are more inclined to spend effort thinking through a decision than people who are low in need for cognition. The Need for Cognition scale asks respondents to indicate the extent to which they enjoy thinking for the sake of thinking, experience intrinsic motivation to think deeply (Cacioppo & Petty, 1982).

Another model that illustrates current thinking about information processing is the Heuristic-Systematic Model of processing (Chaiken, 1980). As in the ELM, the Heuristic Systematic Model indicates that people may engage in relatively low-effort processing referred to as heuristic processing or high-effort/systematic processing. However, the visual representation of this model is orthogonal with high-low systematic processing crossed with high-low heuristic processing. Chaiken (1980) established that people engaged in systematic processing attended to the content of persuasive arguments, whereas people using heuristic processing looked for heuristic cues that could be used. Some of the heuristic cues that have been identified include trusting experts, longer arguments are likely better arguments, and consensus. The models seem quite similar at first blush. However, the HSM's orthogonal nature implies that heuristic and systematic processing are not simply two ends of a single processing continuum. Different mo-

tives change how people might engage both heuristic and systematic processing.

Individuals primed with accuracy motives are more likely to engage in systematic processing, while those who are motivated to make a good impression on others may be more likely to follow the consensus heuristic. Chen, Shechter, and Chaiken (1996) primed participants to have an accuracy motive or impression motive. Participants were told they would be engaging in a discussion with a partner who had a favorable or an unfavorable attitude toward the discussion topic. In this case it was a message focused on whether the media should broadcast the presidential election returns before all polls were closed. Participants read an essay that was balanced towards the issue. The results indicate that when an accuracy motive was primed participants were more likely to engage in systematic processing and were not influenced by what their future discussion partner might think. Importantly, the types of thoughts the participants in the impression motivation condition wrote down did in fact show that their systematic thoughts were biased to be in alignment with their future discussion partner. Impression primed participants who were told their partners were favorable, systematically considered more thoughts that were favorable toward the issue. Impression primed participants with unfavorable partners systematically considered more thoughts that were unfavorable. This illustrates that people can engage in both heuristically based processing and systematic processing that is biased by these heuristics.

For both HSM and ELM the more effort individuals spend processing information the more likely that attitude is to last into the future, predict future behavior, and result in more resistance to subsequent persuasive appeals. Likewise an attitude that is based only on heuristic or peripheral processing may be relatively easy to change by simply presenting information that would change the way in which the heuristic rule might be implemented. Consider someone who is relying solely on the price of a product to determine which product to buy. If the heuristic is to buy the cheapest toothbrush, then all we have to do to get the person to buy a particular toothbrush is to make sure the price is lower than the price of other toothbrushes. However, persons who take their dental hygiene seriously and have put significant thought into all of the features of different toothbrushes, dentist recommendations, consumer reports, environmentally sound practices of the manufacturer, and a number of other factors are unlikely to change their mind based on a change in any one of these factors. Indeed, when given the choice between changing our attitudes and defending them, we are more likely to attempt to maintain the status quo.

RESISTING PERSUASION AND BELIEF PERSEVERANCE

Now that we have some idea of how persuasion and information processing might work, what strategies can be employed to ensure that people, once persuaded, do not change their minds. From the previous section on information processing it would seem quite straightforward to make sure that people engage in systematic or highly elaborated information processing. If companies plan to spend thousands of dollars on a persuasive

marketing campaign how can they be certain that their message will not be trumped by a competitor's campaign?

First, having people engage with (direct experience) and expend effort thinking about a product (systematic/central processing) is likely to result in strong stable attitudes. If you are successful this may work in your favor, but if most of the thoughts and interactions are negative this will likewise solidify attitudes against your product. People may prepare for an attack on their beliefs by preconstructing counterarguments. Other people may experience reactance and resist persuasive attempts that they feel threaten their freedom to believe as they wish (Brehm, 1966). Still others may attempt to avoid exposure to ideas that would be in opposition to their own attitudes. Pariser (2011) outlines many ways in which social media and online information is prefiltered in such a way that people have to really work to find information with which they would disagree on the internet. Search engines and social media make use of elaborate algorithms that return results to particular users based on what information had previously been viewed favorably. At least in today's online world, it may be rather easy to simply avoid having your attitudes challenged by training your search engine and online systems to show you only what you wish to see.

Why would people avoid new information or be closed to new ideas? One answer may stem from thinking about the consequences of attitude change. Attitudes are often embedded in a complex system of other attitudes and knowledge about the self and the world. Consider your attitude towards vegetables and for the moment let's presume that your attitude is relatively positive and strong. You try to eat vegetables as often as you can, you believe they are good for your health, vegetables are not associated with more complex issues involving the treatment of animals, and if you eat locally grown food you can support the economy and a farmer in your community. However, if you discovered that in fact the vegetables

you are so fond of consuming have been genetically modified and this is something you learn more about and determine is not to be viewed favorably there is likely to be a significant amount of dissonance around your feelings toward vegetables. If you made the decision to change the way you feel about vegetables or to limit which vegetables you purchase this is likely to have a ripple or domino effect and impact how you feel about fruit as well! Perhaps it even makes you reconsider pasta ingredients and your favorite restaurants. While it is unlikely that this domino effect is immediate, it is likely that over the breadth of time changing a single attitude may have lasting ripple effects on a variety of previously held attitudes (Eagly & Chaiken, 1993). In this case, changing your attitude may well be far more challenging than trying to resist being exposed to the counter-information in the first place.

Related to resistance to attitude changes is belief perseverance. Once people believe something to be true, it is quite difficult to change this belief even when clear evidence is provided demonstrat-

Image © Glynnis Jones, 2014. Used under license from Shutterstock, Inc.

ing that the information is in fact false. Ross, Lepper, and Hubbard (1975) recruited participants to participate in a study in which they would be asked to read a series of suicide notes and make a determination about which were real and which were not. Once participants completed the task they were given false feedback indicating their performance was successful, average, or a failure. Participants were then immediately debriefed and told that the feedback they received about their performance was only part of the study and was not in any way related to their actual performance on the task. They were then asked to complete a questionnaire asking how they believed they really did perform and how well they thought they might do on a similar task in the future. The results demonstrate that the feedback significantly impacted participant perceptions of their ability to do this task, even though it had been made clear that the feedback was not at all related to their performance. In a second study, Ross, Lepper, and Hubbard (1975) demonstrate that even someone who observes the false feedback and is then told the feedback was not related to performance persisted in believing that the person receiving poor feedback was actually less able to do the task compared to the person receiving success feedback. The only way they could successfully overwhelm the perseverance effect was to debrief participants about the feedback *and* thoroughly explain the belief perseverance phenomena in detail.

It is clear that there are many ways to conceptualize and understand attitudes. The material presented in this chapter provides only the briefest overview and is meant to introduce you to some of the key concepts that guide attitudinal research in social psychology. Marketing professionals spend millions of dollars each year to shift attitudes or persuade people to engage in a particular behavior. Understanding the ways in which persuasion may or may not be effective can also help you be a critical consumer of persuasive information. What persuasion techniques seem more obvious to you now? How might you leverage your newfound knowledge about attitudinal formation and persuasion?

NAME _____ DATE _____

Chapter Questions

1. What persuasion techniques have you used to try to change someone's mind?

2. What sorts of persuasive attempts do you find most compelling?

3. If people spend a great deal of time thinking about technology, will it be easier or harder to convince them to invest in a new technology?

4. If people do not have much to say about politics, do you think that makes them an easier voter to persuade?

5. Imagine two people who are friends, but during election years find themselves campaigning for opposing candidates. What would POX theory predict might occur?

6. According to the theory of reasoned action, what would you need to do to encourage someone to eat more vegetables?

7. How could you use the theory of planned behavior to design an intervention that would encourage people to recycle?

8. If people have an attitude that is closely tied to their value system, can you change that attitude?

9. If you want to make sure your child does not start smoking cigarettes, how might you use attitude inoculation?

10. Based on the research about choices, will you be happier when you choose one of five kinds of Girl Scout cookies, or one of thirty kinds of popcorn sold by the Boy Scouts?

Social Identity

Image © romrf, 2014. Used under license from Shutterstock, Inc.

Dr. Geoffrey Miller is an evolutionary psychologist employed by the University of New Mexico. In 2013 he was a visiting professor at New York University, and on June 2, 2013, he tweeted, "Dear obese PhD applicants: if you didn't have the willpower to stop eating carbs, you won't have the willpower to do a dissertation. #truth." As you might imagine, this erroneous association between the domain of physical appearance and cognitive prowess led to an uproar. Within 24 hours people had launched websites, hashtags, and tumblrs to emphasize the distinction between obesity and intellectual fortitude. Do not make the mistake Dr. Miller made by naively assuming that because persons may not fit the societal mold in one domain (specific), that they are incapable of great success in any other (global). The assumption that people are obese because they lack willpower is problematic, not only because there are multiple causes of obesity, but also because a person might not see their physical state as a basis for self-worth or self-identity and choose instead to exercise immense willpower in other domains of their life (e.g., writing books, practicing piano, doing well in school). Extrapolating global traits from specific temporary states is a common practice when we are forming impressions of others.

Dr. Miller also indicated that he had only sent the tweet as part of a study, though he had no IRB approval to conduct such a study and was censured by the University of New Mexico which involved removing him from the admissions process, developing a plan to attend sensitivity training, and issuing an apology to his colleagues and department. Certainly, there is no evidence that a person's body mass index predicts PhD dropout rates, but there is clear evidence that certain types of bias will not be tolerated.

What Is Social Identity?

Social identity refers to the groups with which a person identifies that in turn impact a person's self-concept. Social identity might be based on a particular demographic characteristic such as age,

or on other types of group memberships. There are both benefits and costs associated with groups that make up a person's social identity. Some groups may provide status, prestige, or privilege. Other groups may result in being stigmatized or experience other negative consequences. What group memberships make up your social identity? You may want to consider sex, age, living situations, relationships, religion, professional organizations, nationality, heritage, and so on. Think carefully about how each of these groups became part of your social identity.

HOW YOU ARE PERCEIVED, NOT WHO YOU ARE

One way in which people think about their social identity, particularly if their social identity might have unfavorable consequences, is to attempt to reject or create distance from their social identities (Brown, 2000). An individual who claims they are an individual which cannot be labeled or grouped with others is someone who is trying to reject so-

Image © Twin Design, 2014. Used under license from Shutterstock, Inc.

cial identity. However, there are other people who use the opposite tactic to reject social identities by claiming we are all "human" or "living organisms" in an effort to avoid being grouped in a particular way. While conceptualizing the self in this way may be beneficial to one's individual perceptions of the self, it is likely not very effective at changing others' perceptions. The reality of one's social identity as experienced by the individual does not always match how others perceive (and consequently treat) that individual. Persons who "look" intelligent because they wear glasses or a certain style of dress may in fact not be as intellectually astute as you might imagine. However, you are still likely to treat them as though they are intelligent until you have sufficient evidence to overwhelm your initial categorization. Further, your willingness to reconsider a first impression is contingent upon your motivation to do so.

CONCEPTUALIZING IDENTITY GROUPS

There are a number of ways we might conceive of social identity. These distinctions among types of groups may in turn impact both how we perceive our own group memberships and how our group memberships are perceived by others. We rarely ask people about their group memberships and make assumptions about who they are and to which groups they belong. People are often treated as though they are members of presumed groups until there is proof otherwise. Consider the case of sexual orientation. People have stereotypes about what someone who is lesbian or gay might be like. If a person (regardless of his or her sexual orientation) behaves in a way that fits the stereotype then people often make presumptions about that person's sexual orientation. Often bullying towards people has little to do with their claimed social identities and much more to do with the perceptions others have about who they are.

Patrick et al. (2013) surveyed students in the 8th through the 12th grade and asked them about their experiences with bullying. Between 9% and 14% of male students reported being bullied for perceived sexual orientation. In addition, this bullying has significant mental health implications for those who are victimized by peers. These bullies do not actually know whether or not a person is gay, lesbian, or bisexual, but tend to bully based only on their perception of their fellow students' sexual orientation. Much of how others treat us may have far more to do with who they perceive us to be than who we believe we really are.

VISIBLE VS. NONVISIBLE. Tsui and Gutek (1999) indicated that demographic social identity can be visible and nonvisible. Visible social identities may be derived from characteristics that others can see and are unlikely to be successfully masked (e.g., sex, race, age, ethnicity, language). Nonvisible social identities might include religion, occupation, professional or social group memberships, disability status/illness, and sexual orientation. While the above lists may be generally true, one can imagine ways in which a religion becomes visible or disability status or an illness may be more or less visible depending on whether there is a physical expression that would be visible to others. It is also important to note that there are cases where it would be desirable for nonvisible social identities to be made visible and vice versa. Further, it may be the case that in some situations people would prefer to not disclose to others their visible social identities.

Image © Marcel Jancovic, 2014. Used under license from Shutterstock, Inc.

Much of the work on stereotypes, prejudice, and discrimination has relied predominantly on visible social identities. However, it is important to understand how nonvisible social categories also impact interactions. Clair, Beatty, and MacLean (2005) provide the compelling example of a woman who has multiple sclerosis and on most days does not have noticeable symptoms, but on a day she is asked to write on a flipchart at work in front of many people she does not know she is experiencing symptoms. Her hands shaking make it difficult for her to write well, but she takes on the task anyway rather than trying to explain. Another example is a woman who would like to take off work for the birth of her child, but because she is not the biological mother, she must divulge

her nonvisible sexual orientation to explain that her partner will be giving birth (Reimann, 2001). One public policy example that encouraged individuals to keep their nonvisible identities secret was the now repealed, "Don't Ask, Don't Tell" policy (10 U. S. C. § 654) enforced by the military to discourage gay and lesbian soldiers in the United States from disclosing their sexual orientation (H.R. 2965, S. 4023).

POSSIBLE VS. IMPOSSIBLE. Some social identity groups are possible future groups, while others are impossible. A person who is born white cannot later become black; race is not a mutable social identity. People who identify as biracial or multiracial may have some latitude with regard to which of their racial identities are salient in a particular moment, but ultimately these choices require rendering the social identity of being identified with more than one race nonvisible in a particular context. Some professional organizations or occupations may or may not be possible social identity markers. For example, a woman who is 5'6" is not likely to ever play for the NBA, thus professional NBA star is not a possible social identity for her. Similarly the WNBA remains closed to male basketball players. However, a 6'0" woman may play for the WNBA. It is also possible (even quite likely) that you will someday be eligible for membership in AARP and join other individuals of advanced age. For

Image © Cameron Whitman, 2014. Used under license from Shutterstock, Inc.

some people, retiree might be a social identity that is possible, while for others economic situations will make retirement an impossible social identity. Being mindful of the social identities that might be possible for us can also change how we think about those social groups.

CHOSEN VS. NO CHOICE. It is quite clear that some social identities are chosen. Most individuals get to choose (and be chosen for) particular professional organizations, living groups (e.g., fraternity/sorority), and occupations. Consider the shift that occurred when alcoholism and alcoholic was perceived as a disease vs. a choice. Once people believed that alcoholism was a disease, there was increased support for individuals struggling to overcome their addiction to alcohol. Compare thoughts about alcoholism and treatment today to a 1981 article by Rodin in which public opinion surveys indicated that there was little consensus about the causes of alcoholism and while there was some concession that it was a disease, it was also not perceived as treatable by intervention.

Stigma toward individuals who are overweight or obese continues to be related to whether people perceive there is a choice to be or not to be overweight. Crandall (1994) reviews and establishes the experiences of prejudice against people who are overweight. People who hold anti-fat attitudes tend to blame fat people for their weight. The idea that individuals in disadvantaged groups are responsible for any negative consequences has been referred to as the "ultimate attribution er-

ror" (Pettigrew, 1979). If we perceive that a social identity is a choice, then we are more likely to hold people responsible for their situation and less likely to see discrimination as problematic. Think honestly about your perceptions of a person who is overweight who is exercising and eating healthy foods and how you would feel if the same person were not getting appropriate exercise and had a poor diet.

TEMPORARY VS. PERMANENT. Indeed one way in which able-bodied individuals are conceptualized by people with disabilities is "temporarily able bodied" or TABs. Age is relatively temporary as well. Persons who have a social identity strongly tied to being in their 20s have only a decade to retain that identity, though during this time it is likely that they will experience some consequences of that social identity. Again, race, sexual orientation, and ethnicity are permanent. Indeed, one way in which we can have social identity threatened is for someone to indicate that our identity as a member of a particular group is in fact only temporary. Most lesbian and gay individuals find questions related to "how long" they have been gay/lesbian or implications that their sexual orientation is a phase quite offensive. While some people do have social identity shifts related to sexual orientation, the majority of people (89%) do not experience shifts from a nonheterosexual orientation to a heterosexual orientation (Diamond 2003). There is also an imbalance wherein stigmatized groups may be more likely to be "assured" that their current social identity is only temporary (e.g., lesbian/gay individuals).

For example, few heterosexually identified individuals are going to experience someone implying that their heterosexuality is only a phase.

Social identities also shift as contexts shift. If you strongly identify with a particular social identity then you are more likely to retain that identity even as your environment changes. However, if you have a weaker tie to that particular social identity group then a new environment may lead to a shift in your social identity. Ethier and Deaux (1994) followed a group of Hispanic students across their first year at predominantly "Anglo" universities. Students who began college with a strong tie to their ethnic identity engaged in activities at the college that were congruent with retaining a strong ethnic social identity even as they began to express their identity through remooring their expression of Hispanic social identity to the university rather than only with friends from home or family members. However, students who were less identified with being Hispanic engaged in activities that allowed them to develop a strong social identity related to the university as a whole.

Stereotypes

Stereotypes are thoughts or beliefs about groups of other people. Stereotypes can be thought of as cognitive in nature and comprise information that we may or may not believe to be true. Having awareness of a stereotype does not necessarily imply that you believe the stereotype applies. On the other hand, if you have no awareness of the stereotype it would be quite difficult to make use of it. In 1798, printing plates came into use that allowed for duplicating print rather than having to rewrite original text again and again. In 1922, Walter Lippman began using the word to refer to the impressions others hold of groups of people.

Stereotypes as conceptualize in social psychology are also socially shared. Let's say that you generally believe that all people who wear green are unruly compared to those who wear other colors. This does not constitute a stereotype unless many other people have a similar belief about wearers of green. In order for a stereotype to be meaningful

Image © XiXinXing, 2014. Used under license from Shutterstock, Inc.

many people have to have a common understanding that a group is meaningful and that the stereotype about the group is widely believed to be true (or to have been true at some point).

COGNITIVE SHORTCUTS TO INACCURACY?

Stereotypes serve a cognitive purpose that allows people to manage the huge amount of information we encounter each time we see other people. There is a clear value in being able to categorize people so that we can avoid others who may present a danger to us. However, there is also a cost to this sort of categorization. Namely, whenever we use a stereotype broadly to make inferences about others who are members of a particular group we are ignoring their unique qualities and likely going to also be wrong much of the time.

KERNEL OF TRUTH. Where do stereotypes come from? Are women really poor drivers? Often historical trajectories of stereotypes point us to a kernel of truth. When cars first became widely owned, men were more likely to be recruited to drive them and were taught how to drive the earliest vehicles. It was thought inappropriate for women to drive, but when women began driving in their adult lives they made many of the same

errors all beginning drivers made. What other examples can you generate?

CATEGORIZING. We are quick to categorize and when we cannot easily understand where to place someone we tend to devote more cognitive energy to try to increase our accuracy. This can occur when it really has very little impact for our own experiences. People often feel very concerned when they cannot discern whether or not someone is male or female, even though many people readily acknowledge that sex is likely not binary for everyone and that gender is in fact occurring on a spectrum from masculine to feminine. This makes being a transgendered person or gender non-conforming person challenging. People attempt to make the binary categories work, even when they simply do not. Public restrooms are at the heart of some of the more disconcerting experiences for people who do not fit a binary definition of sex. For example, a masculine-appearing person in the women's restroom may get second looks, rude comments, or even told they are in the "wrong" restroom. States are actively passing laws that either prevent this type of discrimination or laws that would force individuals to use restroom facilities that match their perceived gender. However, other places simply require that a unisex single-user restrooms should be made available for everyone to use.

How can you make sure your exposures to particular images of individuals are not generalized to everyone who shares their racial identity?

Learned Associations

KNOWING VS. BELIEVING

Associations between particular traits and demographics can be quickly learned. However, it is also possible to know that a stereotype exists and resist believing that the stereotype is true. For example, people are quite capable of understanding that there is a stereotype that people who wear glasses are likely to be smart, but simultaneously understand that wearing glasses does not in fact increase intelligence nor does having a high IQ decrease your visual acuity.

How might these associations be reinforced or changed? Dasgupta and Asgari (2004) conducted a survey of women's gender stereotypes during their first year of college and again in their sophomore year. The results found that if women were attending a women's college their endorsement of gender stereotypes was lower than women who were attending a coed college. Further, the more female professors the students had in their courses, the less they endorsed stereotypes based on gender. This provides at least some evidence that stereotypes can be disrupted by exposure over time to multiple examples that undermine the stereotype.

Given the wide array of people we see each day, how can any stereotype persist once we find someone that is the exception to the stereotypic rule? There are likely two reasons stereotypes are slow to change. First, stereotypes provide cognitive shortcuts that save time and energy when trying to understand and interact with people throughout our day. If these shortcuts have proven useful in carrying out our daily lives, then it is difficult to do away with them if they have served us well the majority of the time. Second, when we do encounter someone who is the exception to the stereotype, rather than adjusting our view of the entire group to which that person belongs we engage in subtyping. Subtypes become their own unique group which we see as encapsulating the exceptions.

For example, the stereotype that gay men are effeminate is not easily remedied by encounters with a few masculine gay men. Rather a subtype of gay men may be created and a new label provided that modifies the original label, "straight-acting gay men." Rather than change the stereotype of gay men as a whole, the stereotype that most gay men are effeminate is maintained while creating a subcategory for what is perceived as a smaller group of more masculine gay men. Subtyping makes it quite difficult to change stereotypes simply by not fitting the stereotype. It seems prolonged and repeated exposure to people who do not fit the stereotypic expectations might create change, but it's not clear how long lasting the changes might be.

If stereotypes were only expectations about how a person should behave and a person who does not really behave in that way is simply subtyped into a different category then it may seem as if stereotypes themselves are not particularly harmful. However, Rudman and Glick (2001) make the point that stereotypes form not only expectations and descriptions of how people in a particular demographic behave, but also are prescription and indicate that this is how people should behave. For example, when women do not fulfill the stereotype there may be negative consequences. A woman who is a professor and leader in a field that is stereotypically masculine may change endorsement of gender roles (positively) for those students in her classroom, create a subtype of women that might be labeled as "career women," and also suffer from negative evaluations and perceptions that she is unlikeable or cold (Wiley & Eskilson, 1985). Notably it will not just be men that negatively evaluate her; both men *and* women are likely to show bias toward women who violate stereotypic expectations (Heilman, Wallen, Fuchs, & Tamkins, 2004).

SOCIAL ROLE THEORY

Social role theory indicates that stereotypes in part stem from the division of labor such that large numbers of people from a particular demograph-

ic take on certain roles or types of labor (Eagly, 1987). These roles are often associated with traits. Once a person is associated with a role, there is then an assumption that the traits associated with the role must be traits possessed by the person who is in the role. For example, we may think of people who take care of children as nurturing. Women tend to be frequently tasked with child-care duties. Therefore there is a presumption that women are uniquely nurturing and innately qualified to fill this social role.

BELIEF IN A JUST WORLD

There are many values that reflect the idea that the world is just. There are two dimensions to this scale. One is focused on the self and involves people believing that their positive and negative outcomes are tied to their actions and deservedness of those outcomes. The other is focused on others rather than the self. For this chapter we are going to be considering how belief in a just world for others impacts how we interact with and perceive other people. People who have a high belief in a just world are likely to endorse items such as, "People usually get what's coming to them." This is also reflected by phrases such as, "You reap what you sow" and "What goes around comes around." It quickly becomes clear how this type of value system would also lead to victim blaming. If a person is doing well, it feels better to believe that they worked hard and are deserving of their good fortune. However, to be internally congruent the

flipside is also seen as valid that those who are suffering must have brought it on themselves. Lerner (1980) found that participants who learn that someone has won a small lottery also believed that person must have been more deserving than the person who did not win. What about the other side of this phenomena? Lerner (1980) showed participants a video of a participant receiving electrical shocks as part of an experiment (all fictitious of course). When asked for their opinion of the person receiving these shocks, they gave negative ratings. Even when the person receiving shocks was portrayed as volunteering to receive these unpleasant electrical shocks and when it was made clear that the person did not have a way to remove themselves from the situation, the person was still rated quite negatively.

Surely everyone does not feel the world is a just place. Rubin and Peplau (1975) found that people who strongly endorsed just world beliefs were also more religious, authoritarian, conservative, and had more negative attitudes toward underprivileged groups. However, for those who do, there are consequences for how they perceive others and indeed their own circumstances.

Expectations and Valence

Expectations shape our outcomes. Whether we expect we will do well or fail, those expectations guide our actions. Perhaps more interestingly is that the expectations that others have of us also shape our behavior and outcomes. If people always had high expectations for us, would that improve our performance? Not necessarily, even positive expectations can be troublesome if they are based in stereotypes and we simply do not fit the stereotype. Let's begin with when expectations are positive and help and then focus on how even positive expectations can lead to negative outcomes.

PYGMALION EFFECT AND SELF-FULFILLING PROPHECY

The Pygmalion effect derives its name from Ovid's Metamorphoses who fell in love with an ivory statue he had made. Indeed he was so enamored with his creation he asks the gods to give him a wife that looks like the statue. The gods grant the request and the statue comes to life. Later, the play by the same name penned by George Bernard Shaw portrays a self-efficacious Professor Higgins who passes off a poor young girl as a duchess at an ambassador's garden party. Social science stepped in to investigate when Rosenthal and Jacobsen (1968) had elementary schoolteachers believe that a randomly selected set of students were showing unusual potential for intellectual growth. Over the course of the year the students who had been identified as having potential had in fact experienced an increase in scores on intelligence tests. The student performance had risen to meet the expectations of their teachers. Students in courses where the standards *and* the expectations for success are high will also rise to those standards and experience success in far greater numbers than those students from whom little is expected.

Self-fulfilling prophecy, on the other hand, involves one's own expectations. If you believe that you will do well at something it is likely that you will put in the effort and do well at the task. However, if you have low expectations for yourself, than it is likewise the case that your performance is likely to suffer. If the expectation that "people like you" does not fare well at particular subjects

Image © Amir Ridhwan, 2014. Used under license from Shutterstock, Inc.

Image © Goodluz, 2014. Used under license from Shutterstock, Inc.

in school, then you may well behave in such a way that the prophecy would come to be reality. For example, a female who believes that girls are not very good at math is likely to do poorly on a math exam, while a boy who believes he is by his very nature mathematically inclined would experience success. Our beliefs shape our behavior and we tend to fulfill our own prophecies about ourselves.

GREAT EXPECTATIONS AND NEGATIVE OUTCOMES

It would seem then that if a stereotype about one's group is good or positive or would lead to high expectations for performance, then the stereotypes should ultimately benefit the target. However, there are also costs to these great expectations when they are based on demographic characteristics. Consider tall people who are not athletically inclined and poor at basketball, or women who do not cook well, or men who cannot fix automobiles or computers. Not only may they be more likely to experience themselves as not being good at those particular tasks, but in fact they may feel they are not very good at being men or being women or even being tall! Further, because stereotypic expectations can be used to identify who you may ask to take part in these tasks, these people may be even more likely to encounter situations in which they decline to engage in the task or engage in the task and do poorly. For example, short people who are not good at basketball are unlikely to be asked

to exhibit their court skills as often as tall people who are not good at basketball. A woman who is not mechanically inclined is not likely to encounter many requests for help with fixing broken-down cars and even if she did would not be expected to be very much help. Indeed women who have training as auto mechanics may have to be pretty vocal about their skills before they are called upon to step in and get a car back on the road.

ARE GOOD TRAITS ALWAYS GOOD? THE EVIL GENIUS

We often think of traits as being either positive or negative. However, when we start to form impressions of others our assignment of traits is also complicated by our social groups. For example, having a friend who is really intelligent is likely to be seen as a positive trait. Indeed, most of us would like people to think we are intelligent. On the other hand we can also assign a trait of intelligence to someone and that trait could have quite negative connotations for us. For example, an evil genius puts a typically positive-viewed trait in a context that makes genius particularly problematic. It should be noted that there is actually very little support for the idea that individuals who are highly intelligent are less likely to be socially affable and in fact are no more inclined to be evil than their average intelligence counterparts (O'Boyle, Forsyth, Banks, & McDaniel, 2012).

In any case, a trait retains its positive valence only so long as it also is beneficial for the self. We would like to be clever, but prefer our enemies to be dull. A leader of a country that is hostile to your own invokes more fear, when perceived as strong and powerful compared to being viewed as weak and vulnerable.

Prejudice

Frequently people use words like *stereotyping, prejudice,* and *discrimination* interchangeably. However, each of these constructs is unique. Remember that stereotyping is a cognitive association between a trait and a group that is socially shared. Prejudice refers to the emotional or affective response that a person has when encountering or thinking about a member from a particular group. The prejudice may or may not have a basis in a stereotype. It may be possible that people have feelings that do not map clearly onto a particular stereotype. However, it is also the case that a belief or stereotype can drive an emotional reaction.

A woman who is walking to her car late at night may have a fearful response to men walking near her that she would not have toward women in her vicinity. In part, this is based on a stereotype that men are more likely to commit violent acts towards women than are other women. However, the fear may also precede awareness of that stereotype. The woman may immediately find her heart beating faster and have an affective reaction before she consciously thinks about sex differences in perpetration of violent crime.

AFFECTIVE RESPONSES

Affective responses do not always have to be fearful, they can be more general. A negative or positive feeling about someone from a particular group or even more generally anxiety may be aroused when encountering a member of a group. Stephan and Stephan (1992) conducted a study in which they found that when individuals had very little knowledge about another group they reported more anxiety about that group than when they

had an opportunity to learn more about people from that group. A more recent meta-analysis has also indicated that contact in and of itself is not likely to reduce prejudice directly, but rather requires a particular set of circumstances or optimal conditions to reduce prejudice toward a particular group (Pettigrew & Tropp, 2006). There are multiple ways in which we can understand the how prejudice is reduced, maintained, or reinforced through contact with members of other groups.

ALLPORT'S CONTACT HYPOTHESIS

Allport (1954) outlined the intergroup contact theory in his text *The Nature of Prejudice*. According to his contact hypothesis, providing individuals from different groups to come into contact with one another would allow for a decrease in prejudice. Allport made it clear that there were four features of a contact situation that would lead to reduction in prejudice. First, groups must encounter one another with equal status in the situation. Second, the groups should share one or more common goals. Third, there should be an opportunity for intergroup cooperation, and finally the groups must feel that working together would be encouraged by authorities, culture, or custom. To illustrate the importance of socially sanctioned support for intergroup cooperation and acceptance, Sims and Patrick (1936) found that the more time white college students from the northern states spent in the South, the higher they were in anti-black prejudice. Thus, contact with African Americans did not reduce prejudice and in this case in particular increased prejudice against African Americans.

The Robber's Cave Study is perhaps the classic example. Sherif and Sherif (1953) along with colleagues held a day camp for 22 boys who were divided into two groups that were created to maximize equality in terms of physicality and skill sets. As the camp proceeded the groups were encouraged to bond with members of their groups and one group came to call themselves "The Rattlers" and the other group took the name "The Eagles."

As time went on, each group engaged predominantly with their own group, but eventually began to seek opportunities to compete with the other group. In the second phase of Sherif's experiment the groups were set up to compete against one another with both group and individuals prizes. After these competitions, each group began to show prejudice against the other group by refusing to eat with the other group, disrespecting the other group, name calling, and general derogation of the other group. In the final stage of the experiment, the groups were provided opportunities to make friends with members of the other group but these efforts at trying to have the groups reconcile their differences were failures. The boys continued to be hostile toward one another. Thus, a superordinate goal was introduced in which the water supply for the whole camp had been compromised. The groups proceeded to work together to solve the problem and when water access was restored the groups continued to be cooperative toward one another with regard to access to the water supply.

However, Amir (1969) noted that contact can reduce prejudice under favorable conditions; however, unfavorable conditions can increase tensions between groups and prejudice. It is important to specify the nature of the contact and the situation in which the contact occurs. Contact that increases knowledge about commonalities may in fact reduce prejudice, but contact that emphasizes difference, competition for resources, or highlights a lack of cooperation may in fact have the opposite effect. Time and again it has been demonstrated that the conditions for contact matter in understanding when contact will and will not reduce prejudice.

SUBTLE VS. BLATANT

Blatant instances of prejudice are easy to identify. Persons who indicate they hate women or a particular group are fairly blatant in their prejudicial responses. Other common negative blatant examples are reports of being disgusted by members of some particular group. Subtle prejudice may be harder to detect and results in actions of discrimination that can be challenging to identify as such. Subtle prejudice often emerges when it is normative not to be blatantly prejudice against a group. Meertens and Pettigrew (1997) demonstrated that subtle prejudice can manifest itself by indicating that there are no differences between groups and therefore no need to engage in any changes to decrease inequality. For some this may take the form of saying that because men and women are in fact equal, there is no need to correct the wage gap based on gender or that affirmative action policies are no longer needed because equality already exists.

As one indicator of subtle prejudice, modern racism (McConahay, 1986) and modern sexism (Swim et al., 1995) demonstrate that people may reject blatant forms of racism or sexism, more subtle or more modern forms of sexism and racism have emerged. One such example is color-blind racial ideology (CBRI). CBRI involves

Image © Howard Klaaste, 2014. Used under license from Shutterstock, Inc.

WHITES ONLY
BY ORDER

Image © runzelkorn, 2014. Used under license from Shutterstock, Inc.

minimization, denial, or distortion of race and racism in society (Neville, 2009). This ideology is often endorsed by white individuals who believe that society has achieved racial equality and that race is no longer a problem in the present.

Color-blind approaches are problematic. People who indicate that they do not see color or gender or religion and take everyone as a unique individual are naïve to the complexity of this approach. First, as you learned in the social cognition chapter categorizing individuals is automatic and difficult to override even with considerable effort. Second, when we come to understand the importance of social identity for understanding the self, it is also important to understand that those social identities come with a diverse array of characteristics which may also be important to our identity. Comas-Diaz and Jacobsen (1991) discuss how a color-blind approach is particularly problematic for clinicians attempting to help a client resolve presenting problems. For clients who are experiencing bias, being blind to the role of cultural or racial identity is not helpful. Further, people exposed to a color-blind message showed increases in stress and for ethnic minorities color-blind messages led to lower cognitive performance (Holoien & Shelton, 2012).

Murphy and colleagues (2012) conducted a study in which a white confederate interacted with either black or Latino participants. Prior to the interaction the minority participants were provided a profile that indicated that the white confederate was surprised by and uncomfortable with diversity on campus (blatant condition) or that the white confederate was excited about diversity on campus (subtle and control conditions). Then the participants interacted with confederates. The confederates were trained to engage in positive or negative behaviors during the interaction. The negative behaviors included sitting further away from the participant, minimal eye contact, and refraining from touching the participant. The positive behaviors were relaxed and friendly and making eye contact. The confederate and participant were then asked to come up with a ranking of several items that are most useful to bring to college. After they completed the task, the pair was separated and participants were asked to complete questionnaire measures and the stroop task. Those individuals who were in the subtle bias condition (read that their partner was excited about diversity on campus and engaged in negative nonverbal behaviors during the interaction) had more difficulty doing well on the stroop task than did individuals who were in the blatant bias condition. Thus, even exposure to subtle bias can impair cognitive performance.

How does subtle discrimination operate in the real world? Do people really behave the ways that the confederates did in the previous study? Cortina and colleagues (2013) demonstrate that modern discrimination in the workplace can be thought of as selective incivility. Incivility has been demonstrated towards working women in a number of settings such as court employees (Cortina et al., 2013) and university faculty (Richman et al., 1999). Examples can be ignoring or interrupting someone, belittling someone's contribution, or using a condescending tone. All of these examples are often dismissed as rude, but not necessarily biased. Incivility allows for people to degrade others while still claiming they are not biased against a person based on their sex or race. Analysis of data from several organizations, including law enforcement, city government and military personnel, demonstrated that women and people of color were more likely to report incivility and that incivility was related to their intention to look for a job elsewhere. This was particularly true for women of color who were likely to experience incivility related to both sex and race (Cortina et al., 2013).

MOTIVATION TO CONTROL PREJUDICE

Once we are aware that we may be having automatic and negative reactions to people with particular social identities and realize that this is incongruent with how we would like to treat others, we may be motivated to control our prejudiced responses. Dunton and Fazio (1997) developed the motivation to control prejudice scale which asks respondents to what extent they take action to avoid having prejudicial reactions. Some items include: "If I have a prejudiced thought or feeling, I keep it to myself." "It's important to me that other people not think I'm prejudiced." "It's never acceptable to express one's prejudices."

Individuals who have higher scores on this scale are likely to effectively avoid expressing overt prejudice or stereotype endorsement. There are two underlying factors in this scale. One is a concern with being perceived or actually being prejudiced in a way that violates one's personal values. The second is an attempt to inhibit one's own expression to avoid disputes with others. However, the implicit attitudes are more difficult to regulate and in spite of good intentions and impression management concerns, prejudice is likely to emerge on more implicit measures.

STEREOTYPE SUPPRESSION AND REBOUND EFFECTS

A person may be quite motivated to control their prejudicial reactions and begin to actively suppress their stereotypic thoughts. However, there is an ironic effect that occurs. The more people attempt to not think about a particular association the more they are likely to do so. If I encourage you not to think about white bears, you are likely to have white bears of all sorts come to mind more frequently than before I had made any request. In fact, polar bears may come to mind at a rate that it would take considerable effort to reduce. This effort in turn sets off a chain reaction of other associations that often increase your thoughts about white bears.

Macrae, Bodenhausen, Milne, and Jetten (1994) propose that this is because in an attempt to suppress a particular thought people begin to monitor their thoughts for these unwanted associations. However, the monitoring itself increases or activates thoughts related to both aspects that are to be suppressed. Going back to the white bear example, you may not only be monitoring for the combination of white bears (e.g., polar bears), but also bears generally and perhaps even the color white. In doing so, you may find koala bears come to mind and you try to decide if that is indeed the sort of thought that ought to be suppressed, after all in pictures they sometimes seem to have white or at least light-colored fur. Then you may start to compare the koala to the polar bear and there you are thinking about white bears in spite of your best intention to avoid such thoughts.

Discrimination

To this point we have discussed stereotypes and prejudice, but both are relatively benign compared to discrimination. Discrimination refers to behaviors or actions that are taken that often stem from stereotypes or prejudice in which a member of a group is treated in a particular way because they belong to a group. Discrimination may not always be directed at a group that is viewed negatively. Indeed, we can engage in discriminatory actions against people that belong to groups about which we have positive stereotypes. If persons have a stereotype that indicates Asian individuals are good at math, and then suggests that they would have no problem in a particular math class, is this discrimination?

Discrimination is a term that is often used to describe behaviors that range from hate crimes, harassment, and violence to micro-aggressions. Micro-aggressions are behaviors that members of groups may experience frequently and which are often done without intent to harm, but nevertheless build up overtime and often have significant consequences on the lives of those who are subjected to these slights. However, there are other considerations that you should consider when determining what language you will use.

From Feeling to Fighting

In the previous sections we have discussed the stereotypes which are cognitive processes, prejudice or affective responses, and discrimination or biased behavior towards others. In the next section, we will discuss how these three constructs intersect in today's society and how critical examination of these three facets of bias can lead to social change.

THE DANGER OF POLITICAL CORRECTNESS: INTRINSIC AND EXTRINSIC MOTIVATION

Some individuals feel that much of the work with regard to modern civil rights and attempts to eradicate racism, sexism, heterosexism, ableism, and ageism is unimportant and derisively discuss political correctness. Political correctness as often been used by the popular media and press to refer to language that is situated to avoid offending. While others have posited that using appropriate language (or politically correct language) helps to minimize discrimination.

First, accuracy is important. The common practice of referring to adult women as "girls" contributes to the position of women as children and incapable of adult decision making. Employers seeking someone to carry out important projects and undertake critical business operations are unlikely to seek a girl any more than they would seek a boy to do the work. When asked what an appropriate wage is for a girl vs. a woman we are likely to receive different estimates. In addition, in your research writing if you indicate that you interviewed 15 girls for your study, there is in fact an age implication that your research is with children. Finally, a note you make about an adult client having a romantic relationship with a girl implies to anyone else reading the note that the adult client may well be a pedophile. Accuracy matters!

Second, the language people use belies their own positioning and attitudes toward groups of individuals. Persons who refer to others by their label as a noun rather than an adjective (e.g., gays vs. gay people) also demonstrate their own awareness of a variety of diversity issues. In this way political correctness can present some concern. If people use the politically correct language but harbor negative attitudes or prejudicial feelings toward a group, members of that group may believe the person is trustworthy but in fact this person may be particularly harmful. Groups of people may use words in offensive ways by taking a label that describes a person and using it to describe things with negative connotations (e.g., "that's so gay" or "that's retarded" or "you play like a girl"). Political correctness can help individuals who are intrinsically motivated to be accepting of a diverse array of people to communicate their good intentions and well-meaning by adopting linguistic cues that demonstrate acceptance (rather than tolerance). On the other hand, political correctness may also provide those who hold quite negative attitudes to appear less prejudicial and hide their biases under the guise of acceptance language.

Candace Parker (yellow) defending against Tanisha Wright (green) during the WNBA playoff game in 2009.

When someone indicates they dislike having to be politically correct, this may demonstrate that they are in fact not intrinsically motivated to embrace diversity and rather are externally motivated to avoid perceived punishment for using inappropriate terms. Many people have adopted a variety of phrases that seem to imply embracing diversity, but in fact present their own problematic implications. The language of tolerance vs. acceptance is one such indicator. For those of you who grew up with younger siblings you may have tolerated their presence when you found them annoying or didn't really want them around but were forced to take them with you. Think of the emotions that you felt when you were tolerating them and how different that is from accepting them and wanting them to be present. Likewise, to say that we want to increase tolerance has a very different goal than to increase acceptance.

A LIFETIME OF SMALL SLIGHTS

Infant mortality rate is often used as an indicator that a group of people is suffering or doing well. African American women in the United States have been experiencing a higher infant mortality rate for some time and the typical explanations that involve economics, education, and access to healthcare are pointed to as causal. However, consider that when comparing black and white women with college degrees that children born to black women have a nearly three times higher infant mortality rate than infants born to white women. What could possibly explain that difference?

Two explanations have received attention. The first is racial bias or discrimination among healthcare providers. In 2007, a Harvard study circulated hypothetical vignettes of patients reporting chest pain during a hospital visit and that examination indicated that the patient had in fact suffered a heart attack. When the patient was portrayed as black the doctors were less likely to recommend life-saving drugs than when the patient was white (Green et al., 2007). The second is that poor health is the outcome of a lifetime of racism experienced through micro-aggressions and overt dis-

crimination. Experiencing discrimination is bad for your health. It is stressful to be ostracized and causes increases in cortisol levels. If your cortisol levels remain chronically high as they would if you were exposed to chronic stressors brought on by racism, this can cause hypertension and other cardiovascular problems. A normal stress response involves a release of adrenaline, endorphins, and cortisol. However, over time the resulting high blood pressure can scar arteries and lead to more plaque buildup and increase the risk of heart attack and stroke (Hill, Neighbors, & Gayle, 2004)

GENOCIDE

Perhaps one of the most extreme forms of discrimination is genocide. Genocide involves the killing of an entire group of people based on their particular social identities or demographic. The Holocaust is perhaps the most widely discussed genocide, during which 6 million Jews were killed during World War II. The methods were truly horrific and the effects of these atrocities continue to impact our understanding of the world today. However, it is important to remember that we are not so separated by distance nor time from genocides, as there have been other such atrocities both in the United States and within the last decade.

While some objections have been raised to labelling the ways in which Indigenous peoples were treated as genocide, it is clear that bias against American Indians in North America led to significant devastation of the population of Indigenous people. In the United States and North America, the mass murder and forced relocation of Indigenous people continues to have severe consequences. As U.S. settlers moved from east to west, they decimated entire tribes and cultures. Dobyns (1983) has estimated that there were over 18 million Indigenous people living in the Americas prior to 1492. Others have listed smaller numbers; the U.S. Bureau of the Census in 1894 indicated that war was the cause of death for 30,000 Indians (Thorton, 1990). What is clear is that the attitudes toward Indigenous populations continued through the 20th century. Similarly, slavery as a practice is not considered genocide as the intent was not to kill but rather to sell people to other people. Sinafasi Makelo has repeatedly asked the UN Security Council to recognize cannibalism as a crime against humanity and an act of genocide, citing the practice of Pygmies being killed and eaten during the Congo Civil War by both sides as they were not viewed as human (BBC News, 2003).

In 2008, the International Criminal Court filed suit against Sudan's president for three counts of genocide when three tribal groups in Darfur were to be destroyed. Black Sudanese civilians were killed in Darfur, Sudan by Arab Sudanese militias. Over 1 million black Sudanese individuals were displaced from their homes and forced into refugee camps where starvation took many more lives. In 2009, the genocide charges were dropped, though crimes against humanity and war crimes remain listed on the warrant issued for al-Bashir's arrest.

There are clear patterns to when and how genocide is carried out. First, there is often some competition for resources that leads to serious and intense conflict (Staub, 1999). This can take the form of economic hardship, insecurity, and perception that one is losing control over one's own life position because of another group's actions.

The second pattern is dehumanization (Waller, 2002). Members of the underprivileged group begin to be referred to in ways that undermine their humanity, for example, as animals, less than human, without values or value. Therefore, these people who are not in fact human are no longer entitled to the rights most often extended to humans. This can take many forms. During war, slang names are often created to dehumanize the enemy (e.g., "towelheads" or "gooks"). Consider, the ways in which similar tactics take place which may lead to "gendercide" (e.g., referring to women as "bitches," a term used for female dogs).

The third condition is that the dominant group believes the claims authorities make about the underprivileged group. That is, the dominant group members buy into the dehumanization and "correctness" of these ideas as reflecting reality. There is rarely an immediate action to kill the underprivileged group, but rather a slow and escalating aggression against the group members. Examples may include segregation, curfews, differential requirements for navigating daily life (e.g., carrying identification papers at all times), and a lack of protection for the underprivileged group when they become victims of crime. The final element is that there are often passive bystanders who bear witness to each of these steps, but stand to the side rather than speak up. Niemoller's poem perhaps captures this final element best:

"First they came for the Socialalists, and I did not speak out—

Because I was not a Socialist.

Then they came for the Trade Unionists and I did not speak out—

Because I was not a Trade Unionist.

Then they came fro the Jews, and I did not speak out—

Because I was not a Jew.

Then they came for me—and there was no one left to speak for me."

—Niemoller (1892–1984)

OSWIECIM, POLAND: Boots of victims in Auschwitz Camp I, a former Nazi extermination camp on October 22, 2012, in Oswiecim, Poland. It was the biggest Nazi concentration camp in Europe.

© Bettmann/CORBIS

This scene at the Nazi concentration camp at Belsen shows part of the endless pile of corpses of some 60,000 civilian prisoners awaiting burial. Following the arrival of British 2nd Army troops, they forced the German SS guards to dig graves and bury their unfortunate victims. Despite the frantic efforts of British medical units, hundreds of diseased and tortured civilians—jammed into the overcrowded camp by the Nazis—died hourly.

Paul Slovic (2007) asks the question that perhaps is most concerning: Why do people stand by and bear witness to genocide without taking action? He begins by quoting Mother Teresa, "If I look at the mass I will never act. If I look at the one, I will." It is also interesting to consider why we are quick to send aid when people become victims of natural disaster, but hesitant to get involved when people or governments kill people. The affect (or emotional) response we experience when faced with the killing of many people is difficult to put into words. When 800,000 people were killed in 100 days in Rwanda, the reaction and media coverage did not result in an immediate reaction from the public. Slovic argues that the numbers are numbing and do not result in strong or specific affect that would lead to taking action. It is challenging to imagine 800,000 people, when we see a single face and consider a single life we can experience deeply the impact that life may have on our world. However, as the numbers climb and we lose the ability to put faces and stories to these numbers, we become numb to the value of their life experience. Showing photographs of the people who are one of the many victims can help to elicit the affective response that will lead people to take action to help that person.

PROTECTING THE SELF FROM DISCRIMINATION

INTERNALIZED "ISMS." Earlier in this chapter we discussed the distinction between knowing a stereotype and believing it is true. However, one of the more psychologically harmful outcomes of stereotypes is when persons begin to believe a stereotype or set of stereotypes about themselves that have negative impact. For example, when lesbian and gay people begin to internalize heterosexist beliefs or when people experience internalized racism or sexism it can be very difficult to maintain self-esteem. In these cases, individuals come to not only know the stereotypes that apply to their social identity but they take them to heart and believe that those stereotypes are in fact true.

Perhaps the clearest examples to consider stem from internalized misogyny. Consider how many times you have heard women and girls disavow themselves of femininity (e.g., I'm not a girly-girl) or femaleness and how often we hear feminization being equated with incompetence (e.g., you throw like a girl). Also consider how often you have heard these two phrases: 1. "I just don't get along with other women." and 2. "I just don't get along with other men." Chances are that you have heard the first far more often than the second. It is just one more way in which women as a group are seen more negatively (even by other women). Szymanski, Gupta, Carr, and Stewart (2009) found that internalized misogyny was related to increased psychological distress when faced with sexist events. Internalized sexism may include accepting traditional gender roles, and denial of sexism both personally

and culturally. Internalized misogyny is hatred of and devaluation of women and female-related characteristics. It is important to understand that both women and men exhibit beliefs and behaviors that promote misogynistic views.

Bryant (2011) examined the ways in which internalized racism impacts African American male youth. Internalized racism for African Americans involves accepting a racial stratification that devalues the intrinsic worth and diminishes the abilities of African Americans. This internalization leads to a decrease in self-worth and shame associated with African identity. While Bryant's work identifies several factors that increase the likelihood that a young African American male would engage in violence, the largest affect size emerged for internalized racism. The more participants had internalized racism the more likely they were to have engaged in violence. However, internalized racism was only predictive of the propensity for

violence, not of violent behavior. The logic here is quite straightforward: If you do not value yourself, then engaging in self-destructive behavior that may lead to the loss of your life or your freedom is not as large a risk as it is for those who hold themselves in high esteem.

What about the model minority in the United States? A model minority is often imbued with positive traits, such as Asian Americans being intelligent, perfectionists, and excellent at math. Even these positive stereotypes can result in negative outcomes—namely, concerns that Asian Americans will take jobs from European Americans who feel entitled to high-paying positions. Anyone who fails to live up to these high standards may be viewed negatively. Anti-Asian racism can also be internalized. This is evidenced when one group may be referred to derogatorily as "fresh off the boat" implying they are not assimilated into American culture enough and also derogatorily "white washed" to imply that a group is too assimilated and has lost touch with being Asian altogether (Pyke & Dang, 2003). What are the concrete ways in which Asian Americans might experience internalized racism? Some examples include dis-identification, attempting to not be perceived as "too" foreign and to seek acceptance by whites and losing any trace of an accent that might belie a second language. This may also lead to segregating oneself from other Asian Americans who are in turn derogated as more stereotypical.

Czopp (2008) found that black participants evaluated white students negatively when they complimented African Americans on their athletic ability. Black participants also evaluated an interracial interaction as more negative when the white actor in the vignette was expressing positive stereotypes compared to when the interaction did not involve stereotypes. Another series of studies by (Kay, Day, Zanna, & Nussbaum, 2013) demonstrate again that positive stereotypes are often regarded as harmless or taken lightly, but the reality of their impact is often just the opposite.

The Martin Luther King, Jr. Memorial located on the National Mall in Washington, DC.

In a positive stereotype condition, participants read a fictitious article that indicated that black people had scored higher on an athletic ability test. In the negative stereotype condition the article made a similar claim indicating that intelligence scores were higher for white people. Readers were then simply asked to write down their thoughts about the article. Many in the negative stereotype condition were quick to recognize the bias in the article (73.9%), but only 44.4% claimed bias played a role in the positive stereotype condition. In a second study participants were asked to complete the same tasks and then participate in a second ostensibly unrelated study in which they completed a questionnaire that asked them to what extent differences between European and African Americans were attributable to "nature." Those who had read the positive stereotype article were more likely to believe that differences between European and African American individuals were due to biological or natural differ-

ences. Those exposed to the negative stereotype condition were less likely to attribute differences to biology (Kay et al., 2013).

However, in the most surprising study of the series carried out by Kay and colleagues (2013), participants were again asked to read passages portraying the positive athleticism stereotype, a negative stereotype indicating black individuals were more violent than white individuals and then asked to what extent they endorsed a variety of other stereotypes about African American targets. Again many participants are quick to note that the negative stereotype portrayed here about violence is likely to be biased and are on guard against stereotyping. Those in the positive stereotype condition were not as concerned about bias in the article. After they completed those tasks they were asked to participate in an ostensibly unrelated study in which materials were being pretested for another experiment on impression formation. They were shown a series of 10 profiles including name, age, personality test scores, and asked to rate persons on how likely they would be to perform an act of kindness, be involved in a crime, volunteer for charity, and cheat. The names were manipulated so that 2 of the 10 would be perceived to be African American. The results show that those individuals who were in the *positive* stereotype condition were more likely to indicate that the profiles with African American names would be involved in a crime. Those who were previously exposed to the negative stereotype about violence were no more likely than the control group to rate the African American profiles higher on negative traits. It seems that positive stereotypes may be particularly dangerous because people do not perceive them as problematic and yet they seem to prime related stereotypic assumptions that are generalized to other situations.

We do not experience social identity piecemeal but live our lives at the intersections of race, age, ability, gender, sex, sexual orientation, nationality, and so on. We are not only Asian American, Afri-

can American, Mexican American, and so on, but also male, female, intersexed, *and* heterosexual, bisexual, pansexual, homosexual. Pyke and Dang (2003) illustrate the unique positioning of males and females in Asian American culture: "…contradictory stereotypes of Asian masculinity—the wimpy nerd and the hypermasculine gangster—as well as Asian femininity—the unattractive, nonsexual nerd and the highly erotic female." Our social identities are complex and the intersectionality of social identity further complicates our experiences of internalized racism, sexism, heterosexism, ableism, and bias generally.

Cheryan and Bodenhausen (2000) asked Asian American women to participate in an experiment. Participants were asked to complete a survey that made either their ethnic identity salient or their sex salient. In the control condition the participants completed a survey about their own individual identity. Afterwards they were given a test of the quantitative skills. The study essentially primes an identity that is stereotypically expected to per-

Gay Pride Parade, New York City, 2013.

form quite well on the task (Asian American) and in the other condition an identity that is expected to perform poorly on the task (female). The results indicate that when ethnicity was primed performance was lower than in the control condition. However, in the sex-salient condition, there was no significant difference compared to scores in the control condition. The results support the idea that there is stereotype threat associated with the model minority stereotype that Asians excel at math. However, the lack of a difference between the control condition and sex-salient condition may point to either no evidence of stereotype threat or that women encountering a math skills test are always aware of the expectations based on sex and the manipulation did not heighten awareness beyond that experienced in the control condition. The researchers suggest that for Asian American women the stereotype about Asian math performance may provide a buffer from the negative math-related stereotypes associated with being female.

THE ROLE OF PRIDE. In discussing the ways in which people tend to view other groups negatively, it is also important to understand how people conceptualize their own group memberships. Believing that a group you belong to is valuable or good may help you maintain high self-esteem. In-group favoritism means that you like your group and think of it as preferable to other groups. While in some cases, liking your own groups better than others may mean that you feel negatively about the other group, but it can also simply mean you feel *more* positively toward your own group. Lee and colleagues (2012) find that people may have nested group categorizations. Bias that can seem evident at one level may disappear when considering a superordinate group. Consider how housing on many campuses divides students into those who live in fraternity or sorority houses and those who live in residence halls. These differences seem to be ameliorated when one college plays another in a rival game and everyone (regardless of living group) identifies with their common affiliation as students attending the same university.

A; Image © spirit of america, 2014. Used under license from Shutterstock, Inc.

B; Image © lev radin, 2014. Used under license from Shutterstock, Inc.

C; Image © Dong Jianes, 2014. Used under license from Shutterstock, Inc.

A: Republican National Convention delegates pledge allegiance. B: Latin American flags during the 43rd New York Pride parade. C: Dancer participating in the 24th Red Mountain Eagle Pow-Wow in 2010.

It can also be easier to exhibit in-group favoritism when mainstream culture also values your group. For example, young people show a very strong implicit preference for their group and relatively more prejudice against the elderly (Dasgupta & Greenwald, 2001). It is important to note that even when explicit attitudes were relatively similar (old and young exemplars equally favored), the implicit measures demonstrate that young exemplars are more readily associated with positivity. However, pride need not only imply prejudice. It is quite possible to have in-group favoritism occur independently of dislike for the out-group (Mummendey et al., 1992).

In addition, pride may be an important factor in social identity development. The vast majority of studies that explore stereotypes and prejudice involve asking individuals of the dominant group about their attitudes and prejudice toward other groups. There a number of reasons this might occur. First, if the dominant group has more power to harm or benefit members of other groups, then it becomes important to understand their attitudes in order to create change. Second, the majority or dominant group may also be a population that is more readily available to participate in experimental studies examining prejudice. However, there are some studies that demonstrate the importance of social-identity development particular for individuals who are from groups that are more likely to experience discrimination based on their social identity.

The development of a social identity related to race/ethnicity, sexual orientation, and disability has proven crucial to understanding how people come to understand their social identity and the ramification of their particular intersectionality of identities. While this may not have received as much attention as other areas within psychology, it is an idea first mentioned by Lewin in 1948 who asserted the importance of a firm sense of group identity as critical to one's well-being.

For example, Sullivan (1998) proposes that heterosexual identity is developed across five stages. In the first stage, there is no awareness of sexual orientation (*naivete*). The second stage involves *acceptance* in which heterosexuality is taken for granted and are typically engaged in heterosexism without awareness. The third stage indicates an awareness of the ways in which LGB individuals are oppressed and realize that there are a diverse array of sexual orientations during *resistance* stage. A fourth stage involves *redefinition* through which people define themselves as heterosexual in such a way that it is not reliant on heterosexism. Finally, the fifth stage is *internalization* in which people integrate their understanding of their heterosexuality as part of a whole self that impacts multiple other identities and parts of life.

Similarly, development of ethnic social identity has been posited to have three stages by Phinney (1989) that involves *diffusion/foreclosure* during which ethnicity is not explored. A second stage during which individuals begin to explore their ethnic identity (*moratorium*). The final stage is when *ethnic identity is achieved*. Campbell (2008) also posited that it is critical for the well-being of individuals with disabilities to engage in identity development in such a way that internalized ableism is rejected and a holistic view of self as one with the body and retains (or regains) agency over one's life.

One reason that it is important to understand how we come to understand our various social identity groups is to understand how we may internalize negative views about ourselves based on society's negative views of our various groups. These negative attitudes toward self are often referred to as *internalized* attitudes, whereby we come to believe that society's assessment of our group membership in fact is something that is true about the self. For example, internalized misogyny occurs when women come to hate femininity because society has indicated that femininity and women are not to be valued. Similarly, internalized racism involves coming to believe that the stereotypes about one's race must in fact be factual and descriptive of the self. Internalized homophobia has been used to refer to individuals who do not identify as heterosexual coming to feel quite negatively about their sexual orientation. The process of social identity development often involves a stage during which a person rejects these negative messages and chooses instead to take pride in their social identity. It is clear that pride in one's social identity serves an important mental health function and may provide some buffer against the onslaught of negativity towards one's group memberships.

STIGMA: SOCIAL MOBILITY AND SOCIAL CHANGE

Social mobility refers to the idea that people strive to leave their current social standing to move "up" into a better social standing—most easily applied to socioeconomic status or class. You know, classic rags-to-riches stories and the small-town graduate who goes to the big city and is a huge success. Individuals who are engaged in social mobility do move up and do have success; however, once successful they do not look back or remind people where they came from. The concept of social mobility also does not accommodate reaching back to those left behind to help them be successful as well. Social mobility is also congruent with beliefs that indicate that hard work will pay off and that through individual success, persons can escape their current social standing and move up in the world. However, our social identities can limit social mobility. For many years (and in some places even currently) being female limited your ability

to move beyond a particular position in an organization or level of education.

Social change, on the other hand, has implications that it is difficult to move out of a particular group. The social change approach indicates that change will occur but often through proactive engagement and conflict. Social change requires people to take control and action to eradicate inequality that would allow an improvement in their circumstances. People who engage in social change are often motivated by hope that inequality based on social identity can be eliminated.

DENYING DIFFERENCE OR EMBRACING DIVERSITY

How do we create change to avoid the negative aspects of prejudice and discrimination? We have witnessed the oscillation between two approaches both which present unique challenges. First, we have the concept of appealing to the superordinate category human. We are all human and if we just leave it at that and do not spend so much time and energy on our differences we could avoid stereotyping, prejudice, and discrimination. While this type of appeal may work in some instances, as a widespread approach, it is not likely to lead to success. Social identities are not only sources of stigma but also sources of pride. Many people are quite proud of their nationality or race/ethnicity or sex. People

People living in Nepal as part of the caste of untouchables make up 7% of the population. On the right, even having a job that pays minimum wage might not allow such persons to improve their circumstances as they live paycheck to paycheck.

Hundreds of thousands of immigrants, Mexican Americans, and Mexicans marched to demand immigration reform in Los Angeles in 2006. Grandparents and grandchildren lighting the Menorah together during Chanukah.

who report they are proud to be American are likely to resist embracing the idea that we are all citizens of the world. Males who pride themselves on being a manly man, for example, may be offended when someone indicates they just see people for people and do not see sex/gender.

The second approach is to embrace multiculturalism. Celebrate the diversity of identities that we each embrace, helping people to live authentic lives at their particular intersectionality. However, there are challenges here as well. If persons pride themselves on a social identity that causes harm to others because of their social identity, how do we find a mutually supportive way to embrace diversity? For example, a person who has hiring power and whose religion indicates women should not be allowed to work may harm the chances for working women to succeed in an organization.

Consider the recent story of a young man attending York University as reported by Mandel (2014). He was enrolled in an online course and for one part of the course, the students were required to meet in groups and carry out a project for the class. The student emailed the professor and indicated that he could not possibly meet with a group of women because his religion forbade him from intermingling between men and women. The vice dean at the university indicated the professor must accommodate the student's request and provide another arrangement. The professor inquired whether the

same accommodation could be requested if a person did not want to intermingle with students of different races, religions, sexual orientations. The faculty member ultimately refused to abide by the vice dean's and human rights office's request and explained to the student that he would need to complete the assignment as stated and meet with the students in his group which included females. The university continues back the student's original request, even though the student completed the assignment by meeting with his female peers without incident. What might your reaction be if a subset of students in the course refused to interact with you because of your sex or your race?

CAPITALISTIC ARGUMENTS FOR SOCIAL CHANGE

Some individuals make choices to be more inclusive and consciously work to reject stereotypes, reduce prejudice, and stop discrimination; however, others will continue to embrace exclusivity or discrimination. While for many there is a moral argument for reducing discrimination, others are unmoved or disagree that there is a moral reason to effect change. For some, the best argument for embracing diversity and decreasing discrimination comes from a business mindset. Employers begin to realize that the bottom line is most impacted by whether or not employees are able to do the work they were hired to do. A healthy and cognitively present workforce is going to deliver a higher quality work product and be less likely to leave an organization.

When people go to work and spend time and energy worrying about whether someone will harass them, exclude them, or find out about a nonvisible social identity, this detracts from the work at hand. Companies that encourage "don't ask, don't tell" policies regarding religion, sexual orientation, or gender identity are in fact asking their employees to be inauthentic, to be dishonest about who they are. This sort of subterfuge requires energy that could be devoted to the work, if an organization were to create a workplace culture that embraced diversity rather than tolerated it. Encouraging employees to learn about one another is likely to result in better customer service, higher quality work, and ultimately a larger bottom line.

Recall that even subtle racism or sexism can result in incivility. In turn this incivility increases the likelihood that employees will leave for jobs in other or-

ganizations. When an employee leaves for another organization, all of the resource invested in that person's training on the job and the organizational knowledge are lost. It is expensive to hire a new employee as it takes time and energy to interview and identify a good replacement and then to train and familiarize that person with the organization and the job. It is often cheaper to retain employees rather than replace them. Indeed the amount that could be saved by creating an organizational climate that does not tolerate incivility and promotes acceptance of (not just tolerance of) diversity, could improve the bottom line over the long term.

MENTAL AND PHYSICAL WELLNESS AND INCLUSIVENESS

It may seem straightforward to indicate that prejudice and discrimination are not good for society, but it is just as important to acknowledge that there are real health consequences for individuals who

endure lifetimes of prejudice and discrimination. Landrine and Klonoff (1996) found that individuals who had more experiences of racism in the past year and in their lifetime was related to increased reporting of psychiatric symptoms including somatization (experiencing physical symptoms that have no clear cause), anxiety, depression, and obsessive-compulsive symptomology.

Black women with college degrees experience an infant mortality rate three times higher than the rate for children born to similar white women (from Wise, 2010). Similarly, black households earning more than $35,000 have higher infant mortality rates than white households earning less than $10,000 (Cohen, Geronimus, Bound, & James, 2005). As summarized by Wise (2010), these and many similar health outcomes occur when racism triggers the brain's hypothalamus which alerts the adrenal glands to release adrenaline, endorphins, and cortisol. These experiences then damage the hypothalamic-pituitary-adrenal axis. This damage and sustained stress raises blood pressure, thus scarring arteries, and increases the probability that arterial plaque will accumulate and hamper circulation, putting these individuals at increased risk of heart attack, stroke, and heart disease (Hill, Neighbors, & Gayle, 2004). The impact of various -isms extends far beyond political correctness.

Conclusion

The ways in which we perceive ourselves and others shape our social world. In many cases the harms caused by what at first seem simple processes are dismissed. However, understanding how even subtle bias can result in significant negative outcomes can also help us consider carefully what needs to change. The question you are left with is, what are you going to do? If you are considering a career in the helping professions, how will you manage the diversity of people who you will need to help? What biases do you have that you think might cause harm to others?

Suggested Activities:

Read Peggy McIntosh's article entitled, "White Privilege: Unpacking the Invisible Knapsack." What other sorts of privilege do you experience? Able-bodied privilege, heterosexual privilege, class privilege, and cisgender privilege are just a few you should consider.

Watch the now classic documentary about Jane Elliot's "Blue-Eyed" demonstration. There are many versions of the film and clips are often available on YouTube; your library may have "A Class Divided."

For more advanced students or to broaden your horizons, watch and then have a discussion with others about the following films: *Pride Divide, The World Before Her, Miss Representation,* or *Training Rules.*

Take the Implicit Associations Test at implicit. harvard.edu to find out what subtle associations you might have. Rather than defending yourself against your results, consider where you may have learned those associations and how you might try to unlearn them.

NAME _____ DATE _____

Chapter Questions

1. When was the first time you were aware that prejudice existed? How did it make you feel to find out that some people were treated differently because of their identity?

2. What might it be like to be a therapist treating someone who is experiencing prejudice? Do you have the necessary understanding to help this person deal with these challenges?

3. What are some of the things that white people or heterosexual people do that emphasize their privilege?

4. Think about how elderly people are treated in our society. Why do you think U.S. culture is different from other cultures (e.g., Native American or Asian cultures) in this regard?

5. Subtle biases are difficult to overcome. How do you think you might try to rid yourself of these biases?

6. If you overhear someone expressing hatred for an entire group of people, do you intervene? Why or why not?

7. Explain the difference between tolerance and acceptance. Which would actually reduce micro-aggressions?

8. Many times our biases stem from a lack of information. What group(s) do you wish you knew more about? What specific questions do you have? Where might you find out the answers to your questions?

9. Given what you know about stereotype threat, how do you think this could be managed in educational settings?

10. Some people indicate they see all people as human and they do not see race or sex or sexual orientation or ability. Why might this approach also be problematic?

Intergroup Relations

Groups: Form, Functions and Considerations

INGROUP VS. OUTGROUP

One of the first distinctions we make between groups is quite simple—that is, the basic category of whether someone is in our same group or in a different group. We refer to those who share our group membership as members of our in-group and those who do not as out-group members. This sort of group membership can include social identity groups, but can also

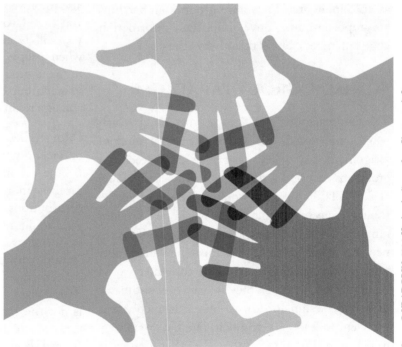

Image © VLADGRIN, 2014. Used under license from Shutterstock, Inc.

include small workgroups, teams, and friendship groups. What groups do you belong to? How do you determine whether someone is an in-group member or an out-group member?

When playing sports uniforms often provide a very clear way for everyone to understand who is with which group. Even fans convey their in-group/out-group status by wearing team colors or insignia. Once people are members of a group we imbue them with characteristics that we believe group

members share. For example, a person who is wearing (perhaps even accidentally) the team colors for the opposing team may well be treated as an opponent. We believe group memberships are important and convey important information about members, but is that always the case?

MINIMAL GROUP PARADIGM

The minimal group paradigm is a method by which people are placed into groups based on random assignment, but believe that they are placed into groups based upon a simple estimation task (Tajfel et al., 1971). Participants would arrive at a lab and be shown a screen. On the screen would be a random number of dots (too many to easily count). The participants would be asked to estimate how many dots were on the screen and then the computer would randomly tell them that they were an over-estimator or an under-estimator. This minimal distinction was sufficient to lead participants to rate the group they were assigned to as better than the other group and assign greater rewards to their own group.

IN-GROUP FAVORITISM

In-group favoritism refers simply to favoring a group you belong to over other groups. This sort of favoritism serves to provide favorable returns (the more your group has, the higher your chances of benefitting). However, in-group favoritism may also improve self-esteem. Belonging to a group that you view favorably can make you feel better about yourself. Lemyre and Smith (1985) found that even when people were divided into groups using the minimal group paradigm they continued to engage in intergroup discrimination and in-group favoritism and as a result experienced increases in self-esteem.

Prior studies of this impact have often created situations in which participants must choose to distribute resources in such a way that their group receives more (and the other group less), equal distributions, or giving the other group more than you would give your own group. However, when we move away from resources and consider simply attitudes towards groups, Feschbach (1994) had demonstrated that patriotism is not the same as nationalism. That is, having pride in your nation is not the same as feeling national superiority or the need to have dominance over other nations. Indeed, Brewer (1999) argues that out-group derogation need not be a part of in-group favoritism.

OUT-GROUP HOMOGENEITY

Out-group homogeneity is the idea that all of the members of the out-group are similar to one an-

other. However, perceptions of the in-group tend to demonstrate that each member of the group has unique qualities. The result is that when a stereotype is applied to the out-group, it is easy to believe that all members of the group are similar and therefore are easily construed as sharing the stereotypic trait. There are several ways in which people perceive the out-group as homogenous. First, each group is expected to fit the stereotypical assumptions about the group. Dispersion is also perceived as group members are similar or different from others in the same group. Low levels of dispersion are often associated with perceptions of greater homogeneity in the out-group. Finally, the similarity or extent to which group members resemble one another also increases the perception of homogeneity.

However, Ellemers, Spears, and Doosje (1997) have demonstrated that when two groups are in competition with one another the in-group ho-mogeneity effect also emerges. This means that people who are strongly identified with the in-group also believe that all members of their group are similar to one another and share stereotypical but valued traits. Further, individuals who were more committed to the group were more likely to see the group as homogenous. Judd et al. (2005) found that some people did not admit to having stereotypes about out-groups and did not demonstrate beliefs about homogenous membership of their in- or out-group; however, the participants continued to believe that the out-group did have these types of biases. The results from Judd et al. (2005) are also context specific. When the groups involved ethnicity or gender, the results demonstrated relatively little intergroup bias or out-group homogeneity, but results for nationality groups found both effects.

It is clear that beliefs about in-groups and out-groups can shape intergroup relations; however, there are also effects that shape how we treat group members within our groups and or when we claim or distance ourselves from group memberships.

BIRGING AND CORFING

Basking In Reflected Glory (BIRGing) occurs when a group or group member experiences success and we make sure that the person claims group membership and that we highlight the fact

P. Olgivlie/A. Whyte

FIGURE 7.1. *Angela Whyte.*

versity students wore clothing that had college insignia on it more frequently on the Mondays following victorious weekend football games than following a loss. In addition, when students were phoned and asked in a survey to recall the outcome from the last football game, they were more likely to use the pronoun "we" when describing victories and "they" when describing losses. Think about the last competition that you watched. Team members who lose, lose alone and the winning team members seem to win together.

Wann and Branscombe (1990) demonstrated that the tendency to BIRG and CORF was moderated by how much a person identified with a particular group. In a study of sports fans, they found that individuals who were diehard fans were less likely to CORF and more likely to BIRG than fair-weather fans who exhibited the opposite pattern. While sports seems to be the domain most frequently studied, Boen et al. (2002) extended the effects to the political arena. This study demonstrated the likelihood that people who had campaign signs in their yards were more likely to keep signs up after the election if their candidate had successfully won their bid for an elected position. Understanding when and how group membership matters is important to understanding how intergroup conflict can be resolved. Some researchers

that we are also members of the shared group. For example, when Angela Whyte, a track star from the University of Idaho (and former social psychology student), participates in the Olympics as a member of the Canadian team, people from the University of Idaho are proud to wear their school logos and support her efforts based on this shared membership. Even when Angela is participating as part of the Canadian team, many United States students root for her success as they seek to bask in the reflected glory she bestows on the University of Idaho.

Cutting Off Reflected Failure (CORFing) refers to denying a group membership when the group fails or excluding a group member who has failed. For example, Cialdini et al. (1976) found that uni-

Image © Maxisport, 2014. Used under license from Shutterstock, Inc.

have focused particularly on how language shapes and reflects intergroup dynamics well beyond the use of "we" and "they."

LINGUISTIC CATEGORY MODEL

Semin and Fiedler (1991) proposed the linguistic category model which demonstrates that intergroup relations are embedded in our language choices. Verb and adjective choice when discussing one's own group and other groups often demonstrates a person's opinion and perception of the intergroup relations between the two groups. The model lays out a series of verbs and adjectives that vary in terms of whether they are concrete or abstract. Verbs that are more specific and concrete often seem to limit the inferences one can make about the people carrying out the action. On the other hand verbs that are more abstract and global allow for inferences beyond the specific situation and lead to more enduring attributions. Someone who helps someone else may have done any number of actions and may in fact be a helpful sort of person.

How does this model play out at the intergroup level? Often people in one's own in-group are described as doing desirable things in ways that lead to a global attribution (interpretive action verbs) and undesirable things using words that lead to a specific and discrete attribution (descriptive action verbs). The reverse pattern is used for behaviors of the out-group. For example, if your student group raised $450 for a local charity by selling pancakes last Sunday, you would probably use language that indicated that your group helped out a local charity. However, if an out-group had participated in the same activity you would be more likely to describe what they did with concrete and specific details. The use of specific and concrete details reduces the likelihood that this positive circumstance will lead to a global attribution that the group is generous, helpful, or service-oriented. On the other hand, if a member of your group cheated on an exam, you may be more likely to use more specific and concrete language to

avoid having the attribution spread to the group: Bob cheated on the third exam in his chemistry class two semesters ago. However, if Bob was not a member of your group you might relay the same information by saying simply, Bob cheats.

The use of these particular linguistic patterns has been studied in lab settings and field studies, from examining ageism (Ng & Chan, 1996) to interaction with healthcare providers (Watson & Gallois, 2002). Now that you are aware of how the model works, what circumstances can you think of that demonstrate the pervasiveness of this pattern?

Membership Accessibility

Attitudes towards some of our group memberships are not always salient to us. For example, when you are attending a college class you may have awareness of the group members as a student at the university, but you may not be as aware of your religious affiliations as you might be when attending synagogue, church or other religious services. Likewise when you are with your friends your familial group memberships are not likely to be at the forefront of your mind. So when do intergroup perceptions and attitudes matter?

TEAM COLORS AND OTHER REMINDERS

Group memberships and intergroup attitudes are most likely to matter when people are aware of their memberships and that those memberships differ from the other group. For example, if you are on a campus with a Greek system and sorority and fraternity members wear letter shirts or hats with their letters on them, you may be more aware of your own living groups that are different from those portrayed by this reminder of group membership. Attending a sporting event is another excellent way to realize that intergroup membership will shape your interactions. However, group memberships can also be made salient by being

Image © RyFlip, 2014. Used under license from Shutterstock, Inc.

Image © Tyler Olson, 2014. Used under license from Shutterstock, Inc.

the only member of your particular group or one of very few members of your group. For example, if you are the only international student in a classroom or the only student of color, it is likely that you are more aware of your nationality or race/ethnicity than you would be if there were more students who shared your nationality or race/ethnicity. Women in majors that are male dominated are often more aware of their sex than women who are in majors that are female dominated or that are chosen at equal rates by men and women.

What other reminders are there of your group membership? How are important group memberships carried with you in symbols or traditions? For example, some individuals have group membership tattoos so that to some extent there is always a marker of that particular identity. Other times people use jewelry to signify religious affiliations or familial markers. Imagine how your perceptions of your classmates might shift if everyone were asked to divide themselves into groups based upon religious beliefs (e.g., atheists, agnostics, Baptists, Methodists, Islamists, Hindu, Buddhist, Mormon, Jewish, etc.) and how that might seem. Now imagine that there were only three groups: atheists, theists, and agnostics. Do you think these different divisions would lead to different perceptions of the individuals in each group? How does the number of people you might have in each group change your perception of what it means to be in that group?

Intergroup Emotions

Intergroup emotions theory demonstrates the ways in which our group membership and relationships with other groups impact our emotional lives (Smith & Mackie, 2008). In their review, Smith and Mackie (2008) examined the basic tenets of the theory. Groups with whom we have significant positive and friendly contact tend to be groups that we view favorably and do not experience prejudicial emotions towards. Perhaps a more interesting aspect of intergroup emotions theory is that our emotions or how we report feeling as an individual tend to be different than how we feel about ourselves when we are thinking as a member of a group. For example, being asked how proud you feel and being asked how proud you feel being an American, will likely result in different responses and perhaps even cause you to experience different levels of intensity. Group emotions (e.g., anger) directed at other groups are more intense if you are highly identified with that group. For example, if you are very patriotic someone insulting the United States may make you far angrier than if you are less patriotic. However, people who strongly identify with a group may avoid entertaining negative group emotions (e.g., guilt). Feeling guilty about a group membership makes this important group membership negative and may have implications for self-evaluation.

People who share group memberships who are asked to report their emotions about their group membership tend to report very similar emotions.

It appears that group emotions are socially shared. Again, if you identify strongly with the group, then you are even more likely to have a similar emotional experience to other group members. While individual levels of emotional experiences do not readily predict individual action, group-level emotions predict group-relevant attitudes and behavioral intentions. Additionally, group emotions help to motivate and enforce group members to behave in ways that conform to the group. Your group memberships will also shape how you feel. If I ask you how satisfied you feel as a citizen of your nation, a man or woman, or fan of your local sports team, you are likely to report a wide array of emotional responses based on the group membership that you are considering.

Some intergroup emotions (e.g., fear) lead groups to avoid other groups, while other emotions (e.g., anger) may lead groups to engage in conflict with another group or attack. Positive group emotions may operate similarly where emotions such as satisfaction or success may not only make group members want to continue to affiliate with other group members, but also to engage with other groups that promote these positive feelings. Feeling pity for another group may lead a group member to reach out and try to help, though this offer of assistance may still be rooted in prejudicial perceptions.

Intergroup Interaction: From Cooperation to Genocide

In an increasingly diverse world, it would seem that the opportunity for intergroup interaction has increased. However, people tend to affiliate most closely with those that are similar to them, which decreases the diversity of our friendship groups and even our awareness about other groups. And yet the internet and media coverage have increased exposure to people from a variety of groups that may or may not be geographically close, leaving most people with enough information about "others" to form some stereotypes and perceptions of people who have different group identities. For social psychologists, it is interesting to explore when interactions between groups will go well and when there are likely to be more negative outcomes.

COMMON GOALS

As demonstrated in the Robber's Cave studies by Sherif and discussed in the previous chapter, there are clear advantages to having groups establish common goals. Common goals can lead to cooperation and intergroup relations that are both

On the left, students in Athens, Greece, demonstrate against new Nazi and far-right Golden Dawn parties on September 26, 2013. On the right, Italian extreme right-wing political association, Casa Pound, honors fallen comrades in Milan, Italy, on April 29, 2012.

peaceful and mutually beneficial. Indeed many of the problems that face the world today cannot be solved by a single group acting alone. Global warming or climate change presents one such problem that absolutely requires cooperation for a common goal of preserving natural resources and a planet that will continue to support the population. Even focusing narrowly on stakeholders within the United States, competing groups have taken up quite distinct positions about how to engage climate change and what actions may be harmful or helpful. For example, fracking which has many people who are looking for new energy resources and capitalist motives excited. At the same time, there are many other individuals who feel that the potential for harm is too great compared to the benefits derived from this process. The inability to establish a common goal between these two groups has led to the continuation of intergroup conflict.

Image © EPG_EuroPhotoGraphics, 2014. Used under license from Shutterstock, Inc.

On February 8, 2014, this Raleigh, North Carolina demonstration included 80,000 to 100,000 people.

SUPERORDINATE MEMBERSHIPS

Intergroup cooperation is also enhanced by taking advantage of superordinate memberships. For example, when groups are called upon as members of the United Nations it highlights the superordinate membership of the nation being a member of the UN, rather than only a nation or group that is distinct from all other nations.

However, being part of a superordinate group is not always viewed favorably by members. Sindic and Reicher (2009) surveyed Scottish participants about their support of independence from Britain and the European Union. The more strongly participants identified themselves as Scottish, the more they wanted independence from Great Britain. Specifically people felt that being part of Britain undermined the power of Scotland and endorsed separatism believing that without independence it would be difficult to sustain a "Scottish way of life."

Gaertner et al. (1990) had two groups of three participants meet in separate rooms (AAA and BBB) and discuss a solution to a problem. The groups then met as one group and members were either seated with one team on each side of a hexagonal table (ABABAB) or in a fully integrated group (ABABAB) seating chart. Participants in the integrated seating acted as one group rather than two groups and demonstrated less intergroup bias and felt more confident in the group's final solution.

INEQUALITY

Social dominance orientation (SDO) is a personality variable, and the scale developed by Pratto and colleagues (1994) measures the degree to which one endorses a hierarchy in which some groups are dominant over other groups. People who are high in social dominance tend to prefer inequality and engage in hierarchy-enhancement in which the power differentials between those who have more power are reinforced and supported. Overall men tend to be higher than women in SDO. It is interesting to note that those who are high in SDO support their country going to war primarily as a method of exerting national dominance and are less motivated by war undertaken as part of humanitarian efforts.

On March 31, 2012, a Sanford, Florida woman joins a rally in support of Trayvon Martin.

For people who are high in SDO it is not sufficient to see their own group as dominant, but to increase the distance between their superior group and subordinate groups. Consider the following choice. You can choose one of these options: Assign your group $10 and the other group $8 or assign your group $10 and the other group $2. People high in SDO are likely to take the second option, even thought there is no increased monetary reward for doing so. For someone high in SDO, there is value in denigrating the other group, even when there is no concrete reward to one's own group.

DEHUMANIZATION/INFRAHUMANIZATION. In the previous chapter we discussed the role of dehumanization in genocide; however, there are other aspects of dehumanization that we have not yet covered. More broadly dehumanization occurs when a person's very humanity is disregarded (Haslam & Loughnan, 2014). For some researchers, dehumanization results in moral exclusion or moral disengagement (Opotow, 1990). This means that others are seen as beyond the realm of moral restraint; it is therefore unnecessary to behave towards these individuals as we would morally consider a human. Rather a morality that may be akin to how we feel about animals is employed. When harming someone that is perceived as dehumanized or morally excluded it is unlikely that the moral emotions of guilt and shame will be experienced or will come into play while carrying out aggression towards these people.

Another approach is demonization, in which the members of the other group are in fact not human, but rather than being animal-like, they are evil and demonic. They may be described as monsters or in other ways hated (Bar-Tal, 2004). Consider the language white pioneers used when referring to Indigenous people as "Savages." How did the use of this language make it easier to commit genocide against Native Americans? Other examples include using labels and traits to legitimize treatment that would not be considered reasonable for those who were viewed as within the realm of groups that are normative. This extreme "othering" provides justification and resolves dissonance, guilt, and shame that would otherwise plague those carrying out these actions against another person or group (Bandura, 1999; Kelman, 1973; Staub, 1989).

Harris and Fiske (2006) have proposed a stereotype content model that indicates the ways in which groups are stereotyped leads to emotional responses and dehumanization. Most stereotypes vary in terms of whether they describe warmth (vs. cold) and competence (vs. incompetence). When a group is stereotyped as both incompetent and cold, the likelihood of dehumanization is increased. They may evoke disgust and do not activate parts of the brain that engage in social cognition (or perceiving other people). These people then become inanimate objects rather than human beings. Harris and Fiske (2006) report that drug addicts and homeless people may be perceived this way. What other groups do you think have a stereotype that invokes both cold and incompetent perceptions? What strategy might overcome these perceptions?

Infrahumanization may be a more subtle form of dehumanization. Leyens and colleagues (2000) proposed that there are primary and secondary emotions. Humans are unique from animals in that we feel secondary emotions like nostalgia or delight. Animals and humans both experience primary emotions such as happiness, sadness, and anger. People often believe that the experience of these secondary emotions are at the core of what it means to be human. Out-groups are subtly dehumanized when they are perceived as less likely to experience secondary emotions. Out-group members are particularly likely to be perceived to lack those uniquely human emotions. The label infrahumanization is that out-group members are perceived as more similar to animals than to in-group members (and the self).

Haslam (2006) went beyond emotions and found that other subtle forms of dehumanization or infrahumanization include denying people attributes that are considered to be central to what it means to be human—namely, unique human attributes such as secondary emotions, refinement, sophistication, and rationality. Human nature attributes may involve imagination, vivacity, warmth, and emotion. When groups are denied these uniquely human attributes they are implicitly likened to animals and when they are denied human nature attributes they are likened to machines or robots. In each case, the harm is that the other is not viewed as human. While we may experience some emotional response to the harm of an animal or even a machine that malfunctions, it is unlikely to be the same sort of empathy we have if the harm or malfunction were happening to our closest family member or friend.

The research has addressed a variety of groups that are subject to dehumanization by other groups. Mentally ill individuals (Martinez et al., 2011) and lower class individuals (Loughan et al., 2014) and even medical patients (Lammers & Stapel, 2011; Vaes & Muratore, 2013) have been targets of dehumanization. It is clear that dehumanization occurs to wide swaths of the population and it is unlikely that anyone is immune from the impact of dehumanizing thoughts and actions.

When people are dehumanized they are less likely to be helped (Vaes et al., 2003). People who believed that other-race hurricane Katrina victims did not experience uniquely human emotions were less likely to volunteer to help with relief efforts (Cuddy et al., 2007). People who are dehumanized are less likely to receive help and more likely to be subject to antisocial treatment. Children who bully others (Obermann, 2011) are likely to dehumanize their victims and do not experience anticipatory guilt before they bully someone (Bandura et al., 1996). Men who report greater rape proclivity and likelihood to sexually harass women are more likely to have implicit associations between women and animals (Rudman & Mescher, 2012).

However, it is not just men who dehumanize women. Vaes, Paladino, and Puvia (2011) had participants take an Implicit Associations Test in which people were presented with either male or female photos. In some of the photos the men and women were objectified, while in other photos the photos were not objectifying. Participants were also presented with words related to humans or animals. As each word or photo appeared, participants had to press a key to indicate whether the photo was of a male or female person or if the word was a descriptor of a human or non-human animal. Results found that objectifying female photos were strongly associated with the animal words compared to photos of females who were not objectified and photos of men. This means that on trials where a photo of an objectified female was shown, participants could much more quickly and correctly categorize an animal-related word and that it took longer to correctly categorize a human-related word, than when other photos were shown. It is notable that the effect occurred for both male and female participants.

Are there any cures for dehumanization? Perhaps humanizing social targets and reminding people that members of the out-group are in fact human.

Another solution might be to encourage the consideration of a superordinate group. For example, when people dehumanize homeless people or people living in poverty in the United States, a reminder that we share a nationality might reduce dehumanization. Relating particularly human stories about members of the group can serve to humanize members of a group previously dehumanized. Ultimately there have been few studies exploring how we can reduce dehumanization. What suggestions can you offer? How might you test your suggestions for intervention?

Conflict

Groups often experience conflict with other groups. Whether this is formalized competition we might see in sports, or simply groups that share space or resources. A great deal of research has explored how people navigate these conflicts and

On August 31, 2008, a Community Emergency Response team gathers before hurricane Gustav hits the coast.

particularly why groups may engage in conflict differently than individuals.

SOCIAL DILEMMAS

Social dilemmas are situations in which one's individual interest is at odds with the collective interest. Doing what is good for the group may not be what is best for you. There are several kinds of social dilemmas. One is called a **commons dilemma** (also called **tragedy of the commons**) in which a commonly used resource is used by all in the group. However, if one person overuses the resource there will not be enough for the group to use. Perhaps a common example is hot water shared by a household. During critical times of day when everyone is getting ready to go to work or school, there is a demand for the common amount of hot water in the house. If one person takes a long shower it may leave those who follow without any hot water. So while one person enjoyed the luxury of a long hot shower, others are left to briskly wash and rinse with tepid or cold water.

Another kind of dilemma is referred to as a **public goods dilemma** in which everyone contributes to a resource so that the resource is able to serve the group. Public radio stations like KRFP in Moscow, Idaho, is one such example. The radio station is supported by listeners who make donations so that everyone can benefit from the local news, feature stories, local DJs, and community updates. However, if enough people begin to believe that someone else will contribute and fail to send in their own support, then the radio could quickly be off the air. Cooperative farms and gardens work similarly. With increased interest in local food there are many cooperative farms in which volunteers take turns planting, weeding, watering, harvesting, and in return receive a share of the harvest. If volunteers stopped doing their part, then everyone would suffer as the harvest would likely be poor and everyone would get less or perhaps even be without any food in return for their work.

PRISONER'S DILEMMA. Both types of these social dilemmas represent a mixed motive problem in which there is a conflict between one's own interest and the good of the group. Prisoner's dilemma games are one way that researchers have explored the social dynamics and decision-making processes of those facing these types of conflicts. The name comes from a setting that is easy to imagine. Two individuals are taken into custody for a crime and questioned separately. If both individuals keep silent and refuse to answer questions—that is, they cooperate with one another—then there may be little chance of moving forward with formal charges. However, if one of the prisoner's defects (or competes) and starts blaming the other person for the crime, then the person who was cooperative will likely be charged and sentenced more harshly than the confessing suspect. If they both start pointing fingers, then it reduces the chances that either will be able to escape charges. Similar decision-making schemes are presented to participants under a variety of conditions to help us understand how people manage these mixed-motive conflicts.

FIGURE 7.2

Illustration by Max Dusky.

COMPETITION

Schopler and Insko (1992) determined that people behaved differently in interpersonal contexts compared to intergroup contexts. When two individuals were asked to play a prisoner's dilemma game in which cooperation yields the highest rewards, they often found ways to cooperate. Draw your own diagram of a mixed-motives task. Using the prisoner's dilemma image depicted in Figure 7.2 might help you think through a variety of scenarios that might change who would cooperate and who would not. If one competes and the other cooperates, then the competing team earns 100 points and the cooperative team only half as many. If both teams choose to compete they both earn only 60 points. Some research by Schopler and Insko (1992) demonstrated that when individuals played they would learn to cooperate, but groups or teams that played on another tended to compete and often earned lower payoffs.

Other researchers have proposed that it is not always the case that groups are more likely to compete than individuals, but rather that groups are adapting to a more complex intergroup dynamic. Lodewijkx et al. (1999) found that when cooperation was incentivized groups were more likely to cooperate. Rather than changing the relative point value, half of their participants were told the numbers in the game matrix (like the one above) represented points which were considered relatively low incentive and the other half were randomly assigned to read that the points represented money (Dutch cents), a much higher incentive. Those in the money condition were told that they would be awarded individually the money earned through the course of the interaction. Groups made decisions together after discussion and through consensus. Individuals made their choices alone. Their results demonstrated that individuals were more likely to cooperate than compete, which is the same result reported by Schopler and Insko (1992). However, groups in this experiment were most likely to cooperate when the incentive was money and more likely to compete when they believed they were playing for points.

It may seem at first hopeful that if there were choices that mattered and were valuable that the importance of the rewards may lead to more cooperation. However, Lodewijkx et al. (1999) conveyed to everyone in the room that their opponent was ready to cooperate on every trial and it was after receiving this information that groups and individuals made their choices. Now part of this game requires trust in your opponent, but if you believe that your opponent will cooperate the best individual payoff is to then compete. However, the results demonstrate that more often than not if the incentive was money both individuals and groups engaged cooperatively. In the real world, intergroup conflict there may be less trust and more violations of trust that have occurred historically that shape how choices are made and conflicts resolved.

REALISTIC GROUP CONFLICT THEORY

Realistic group conflict theory is the idea that prejudice or bias against other groups is often the result of conflicts of interest between groups (LeVine & Campbell, 1972). When there is a limited resource and groups perceive that other groups are using this already scarce resource, hostility and conflict develop. This hostility intensifies as groups have more contact with one another and are relatively proximal to one another. There does not actually have to be a scarcity of the resource, only the perception that the resource is scarce. For example, consider two groups of children who are on opposing teams of a soccer match. During a break there appear to be a limited number of orange slices and as the groups begin to perceive that there may not be enough oranges for everyone to have their fill, teams begin pushing and arguing with the members of the other team. This can occur, even though these children may know they can shortly have more oranges once they are home or even that there are probably more in a cooler, but during the break the perception of scarcity is enough to cause hostility to arise.

Image © spirit of america, 2014. Used under license from Shutterstock, Inc.

Image © Ryan Rodrick Beiler, 2014. Used under license from Shutterstock, Inc.

In May 2006, hundreds of thousands of participants march for immigration reform. Four years later immigration reform remained at the forefront of national debate. In May 2010, this woman holds a sign referencing the Dream Act. What perception guides concerns about immigration? What resource is perceived to be limited that causes the conflict?

Duckitt (1994) identified two additional considerations that realistic group conflict theory must

take into account. First, conflict can occur in the form of competition with an equal group. Much like the soccer teams described in the previous paragraph, the in-group sees the out-group as a threat to the in-group's ability to acquire some resource. On the other hand, conflict can also arise when there is domination of the out-group by the in-group. Now the groups are no longer equals, but rather one group dominates or exploits the other. It is likely that the dominant group will now see members of the subordinate group as inferior and may begin to stereotype them and exhibit bias towards them based on the stereotype.

The stereotypes that result from one group dominating the other can differ. If the view of the subordinate group is that they have low power and status this may legitimize various types of discrimination toward this group that is perceived as weaker. The dominant group may see members of the subordinate group as unable to handle responsibility or in need of protection by the dominant group. In response, members of the subordinate group may in turn see this domination as legitimate and avoid conflict by submitting to the dominant group. Jost (1995) supplies the term **false consciousness** to describe a person believing falsely or inaccurately in ideas that are contrary to self-interest and thereby maintaining the power imbalance. The discussions in the previous chapter about internalized racism and sexism are examples of false consciousness.

On the other hand, if the oppression by the dominant group is destabilized, the subordinate group may see the dominant group as oppressive and hostile and mobilize to challenge the dominant group and their stereotypes. This leads the groups to reengage in conflict in an attempt to challenge the existing power structure. This challenge in some cases is viewed as competition to have power over the other group, but can also be a challenge to simply be viewed as equal to the dominant group rather than dominating the dominant group. In turn, the dominant group's response to the subordinate group's challenge can also vary. In some cases the dominant group fights to maintain its position and continue the pattern of oppression. In other cases, such as the U.S. civil rights movement in the 1960s, the dominant group concedes that there is no basis for this power differential and at least begins to demonstrate tolerance (if not acceptance) of the other group as equal.

POWER AND STATUS. Conflict can occur for a number of reasons, but power and privilege are often reasons that conflict arises. When groups feel they have more power than other groups it is typically limited to particular dimensions often related to ability or competence. When people are asked to rate their own groups and other groups on traits or skills that are relevant to maintaining a power differential between their group and another group, they will demonstrate they are better than the other group on these valued dimensions. However, when asked to rate their own group and the other group on items unrelated to the power differential they may indicate there are few differences between the groups.

Consider men as a group and women as a group. When asked to complete a measure of how skilled men are and how skilled women are on a variety of tasks, men are likely to make a point of being better at women on a variety of tasks that help maintain male dominance and masculinity as powerful (e.g., physical strength, intelligence, rational thinking). However, men may be more than willing to rate women as equals or even better skilled at tasks that are not viewed as powerful (e.g., nur-

turing, caretaking, socially skilled). When a group is maintaining the patterns in which they have power, they tend to focus more on traits that are important for maintaining those differences.

RESOURCES. Group conflict often centers on perceived or real distribution of resources. **Resource stress** refers to the perception that access to a resource is limited for certain groups. Some of these resources may be money or jobs or other forms of economic power (Esses, Jackson, & Armstrong, 1998). Unequal distribution of resources enhances the perception that those with low power will not have access to resources and that those with more power cannot risk losing status and the access they currently enjoy. When there is a perception that a resource is scarce, which groups are seen as competitors for that resource? Esses, Jackson, and Armstrong (1998) propose that salient and distinct groups are more likely to be viewed as in competition for valued resources. The more similar an out-group is to the in-group, the more likely the groups will view the other as competition.

Attitudes toward immigration are often guided by resource stress. Espenshade and Hempstead (1996) reported that between 1946 and 1993 attitudes toward immigration were more positive when the unemployment rate was relatively low and more negative as unemployment rates rose. People who believed the U.S. economy was doing well were more likely to support immigration. In a clever study by Esses, Jackson, and Armstrong (1998) participants were presented editorials

Image © Glynnis Jones, 2014. Used under license from Shutterstock, Inc.

Image © spirit of america, 2014. Used under license from Shutterstock, Inc.

In July 2012, the Occupy Wall Street movement participants refer directly to the role of power in U.S. society and reference the Common Good directly. Donald Trump endorses Mitt Romney for U.S. president. How do these images reflect the rejection and reinforcement of power differences between groups?

containing information about immigration and the recent immigration of Sandirians (a fictitious group). Sandirians were described in positive terms as ambitious, hardworking, smart, family-oriented, spiritual, and religious and were likely to fit in well in Canada (where the study was conducted). One group read an article that inferred possible competition and focused on the scarcity of jobs and that skilled immigrants in Canada were still able to find employment. The other group in the no-competition group condition read a similar editorial without the mention of the job market. In the competition condition, it was clear that the hardworking and positively described Sandirians were seen as a threat and the attitudes toward them were significantly more negative, as were the attitudes toward immigration generally. Participants in the no-competition group remained positive about the Sandirians, their traits, and immigration in general.

Can we stop intergroup conflict by making sure that inaccurate perceptions about scarcity and competition are eradicated? Well, this might help. However, in some cases the competition and scarcity are real. Based on your reading so far what might you propose? Perhaps reminding people of superordinate common group memberships could ameliorate some of these differences.

COMMUNICATING MOTIVES

Halevy, Bornstein, and Sagiv (2008) were interested in how individuals participate in intergroup conflict. They explored this idea by creating a new version of the prisoner's dilemma game. In this case, each person is provided some funds that they can contribute. It is up to them to keep their funds or contribute funds that benefit the in-group (at a personal cost) or to another pool that benefits the in-group, but harms the out-group as well. Half of the groups participated without communicating with anyone else in their group, the other half were given the opportunity to discuss their strategies for a brief time before they made their individual decisions. Participants were more likely to contribute their funds (rather than keep them) if the group had communicated with one another.

MIRROR-IMAGE PERCEPTIONS. In understanding the ways in which two groups view one another, it may often be assumed that the perceptions of groups who are in conflict are precisely the mirror images of one another. Shamir and Shikaki (2002) report that in the Israeli-Palestinian conflict both sides see the others acts as terrorist acts and their own violent behavior as justified and in reaction to the other. Mirror-image perceptions such as these can keep groups at a stalemate. In order to even begin to negotiate, sides must be willing to communicate clearly that they are open to discussing a solution.

The concept of mirror images relating to intergroup relations began in 1961 when Brofenbrenner coined the term "mirror-image perceptions" to describe American's and Soviet's perceptions of one another. This can include seeing the other as extreme, irrational, and power-hungry, while one's own group is moderate, reasonable, and engaging in an ethic of care for others.

Following the violence in Indonesia in 1997, participants were asked to complete the Mirror-Image Semantic Differential Scales and a conflict inventory by Nasroen and Suwartono (2014). This period was thought to be a post-crisis phase, during which mirror-image views of the other may be placated and superordinate group memberships might take hold. The conflict was between the Dayak and Madura ethnic groups and resulted in communal violence. Two youths were stabbed, houses were burned, decapitation occurred, along with other atrocities. The death toll was estimated to be 500 and the majority of the dead were Madurese, though several Dayaks died as well. The results demonstrate that both groups rated the in-group more favorable, but the out-group was no longer perceived as the mirror image of the in-group. Indeed there was far more similarity in their patterns than mirror images. However, participants who were more educated made more similar ratings between their in-group and the out-group. However, the relatively less-educated Madurese participants maintained some level of difference, though not precisely a mirror-image effect.

However, groups do not always have equal amounts of power and the perceptions each group has may be highly contextualized by the power dynamics and larger social and cultural setting in which the groups operate. Rouhana and Fiske (1995) collected data in 1989, which is after the Beirut Massacre but before the 1993 PLO-Israel agreement was reached. The research examined the relationship between Jewish and Arab citizens inside Israel (not in the West Bank and Gaza). Participants were asked to complete a questionnaire. The survey involved questions that were derived after preliminary interviews with people from both communities about the meaning of power, threat, and the relative power status between groups. The factor analysis revealed some evidence of a mirror-image perception in that what one group perceived as threatening the other felt provided security. On the other hand, a second factor which was threatening to Arab students resulted in neither threat nor security for Jewish students. The authors conclude that the mirror image even if only partial undermines the development of a common identity or sense of common fate. For common fate to become a reality the two groups must begin to share a perception about their circumstances and joint outcomes.

HOSTILE MEDIA BIAS. According to a *New York Times* article published on September 26, 1982 and written by Thomas L. Friedman, more than 300 Palestinian and Lebanese men, women, and children in the Sabra and Shatila refugee camps were killed by Christian militiamen. The Israeli army allowed the Christian militiamen to enter the refugee camp and provided them with arms, provisions, and flares to assist their nighttime mission. On September 16 the Israeli army became aware that the militiamen were killing Shatila civilian refugees. On September 17 the Israeli com-

mander ordered the militiamen to stand down, according to the Israeli government. According to Defense Minister Sharon the militiamen were told they could stay inside the refugee camp until Saturday morning. They continued to kill refugees through the night and until they left. The media coverage was widespread and Vallone, Ross, and Lepper (1985) asked participants some of whom were pro-Arab and others who were pro-Israeli to view the media coverage and report back which side they believed the media was favoring. Their results indicate that everyone believed the media was hostile to their viewpoint. Pro-Arab participants felt the news coverage to Israel's side and pro-Israeli participants felt the news was just as biased against them.

In 2012, Pew Research Center coded the news from August 27 through October 21 about the presidential election that year, and found that

This man clearly believes some media to be hostile.

FOX News provided more news stories with a positive tone about Romney (28%) compared to Obama (6%). In the same study, MSNBC showed a similar bias in the other direction with only 3% of stories about Romney being positive and 39% positive Obama stories. CNN was a bit more balanced with Obama coverage that had a positive tone 21% of the time and negative tone 18% of the time, but stories for Romney were coded as having more negative (36%) than positive (11%) tones. CNN provided more balanced attention with 61% balanced or mixed Obama stories and 53% balanced or mixed stories for Romney. What do you think media coverage will be like in the next election? How does your view demonstrate expected hostile media bias effects?

However, it is not only the media that we perceive as against us, there was a much earlier study by Hastorf and Cantril (1954) in which participants watched Dartmouth and Princeton play football. The game was rough as the teams were rivals. The Princeton fans saw that Dartmouth was committing personal fouls and playing particularly rough with some noted retaliation from Princeton. Dartmouth fans watching the same game reported Princeton's team was actively provoking their team and Dartmouth's actions were measured responses to these brutal Princeton players. In this case, the perception of the game was that one's own team were the heroes and the other side was made up of villains. In this case, when people are watching the game itself they see their group positively and the other group negatively. However, when the media provides a report of the events, it seems everyone believes the coverage of their team paints them in a relatively negative light.

Waging Peace

Peace psychology emerged during the cold war when there was much concern about the outbreak of nuclear war. The focal concerns of peace psychology are deeply engaged in the historical and geographical contexts in which violence and intergroup conflict erupts. Some researchers are concerned primarily with how people behave in these situations and others focus on structural and systemic dynamics. Christie (2006) identifies three emerging themes in peace psychology. First is the sensitivity to geohistorical context. That is, peace psychologists recognize that conflicts that occur between groups are often the result of only recent events and instead occur in a rich context in which historical intergroup interactions and geographical shifts impact how groups perceive and behave toward one another.

Secondly there is a greater distinction made within the constructs of violence and peace. Violence can

Left, G20 protestors seek gender justice for all in Toronto, Canada in 2010. Right, the 2009 Washington, D.C. march to the Pentagon as part of an anti-war protest. What is the distinction between people who protest against war and those who do not support the military? Do you see these as distinct ideologies? Can a person be pro-soldier and anti-war? How has the return of our military men and women shaped perceptions of the damage of war on mental health?

involve bloodshed and acute, horrific acts of aggression. However, violence can also be embedded structurally and social inequalities that deny basic human need satisfaction and mental wellness can also be a form of violence. The research covered in the previous chapter on the health consequences of a lifetime of micro-aggressions is one such example. Likewise waging peace can take the form of direct negotiation and amelioration of harms or preventing violence. Or it can be focused on providing sustainable social justice structurally to increase equitable access to resources and rights needed to meet basic human needs (Christie, 2006).

Finally, Christie (2006) notes that peace psychology is becoming increasingly interdisciplinary. At the intersection of political psychology and social psychology, peace psychology has focused on decision making and conflict management. The focus of much of this work is on resolving conflict and understanding how solutions can be derived that will induce cooperative and peaceful intergroup interactions. Importantly, peace psychologists are not only interested in nations and their conflicts, but also interpersonal violence, such as patriarchal terrorism. The violence of men toward women continues worldwide as women often have lower status, restricted choices, and remain vulnerable and dependent up on men (Bunch & Carillo, 1998; as cited in Christie, 2006).

SUPERORDINATE GOALS AND COMMON ENEMIES

Much of the work in peace building has focused on identifying ways for groups to engage in peaceful intergroup contact that sets the stage for future nonviolent interactions. Often groups are willing to engage in this interaction in pursuit of a common goal. There may be two types of goals that could be considered paths to peace between groups. One is to exist as two neighboring groups who live at peace with one another and have mutual respect for each other. The other is to have a single unified society that includes individuals

who were formerly identified as members of separate groups (Nadler, 2002).

Reconciliation in the years following the genocide in Rwanda has had to focus on healing and understanding the roots of this violence (Staub, 2008). Finding a way to heal these wounds involves those who survived genocide in their lifetimes gaining public acknowledgement that the actions that took these lives were absolutely wrong and were not in any way morally justified in their actions. When this acknowledgement is public and comes from local, national, and international groups, and communities and leaders, there is some alleviation of discrimination against victims. We may often believe that genocide is a one-sided event, but historical context often complicates which groups frame themselves as victims. After a conflict groups tend to blame the other group for their suffering and not acknowledge their own role in the suffering of others. Reconciliation requires acknowledgement of the larger historical context and mutual suffering and victimization that has occurred on both sides.

In 1995 after the first election by vote, there was a Truth and Reconciliation Commission that allowed people to tell their stories of Apartheid and violence. This opportunity to have a voice allowed others to hear and essentially became respect rituals in which people could be seen as recognized as humans and as included in the new South Africa (Janoff-Bulman & Werther, 2008). This particular type of respect is often referred to as categorical respect. By virtue of being a member of a particular category, they are deserving of respect. Language that focuses on human rights and human dignity makes use of the idea that humans deserve respect categorically.

> "With the gift of listening comes the gift of healing."
>
> —Catherine de Hueck Doherty (1896-1985)

Prior to reaching a peace agreement, it can be useful to find a common moral consideration upon which both groups can agree that peace is a part of the common goal (Kelman, 2008). It is necessary to appeal to principles and morals upon which both groups can agree that peace is absolutely the right ultimate solution to the conflict even as tensions must be worked through.

While certainly not the perspective that peace psychologists would promote, some early research has demonstrated that conflict from outside of a group can increase cohesion within the group. Consider Brophy's (1945) results that racial prejudice among white seamen towards black seamen decreased when they served together and even more so when they worked together on dangerous operations. The superordinate category of nationality and the "allies" working together against the common enemy, Germany created a decrease in racial conflict.

Similarly, immediately following the events of 9/11 and the identification of the hijackers by the media as of Middle Eastern descent, non-Muslim African Americans reported a general decrease in perceptions of prejudice or concerns as the new "common enemy" were those who appeared Middle Eastern. Unfortunately, this included increases in prejudice against Americans who were Middle Eastern (regardless of nationality) and practicing Muslims (even those born and raised in the United States) (Disha, Cavendish, & King, 2011). So while a common enemy may unite some groups, some former in-group members may now become the enemy.

The Japanese internment camps in the western United States serve as another example of when in-group members (Japanese Americans) were seen as more Japanese than American. This perception was in spite of the fact that the census at the time indicated that of the 120,000 Japanese Americans living on the West Coast, 80,000 were second or third generation Americans and U.S. citizens. Of those placed in internment camps

from 1942 to 1945, estimates are that 62% were in fact U.S. citizens (Park, 2008). The United States again had a common in-group, the Allies, and a common enemy, the Axis. For many U.S. citizens the superordinate identity as an American did not overwhelm their descent or relationship to those who might be part of the out-group.

MEDIATION AND NEGOTIATION

Deutsch and Kraus (1960) devised a game in which participants were assigned to play the role of a trucking company manager. There were to be two companies and the goal of the game was to move the trucks back and forth so as to maximize the trips. The game map was set up so that there was a shortcut but it involved a portion of one-lane road. If two trucks met coming from different directions one would have to back up to let the other through, otherwise there would be a stalemate. In the *unilateral threat* iterations of this game one of the company managers was given a gate to effectively shut off access to the one-lane road. In the *bilateral threat* condition, both company managers had a gate to shut off access to the road. The outcome was that the companies made significantly less money when one gate was involved and even less than that when they each had a gate. People tended to meet threat with threat even when it sabotaged their own profits. Similarly international relations are plagued by such stand-offs. However, threat does serve an important role. If a subordinate group makes a threat, there is likely to at least be some access to negotiation rather than no communication.

In a later study carried out by Deutsch and Krauss (1962) again using the trucking game, participants had to communicate to one another on each trial. Communication worked when there was only one gate in the game, but if both companies were equally armed with a gate, communication served to escalate the conflict. In 1966, Deutsch and Krauss conducted yet another version of the experiment, this time training participants in how to communicate constructively. Participants who

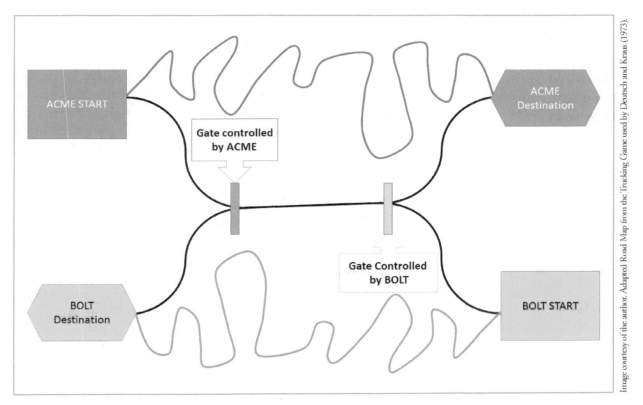

FIGURE 7.3 ACME Trucking game board. Adapted Road Map from the Trucking Game used by Deutsch and Kraus (1973).

Image courtesy of the author. Adapted Road Map from the Trucking Game used by Deutsch and Kraus (1973).

had received this tutoring now communicated fair proposals and had better outcomes than those who communicated without the benefit of training.

Not everyone approaches conflict in the same way. Wade-Benzoni and colleagues (2002) found that Japanese participants were more likely to cooperate when faced with a conflict compared to American participants who were less likely to do so. People from more collectivist cultures may be more likely to try cooperative approaches when faced with conflict compared to people from individualistic cultures. This individualistic approach is likely to escalate conflict and lead to mistrust of the other group. This is due in part to the perception that American participants see their behavior during the intergroup interaction as fairer, while Japanese participants believed that everyone was attempting to be fair (Gelfand et al., 2002).

> "Work on developing a cooperative relationship, so when conflict comes, you believe you are allies."
>
> – *Dean Tjosvold*

Communication may serve many purposes in deescalating conflict and helping groups find mutually acceptable agreements. This communication is typically slow moving and negotiation takes time. The African National Congress began by issuing real threats to South African leaders in opposition to Apartheid. These threats eventually led the South African government officials to take the ANC seriously. After the release of Nelson Mandela in 1990 communication commenced and it took four years, but in 1994 there was an agreement to hold a democratic election (one person/one vote).

GRIT

GRIT stands for Graduated and Reciprocated Initiatives in Tension-reduction. In this approach to conflict resolution, rather than making large concessions or final agreements, one group begins by making a small one-sided concession. The other side then does the same. In response to reciprocation by the other side, the first group makes a slightly larger concession, and hopes the other side will meet the concession with a concession of their own of equal magnitude. If the first group to offer a small concession is not met with a reciprocal gesture by the second group, a second concession is offered in hopes of beginning a pattern of behavior that will build trust, will not be overly costly if the concession is unreciprocated, and does not communicate weakness (Osgood, 1959).

Osgood (1970) explained GRIT by using the analogy of a seesaw on which one person is standing at each end and the seesaw is balanced. However, it does not take much to throw or launch the other person off balance. Likewise someone running toward the middle could also be disastrous. It is through each side taking small steps toward the middle that balance can be maintained without upsetting either party.

Conflict is a part of human history, though we have declared World Peace Day to be celebrated on September 21. By some accounts we have only experienced 268 days of peace in the last 3,400 years (Hedges, 2003). The goal of world peace is a lofty one, but one worth pursuing. Americans are largely supportive of war and reports of public support for a war run between 65% and 85% once troops are engaged. Though national support levels for both Vietnam and Korea were only 30% by the time the conflicts concluded and tend to decrease when our troops' death tolls rise (Hedges, 2003). There continues to be war, as well as efforts made to find peaceful reconciliations. Social injustice exists and people continue to persevere in the pursuit of a social equality and human rights. However, conflict may also serve a purpose. Provided we were asked to choose between peace that required maintaining a socially unjust status quo and conflict at the end of which social justice may go hand in hand with peace, surely we hope people choose the latter.

"Change means movement. Movement means friction. Only in the frictionless vacuum of a nonexistent abstract world can movement or change occur without that abrasive friction of conflict."

– *Saul Alinsky (1909-1972)*

NAME _____ DATE _____

Chapter Questions

1.   What group memberships are most important to you?

2.   Are there particular social identity groups that make you proud?

3.   Think about what it might be like to have a social identity that is different than your own. How might it feel to belong to these different groups?

4.   When you are in a group what strategies does your group use to get along with other groups?

5. What do you think can be done about psychic numbing as it relates to genocide?

6. Give some examples of positive intergroup relations and how these relations became or remain positive?

7. What strategy would you use when playing the ACME trucking game?

8. If you intend to enter the helping professions, how might you help individuals who belong to stigmatized groups (e.g., people with mental health concerns) deal with this negativity?

Group Dynamics

Understanding Small Groups

Image © gyn9037, 2014. Used under license from Shutterstock, Inc.

In this chapter the focus will be on groups and interactions within small groups. Rather than focusing on social identity groups in Chapters 5 and 7, this chapter examines small interacting groups. Groups might be families, juries, work teams, sports teams, or friendship groups. There are some essential components for us to consider when deciding whether a collection of individuals should necessarily be considered a group and would fit with the sort of research findings that we will cover in this chapter.

Group members typically interact with one another. They communicate, act in concert, and engage with one another on a variety of levels. Group members often physically, emotionally, and cognitively touch one another and impact the outcomes of other members and the group itself. Technology may be changing what it means to be in a group, but certainly online groups in some cases may be considered groups even though they do not physically interact.

Groups also are typically interdependent. It is hard to consider people to be members of a group if there is not some interdependence. Interdependence means that members are mutually influential on the outcomes of others. The experiences of being in the group, emotional and cognitive experiences are reliant in part on how others in the group behave, perform, think, and communicate.

Structure is also part of understanding which collections of individuals might constitute a group and which do not. If you are waiting for a bus and there are several other people also waiting you are not likely to think of or meet the definition of a group. However, if a bicyclist were hit by a car right in front of all of you and all of the witnesses began to take action to care for the injured you might suddenly begin to form a group. You would

begin interacting with others, the ability of one member to carry out a task is dependent upon the ability of others to assist and cooperate or get out of the way and take on another task. There will be some moment in which a leader will emerge, when someone begins to assign tasks to other bystanders and speak to the authorities or EMTs when they arrive, there will be roles taken on by each member of what has suddenly become a group. The person handing out task assignments may be fulfilling the task-leader role. Others may work at comforting others who are distraught and take on a socio-emotional leader role. Someone else might fulfill a role of contacting others outside of the group (911, police, loved ones, or others who might be able to provide eyewitness accounts). There may also suddenly emerge a norm that this group is one that is going to cooperate and help. A norm is typically an implicit standard about how the group should behave. I

Groups come together for many reasons, to celebrate their culture, to engage in traditional ceremonies, or to cooperate on projects.

have painted a rather generous story in which the random strangers at the bus stop come together as a group and endorse an ethic of helpfulness. However, it is probably just as easy to imagine another series of individuals who would adopt a norm of minding your own business and ultimately not form a group nor help the person in need.

Are these people a group?

Groups are also often together for the purpose of serving a goal. Sports teams may have the goal of performing well and winning competitions against rivals. Other groups may have a primary goal of being friends and having fun or providing support for one another. There are many possible goals and tasks that groups may perform in pursuit of their goal. Later in this chapter we will discuss the particular types of tasks that groups are often asked to do.

ARE THREE HEADS BETTER THAN ONE?

We rely on groups for a variety of decision-making tasks because we believe that groups present a fairer process. Consider the following two situations:

1. A single person working alone uses established criteria to determine which students should receive scholarships.

2. A committee works together using established criteria to determine which students should receive scholarships.

There is likely a perception that the second process is fairer: that the committee members serve as an internal check and balance to avoid bias and favoritism. Jury trials are thought to be more just than a judge ruling alone. Finally, we often believe that a group of experts may be more likely to generate a better solution or to at least catch errors that others overlooked because so many sets of eyes have reviewed the problem and solution.

When trying to understand both the value of groups and the inherent pitfalls of group membership, I am reminded of a colleague who was serving on a committee. He had volunteered to draft a letter that would be sent from the committee to the dean of the college. In drafting the letter to be sent around for review, he added a line of gibberish in the last paragraph, expecting his co-committee members to write back with either a correction or a laugh about it. Much to his surprise, he received emails from every member of the committee that the letter "…sounds good. Where should I sign?" and "…looks great, let's move forward." It became increasingly clear that no one had actually read the document. Thus, a group is sometimes better than an individual, but group dynamics matter!

NOMINAL VS. INTERACTING GROUPS. Do groups do better than individuals working alone? One way to determine whether groups outperform individuals is to use nominal groups. Nominal groups are literally groups in name only. Typically individuals are brought into a laboratory setting and asked to complete a task. Their performance on the task is then combined with the performance of other individuals with whom they did not interact. Scores are then compared to determine if three people working independently are outperformed by an interacting group of three working together on the same task.

Brainstorming or decision making?

Brainstorming is a Type 1 creativity task, falling within the Generate Quadrant and involves conceptual work and cooperation. This is a task that lends itself well to exploring the question about whether groups outperform individuals. In one such study by Diehl and Stroebe (1987), interacting and nominal groups were asked to generate as many ideas about how to improve the relationship between the German population and foreign workers as they could. The individuals working alone whose score together comprised the nominal group score generated an average of over 74 ideas; the interacting groups came up with only 28, thus providing evidence that while groups are thought to be better, nominal groups actually produced more and better ideas.

Why would the group fall so far behind? First, in a group people have to take turns contributing their ideas so as not to interrupt others. While group members are waiting for their turn and listening to other members' suggestions a member may forget what he was planning to contribute to the conversation. People may have social anxiety about speaking up in a group (Camacho & Paulus, 1995). All of these reasons are referred to as process loss or production blocking (Mullen, Johnson, & Salas, 1991). Groups lose some of their ability to process information because some time and energy must be spent on coordinating their efforts with one another. Some solutions were attempted to help groups reach the same levels of performance that nominal groups were able to achieve. Group members were provided notepads to write down their ideas in addition to saying them aloud to the group. Groups were also given more time so that each member of the group was allotted the same amount of time as the individuals in the nominal groups were allowed. However, these solutions were not sufficient to improve the performance of interacting groups (Diehl & Stroebe, 1987 as cited in Forsyth, 2006).

More recently Henningsen and Henningsen (2013) have investigated whether brainstorming groups might provide other valuable outcomes beyond simply using the number of tasks generated as the only way to determine which is more important. In their study they had nominal and interacting groups work on an idea generation task for two separate 10-minute periods. In the first 10-minute session the nominal groups outperformed the interacting groups. However, there was not a difference between nominal and interacting group performance in the second trial. Perhaps something about working with the group at time 1 allowed the group to learn how to coordinate their efforts and improve their performance to meet the levels attained by the nominal group members.

GROUP DEVELOPMENT

In the bus stop example we discussed how a collection of individuals might become a group. However, groups under more calm and nonemergency situations often go through a development process that involves five stages. The stages are often encountered in order but it is often necessary for a group to revisit previous stages as group membership shifts or new goals or tasks are encountered.

FORMING. During the forming phase the group is essential, drawing a boundary around who is considered a member of the group and who is not considered a member of the group. This is also called the orientation stage in which group members may not be particularly close to one another or open with other members. There is often some tension as the group is determining whether it will be a group and who will or will not be included. Depending on the group this may occur within only a few minutes or take some time to sort out. Think about team building exercises and how they are meant to break the ice and help the group get past this stage. In some cases, the forming stage can be as simple as someone declaring which people are going to be in the group. For example, a coach assembling a team has already drawn the line around the group and determined who will make up the team for the season.

Some groups form informally, while others may make more formal declarations of who is and is not a member.

STORMING. Storming is also referred to as the conflict stage. This is what happens once a group has members who understand they are going to be interdependent with other members. Now the tension is focused within the group and determining who will fill which role. Members develop appreciation for other members' strengths and determine how the group might make up for weaknesses. If there is no explicit leader for the group, an emergent leader will often be identified (or self-identify). In some cases, at this stage small factions might develop within the group as people position themselves to align with particular ideas about how the group should function and who should take on what roles. This is also the moment when members may feel hostile towards the group or withdraw from the group.

Student organizations often experience a storming stage as elections for officers come around and then again at the beginning of a new school year as new members join. While it is tempting to frame the conflict as a negative, conflict may also help the group become more solidified by bringing together loyal and core members who will feel more attached to the group as a result of withstanding the disagreements that arise (Wheelan, 2003). It is certainly easier to manage group conflict when members air their differences and have engaged discussion about those issues than to have people who are disgruntled members of the group that prefer to avoid conflict and remain dissatisfied members of the group and potentially shaping group outcomes and climate.

NORMING. During the norming stage a group is often stable and organized with members who are attached to the group. Mutual trust and support increases and norms about how the group will move forward are established. Communication tends to be more open and as disagreements arise they are readily aired and settled. Consider a friendship group in which you now have a routine set of activities the friends do together. It may be normative that one person will be responsible for settling the bill and gathering the funds to do so from members and a norm that everyone trusts this person in their role and readily hands over the amount necessary. It may also be the case that another member of the group is chronically late, but rather than exclude this person or create conflict, the group may accommodate this by telling the member that activities will start earlier than they are scheduled, or sending someone to bring this person to the group activity.

PERFORMING. During the performing stage of group life, groups are engaged in tasks and striving to reach group goals. Group at this stage are doing the work that they were formed to do. Groups that make a name for themselves often do so at this group development stage and often hit their stride and can coordinate the efforts of members. In this stage a group might focus more on the task at hand than on socializing or managing conflict within the group. Some groups never reach this stage and seem to dissolve before arriving. Group development takes time and groups that are developed under time pressure may find the stages are simply too much to manage on the timeline they have to perform the task assigned. Some groups may skip some of these stages altogether. However, longstanding groups may also experience periods of time in which they are in the performing stage and then after a success move back into the norming stage for a period of time (McGrew, Bilotta, & Deeney, 1999).

ADJOURNING. The final stage is perhaps the most difficult to study as this is the stage at which groups dissolve or members leave as tasks are finished or groups are unable to successfully coordinate efforts. During this dissolution, group members become reluctant to complete surveys or questionnaires related to the group as they are already moving on to their next group or enjoying working independently. In some cases dissolution is planned, as when a team of experts is assembled to solve a problem or compete in a tournament, once the problem is solved and the tournament played the group no longer has a purpose. At other times, groups are disbanded by external forces beyond their control, as when work teams are laid off or put on other teams to tackle different tasks. In some cases, the members themselves

simply disband as the group no longer meets the needs of its members. For example, a support group formed after a tragedy may eventually find that many members find a way to move on and the group dwindles until it is unable to sustain any semblance of a group.

When groups dissolve there are often members who will be upset by the group no longer meeting or working together. And in some cases turnover in the group may be sufficient for someone to abandon a group. Consider student government on your campus. There are likely years when the officers have some considerable success an encouraging student engagement and really make headway on important issues. However, in the very next year if the previous year's officers have all graduated and no one from that group is left, the next group of officers must start again from the ground up. Greek chapters often have some of these feelings when seniors prepare to graduate they begin to be less engaged in the house and the chapter. Members who are being left behind when seniors graduate and move out of the house often feel upset by this seeming disregard for the group.

Group Tasks

Many groups are assembled with the explicit tasks and goals laid out for them to accomplish. The

Image © Igor Bulgarin, 2014. Used under license from Shutterstock, Inc.

Image © bibiphoto, 2014. Used under license from Shutterstock, Inc.

Performing groups engage a wide variety of tasks, but most require some level of coordination among members.

nature of these tasks shape much of how groups will engage with one another and what type of leadership will be effective. Communication within the group will also be impacted by the task they are given. Finally, some groups may be given a single discrete task, while other groups may encounter more complex goals that require them to take on a wider array of tasks. In the next section, the types of tasks that groups undertake will be explored.

TASK CIRCUMPLEX

McGrath (1984) has provided a **circumplex model of group tasks**. In the circumplex we can easily place tasks and understand group dynamics by understanding the tasks they are doing. Some tasks engage a group in conflict and others are benefitted by group cooperation. Tasks might also be more conceptual and others require a group to engage in behavioral tasks. There are four primary quadrants to the circumplex: generate, choose,

negotiate, and execute; and within each of these quadrants are additional tasks that vary on the conflict-cooperate and conceptual-behavioral dimensions. Can you think of some tasks that fit each of these octants?

ADDITIVE, DISJUNCTIVE, AND CONJUNCTIVE

There are other distinctions made between tasks as well. Tasks may be additive, disjunctive, or conjunctive. Each of these task types benefit from different group dynamics, leadership styles, and situational factors. Most research is interested in understanding how we can optimize group performance, but the answer about what will help groups succeed requires us to have a deep understanding of the type of tasks the group will do.

Additive tasks are those in which the group's output is a direct result of the summative efforts of all of the individual members. For example, a group

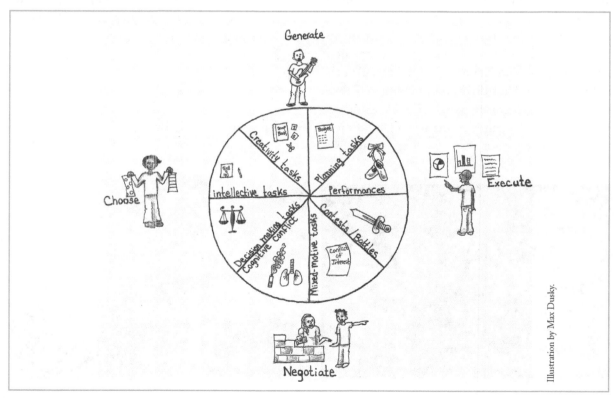

Illustration by Max Dusky.

FIGURE 8.1

is tasked with folding brochures for an upcoming event. The group's performance would be how many brochures were folded and we could easily find out by simply knowing how many brochures each member folded. Additive tasks are also characterized by all members performing the same task often at the same time as part of a group effort.

What tasks might these men be doing? Do you think the task is additive, disjunctive, or conjunctive?

Disjunctive task performance is contingent upon the group's best performer. For example, an academic trivia bowl might function in this way. The group will get credit for the answer if they simply have their best person answer the question. However, other factors can influence performance. For example, if the best person in the group is not identified or asked to provide an answer the group loses an opportunity for optimal performance. Disjunctive tasks involve those that have an objectively correct answer as well as those that require decision making or creativity. A game of Pictionary tends to be disjunctive as the team who has an expert artist is likely to do well, but only if given the opportunity (and takes the opportunity) to draw.

Conjunctive task performance depends on the group's weakest member. For example, if a team is to make it through an obstacle course the team's time cannot be any better than their slowest member. Often the tasks on the game show *Survivor* are conjunctive. Perhaps a familiar example would be to consider a classroom. The professor may only proceed to the next topic once everyone has grasped the basic concept. The person who takes the longest to grasp the concept sets the pace for the course.

Earlier we discussed whether groups would outperform individuals. Task type might matter here as well. For additive tasks, we have to take into account group dynamic concepts from earlier in this text. Social loafing and social facilitation might well impact how productive a group is on an additive tasks. If it seems that others are working diligently at the task, then some members may slow down or engage in social loafing letting a few pull the weight of the group. On the other hand, doing some tasks while others are doing the same may motivate everyone to work quickly or efficiently. For conjunctive tasks, most individuals will perform better than the group. These tasks hold a group's performance back to the worst performer in the group. The opposite is true for disjunctive tasks, where everyone in the group benefits from one member's expertise. Groups performing disjunctive tasks would likely perform better than individuals.

TASK CONTEXTS

Certainly, knowing the type of task the group will perform is a first step to understanding group dynamics. However, there are a number of other factors that influence a group's performance. The organizational structure the group is in might change how groups carry out tasks. Compensation systems and accountability also change how groups engage a task. If a group fails to accomplish a task, what are the consequences? If individual effort is identifiable and the social loafer could be pointed to as the cause for a poor performance, then everyone is likely to do their fair share. However, if the group effort does not make individuals within the group accountable, then some group members may disengage or not try as

"Woohoo, everybody made the meeting!"

hard as they might otherwise. Let's consider two more task contexts that change how groups engage: time pressure and affect.

THE ROLE OF TIME PRESSURE. In real-world settings, groups are often under some level of time pressure to perform the tasks they are assigned. Corporations put together teams of experts to tackle emergent problems or creative teams to come up with the next big idea before the competitor organization launches a new product. Rarely are groups set to task and told to take as long as they need. Even juries who are asked to make decisions impacting life, death, and imprisonment will be declared "hung" if they cannot reach a decision in what is considered a reasonable amount of time. What is the impact of this time pressure on group performance?

Kelly and Karau (1999) have explored the role of time pressure on group decision making. Group members were given information about two possible drugs that would reduce cholesterol. Each group member received positive, neutral, and

Does time pressure make us less apt to work or engage with group members?

negative information about each drug. The task was to determine which drug the pharmaceutical company should market. Time pressure was induced by telling the group that the president of the company was asking them to come to a final decision during their meeting today. Group discussion under time pressure was more focused on the task at hand. Members seem to focus on reaching a conclusion rather than carefully considering all information. When members entered the discussion with a preference for one drug over the other, the focus of the discussion was the preferred drug rather than the alternative. Kelly and Karau (1999) concluded that time pressure may help groups efficiently come to decisions when the decision is straightforward. However, for more complex decisions time pressure limits the probability that the group will fully explore all possible facts that impact the decision. Do you think there are implications for jury decision making?

Amabile, Hadley, and Kramer (2002) have also found that creativity both in teams and for individuals is harmed by time pressure. People who are supposed to generate new ideas or come up with creative solutions do not do their best work under time pressure. Given that time pressure is not likely to go away any time soon, what can be done? People who can find time to focus their efforts on the task requiring creativity without interruption do have success (even under time pressure) at generating novel ideas and solutions. The interruption-free workday in most organizations is rare and requires the organization leadership and others to respect this need. However, the relationship between time pressure and creativity may be curvilinear. Moderate levels of time pressure may motivate a person to engage creatively, while both high and low time pressure might result in decreased creativity.

Chirumbolo and colleagues (2004) had participants in small groups complete a creativity task under time pressure and found that these groups were less creative. One possible outcome of time pressure is that it increases need for closure. To test this, Chirumbolo and colleagues (2004) creat-ed groups where the individuals in the group had scored high on an individual difference measure of need for closure and groups where the individuals had low need for closure scores. The results demonstrate that high need for closure groups were less creative. Therefore, time pressure seems to operate by increasing the need for closure.

Clearly, many tasks on the execute side of the task circumplex have built in time pressures. Sports often involve timed games or competitions and even artistic performances are scheduled to last a particular amount of time. For these tasks, time pressure is by definition part of the task rather than a contextual or situational factor.

GROUP AFFECT AND MOOD. If you have been part of a group you have likely experienced a group level mood. Whether a team wins or loses a game can shape how people feel as a group. These group level moods and emotions are not quite the same as an individual experience of a mood or emotion. For example, a team member plays the best game of a lifetime in a championship match and sets personal best records, but ultimately the team loses the game. The team is likely to feel disappointed and sad, but the individual who had a great game may experience both disappointment at the team loss but some level of happiness about their own performance. In this chapter, we are concerned about the group-level experience of mood and emotion. What purpose do these group-level emotional experiences serve?

Emotions and moods are important for understanding how to coordinate our efforts with others (Cosmides & Tooby, 2000). Shared emotional states may help a group continue to work well together. If everyone in the group is in a great mood, it may help determine what the group will do next. Spoor and Kelly (2004) have proposed that emotions and moods both help groups coordinate and foster group member bonds. Often friendship groups that suffer a loss or trauma report it brought them closer together. The same is true for teams that have won championships.

In 2013, Belarus gymnasts win the Gymnastics World Championships. In 2011, Team USA celebrates a win at the Football World Championships.

What about those situations in which group members are experiencing a diverse array of emotions? Some people are happy, others are upset. What is a group to do? Emotional contagion may provide some insight about how groups experience emotions and moods. Emotional contagion refers to the idea that emotions experienced by one person can be passed on to others. People often talk about someone who is very cheerful and how their love for life was contagious. However, it is also clear that negative affect is likely more contagious than positive affect (Spoor & Kelly, 2004). Further, when group members are not in sync with their emotional states, this may lead to important communication about how the group operates and status within the group.

Tiedens et al. (2000) found that people expect high status and competent individuals to experience pride when the group is successful and anger when the group experiences poor outcomes. Low status individuals are expected to experience gratitude when the group is successful and sadness in response to failed group efforts. For example, a group that wins a game may have a team captain proud that her team won and team members grateful for the opportunity to have had a successful game. This emotional mix may serve to communicate status, but also to bond group members to one another. Group moods may help coordinate their efforts in goal directed ways. If there is a negative affective state it may help a group come

Groups who share similar affective states may find their experience in the group intensifies these feelings.

together against a common enemy or for a common cause. Consider a group where one member is fighting cancer, the group may be sad and angry that this is happening, but that emotional response may lead them to raise awareness through community organizing. By the same note a team that seems to have turned the corner in a close game, but finds the positive affect associated with success helps them to stay in the "zone" and win.

Group Composition

We have explored how tasks and contextual factors shape performance. In this section, the people who compose the group will be the focus. Groups are not assembled from people with homogenous skill sets. Rather, groups are often formed with the express intent of having diverse individuals bring their unique skills, experiences, and perspectives to the task at hand.

GROUP SIZE

Much of the research exploring group dynamics has focused on relatively small groups, work groups, sports teams, and so on. However, there are clearly larger groups that also have particular dynamics, such as unions, student organizations, companies, and community groups that operate much like small groups. However, there are some clear distinctions.

Group members are more likely to contribute equally in small groups as composed to large groups. For example, in a group of five or even a dozen, everyone might have an opportunity to weigh in on an important decision. A larger group like a worker's union may hold a vote, but it is not likely that 100% of the members would cast a ballot.

Isaac, Walker, and Williams (1994) explored the role of group size in a public goods dilemma. Public goods dilemmas (as discussed in Chapter 7) typically involved relatively small groups (~10 person

		Everyone Else	
		Group Acct	Personal Acct
My Decision	Group Acct	If everyone contributes everything to the group, everyone will receive the Maximum possible group earnings. ($1.50)	If I contribute to the group, and everyone else contributes to their personal account then I will receive minimum possible earnings. ($0.15)
	Personal Acct	If I put all of my tokens in my personal account and everyone else contributes to the group account, then I will have the Maximum possible earnings. ($1.85)	If everyone keeps their tokens and no one contributes to the group account, then I will receive the minimum possible group earnings. ($0.50)

FIGURE 8.2

groups). In their study each member is provided a number of tokens that are to be divided between their own account and a group account. Free-riding refers to some members of a group keeping their own tokens, contributing nothing to the group, and letting others support the group effort while building their own resources. This effect emerges even in small groups, so do you think the effect would be larger or smaller in larger groups (~100)? In this clever experiment, participants logged into a system in which they would be offered the opportunity to contribute or keep their tokens. Participants were provided with the following information about how their allocations shaped their outcomes:

At the end of all 10 rounds, the tokens were converted to extra credit points for the course. Groups with 40 or 100 participants allocated more tokens to the group account than did members of small groups. Larger groups were more efficient in providing for the public good (group account) than were smaller groups (Isaac et al., 1994).

Group decision making also changes as group size increases. A small group may provide sufficient time for all group members to contribute their thoughts. However, a larger group may only have time for a few key group members to contribute to the group discussion and some people may be less likely to contribute than others. Gallupe and colleagues (1992) conducted a study examining the impact of group size on electronic-mediated brainstorming tasks. In this case group sizes ranged from 2 to 12 people. The groups then participated in electronic or face-to-face brainstorming to generate ideas. Gallupe and colleagues (1992) thought that electronic mediated brainstorming might eliminate the sort of production blocking or process loss that we see in face-to-face groups. Indeed groups in electronic mediated brainstorming sessions outperformed face-to-face groups. In addition, larger groups produced more ideas than smaller groups and this was especially true in the electronic mediated groups (see Figure 8.3).

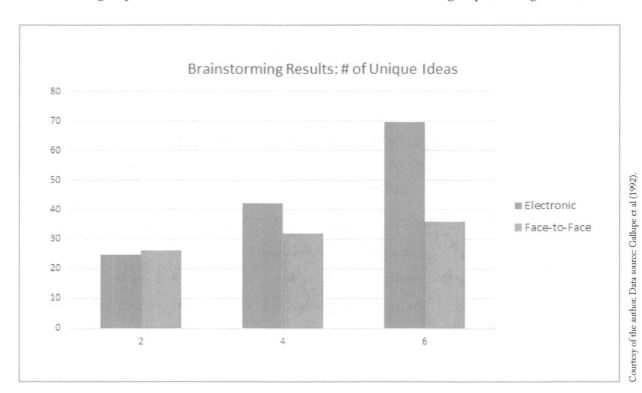

FIGURE 8.3. *Larger groups were more productive than smaller groups and even more so when communication occurred electronically.*

Courtesy of the author. Data source: Gallupe et al (1992).

Image © Cartoonresource, 2014. Used under license from Shutterstock, Inc.

"Diversity is good. Pass it down."

DIVERSE EXPERTISE

Group members may share some commonalities, but are also likely to be selected for group membership based on their particular expertise areas. There are two types of diversity to consider. First, we will consider surface level diversity. These are surface level characteristics that tend to be visible and about which people may have stereotypes. Surface level diversity includes demographic information such as age, gender, race, and other visible social identities. The second type of diversity is referred to as deep diversity. Deep diversity refers to the expertise or other psychological qualities a person brings to a group.

Harrison, Price, Gavin, and Florey (2002) examined how surface level and deep level diversity impacted group dynamics and team outcomes. The results demonstrate that team diversity both surface level and deep level diversity were related to lower team social integration. Social integration (cohesion) or the extent to which a group felt they were an integrated group was positively related to performance. Thus, the challenge for diverse groups is building a cohesive group that integrates the range of diverse members to optimize performance.

Diversity within a group can also create fault lines within a group (Lau & Murnighan, 1998). A group that is diverse across only one or two dimensions may create factions within the group. Fault lines may develop when a group that is composed of relatively similar individuals and balanced across sex with equal number of males and females, may find that the men in the group and the women in the group form two "sub-groups." However, a group that is diverse in such a way that identities do not lead to clear demographic based factions may have conflict but it may avoid some of the political ramifications produced by fault lines. Conflict that arises as a result of diverse perspectives can also lead to improved creativity. It is important when fault lines emerge that groups stay engaged in the central task and are reminded of the shared group memberships.

SHARED VS. UNSHARED INFORMATION. For most groups, the goal of optimizing performance would benefit from being able to accurately identify the expert in the group to perform an intellective task (one where there is a correct answer). Henry (1995) suggests that groups may take two approaches to identifying the expert. One strategy is to encourage groups to determine which member is most accurate.

How do groups share information about their points of view? From work teams to national gatherings, groups are sharing information.

The second strategy is to explicitly encourage group members to share information relevant to the decision. While both strategies improve performance, groups were not very good at identifying the best member or expert in their group. It is important for groups to get feedback about which of their team members is in fact an expert. Over time, groups may well learn who the go-to person might be.

Stasser and Titus (2003) conducted a series of studies using a hidden profile method. In this method each group member is given several pieces of information about a decision that the group will make. Some of the information they are given is provided to all members. Other facts are provided only to the one member. Still other information is provided to more than one but not all of the members. Findings from studies using this paradigm indicate that group members spend more time discussing shared information and begin discussion by expressing information that everyone knows. Unshared information or the unique to individual information is less likely to be mentioned at all and if it is only at the end of the discussion.

Does this sort of shared vs. unshared information matter? Consider a study by Larson, Christensen, Abbot, and Franz (1996). They had teams which included a resident physician, intern, and a third-year medical student watch videos of a patient's intake interview in the emergency room. Each member of the team watched the video alone. Approximately half of the symptoms were shown to all three members, and the remaining were shown to only one member of the team. The team then met to generate a diagnosis. Symptoms everyone had viewed dominated initial discussion and 70% of the symptoms mentioned were symptoms everyone knew about. It was not until later in the conversation that the unique symptoms were brought up in equal proportion to shared symptoms. It would seem that this type of discussion could have real consequences and the key to an accurate diagnosis may well be in the unshared information!

TRANSACTIVE MEMORY SYSTEMS. Transactive memory systems are systems of information processing and storage that function across multiple people. Imagine a simple case, in which your heterosexual grandparents who endorse traditional gender roles divide up routine tasks and events. Perhaps your grandfather is in charge of having the oil changed in the car and your grandmother sends out the birthday cards to all of the grandkids. It is likely that your grandfather may not remember the birthdates for everyone, but he certainly knows that all of the grandchildren have a birthday. He relies on your grandmother to take care of that cognitive labor. Likewise your grand-

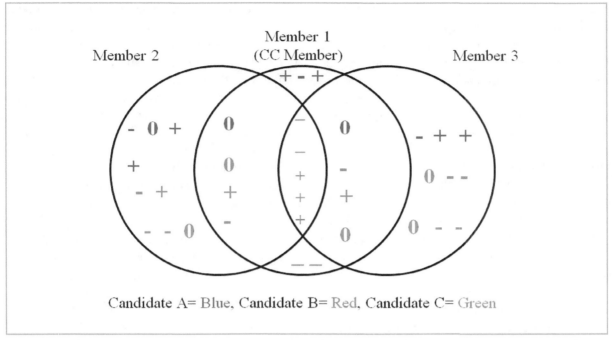

Candidate A= Blue, Candidate B= Red, Candidate C= Green

FIGURE 8.4 *Plus signs indicate positive information, negative signs indicate negative information, and 0 indicates neutral information. Each member receives the same number of facts about each of the three candidates (A, B, and C). What decision is the best decision? What decision will the group make?*

mother certainly knows that the oil needs to be changed in the car, but doesn't necessarily track when it might be time for another oil change as she leaves this cognitive labor to your grandfather. This division of cognitive labor allows both members of this transactive memory system to carry out necessary tasks and efficiently make use of the other's expertise. If your grandmother finds a coupon in the newspaper for an oil change, she might tell your grandfather to look for it as she still attends to the need, but relies on your grandfather to take the lead on tasks in his domain.

Wegner, Erber, and Raymond (1991) studied transactive memory systems in romantic couples to determine how these systems operate. They invited couples to the lab and either had them complete a task together or separated the couple and had them complete the task with a member of another couple. Participants were asked to recall underlined words appearing on a series of cards. For half of the pairs they were assigned areas of expertise and for the oth-

er half there were no specific instructions regarding expertise. The results showed that natural couples recalled more items when they were allowed to use their existing transactive memory system (no expertise was assigned). Indeed, couples provided expertise assignments had the lowest recall scores in the study. Strangers working on the task recalled more words when they were assigned particular expertise domains.

How does this function in groups? Initially, in groups people may rely on surface characteristics to determine who might know what bits of information. For example, a particularly athletic and tall male group member might be presumed to know more about basketball than a petite female group member. This may be inaccurate, but when groups are just beginning to work together these surface characteristics may be used to fill in the blanks. Consider a workplace in which teams are to court client accounts. It may be that when the team is first put together there are only surface characteristics available. So the males on the team may attend to the client's favorite scotch, golf handicap, and sports team preferences. The females might be expected to make note of the client's marital status, partner's name, and anniversary. All of this information may well be critical to persuading a client that your company cares about them, but the gender division of this information may reinforce gender stereotypes.

Hollingshead and Fraidin (2003) had dyads complete a transactive memory task in which they had to indicate whether they or their partner would remember words from a particular category. Their results demonstrate that participants expected their partners to remember information congruent with gender stereotypes and they themselves lived up to the expectations for stereotypes about their own gender. While the authors suggest that it is possible to overcome these initial presumptions, in the real world this may be unlikely as once we prove we are living up to the gender stereotype it can be difficult to get the opportunity to demonstrate we have other areas of expertise as well.

LEADERS

Leadership is often used as a hallmark of success and excellence. People are discussed as having excellent leadership skills, being a leader is imbued with positive connotation, and leadership seminars and trainings continue to provide substantial income for those delivering them. While leadership training and discussions about leadership focus on the individual, the leader only exists if in fact there is a group to lead. Some smaller or short-term groups do not in fact have a leader and members are able to organize around collaborative consensus or through division of leadership areas among all members (Pearce & Conger, 2003). However, large groups often find it difficult to remain a group without some leadership.

In some cases, leaders are imbued with a great deal of power of the outcomes of the groups, while in other cases leaders adopt a style in which power is shared. The concept of transformative leadership continues to resonate with people who be-lieve that there are great leaders who have great impact. However, it may not be a specific leader who changes the trajectory of a company or sports team, but rather having a "new" leader or a change in the organization that in and of itself creates positive (or sometimes negative) change. The reality for most leaders is that they share power with others in the organization and while they may have some influence, it is not as great as we might imagine. It is unlikely that any leader shoulders all the blame for a group's failure nor should a leader receive all of the credit for a team's success (Meindl, Ehrlich, & Durkerich, 1985). In this section we will examine who becomes a leader, what makes for effective leadership, and how diverse leaders face particular challenges.

EMERGENT LEADERSHIP. Emerging leaders are those members of a group who become leaders. These types of leaders can emerge without any formal process or appointment and they may or may not be recognized officially as the leader. Friendship groups do not typically elect a leader, but most members of the group come to know who the leaders of the group are. Emergent leaders are not chosen by membership nor are they appointed by someone outside the group. Rather, they emerge organically from within the group. Group members may or may not have clear awareness of why they are choosing to provide a particular person with the responsibility and opportunity to lead the group. Great person theory posited by Carlyle in 1841 suggested that there must be characteristics that would predispose someone to leadership. He proposed by studying great leaders that these traits could be sorted out. While the idea of merit-based leader selection may be attractive, demographic expectations about "who leads" tend to shape leadership selection. Even when leaders are emergent rather than elected, there are a variety of factors that increase the chances that someone will be chosen as the leader of the group. Leaders tend to be older, taller, and heavier (Stogdill, 1948, 1974). People who are in the numerical minority with regard to shared race or ethnicity are less likely to emerge as leaders (Bass, 2008;

Different types of tasks and groups require different kinds of leadership.

Landau, 1995; Roll, McClelland, & Abel, 1996). Talkative people are also more likely to emerge as leaders (Mullen, Salas, & Driskell, 1989). In this case, participation or frequent communication increases the chances that someone will be selected as the leader of a group. However, the content of what these talkative individuals say is less important than the sheer amount of talking that they do (Van Vugt & Ahuja, 2011).

There are in fact two primary areas of leadership: relationship (or socio-emotional) leadership and task leadership (Yukl, 2013). Socio-emotional leadership which refers to a leader who provides a support for the group members, makes sure that everyone feels included, and helps to resolve intragroup conflict. The other type of leadership is task-focused leadership. This is a person who keeps the group on task, delegates tasks to others, or otherwise ensures that the tasks set before the group are accomplished. In some cases, a different person fills each role. In other cases, one person may fulfill both leadership roles. While both types of leadership qualities are desirable, members tend to put more emphasis on the need for a task leader (Nye & Forsyth, 1991). Given stereotypes about women and men, this leads men to be more frequently perceived as fitting the prototypical expectations of leadership roles.

Implicit leadership theories are in fact the idea that we have ideas about the qualities we expect leaders to possess (Lord & Maher, 2002). Our implicit theories shape how we see leaders. If we believe that leaders are to be dominant, we pay particular attention to cues of dominance and dismiss signs that disconfirm our beliefs about how leaders ought to behave. If our implicit leadership theories are biased to favor tall, masculine, white, heavier, talkative, men then it is likely this sort of person may be selected to fulfill this role even if he is not otherwise qualified (Forsyth, 2006).

CONTINGENCY MODEL OF LEADERSHIP. The contingency model of leadership proposed by Fiedler (1978) suggests that different types of groups need different types of leaders. Again, the distinction between relationship vs. task–motivated leaders becomes important for understanding a group's leadership needs. How do you know if you are a relationship-motivated or task-motivated leader? Fiedler used the *Least Preferred Co-worker Scale*.

The first part of the measure asks you to identify the person with whom you have the most difficulty within the group. Then you rate this person on a variety of traits (e.g., pleasant-unpleasant, friendly-unfriendly). Relationship-motivated people are more likely to give this least preferred person more positive ratings, while task-motivated people gave this least preferred person more negative ratings. Which type of leader are you?

It is not the case that one type of leader is better in all cases, but rather the type of leader needed is contingent upon the group's current situation. In situations that are either quite positive or quite negative, task-oriented leaders may serve the group quite well. On the other hand, when the group is experiencing situations in which things are neither extremely good nor extremely bad then relationship-oriented leaders can help a group stay the course.

Bass (2008) forwarded the idea of transformational leadership whereby a charismatic and inspiring form of leadership improves motivation, confidence, and satisfaction and unites a group around a common goal. Leaders who are transformative do not simply reward positive behavior and punish failures, but rather through their own confidence in a course of action and value-based decision making, inspire members. They are able to articulate their vision of the future, are optimistic, and imbue the tasks ahead with meaning. They

Image © Corepics VOF, 2014. Used under license from Shutterstock, Inc.

Formal training may also mean that leaders are already in place, while impromptu group efforts may have a rough start to figuring out who will take the lead.

are willing to question assumptions and traditions and see each group member as an individual with unique needs and abilities. These four components of transformational leadership (idealized influence, inspirational motivation, intellectual stimulation, and individualized consideration) allow leaders to lead across a variety of situations and group types.

GLASS CLIFFS: LEADERS AND GENDER. Can anyone be a leader? Is leadership simply a set of skills or abilities that a person can master and then take on leadership roles? Unfortunately the answer is not simple. While gender roles continue to evolve, the implicit theories of leadership remain a challenge for women seeking leadership positions. Groups asked to choose a leader more frequently opt for a man than a woman (Eagly & Karau, 2002). Even when performance measures are held constant, female leaders are rated as less effective and receive fewer promotions than men (Heilman, Block, & Martell, 1995; Heilman, Wallen, Fuchs, & Tamkins, 2004).

Butler and Geis (1990) trained eight confederates (4 male, 4 female) to act out particular roles. Each confederate memorized the same arguments and discussion points. Groups of four were comprised of two confederates from the original trained group of eight (1 male and 1 female) and two participants (1 male and 1 female). The group was tasked with completing a group task in which they must decide which items were most important for survival after a crash-landing on the moon. There were two leadership scripts that the confederates would enact. In eight out of nine discussion points the two confederates would congenially disagree with one another. Half of these disagreements were resolved with one confederate successfully making a point and half in which the other confederate's suggestion won out. In conditions where one confederate was to be the leader, she or he would provide rationales for all eight of the conflicted items, even when they had originally been proposed by the other confederate. All sessions were recorded and videos were coded

by independent coders for nonverbal cues such as furrowed brow, tightening of the mouth, nods of agreement (or disagreement), smiling, and frowning expressions. The results indicate that when the male confederate took on a leadership position he was rated as showing more leadership than the female confederate who took on a leadership position. Female leaders were more likely to be challenged by the participants in the group. Members also displayed more displeased nonverbal behaviors when there was a female leader.

You may already be familiar with the concept of the glass ceiling. The **glass ceiling** is a term used to describe the invisible barrier that prevents women and ethnic minority employees from rising to the highest level of leadership within organizations (Kanter, 1977). Alternatively, the **glass escalator** refers to the invisible organizational structure, whereby men in traditionally female dominated professions are promoted more quickly and over the heads of women with more experience and better skills (Williams, 1992).

In recent times, it is clear that women are not completely excluded from leadership positions, but this does not mean women and men have equivalent experiences in the highest ranks. More recently archival analysis has uncovered yet a third hurdle for women seeking leadership positions in the workplace: the **glass cliff**. Haslam and Ryan (2008) found that women are more likely than men to be appointed to leadership positions when companies face precarious economic situations or other challenges that increase the probability of failure and criticism.

The most compelling data comes from Ryan and Haslam's (2005) archival analysis examining the FTSE 100 organizations financial situation before and after women were appointed to high profile positions within some of these organizations. First, they examined the fluctuation in stock performance in the 12 months preceding data collection and the average monthly shared price divided by the number of shares traded. They calculated

Shirley Chisolm, Hillary Clinton, and President Barak Obama present exceptions to this finding. Perhaps one reason we talk about their demographics so frequently is because women and people of color are so rarely in leadership positions. When they are, it becomes the focus of the headlines!

the average monthly share price for the six months before and after appointment of a board member. The results indicate that for companies appointing men to their boards the performance indicators were relatively stable. In contrast, companies where women were appointed were more likely to have had significant fluctuation in performance indicators prior to her appointment. Perhaps more interestingly, contrary to a headline in 2003 indicating women in top positions were destroying company bottom lines, this analysis demonstrated that if stocks were down when a woman stepped in there was actually an increase in share price after her appointment, and if she was appointed when stocks were up, that the share price stabilized. However, as with all real-world and archival studies, causation cannot be made so clear.

Haslam and Ryan (2008) presented participants with scenarios in which companies were experiencing troubled times, stable outcomes, or success. They were also given two profiles of potential leaders that were equated on all dimensions with one leader identified as male and the other female. Participants included business leaders and students who had graduated from management programs. When a company was poised for success there was a slight advantage (though not quite significant) given to the male candidate. However, the results were clear when the organization's performance was poor, participants were more likely to select the female candidate over an equally qualified male candidate to take these risky leadership positions. Participant selections indicate that they believed that these positions suit the distinctive leadership abilities of women, providing women with good leadership opportunities.

It seems that there is an implicit leadership theory that indicates women may be particularly skilled at crisis management. Given the relative few number of leadership opportunities made available to women, it may be that when a woman is offered a precarious leadership position she feels more pressure to accept as declining the position may be read by the larger public and the company that she is not interested in leading. However, a man who declines the offer may not have his ambition questioned and he may be perceived as waiting for a better offer.

Image © Cartoonresource, 2014. Used under license from Shutterstock, Inc.

"Helen, you're the Team Leader, why don't you jump first?"

Should women "lean in" to these challenges or opt out? Sheryl Sandberg, COO of Facebook, draws on her own leadership experiences and encourages women to "lean in" at the workplace. The controversy aroused by her book *Lean In: Women, Work, and the Will to Lead,* has caused women around the world to rethink how they navigate the workplace and leadership opportunities. Some women believe she is on the right track, while others believe that other solutions to workplace challenges would be more appropriate. What is clear from the current discussion about this book is that the conversation about women in the workplace needs to evolve away from maintaining the status quo to a call for changing how we think about the workplace and the role of men and women in today's society.

Interacting Groups

The previous sections have laid the foundation for understanding the core of group dynamics. We have an idea about the role of particular tasks, group development, group composition, and leadership styles. This section is going to focus on the group itself. How do groups interact? What does group life look like? Why do people stay in groups? What are some of the problems groups encounter?

ENTITATIVITY

Entitativity refers to how groups perceive themselves as a group. Essentially, how much of an entity is the group? What makes a group a group rather than a collection of individuals? Do others perceive the group as an entity? Does the group see itself as an entity? Campbell (1958) first forwarded the idea of group entitativity as the extent to which a collection of individuals are seen as bonded together in a coherent unit.

Lickel and colleagues (2000) took this a step further by asking participants to rate entitativity of groups that varied on a number of dimensions. Participants consistently rated sports teams, families, gangs, the cast of a play, and so on as having more entitativity than social identity groups (e.g., women, U.S. citizens) or occupational groups (e.g., doctors, teachers). The lowest ratings were given to people waiting at a bus stop or in a line at the bank. Further, ratings of entitativity were related to the extent to which group members interacted with one another, the importance of the group, shared goals and outcomes, and similarity within the group. Size, duration of the group, and permeability also played a role, though were more weakly related to entitativity. Larger groups were seen as less entitative. Permeable groups, those with boundaries that are more open and who would be more accessible to new members, were rated as lower in entitativity. Cluster analysis revealed four major types of groups ranging from high levels of entitativity to low levels: intimacy groups, task groups, social categories, and loose associations.

Does it really matter whether groups are high or low in perceived entitativity? Lickel and colleagues (2000) would say yes. When people are asked about groups to which they personally belong, those that are important to them are most likely to fit intimacy groups (family groups, friendship groups) and those that are relatively less important include social identities (nationality, gender, physical attributes) or loose associations (waiting groups). We perceive groups that are entitative as important and perceive groups as more entitative when they are important to us. How do you imagine different group structures, values, and functions playing out with groups with high vs. low levels of entitativity? Are family groups more relationship-oriented and task groups more task-oriented? Does this have implications for leadership styles for different levels of entitativity?

COHESIVENESS. Cohesiveness in the general case can be thought of as the degree to which group members feel attached to the group. Team building exercises are typically focused on building cohesive groups with the expectation that cohesiveness will increase coordination of efforts and loyalty to the group and tasks at hand. In addition, cohesiveness may also reduce process loss. At first pass this all seems perfectly reasonable, but Zacarro and Lowe (1988) present a slightly clearer if more complex understanding of cohesiveness. They propose there are two types of cohesiveness

What makes these groups seem like groups to you?

that should be taken into account: interpersonal cohesiveness and task cohesiveness.

INTERPERSONAL COHESIVENESS.

Interpersonal cohesiveness refers to cohesiveness or attachment to the group which stems from positive interpersonal relationships that exist between members of the group (Festinger, Schacter, & Back, 1970). This type of cohesiveness can be built through team building that encourages group members to get to know one another and interact on a personal level. Friendship groups are likely to be primarily interpersonally cohesive, while work groups may not get along as well with one another. A group has high interpersonal cohesiveness when group members would choose to do something with other members of the group, even if the task to be done was not appealing. You might also conceptualize interpersonal cohesiveness as commitment to the group.

How does interpersonal cohesiveness fit with other aspects of group performance? Would this help performance on some types of group tasks? Where might it be counterproductive?

TASK COHESIVENESS.

Task cohesiveness is attachment or commitment to the group task or when the tasks carried out by the group have personal relevance to members. This might be the case when you participate in a group activity to volunteer for a charity that you deeply care about, even though you might be neutral or even not care for the other volunteers in your group. This type of task cohesiveness is often heightened when groups believe the task itself is important or provides some extrinsic reward. For example, a group of firefighters working to extinguish a fire with multiple fire houses responding, might all stay committed to the task to get the blaze under control. However, they might have more difficulty working together when the task is less critical (e.g., raising money for a charity).

How does task cohesiveness impact performance? When would this type of cohesiveness help or harm group tasks?

ADDITIVE TASKS.

Zacarro and Lowe (1988) set out to demonstrate which type of cohesiveness would be beneficial on additive tasks. Remember this is a task where the group performance is quite simply the sum of inputs from each group member. In their study they put participants into groups and told them they would be working together. Those in the high interpersonal cohesiveness conditions were encouraged to write their name, major, class year, home state, and hobbies on a card that they would then wear as a name

Would these tasks go better if the group members liked one another? Why or why not?

tag during the experiment. They then introduced themselves to one other person in the group and then when the group convened each person introduced someone else to the group as a whole. This allowed group members to get to know one another and increased interpersonal cohesiveness. Groups in the low interpersonal cohesiveness conditions were told to work alone and create a list of good and bad points about their university. They were not given an opportunity to get to know one another and levels of interpersonal cohesiveness were low.

Task cohesiveness was manipulated by providing students with a cover story. The story emphasized that being able to work in a team was critical to economic success and participation in the American workforce (high task cohesiveness). Participants were then told they would receive a bonus experimental credit if their group did well (high task cohesiveness). Those in the low task cohesiveness did not read the cover story nor were they told about an opportunity for bonus credit.

Groups were then given the task of making origami moon hats and were given instructions and materials to do so. The goal was to make as many quality moon hats as possible during the experimental period. The results were quite clear groups in high task cohesive groups produced more moon hats than those in the low task cohesiveness conditions. However, the group producing the least hats were those who were high in interpersonal cohesiveness and low in task cohesiveness. Here high interpersonal cohesiveness actually harmed performance on an additive task. Why do you think this was the case?

DISJUNCTIVE TASKS. The role of interpersonal and task cohesiveness also changes when we consider other task types. Zacarro and McCoy (1988) again manipulated cohesiveness as described above, but then had groups complete a disjunctive task. The disjunctive task in this case involved a subarctic survival scenario in which groups are asked to rank a number of items in terms of importance for survival in the subarctic climate. Performance was judged based on how close to the expert rankings the group's final ranking were. For this task type, groups with high task and high interpersonal cohesiveness outperformed all other groups. Groups who were high in one or the other types of cohesiveness also did better than groups who were neither task cohesive nor interpersonally cohesive.

CREATIVITY TASKS. Craig and Kelly (1999) manipulated both task and interpersonal cohesiveness in three-person groups using procedures similar to the manipulations used by Zacarro and McCoy (1988). This study involved a creativity task in which three overhead projectors were focused on the same screen (see Figure 8.5). This skewed the projection for the two group members on each side and forced the person in the middle to either draw upside down or avoid blocking the projection from the projector. The groups were asked to draw either a mansion or a bridge. The rules were that only one person could work on each project for the duration of the drawing and that the colored marker available on a particular projector (green, red, blue) could only be used on that projector. This task then required not only creativity but also coordination of effort. The results indicate that both interpersonal and task co-

Illustration by Elizabeth King

FIGURE 8.5

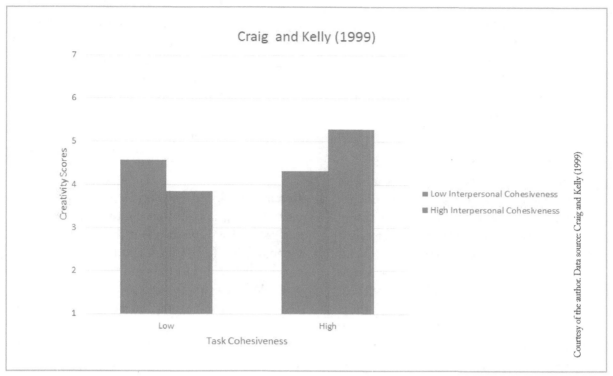

FIGURE 8.6

hesiveness were necessary for a group to produce a creative drawing (see Figure 8.6).

DECISION-MAKING GROUPS

Perhaps the most common type of task that groups are asked to do involves decision making. We have already discussed how groups might share information during group discussion and how that might introduce particular types of bias. There are two other common occurrences in group decision making that have important impacts for group decisions. The first is group polarization and the second is groupthink.

GROUP POLARIZATION. Group polarization was originally referred to as "risky shift." The early findings of Stoner (1961) indicated that when groups were asked to make a decision about how much risk should be undertaken, the group's final decision represented far more risk than their ini-

tial individual ratings of how much risk would be acceptable. This work used the Choice Dilemmas Questionnaire in which a scenario is presented and participants are first asked to respond individually and then after group discussion the group is to come to a consensus. The classic result is that groups were willing to encourage people like Chris in the sample question to take the risk, even when the probability of success was relatively low.

Later work demonstrated that in fact the shift was not *always* more risky. In fact, if the group began by discussing more conservative options then the group would often exhibit a conservative shift. It was after these findings came to light that the phenomena was renamed group polarization. Group polarization indicates that whatever a group discusses first or the direction the majority of group members lean will likely become exacerbated over the course of the discussion and the group decision will be more extreme or polarized than the initial ratings.

SAMPLE QUESTION FROM KOGAN 1961

Below is a modernized adaptation of a typical choice dilemma item from Wallach and Kogan's (1959, 1961) original measure:

Chris works in software development. Chris is married and has one child. After graduating from college five years ago, Chris has been working for a large electronics corporation. The job is with a large firm and there is considerable job stability, though the pay is modest it is adequate and the retirement package is quite good. On the other hand, it is very unlikely that there will be a promotion or raise in the future. While attending a conference, a small start-up extended a job offer. The company is small and newly founded with a highly uncertain future. The new job would pay more to start and would offer the possibility of a share in the ownership if the company is successful. Imagine that you are advising Chris on how to proceed. Please check the lowest probability that you would consider acceptable to make it worthwhile for him to take the new job.

__ The chances are 1 in 10 that the company will be a success.

__ The chances are 2 in 10 that the company will be a success.

__ The chances are 3 in 10 that the company will be a success.

__ The chances are 4 in 10 that the company will be a success.

__ The chances are 5 in 10 that the company will be a success.

__ The chances are 6 in 10 that the company will be a success.

__ The chances are 7 in 10 that the company will be a success.

__ The chances are 8 in 10 that the company will be a success.

__ The chances are 9 in 10 that the company will be a success.

__ Check here if you think Chris should not take the job regardless of the probabilities.

Recently, Yardi and Boyd (2010) examined the impact of group polarization on Twitter. The study analyzed 30,000 tweets about the shooting of Dr. George Tiller (a late-term abortion doctor). The tweets included pro-life and pro-choice advocates. When a tweet was followed by a subsequent like-minded tweet group, identity was strengthened, though people were generally less likely to reply to someone who shared their perspective. When someone with a different perspective added their 140 words the divide between the groups became the focus of the exchange. By examining tweets and direct responses they were able to determine what type of response was more common. The majority of responses were coded as pro-life or pro-choice, with fewer coded as strong pro-life or strong pro-choice advocates. Overall, it showed that within the first 24 hours the Twitter feed involved 20% to 40% of like-minded replies. However, there were a similar number of replies to those with different perspectives. It appears that some topics, for which people have strong attitudes prior to discussion, there is not likely to be much group polarization or consensus. Another possibility is that the nature of Twitter and perhaps other digitally mediated communication prevents group interactions that lead to group polarization.

Group polarization can happen when groups are thinking deeply about the decision. In these cases, where the group is devoting significant cognitive effort and engaged in systematic processing, listening to other's reasons for their decision may provide good solid arguments for one side over the other. In this way, there may be far more good strong ar-

What will constitute success for the various groups in these photos?

guments for the side that the majority of participants present at the beginning of group conversation. However, group polarization can also occur heuristically or when groups may not care too much about a decision. In groups where the decision does not weigh heavily on the group, they may simply be doing a poll as persons each present their choice and group members may go along with the majority. In both cases, the resulting group decision is likely to be more extreme than the average of the individual's initial decisions.

Groupthink. In 1972, Janis coined the term *groupthink* to refer to the ways in which a charismatic leader of followers who are similar to one another simply agree to decision without considering alternatives or disagreeing. This sort of behavior may be helpful if a leader does not want the group to think for themselves, but often the resulting decisions are not optimal.

Groups that fall prey to groupthink tend to see themselves as invincible and incapable of failure. They ignore warnings of danger and are prone to make risky decisions. When a group encounters information counter to the group's decision it is often dismissed as irrelevant or unreliable. Groups may ignore ethical considerations and in fact believe that because so many of them seem to agree it is improbable that this many people could be wrong. Groups begin to hold stereotypes about those who are in the out-group and often a member of the group begins to guard the group from other ideas. There is often pressure

to conform and members often do not present their dissenting opinions or offer counterarguments. This leads to false consensus in which everyone believes that everyone else must agree since no one seems to be disagreeing, even while each person is holding back their own concerns.

There are some solutions that can remedy some of the trouble with groupthink. First, appoint a devil's advocate so that the group at least hears what other possibilities or flaws might exist beyond the current solution. Second, allow for authentic dissent by having a leader who encourages and supports a person who disagrees with the party line. Because much of our group life now occurs online, what digital discourse are we engaged in and how does groupthink and its solutions fit with today's world?

Pariser's (2011) book, *The Filter Bubble: How the new personalized web is changing what we read and how we think*, provides some insights into how and when we may actually encounter people who express opinions that diverge from our own. Consider Facebook's lack of a thumbs down button. If you are going to do something with a Facebook post, your options are to share, like, or comment. The more you click "like" the more posts from that person you will see. Similarly, Google search results use your IP address and search history to provide you with a tailored list of results. This sort of exposure to people like us and things that are congruent with what we like and what holds our interest, feels really great. We enjoy seeing our opinions validated

"Today's theme is 'Getting Beyond Group Think'."

Image © Cartoonresource, 2014. Used under license from Shutterstock, Inc.

and people who share our values show up in our newsfeed. However, this also means that we are not being exposed to very many diverse thoughts or opinions. When we do encounter some divisive issue, it rarely is rationale conversation or dialogue, but rather a series of comments (often anonymous) that resort to name calling, stereotyping, and all of the other symptoms of groupthink. Google and Facebook are de facto playing the role of the member who guards us from competing ideas.

How do we get past the filter bubble? Some solutions might be to maintain diverse friends on your Facebook page rather than deleting them the first time they post something disagreeable to you. Occasionally actively seek information on Google that is counter to your own opinion or thought about an issue. The internet provides an unprecedented opportunity to access an unfathomably diverse number of people and ideas and at the same time works to show us only what we might be most interested in seeing.

Summary

As social beings, groups are a large part of our lives. Families, sports teams, work groups, and student organizations are just some of the examples of groups that we encounter daily. However, we also rely on groups to make important decisions (e.g., juries) and to innovate for our future. Understanding the ways in which groups develop, encounter tasks, and work together can help us find ways to leverage groups to do work that would be made more difficult if we were to do it alone. Groups also present us with unique challenges as we strive to be (or at least elect) leaders who will help us move forward and accomplish goals without undermining our entitativity. Groups are in fact dynamic with many moving parts and multiple considerations. Deep understanding of how groups engage with one another and the tasks that lay before them can help us to appreciate the challenges and possibilities of working and living together.

NAME _____ DATE _____

Chapter Questions

1. Think about each of the following tasks and where they might fit on the task circumplex:

   • Deciding which items to take after a crashed moon landing

   • Adding up all of the numbers 1 through 100 (inclusive of 1 and 100)

   • Solving a word problem

   • Electing a team captain

2. What are some strategies you might employ to avoid the glass ceiling? What can you do as an employer or CEO? What can you do as an employee or colleague?

3. For each of the eight task types on the task circumplex, come up with a group project and way to score that project so that grades reflect each performance type.

4. Give an example of a group you belong to where there is high interpersonal cohesiveness. How did interpersonal cohesiveness develop within the group?

5. Provide an example of a group you belong to where there is high task cohesiveness. How did your group develop task cohesiveness?

6. What group memberships are most important to you?

7. How do you feel when you are wearing insignia for your school and your school wins? What about when your school is viewed negatively?

8. Have you ever left a group? What were some of the consequences for you? What were the consequences for the group?

Interpersonal Relationships

Forming and maintaining close relationships is an important part of human life. Our first relationships are often formed in infancy with a primary caregiver. From this point forward we often seek to engage in and seek close relationships with others. Familial relationships with siblings, cousins, and others develop alongside friendships with peers. During this period of time we begin to develop the skills necessary to develop and maintain close relationships with others. As we approach adolescence and throughout adulthood there is often a focus on establishing close dyadic relationships of

Image © Andrea Danti, 2014. Used under license from Shutterstock, Inc.

a romantic nature. The experience of love and intimacy is a core part of what it means to be human.

Inclusion and Ostracism

It is likely that we have an idealized concept about our social relationships in which our friends and loved ones are accepting and kind and that we can easily form and maintain these relationships. However, we also often experience quite the opposite when we are excluded from friendship groups or rejected by a romantic partner. Some of the material in this chapter will focus on friendships, far more content is devoted to romantic relationships. Far more research is conducted examining romantic relationships in adults and friendships in children. This should not indicate that friendships do not form an important part of adult life, only that the research examining these relationships is sparse.

NEED TO BELONG

Survival and reproduction of many species (including humans) requires people to engage in relationships with others, whether this is for the sole purpose of reproduction or more likely an opportunity to share resources and be cared for if one were to become unwell. Shelter, food, and other survival necessities are provided by others or by cooperation with others. Even when we are not aware of the need for others in these evolutionary terms, we often experience a strong desire to be liked and accepted by others. The need to belong is the desire to develop and maintain close and long-term relationships with other people (Ainsworth, 1989).

> "In two decades of studying loneliness, I have met many people who say they have no friends. I have never met anyone who didn't want to have friends."
>
> *–Warren Jones (1989)*

Loneliness is not just about being alone or in solitude. It is indeed quite a different thing to be lonely. People report they feel alone in a crowd or being surrounded by others and yet have a deep sense of not belonging. Loneliness is an emotional experience that drives us to seek connection and motivates us to form relationships with others (Parkhurst & Hopmeyer, 1999). Between the ages of 7 and 10 years, children begin to understand that being alone is not the same as being lonely, but they still struggle to identify any benefits to solitude (Galanaki, 2004). On the other hand, children were quick to point out that being socially isolated was often used a punishment. Indeed, the use of solitary confinement is one of the harsher penalties doled out to prisoner's for misconduct.

Solitude is, however, also thought to be necessary for human life. The Wilderness Act of 1964 (U.S. Public Law 88-577) indicates that the preservation and management of wilderness areas are designated to promote opportunities for solitude. We spend almost 30% of our waking time alone as adults (Larson, 1990). Solitude is often a desired state to be alone with one's thoughts or to have some time away from others. People may seek solitude to work through challenging decisions, create something new or novel, or to synthesize information without feeling influenced by what others would want them to do. Freedom is also a frequent theme associated with solitude (Long & Averill, 2003). This type of freedom includes freedom from constraints that others may place on our behavior or choices and freedom to pursue desirable activities. Solitude

Image © Ksenjavka, 2014. Used under license from Shutterstock, Inc.

Image © Jeff Thrower, 2014. Used under license from Shutterstock, Inc.

may also provide an opportunity for people to focus attention on the self. Sensory deprivation often leads to a focus on the self and the opportunity to take a break from overstimulation.

The quietest room (-9 db) in the world is referred to as an anechoic chamber and is housed at Orfield Laboratories in Minneapolis (Klimas, 2012). This room absorbs sound and many people cannot bear to be in the room for more than a few minutes, the record is 45 minutes. This sheer quiet is unnerving and the only source of sound is your internal bodily states, your breath, heartbeat, and digestion. Thus, while solitude at some level alleviates overstimulation, at extremes even the physical experience of solitude can be disquieting.

Even as we may desire solitude, few people desire loneliness or solitude over long periods of time. There is a need to be known by others to be situated in a social network of others. Others help us understand who we are. When we ask people who they are, some of the first answers will relate to who they are to others (e.g., sister/brother, parent, friend, group member). Beyond locating ourselves in relation to others, what is it that we desire in our friends, family, or intimate partners?

In Japanese, the word *kenzoku* translates most easily to "family." It implies a shared commitment and shared destiny (Lickerman, 2013). We might refer to people with whom we have this type of relationships as a best friend, this person may be a relative, or even a school friend. However, there is a distinction between *kenzoku* and what we might think of as regular friends or acquaintances. There are often shared interests and values, a history of experiences, and equality and mutuality of support within the friendship. Think about your various friendships and relationships. Which of those might be of this type? What about other relationships? What makes them different from this description?

Baiocco and colleagues (2014) provide robust evidence that having best friends are helpful to the psychological adjustment of young adults. In their survey of Italian young adults, they found that heterosexual individuals had primarily same-sex best friends, while lesbians and gay men were more likely to report both same-sex and cross-sex best friendships. However, heterosexual women were more likely to have men as best friends, while heterosexual men reported having fewer female best friends. In addition, gay men and lesbians were more likely to have heterosexual best friends than heterosexual participants were to have gay or lesbian best friends. For gay and lesbian adults having a heterosexual best friend reduced social anxiety and internalized homophobia. Having a heterosexual best friend may provide gay and lesbian young adults with a signifier of acceptance beyond the LGB community.

Galupo and Gonzalez (2013) found that adult men and women who had friends of different races put less importance on having friends with similar lives and experiences. However, all respondents valued friendships that include trust and honesty, respect for one another as people, and providing support when needed. Women rated these friendship values as more important than men. Lesbian and gay men also rated these friendship values as more important than heterosexual respondents. Clearly friends play an important role in our lives and help us feel as though we belong.

Even when we cannot have in-person interactions with our friends, we still find ways to connect and keep up with one another. Often we think of friends that we have not seen for years, but then once we see them again it is like time has not passed. This sort of "chemistry" between friends is in part what is referred to as *kenzoku* in Japanese. The modern world provides a number of opportunities to be with others in mind if not in body. Online chat rooms and discussion forums can provide one way for people to interact with others (McKenna & Bargh, 1999). Software and technology that allow us to make social connections continues to be widely popular providing another indicator of our need to belong.

BEING EXCLUDED

It is perhaps this motive to belong to groups, have meaningful social relationships, and maintain relationships over time that makes the pain of exclusion more painful. Whether we are bullied at school or work, subjected to indirect aggression through exclusion, or simply left out or forgotten the emotional responses to these experiences are often hurtful. Violence and bullying will be covered more directly in the chapter on aggression, but for this chapter we will cover the research on ostracism.

Kipling Williams received his PhD in social psychology from Ohio State University after completing his undergraduate work at the University of Washington. This line of research has a quite simple beginning. One day while sitting at a park with his dog, a Frisbee hit him in the back. Dr. Williams returned the Frisbee to the pair playing Frisbee. Unexpectedly, one of the players throws the Frisbee back to Dr. Williams and they played for three or four rounds of tosses. Then without explanation the two players return to passing the Frisbee back and forth between themselves, excluding Dr. Williams. In that moment he felt rather awkward and soundly excluded and returned to his dog. In the days that followed, he worked on developing a paradigm that would use a similar procedure to elicit feelings of exclusion in a lab setting.

Williams and Sommer (1997) had participants play an in-person ball toss game. Three people would play the game, two confederates and one participant sitting in chairs in a lab room waiting for an experiment. One of the confederates begins tossing the ball to the other and in some conditions the participant would be excluded completely, in other conditions the participant would also be given an opportunity to catch and toss the ball. Then in the last five minutes before the experi-

ment all of the participants were excluded from the game and ignored (no eye contact from the confederates). It was during these five minutes of exclusion that males begin to engage in face-saving, looking in their wallets, playing with pens or other nearby objects. Females continued to make eye contact and smile. However, by the end of five minutes, all participants were slumping in their chairs and feeling rejected. If we are hurt by strangers not throwing us a ball in cyberspace, then rejection from others we care deeply about is clearly even more painful.

Cyberball is an online ball toss video game that involves two or three other players besides the participant. The participant is instructed to play a simple game and pass the ball back and forth by using the mouse to throw the ball to the other players. The program also allows researchers to control how often each person will receive the ball and to whom the nonparticipant players will throw the ball. In this way, researchers can de-

termine who will be ostracized (the participant or another player) and how frequently each person will be participating in the game.

Later research using both the face-to-face ball toss paradigm and the Cyberball version demonstrated that being excluded by the Cyberball players was similarly aversive, even in a study where participants were explicitly told that the game was rigged and they were just playing against a computer or against other players who would have to follow a particular script. Participants were explicitly told that the other players would not get to choose how to play as they had to follow particular instructions telling them to whom they should toss the ball. The ostracized participants in all conditions reported similar levels of negative mood, heightened needs for belonging, more hurt and anger, and less enjoyment (Zadro, Williams, & Richardson, 2004).

Smith and Williams (2004) went beyond Cyberball to explore the impact of text messaging exclusion.

In this study participants were introduced to two confederates, then the participant was left alone in a room and told they should begin by texting the other people in the group (confederates) using a provided cell phone. Of course the text messages that were received were controlled by the experimenter. In the ostracism conditions, participants viewed text messages indicating that the two confederates were texting one another back and forth, but without responding to the participant's texts. Participants had a variety of reactions to this, some would try to provoke a response from the others, "Are you people not speaking to me? I am being oppressed." Some claimed they were bored by the conversation or that they thought this must be part of the experiment. Still others thought perhaps their phone was not actually transmitting texts and tried to attribute the ostracism to faulty technology. Taylor and Harper (2003) found that not receiving expected texts from friends left individuals feeling excluded and dejected.

Eisenberger (2003) had participants watch a game of Cyberball while in an fMRI chamber and found that just watching a demonstration of the game where the self was not included resulted in negative feelings and activation in the anterior cingulate cortex. The anterior cingulate cortex is also activated when people are experiencing physical pain (Panksepp, 2003).

People are clearly hurt when they are excluded, but we also report more negative affect when we see others being excluded. Wesselmann, Bagg, and Williams (2009) asked participants to simply watch a game of Cyberball while taking the perspective of the ostracized player. Those asked to take the ostracized player's perspective reported more negative affect than those who watched the game without perspective taking instructions. Still other research has shown that even being ostracized by people that we do not like can be painful (Gonsalkorale & Williams, 2007).

Jones, Carter-Sowell, Kelly, and Williams (2009) had participants work in groups to complete a de-

cision-making task. In some conditions, participants were excluded from having full information, leaving them out of the loop. When participants believed that the other group members had intentionally left them out, they reported feeling less liking and trusting of group members and felt more angry and sad. Being ostracized is something we seem particularly keen to avoid. Our need to belong and sensitivity to ostracism could have roots in our evolutionary standing, or more recent history in which survival required relying on others for protection, food, and shelter. Being left out when we want to be included is uncomfortable and painful. People are highly motivated to build social connections and feel a sense of belonging.

Friends and Partners

Social connections can take many forms, from familial connections to friendship. In this section, we are going to focus on dyadic interactions that occur with friends and partners. Some of the theories and findings we cover may also be applied to friendships within family groups. It is important to understand how we meet other people and then how our interactions also build relationships.

MEETING

The term *meet-cute* refers to the first time two people meet and later form a romantic relationships. Meet-cute is typically used in the film industry to refer to a scene in which the couple-to-be first interacts and typically involves some level of serendipity. However, there are even in these films some narrative that reflects the findings from basic social psychological research.

PROXIMITY. Proximity is quite simply the distance between two people (Newcomb, 1960). People who are physically closer (share neighborhoods or work spaces) are more likely to become friends or partners than people who are geographically separated by long distances. If you share space and are frequently co-located this increases the chances that you will meet the other person and interact with each other. This all seems very reasonable, but you may be thinking that the internet has changed this. Internet dating sites, chat rooms, and forums provide a way for people to interact with others who live across the globe. Yet, Amichai-Hamburger, Kingsbury, and Schneider (2013) found that in fact most of the online relationship interactions still occur with people who are geographically close and most people who maintained online interactions over a sustained period of time were from the same city or the same state.

Baym (2010) also posits that being physically near someone allows a relationship to be established quite differently than an online relationship. The nonverbal signals that we are able to read and send when co-located with another person's body are important for developing and understanding relationships. Online people may be more likely to disclose information more quickly and even use emoticons, videos, or photos to communicate with others (Burgoon et al., 2002). Online relationships also allow for friendships and relationships to form that are quite different than those we might form in person. There are more cross-sex friendships online than we would typically see otherwise (Parks & Roberts, 1998). Online relationships may also provide at least some opportunity for relationships that transcend preconceptions about age, race, religion, and other social identities. However, people do not often take advantage of this opportunity by extending those online relationships into their offline social world.

MERE EXPOSURE. One way that proximity functions is by capitalizing on the mere exposure effect. The mere exposure effects demonstrates that people we see frequently may be viewed more positively and more similar to the self. If you are a person who really dislikes the way you look in photographs and your friends and family think the very same photographs are beautiful depictions of you, you may be experiencing the mere exposure effect. The most frequent encounters we have with our visage is in the mirror and that is often the way we "see" ourselves. Mita, Dermer, and Knight (1977) photographed female students and showed each woman the photograph and a

Image © Beatrice, 2014. Used under license from Shutterstock, Inc.

mirror-image photograph. Participants overwhelmingly chose the mirror-image photo, but when their friends were asked to state their preference, they preferred the actual photo. It is likely that if you put a photo of yourself in Photoshop and flipped it to be the mirror image, you would like the photo much better!

Moreland and Beach (1992) had four women who were similar in appearance attend a class as though they were students in the course. The women did not interact with any of the students. These women attended either 5, 10, or 15 class sessions during the semester. The fourth woman did not attend any of the class sessions. At the end of the course, the class was shown photos of the women and rated the women who had attended the course more frequently as more attractive and similar to themselves. Simply seeing someone over and over makes them more attractive. This preference for the women attending 10 or 15 class sessions occurred even when none of the students reported that they knew her and very few reported they had ever seen her at all! People are more likely to agree with others that they see more often (Bornstein, Leone, & Galley, 1987) and disclose more information to others they have been exposed to more frequently (Brockner & Swap, 1976).

Proximity and mere exposure are clearly related. If we are to see someone frequently even with little or no interaction, they are more likely to be co-located in the same geographic area. However, the outcomes of mere exposure and proximity are not always positive. In some instances those who are close to us and people we see frequently may in fact be people we dislike. Ebbesen, Kjos, and Konecni (1976) had participants identify three neighbors they liked and three they disliked. They examined the distance of these neighbors from the participant's home and found that both liked and disliked neighbors were likely to live in close proximity. Even our romantic partners, who we care deeply about, have annoying habits and idiosyncrasies and repeated exposure can exacerbate our negative feelings about them (Cunningham, Shamblen, Barbee, & Ault, 2005). Social allergies refers to the increasing feelings of annoyance when exposed to repeated instances of our partner's habits that we find irritating. The more we are exposed to these social allergens (e.g., poor grooming, bad manners, inconsiderate self-focus, or bad behavior) the more sensitive to their occurrence we become and the more intensely we feel annoyed and hurt by our partner's actions.

SIMILARITY. Believing that we are similar to others also increases liking. If you are told that you have something in common with someone, you will enter into an interaction with a more positive expectation about the potential for friendship. However, even people with incredible self-esteem probably do not want to date themselves. How do we balance the attractiveness of similarity with the need for a partner who complements our strengths and weaknesses?

Optimal distinctiveness theory posits that we strive for an optimal balance between maintaining those things about ourselves that make us unique

Image © Aletia, 2014. Used under license from Shutterstock, Inc.

Image © Studio10Artur, 2014. Used under license from Shutterstock, Inc.

individuals and finding ways to see the self as part of relationship units (Brewer, 1991). When we feel satiated in our relationships, we may seek ways to emphasize our individuality and when we begin to feel dissimilar from our partners we may seek to re-establish affiliation with our partners. Slotter, Duffy, and Gardner (2014) conducted a study to examine how optimal distinctiveness theory was managed in romantic relationships. Participants were asked to write down their thoughts and feelings about a time when they felt quite similar to their partner. The other condition asked participants to focus on how they were unique and different from their romantic partner and how they thought and felt about those differences. Participants then had the opportunity to enter one of two drawings to win either a gift certificate for a romantic dinner for two or a gift certificate to a clothing store. Participants who had just reported how similar they were to their partner entered the drawing for the clothing store gift certificate and those who had focused on their distinctiveness from their partner opted for an entry for the romantic dinner for two. Congruent with optimal distinctiveness theory people actively attempt to strike a balance between being similar and maintaining individuality while maintaining satisfying romantic relationships.

PHYSICAL ATTRACTIVENESS. One of the first things we notice about others is the way they look and it is almost immediately that we evaluate their physical appearance in general. We do not necessarily dissect their entire appearance in that brief amount of time, but we do have a general impression of whether they are attractive or not after only a brief glance. What makes someone attractive? Is beauty in the eye of the beholder, or are there clear indicators of what most people find attractive in others?

Most research has focused on what heterosexual men and women find attractive. However, there may be interesting differences in what lesbians, bisexual women, and heterosexual women have to say about physical attractiveness. Women may seek female partners through personal advertisements (both online and in print newspapers). Bisexual women are more likely than lesbians or heterosexual women to be specific with regard to physical attributes and weight descriptors (Smith & Stillman, 2002). One conclusion is that bisexual women seeking female partners put more emphasis on physical traits than do lesbians or heterosexual women seeking male partners. Morrison, Morrison, and Sager (2004) found that lesbians and heterosexual women were similar in body mass and there was only a slight difference in body satisfaction. This difference was such that lesbian women had slightly higher body satisfaction scores.

Gay men and heterosexual men also have different experiences with regard to body image. Gay men focus more on muscularity when evaluating their own bodies and report their physical appearance matters to others (Yelland &

Tiggemann, 2003). Morrison also found that heterosexual men were more satisfied with their bodies than gay men when controlling for weight. In addition, gay men were leaner overall and closer to the muscular mesomorphic ideal and were as satisfied with their bodies

Legenbauer and colleagues (2009) conducted a study examining the importance of physical attractiveness. Their results demonstrate that heterosexual men had the highest expectations for an attractive partner and gay men the second highest expectations for attractiveness. The implications for the women and men sought by male partners is clear in that physical attractiveness will be emphasized. Both heterosexual and lesbian women were equally like to emphasize attractiveness and less likely than men to do so.

In general we value symmetry in body and face. A photo in which we take the right and left side of the photo and duplicate one side, the resulting perfectly symmetrical face will be perceived as much more attractive. Symmetry may be an indicator of health and therefore seen as a sign of possible fertility and healthy offspring. Indeed this is one sign of attractiveness that does not vary across cultures (Rhodes, Yoshikawa, et al., 2001; Rhodes et al, 2002).

Body shape is also quantifiable for men and women. Men find women more attractive as their waist-to-hip ratio approaches .7. This is also a ratio that is correlated with fertility and therefore may have some evolutionary foundation (Singh & Singh, 2006). Women prefer men with a waist-to-hip ratio closer to 1.0, but height seems to be a better indicator of at least initial attraction (Singh, 1995). The preference for thinness is not the same as a preference for a particular body shape. In some cultures there is stigma associated with being overweight, while in other cultures being plump is more attractive (Symons, 1979). However, the waist-to-hip ratio dating back to ancient cultures and times (32,000 B.P.) to current dates reveals the .7 wait to hip ratio for depictions and sculptures of women even (Singh & Singh, 2006). However, total body fat percentages do vary by culture and seem to be sensitive to food supply and the labor required to acquire food.

Height also plays a significant role in what is attractive particularly for women judging men (Berschied & Walster, 1974). Women rated men who were 5'9" to 5'11" as most attractive and men taller or shorter as less attractive (Graziano, Brothen, & Berscheid, 1978). However, it may be interesting that one of the things associated with height

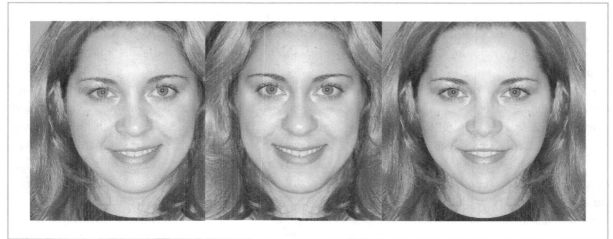

FIGURE 9.1 The picture on the left is the original photographic image, the other two are symmetrical iterations created by taking the left half of the photo, duplicating it, and pasting the photo back into the image. The photo on the right is two right-sides of the photo. In the two images on the right the perfect symmetry would typically be seen as more attractive than the original photo on the left.

for men is dominance, status, and earning power. Further, women tend to select men who are taller than them for romantic relationships; taller men therefore have a larger pool of women who are interested in dating them and therefore may be seen as more desirable partners.

Attractiveness may be the first factor in determining whether we pursue a conversation or further interaction. However, relationships are built on the combination of many factors and it is rare that one factor alone will save or end a relationship. For example, similarity in attractiveness matters and White (1980) found that both causal and serious couples were more likely to end relationships when the partners were not equally attractive. The preference for a similarly attractive partner or friend is typically referred to as the matching hypothesis and is not limited to heterosexual romantic relationships; similar patterns of relationship dissolution occur among friends and same-sex romantic couples (Bar-Tal & Saxe, 1976; Feingold 1988).

WIBIG

What Is Beautiful Is Good, or the WIBIG effect, refers to the idea that people who are attractive are assumed to also possess a number of good qualities related to social competence (Eagly, Ashmore, Makhijani, & Longo, 1991). People who are more attractive are thought to be more socially skilled, so this expectation combined with self-fulfilling prophecy may mean that attractive people are afforded more opportunities to develop and refine their social skills. Therefore, attractive people may in fact be more socially skilled. Feingold (1992) conducted a meta-analysis and found that more attractive people were less likely to report loneliness or social anxiety. However, there may be limits to the stereotype such that attractive adults are not necessarily more competent than unattractive adults (Feingold, 1992).

Snyder, Tanke, and Berscheid (1977) showed male participants (all presumed to be heterosexual) photographs of women and then had the participants talk on the telephone with the female confederates. However, the women on the other end of the phone line were not in fact the women in the photographs and had no idea that the men had been shown a photo. The men were asked to rate their expectations about the women prior to the phone conversation. Independent judges and the women then rated the men's behavior toward them during the conversation. When men were shown a photo of an attractive woman they thought the partner would be more sociable, poised, and funny. In turn the men were more interesting, independent, funny, and sociable in their conversations with these women. The women also behaved in ways that fulfilled the expectations of their conversant partners. Even attractive babies are thought to be smarter and less difficult (Stephan & Langlois, 1984).

Does the attractiveness stereotype we have in the United States hold across cultures? Some research shows that in general attractive others are viewed more positively, but traits that are positive may vary by culture. In Korea, attractive people are presumed to be more concerned with the well-being of others and to have more integrity (Wheeler & Kim, 1997). In other cross-cultural contexts; Chinese immigrants to Canada do not demonstrate the WIBIG stereotype (Dion, Pak, & Dion, 1990). Consider the television show *The Voice* and how the auditions that go viral on YouTube are often those where someone who was not attractive or for whom the WIBIG stereotype was not working in their favor manages to wow the judges and the crowd with their vocal skills. Zuckerman and Driver (1989) also found that vocal attractiveness operated much like facial attractiveness.

COGNITIVE DISREGARD

Rodin (1987) conducted a series of five experiments in which participants were shown photos or had brief interactions with confederates. The first study involved having participants view photos in a lab setting in which some photos who had some relevance to the participant and other photos that were less relevant. Participants were better at recalling the photos that were relevant to the self. People tend to attend more to peers of the same age in a similar task. College students had a brief encounter with someone close to their age or someone older and had better recall for the person that was closer in age. Rodin (1987) refers to this cognitive disregard as the invisibility of others who do not serve a particular purpose that is relevant to our lives.

As you are walking to class you likely encounter dozens or even hundreds of people. However, if you were then presented with photos of people you had seen or had not seen during your walk to class, chances are you would not be certain which people you had encountered. When we first see someone we quite quickly determine whether we need to attend to them because they represent a threat or an opportunity. People who do not seem at first glance to matter for our own lives are cognitively disregarded.

BEING LIKED. We like to be liked. If you were told that others liked you, chances are that you would actually interact with them in such a way that you would come to like them and in turn their liking of you would increase. In one study participants were primed to associate other group members with positive words (*favored, cheerful, sincere*) or negative words (*arrogant, mean, annoying*) (Krause et al., 2014). Then they worked on a task with their fellow group members and liking was measured. Those who were primed to like one another reported behaving in ways that were friendlier toward the liked group members than those primed with negative words. When making use of Cyberball as a measure rather than manipulation, the same study found that when group members were associated with positive words they were more likely to be thrown the ball than when they were associated with negative words.

Kelly's covariation theory (covered in Chapter 3) also tells us that we are even more likely to like others who like us in particular. Eastwick and colleagues (2007) conducted a speed-dating event

and asked participants to complete a variety of measures, including desire to see someone again they had met during speed dating. When people expressed interest in only one of the people they had met that evening and the other person also expressed reciprocal interest in only that person, they often reported more chemistry. However, when people reported they were interested in a number of the people they met, it was less likely that there was actually anyone who reciprocated this interest and a lack of chemistry with anyone else.

Imagine that you like someone who is friendly, nice, kind, and attractive. This person is nice to everyone and pleasant to be around. There is a second attractive person who is friendly, nice, and kind towards you, but not necessarily the same with others. Most people find the second person more desirable. Your attributions for the second person's behavior is that there is something about you in particular that brings out these positive traits in this person. The first person might like you, but then again likes everyone, so the person's positive qualities are really not about you.

When we find that others are critical of us, it decreases our liking of them, even when the critique is mild. Berscheid and colleagues (1969) had students read a list of eight positive things someone else had written about them or seven positive things and one negative thing someone else had written. Students like the all-positive writer much better than the one who also had one negative thing to say. Negative information stands out to us as it is more unusual and we are likely more attentive to negative information as it is a signal that all is not well (Yzerbyt & Leyens, 1991). Further, we are more likely to believe that critique is honest and praise might just be flattery or politeness (Coleman et al., 1987).

INTERACTING

Once we meet a person and begin the process of forming a friendship or romantic relationships we encounter an array of norms and expecta-

tions about how we should communicate, how frequently we should interact, and what sorts of interactions are appropriate. If there is too much communication or contact early on that is not mutual, the person making less contact may discontinue the association. On the other hand if interaction preferences are mutual you are well on your way to the beginning of a new relationship.

You may have heard a variety of "rules" about how soon after a first date you can call or text or email the other person about the possibility of scheduling a second date. Who should pay for the date? When is it okay to split the check? However, these rules are largely social convention and do not necessarily guarantee success or even positive outcomes in the long run. If both people have similar expectations about contact and similar dating scripts, however, then following those expectations may be an important marker of similarity. It is also important to remember that the rules or dating scripts that are more pervasive are based on heterosexual relationships. Klinkenberg and Rose (1994) found that lesbians and gay men had different scripts from one another and patterns of social interaction that were distinct from heterosexual relationships.

When interaction frequency is particularly high, you may also find that this relationship may interfere with preexisting friendships. If you typically go to dinner with someone two nights a week and prior to the entry of this new relationship, you went

to dinner with your roommate and on the other night you went with a group of friends, it may be the case that one of those two relationships will be supplanted by the newest person in your life.

Technology has also influenced how we manage interactions both at the early stages of a relationship but also as the relationship develops over time. Most women report that as relationships progress they interact through different types of technology at each stage (Yang, Brown, & Braun, 2013). Communication with new acquaintances may begin largely through Facebook, then instant messaging. As the relationship or friendship begins to develop they may exchange cell numbers primarily for texting and then after some time arrange a time to meet in person.

EXCHANGE AND COMMUNAL RELATIONSHIPS. Once we begin a relationship it is typical that we will begin the relationship on an exchange basis. Think about your first roommate and how you negotiated costs for shared household items early on. Perhaps you agreed to buy the dish soap the first time and made an explicit agreement about your roommate buying the dish soap next time. After a few months, you may not be keeping such close track of whose turn it is to contribute the dish soap to the household. This shift represents a more communal orientation to your relationship with your roommate. As the lease nears an end or when you begin to think about moving out the relationship may shift back to an exchange model, where you ask for compensation for contributions you made that were not returned in kind.

Exchange approaches to dating can have severe and often negative consequences in the hegemonic heterosexual culture. Social norms that have persisted into this century include ideas about the man paying the bill for a night out with a woman and in return she must then "owe" him something (e.g., a goodnight kiss, her phone number, a second date, sexual behavior). Anderson, Simpson-Taylor, and Hermann (2004) suggest that social rules governing heterosexual interaction indicate that boys and men are more likely to endorse these rules than are girls and women. Perhaps more importantly endorsement of these rules about exchange relationships and the initiation of sex was related to male self-reports of engaging in sexually coercive behavior.

Even in less formal dating arrangements, people who purchase drinks for an attractive other may well be an attempt to gain access to further interaction with that person in an exchange rela-

tionship dynamic. In communal relationships the focus may be more on how choices and behaviors impact the dyad, while an exchange relationships may bring to mind the individual contributions of each member of the pair (Clark & Mills, 1993).

Heterosexual singles are faced with books, blogs, and magazines offering traditional advice encouraging women to be indirect and passive. Men are encouraged to take the lead and women are encouraged to focus primarily on attracting men with physical beauty rather than competence or intelligence. Men likewise are told to act in control and maintain control in their dating lives. While a few books reviewed by Eaton and Rose (2011) did allow for women to initiate a date, far more advice was consistent with very traditional gender stereotypes. One book warned women, "don't object to his plans unless you really have to" (Spindel, 2007, p. 43).

Eaton and Rose (2011) suggest that shifting scripts that are embedded in traditional gender roles to a less gender stereotypic friendship script

Image © Lisa F. Young, 2014. Used under license from Shutterstock, Inc.

Image © Rikke, 2014. Used under license from Shutterstock, Inc.

Image © CREATISTA, 2014. Used under license from Shutterstock, Inc.

Image © mast3r, 2014. Used under license from Shutterstock, Inc.

might lead to more egalitarian relationships. Gay and lesbian couples may be more likely to use friendship scripts as the basis for egalitarian relationships with considerable success (Blumstein & Schwartz, 1990). Dating scripts for lesbians and gay men tend to follow other rules; for example, whomever asked the person out, pays the check or they explicitly negotiate splitting the check. There tends to be a bit more awareness about how power and equality function in relationships where maleness or femaleness does not dictate a particular role and adopt patterns of interaction that one might with close friends.

Relationship satisfaction is largely based on equity. Equity theory is the idea that there is balance and fairness in terms of what you put in and get out of a relationship (Walster, Walster, & Berscheid, 1978). When people believe that the benefits they are receiving from the relationship are similar to the benefits the other person is getting and both people are contributing equally then the relationship is likely to be more satisfying. Walster, Walster, and Traupmann (1978) asked partners in romantic relationships about their contributions to their relationships, the benefits they individually derived from their relationships, and about their sexual intimacy. Couples that were in equitable relationships reported increased sexual intimacy and that intimacy in these relationships was mutually desired by both partners.

SELF-DISCLOSURE. One way in which we establish relationships is through reciprocal self-disclosure. When you first meet someone you often begin an exchange of information about relatively basic types of information (e.g., career goals, favorite music). However, as people get closer to one another they begin to disclose their emotions and feelings (Reis & Shaver, 1988). If norms about self-disclosure are violated, however, we may feel very uncomfortable. If someone you have only just met begins to self-disclose a great deal and you are not comfortable reciprocating, the interaction may feel unbalanced and the obligation to reciprocate disclosures can be off-putting.

Dindia and Allen (1992) conducted a meta-analysis to determine if there were sex differences in self-disclosure. Overall, women tend to disclose more information than men to both strangers and known others, though the effect size is small ($d = .18$). Both men and women disclose more to women and same-sex partners than to opposite-sex partners or men. There are a number of possible explanations, but the relatively small effect size makes the sex difference less important than we might otherwise believe. Stereotypical expectations about men being stoic and women being talkative may play a role, though these traditional beliefs may not in fact carry enough weight to explain even this small sex difference. Though notably, women are not in fact more talkative than men (Mehl et al., 2007).

Self-disclosure no longer requires other people to even be in the same room with us and research has increasingly examined self-disclosure on social networking sites. Facebook's popularity is based largely on connecting people to one another through self-disclosure. The prompt for a status update is, "What's on your mind?" which encourages people to disclose to others their thoughts. Most studies have not found sex differences in motives for using Facebook (Fox & Warber, 2013; Hollenbaugh & Ferris, 2014; Baek et al., 2011). However, it is clear that one motive for using Facebook is to maintain existing relationships by engaging in self-disclosure and being responsive to the self-disclosure of others.

Love

Love can be described as an intense feeling of deep affection and while used to describe familial relationships, it is also frequently used to distinguish friendships from romantic relationships. This does not mean that we do not love our friends, but rather that when you indicate you love someone to whom you are not related that there is often an intention to signal

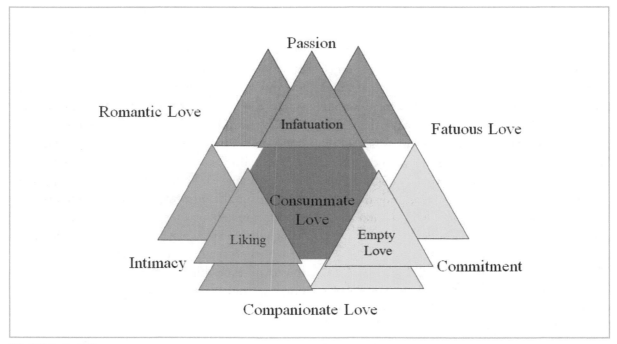

FIGURE 9.2

STERNBERG'S TRIANGLE THEORY

Sternberg has developed a theory of love that involves three components and is often referred to as the triangular theory of love. Three components of love are identified: intimacy, passion, and companionship. Intimacy indicates high levels of mutual self-disclosure and care about another person. We often have high levels of intimacy with romantic partners, but also our best friends and family members to whom we feel close. Intimacy may also include how attached, close, and connected we feel with another person. Passion often involves sexual attraction and desire for another person. Commitment includes both public commitment, private loyalty, and even obligations to continue a dyadic relationship.

The triangular theory leads to seven types of love created by the combination of these different components of love.

1. Liking is a relationship in which there are high levels of intimacy but no commitment or passion.

2. Infatuation occurs when relationships are predominantly based on passion without intimacy or commitment. The feelings involved in infatuation are often colloquially characterized as having a crush on someone that you may not know well.

3. Empty love is a relationship in which each member is bound to the other by commitment but without any passion or intimacy. Couples who stay in marriages for the sake of the children or who have a value system that prevents divorce are often experiencing empty love.

4. Companionate love involves both intimacy and commitment but may lack passion. These relationships are often more durable than friendships without commitment and might often occur between best friends or close family members. Some long-term relationships also evolve into a companionate love and it may be the sort of love that you think your grandparents enjoy,

but you would likely be falling prey to a stereotype. A study published in the *New England Journal of Medicine* reported that in the United States more than a quarter of seniors over 75 were still having sex and over 40% of people between 57 and 64 were having sex two or three times each month (Lindau et al., 2007).

5. Fatuous love includes both passion and commitment. Whirlwind courtships that lead to cohabitation or marriage before intimacy is established might characterize this type of love. Some friends-with-benefits who are exclusively physical with one another without necessarily being very intimate in terms of sharing feelings, emotions, or developing intimacy.

6. Romantic love involves both passion and intimacy without commitment. Early on relationships prior to the declaration of a commitment may easily fit this love type.

7. Consummate love is the relationship that includes passion, intimacy, and commitment and often presents a Western ideal and is the sort of relationship portrayed as a goal in most film and popular media. It is thought that striving for this ideal or having expectations for this in our relationships may lead to dissatisfaction with our relationships as they change over time or ebb and flow among these facets of love.

Romantic love includes both intimacy and passion, but has not yet resulted in a commitment to the other person. Some romantic love endures without moving on to include commitment, but for some people romantic love is a precursor to a relationship that will include commitment as well. When a relationship includes all three components (intimacy, passion, and commitment) we refer to this as consummate love.

LOVE STYLES

Lee (1988) developed a taxonomy of love styles that are in some ways similar to Sternberg's (1986), but focuses instead on how individuals might approach relationships. There are three primary styles of love: eros, ludus, and storge. The *eros* person approaches love as central to life. Physical connection and verbal expressions of love are important and both physical and emotional intimacy are established quickly and intensely. *Ludus* refers to people who are not interested in commitment and are motivated to engage in relationships primarily as a game of courtship. Sex is often viewed as fun and not about commitment or emotional intimacy per se. A person who is distant or overly attentive might be less fun to pursue than someone who is equally engaged in a game-playing approach to romance. *Storge* is the type of love that you might have for a sibling or friend. People who have known one another for a long time have a relaxed emotional intimacy with one another. It is rarely driven by the excitement that characterizes the other two primary styles.

Image © Kiselev Andrey Valerevich, 2014. Used under license from Shutterstock, Inc.

Image © Burlingham, 2014. Used under license from Shutterstock, Inc.

Image © Dubova, 2014. Used under license from Shutterstock, Inc.

There are three additional styles of love that are comprised of combinations of the primary styles listed above. *Mania* is a combination of eros and ludus approaches and these people may be pre-occupied with the object of their love and are often possessive. There is inevitably a great deal of pain associated with manic love as it rarely leads to a lasting and mutually engaged relationships. *Pragma* is a love style that is concerned first and foremost with compatibility or fit with a partner. The approach is quite pragmatic and people with this style will do the work to make a relationship work, but are not likely to take many risks in their pursuit of relationships. Finally, *agape* is a love style that is characterized by selfless giving of one's time, energy, and resources to the beloved.

FALLING IN LOVE

Falling in love is often described as an uncontrollable experience. We use the word *falling* as it indicates that it seems to happen without planning or strategy. Falling in love also makes you less able to perform well. Cognitively the frontal lobe of your brain involved in decision making may become less active when you are in love (Steenbergen, Langeslag, Band, & Hommel, 2013). Dopamine levels are elevated and serotonin levels drop, making people anxious and jittery when in love (Aaron et al., 2005). The increase in adrenaline may also lead to the sweaty palms and dry mouth that plague you when you are in those early romantic encounters. Falling in love also activates parts of the brain in the same way that painkillers might, leaving us less

vulnerable to pain; and even holding your partner's hands decrease activation of areas of the brain that activate during pain or threat (Coan, Schaefer, & Davidson, 2006). Your heartbeat synchronizes to the speed of your partners (Ferrer & Helm, 2013). In general, we experience love with a sense of euphoria (Aaron et al., 2005).

SYMPTOMOLOGY. We tend to think of falling in love as a predominantly psychological process. However, there are physiological indicators that falling in love also changes our hormone levels which may be linked to behavioral changes as well. Marazziti and Canale (2004) found that individuals who had recently fallen in love showed higher levels of cortisol. Men showed lower levels of FSH and testosterone if they had recently fallen in love and women showed higher testosterone levels when falling in love. Higher cortisol and FSH levels are indicative of increased "stress" which may be associated with the initiation of social contact. A year later individuals in the same relationship showed that their hormonal levels had returned to levels equivalent to singles and long-term relationship partners from the control group.

ATTACHMENT STYLES

Adult attachment styles may also shape our interactions with our partners and whether our relationships last. The two-factor theory of attachment includes two independent axes: anxiety and avoidance (Bartholomew & Horowitz, 1991; Collins & Feeney, 2004; Simpson, 1990). The anxiety

axes can be thought of whether you see yourself positively (low anxiety) or negatively (high anxiety). The second axis is avoidance and captures whether you see others positively (low avoidance) or negatively (high avoidance). If you are low in anxiety and low in avoidance then you are similar to about two-thirds of the population in being securely attached. You ask for what you want when you want it and expect that your partner will provide for your needs in the same manner. If you are preoccupied (anxious/ambivalent) this means that you believe other people are good (low avoidance) but that you may not be deserving of their goodness (high anxiety). This attachment style often leads people to be concerned that their partners will leave and seek closeness. Preoccupied people will provide comfort and support for their partners, but it can feel overwhelming at times.

People who think they are good (low anxiety) but others are not to be trusted (high avoidance) are described as having a dismissing avoidant attachment style. They are more independent and view partners as unreliable and uncaring. They may seem withdrawn and unavailable to their partners and provide little support for their partners.

Finally, fearful avoidant attachment is characterized by having both high anxiety (negative self-perception) and high avoidance (negative other-perceptions). Not only do these people not trust others, they also do not see themselves as worthy of love. In general they avoid getting involved in relationships as they feel the relationship is not likely to be a success.

The good news is that attachment styles are not fixed and every relationship that we have in some way informs us about what we can expect from partners and ourselves. Securely attached people can be made anxious or avoidant by being in a relationship where the partner is not also secure. On the other hand having a relationship with a securely attached person may encourage the anxiously attached person he or she is worthy of love and the avoidant person that people can be trusted. There are also some symbiotic pairings in which relationships are maintained, though the attachment style might be reinforced. When a preoccupied person and a dismissing person are in a relationship they both believe that one partner is good and the other is not worthy and have a shared mental model for how the relationship dynamics will function. In line with self-verification theory this may actually feel good as the partner's perception of the other feels accurate and here is a person who sees you accurately and persists in the relationship.

Interdependence Theory

Interdependence theory was first proposed by Kelley and Thibaut (1978). Interdependence indicates that people in relationships with one another are interdependent on the ways in which their partners behave as well as how they interact with their partners. Rusbult and Buunk (1993) extended interdependence theory to close relationships and proposed the investment model of commitment. People receive rewards from their partners and in turn provide investments that produce rewards for the other. Benefits and costs may be emotional, social, instrumental, or even opportunistic. For example, if one partner provides the other access to a vehicle this might be a benefit for one partner and sharing the vehicle might be considered a cost to the other. However, perhaps the partner uses the car to go to high-end grocery stores and subsequently makes delectable dinners, the benefit may balance out the cost. In current economic times, a partner with an income might mean that home ownership becomes a possibility that would not present itself to someone with only one income. Some people find dating a high status person to be socially rewarding and enjoy attending professional or society functions with the partner; for others this need to maintain a public image can be draining and feel more like a cost than a benefit.

There are three components to interdependence theory that work dynamically in relation to one another: Current Outcomes (OC), Comparison Levels (CL), and Alternatives (CL-Alt). For ease of explanation you might think of a 10-point scale, where 1 indicates a relatively poor rating and 10 a very high rating. Current outcomes are simply the rating of how your relationship is currently, taking into account all of the possible costs and benefits of being in the relationship. Perhaps for your relationships this would be a 7 on a 10-point scale (OC = 7).

Your comparison level is what you believe or expect that you should be rating a relationship. This comparison level is comprised of all the possible experiences of relationships, including your own past relationships, those of your parents, friends, and even those you have read about in books or watched in movies. All of these inputs comprise your perception of what someone like you should be able to expect in a romantic relationship. Let's say that your comparison level is quite positive (CL = 9).

Finally, the alternatives to your relationship come into the equation. If you ended the current relationship what would be your next best alternative? This might include other people you might date or even being single. The investment model goes one step further than interdependence theory, by discussing the investments that a person might make to the relationship which would be lost if the relationship were to end are also bound up in the understanding of current outcomes and quality of alternatives. It also includes any losses that you might incur by leaving your current partner (e.g., belongings, emotional stability, friends, social support). For this example, let's say that your alternatives are not very good (Cl-Alt = 4). Now what do you do with all of these numbers?

Relationship satisfaction can be calculated by subtracting the comparison level from the current outcome (OC-CL). If the result is positive then you are likely pretty satisfied with your relationship, you are doing better than you would have expected. If the result is negative then you are dissatisfied with the relationship and had really believed that you deserved better outcomes. Better outcomes might mean a higher return on what you have invested into the relationship or requiring fewer investments and resulting in less costs than you are currently experiencing. In the example above your satisfaction would be a -2, meaning you are somewhat dissatisfied.

Dependence or commitment to the relationship can also be calculated by subtracting your alternatives (CL-Alt) from your current outcomes (OC). If the result is positive then you are likely dependent on this relationship and this is as good as you can do in your current situation. A negative result would indicate that you are likely to leave the relationship for that alternative option. In the case above your dependence score would be 3, indicating that you are likely to remain in this relationship.

FIGURE 9.3 *What alternatives might you consider? Some alternatives may be weighted more than others.*

Illustration by Max Dusky.

LEAVING TO BE LESS UNHAPPY

You have likely encountered friends who are unhappy in their relationship, but continue to stay with their partner. They might have an equation similar to the one in the previous example. They are unsatisfied but dependent, there are no better alternatives. However, we also know that some people seem to go from one unhappy relationship to another and never seem to be satisfied. In this case it is likely that they might have the following pattern (OC = 7, CL-Alt = 8, CL = 9). The formula in this case would result in a negative satisfaction score of -2 and a negative dependence score -1, indicating they are both independent and dissatisfied and will leave. The problem of course is that when they leave for the alternative which is

better (8 rather than 7), the alternative is still less than their comparison level (9) meaning they are now dependent and still dissatisfied. Sometimes people leave a relationship not to be happy but to be less unhappy.

UNDERSTANDING WHY PEOPLE STAY IN VIOLENT RELATIONSHIPS

One frequent question that comes up is why do people stay in violent relationships, why don't they leave? Interdependence theory provides us with some insight. There are stereotypes that indicate that people who are in abusive relationships have no self-respect or lack self-esteem. However, that is not necessarily the case. In fact, persons who have a very high comparison level and know that they deserve and should expect better treatment from their partners, may not have an alternative that would be better. People who are abusive will often make it clear to their abused partners that

FIGURE 9.4 *What are the costs and benefits of leaving?*

nitively disregard opportunities for another relationship. If an alternative emerges, committed people may simply think through how hard it would be to start over or whether this new person would really be able to fulfill their long-term needs the way the current partner will.

Our partners may also derogate alternatives for us. There are both healthy and unhealthy ways to derogate a partner's alternatives. One way is to tell our partners what is wrong with the alternative: "He seems a bit cheap." Another is to tell our partners how poor a fit that person would be: "I bet he wouldn't take you on the sort of vacations we go on." In one study of derogation of alternatives, Schmitt and Buss (1996) found that heterosexual couples often used evolutionarily relevant characteristics to derogate potential rivals. Typically a rival male's resources, status, sexual orientation, and generosity would be used as grounds for derogation by indicating he was poor, gay, lacked status, and cheap. On the other hand, female rival's sexual fidelity and availability was attacked by others referring to her as either a prude, frigid, lesbian, or sexually promiscuous.

their alternatives might involve death threats, stalking, further abuse, embarrassment, losing their children, losing their job, and financial ruin. Programs that provide help to people in domestic violence situations are more helpful to the extent that they provide viable alternatives rather than trying to build self-esteem or raise expectations about how a healthy relationship might function.

Commitment

How then do people stay committed to relationships? If we are exposed to alternatives, how can people maintain satisfying and committed relationships? Derogation of alternatives presents one way that we demonstrate commitment to our partners. Those who are invested in maintaining a long-term relationship will derogate their own alternatives. In some cases, people in relationships do not even notice alternatives or essentially cog-

In abusive relationships, the derogation of alternatives might focus on the partner rather than the rival. For example, an abusive person might tell the partner that he is not good enough to have a relationship with a woman like that or that she is too ugly to even think another man might be interested in having a relationship with her. This sort of derogating the partner in order to derogate the perception of alternatives is clearly meant to harm the partner and maintain the relationship. This sort of derogation should be a red flag that the partner's regard for the other is less than one might expect and sets the stage for continuing psychological and possibly physical abuse. Rusbult and Martz (1995) refer to this as nonvoluntary dependence.

Miller and Maner (2010) conducted a study in which men who were in romantic relationships and men who were not interacted with a female confederate. The female confederate's menstrual cycle was tracked to determine when she would be optimally fertile. Findings indicate that single men rated the confederate as more attractive when she was at the fertile stage of her menstrual cycle and men who were in romantic relationships were less likely to find her attractive. The authors conclude that female fertility cues may trigger relationship-maintenance and alternative derogation in men who are already in committed relationships. Still other research has found that when women are experiencing heighted fertility male partners are more likely to engage in mate-guarding behaviors by deterring other men from expressing interest and making it clear that he is in a committed relationship with her (Haselton & Gangestad, 2006).

There are clear and healthy ways to increase both relationship satisfaction and commitment by improving outcomes in our relationships, decreasing costs, and increasing investments. Derogating our own alternatives is also one way that we maintain our relationships. While we may like to think about our relationships as based on love, there are clearly more concrete considerations in our daily lives that shape our relationships.

INVESTMENTS: CAN YOU TAKE IT WITH YOU WHEN YOU GO?

Goodfriend and Agnew (2008) proposed that there were four types of investments that we make in our close relationships: past tangible, past intangible, planned tangible, and planned intangible. Tangible investments refer to physical and concrete investments that are tied to the relationship (e.g., jointly owned furniture, shared debts, and

pets). Intangible investments are not necessarily material and may include time, love, self-disclosure, and effort one exerts to maintain the relationship. Past investments are those investments that you have already sunk into the relationship. Planned investments include things that you intended to do with your partner in the future (e.g., buy a home, have children, launch a business) that might be lost if the relationship were to end.

Couples with high levels of planned investments were less likely to have broken up four to six months later compared to those with fewer planned investments. Participants reported an increased chance of reuniting with a past partner when past intangible and planned investments were higher. Past tangible investments were not predictive of breakup or intent to reunite with a past partner. Buying a couch together won't keep your relationship together, but investing quality time might have long-term implications for commitment.

PRONOUNS AND OTHER COMMITMENT MARKERS

Cognitive interdependence refers to the ways in which we think of ourselves as part of a romantic relationship. Agnew and colleagues (1998) have found that individuals who are more cognitively interdependent are likely more committed to their relationships. One sign of cognitive interdependence is when couple members use plural pronouns rather than singular pronouns when thinking about their relationships. Participants are asked to share their thoughts about their relationships by making a list of thoughts and using complete sentences. The sentences are then coded for whether they use more plural pronouns or singular pronouns. For example, "We have a great time together" and "We tend to fight over silly things" would both be coded as using plural pronouns and represent more cognitive interdependence (and commitment) than the same thoughts expressed using singular pronouns (e.g., "I have a great time with Kelsey" and "Kelsey and I fight over silly things").

The way we talk about our close relationships might also convey our degree of closeness to others. Fitzsimons and Kay (2004) found that participants reading a passage about two friends that made use of plural pronouns rated the friends as much closer and happier than those reading the same information using singular pronouns. Discussing our partners using plural pronouns may provide yet another way we might mate guard or demonstrate to others that we are committed to our relationships.

Aron and colleagues (1992) developed the Inclusion of Other in the Self (IOS) scale that uses a visual representation of the relationship as a series of seven images of two overlapping circles to determine how much the partner is connected to the self. Participants are asked to indicate which set of circles best describes their relationship with their partner. Participants who choose circles with greater overlap as representative of their relationship also report higher levels of intimacy and feeling close to their partner.

There are many ways in which we communicate and think about our relationship partners. In some cases this reflects how we feel about our partners and in other cases provides a way to communicate our feelings to others. It may also be the case that if we behave as though we are committed to the other we may become committed to the other. When Agnew and colleagues (1998) asked participants to complete sentence stems that used plural pronouns or singular pronouns, those using plural pronouns reported more cognitive interdependence than those provided singular pronoun stems. What other subtle cues help us understand whether our relationships are long lasting or in trouble?

Historically, jewelry or shared clothing might be a marker of commitment (though typically this involved men buying women jewelry or giving women letter jackets or pins to wear). Rarely was there anything that women gave to men that indicated to others he was in a committed relationship (at least not until the exchange of rings). Face-book has provided more opportunities for people to explicitly declare their commitment by becoming "FBO" (Facebook Official). Papp, Danielewicz, and Cayemberg (2012) examined the implications for couples who declare their commitment by changing their relationship status on Facebook. For men, having relationship status listed on Facebook was related to increased relationship satisfaction. Women who posted a profile picture that included the partner was also related to higher levels of relationship satisfaction. The couples in this study were all heterosexual, so gay and lesbian couples may provide more insight about the nature of this sex difference.

Facebook also presents unique and new challenges for couples. Disagreements about whether to become Facebook official led to lower levels of relationship satisfaction for females, but not males. People have begun to develop an etiquette around the relationship status update and breaking up. It may be the case that you are more likely to see

a new relationship announcement (in a relationship, engaged, married) in your newsfeed than a breakup. This is because people tend to hide their relationship status and then change the status more privately. Facebook uses an algorithm called Edgerank that mathematically determines what you will see in your newsfeed. Relationship status updates are heavily weighted updates and are highly likely to appear in your newsfeed and breakups often result in far more comments than almost any other type of post.

Facebook also has collected enough data to be able to predict the timeline for which a couple will change their relationship status from single to in a relationship (Diuk, 2014). By examining the types of posts and how often two people are posting on one another's walls and sharing events, the Facebook Data Science group was able to show that there is a slow but steady increase in posts peaking at about 1.67 posts per day before the relationship will be declared. Then while in a relationship the mutual posting tapers off as the couple spends more time together offline.

Schade and colleagues (2013) found that texting also impacted relationship satisfaction. Most couples used testing to express affection and was associated with higher levels of attachment to their partners. When partners used texting to hurt one another or to regulate the relationship texting was associated with negative relationship quality. It is clear that technology is shaping our relationships and how we interact with one another. Technology provides the opportunity for immediate and almost constant contact with our partners even when they are not with us, but at the same time relationship development may also include in later stages the desire for optimal distinctiveness and time to be away from the partner.

MOTIVATIONS AND ATTRIBUTIONS

Our interactions in relationships are often motivated by a desire to maintain or improve our relationships. However, even when we are well meaning we can find ourselves at odds with those we love. How do these misunderstandings occur? You thought you were doing something that would make your partner happy or that would be fun, but in the end it starts an argument. Understanding how motivations and attributions impact our perceptions about why people engage in particular behaviors may smooth the troubled waters.

INTRINSIC VS. EXTRINSIC MOTIVATION. DeBeers found that diamond sales were lagging in 1938 after the Depression and so they launched an advertisement campaign that told men and women that engagement should be commemorated with a diamond ring. Not just any diamond ring, but a diamond ring equal to two months of the man's salary. In 1947, the slogan "A Diamond is Forever" again increased sells. By 1965, 80% of new brides had a wedding ring and an engagement ring. Thus was born the concept of the engagement ring and a billion-dollar industry. And the law is also involved. In most states, the engagement ring is considered a conditional gift, so if the engagement is broken off the ring should be returned (*Meyer v. Mitnick*, 625 N.W.2D 136; Mich. App., 2011).

Did this person provide his beloved the engagement ring because he was intrinsically motivated, and felt in his heart it should be given to her? Was the giving of the ring driven purely by love? Most likely not. It is much more likely that extrinsic factors led to the purchase and giving of the engagement ring. The desire to marry one's partner is likely intrinsic, but the ring itself may be provided more out of obligation or expectation than it is the appropriate thing to do. When we do things because we are supposed to or expected to, they may be appreciated and avoid the negative experience of not meeting a partner's expectations. However, we do not necessarily reap positive rewards for these extrinsically motivated gifts.

Perhaps you buy your partner chocolate on St. Valentine's Day. This token of your love meets an expectation that you should celebrate the holiday and give sweets to your sweet. Certainly, showing up empty handed or forgetting about the holiday altogether is likely to be met with some consternation and even disappointment. However, your partner is still going to assume that you were extrinsically motivated to give this gift and it will be seen more as your following social convention than a sign of true love.

Intrinsically motivated behaviors lead to internal attributions. If on a randomly selected Tuesday you gave your partner a copy of a book she had been wanting to read or took her to dinner "just because," your partner is going to assume this has more to do with your feelings for her. After all, there was no external or extrinsic reason to do this; therefore, the only reason you could possibly have been so romantic is because you do in fact care deeply for your beloved.

RELATIONSHIP ENHANCEMENT AND IDEALIZATION. People often wonder how to maintain a relationship over the long term. Some research that focuses on happy couples with long-term relationships has provided us with ideas about the way they interact with one another. Srivastava and colleagues (2006) found that optimists reported more relationship satisfaction and that partners who were optimistic felt they could resolve conflicts through constructive engagement. Murray and Holmes (1997) found that partners in satisfying and stable relationships were more likely to have some positive illusions about their partners. Couples tend to believe that their relationship has a brighter future than the average relationship and

in part this optimism increases relationship satisfaction and longevity. Relationship illusions were better predictors of relationship stability than relationship satisfaction or relationship quality. One key to long and satisfying relationships is to maintain positive illusions about the partner rather than trying to be accurate or see the person on a deeper level.

Notarius and Markman (1993) have provided a series of communication patterns that can help promote healthy relationships for couples. Rather than responding to conflict by escalating a negative verbal exchange, couples should try to engage each other differently. The research resulted in some polite alternatives to manage conflict. For example, couples can thank their partner when they do a household chore rather than critiquing the way the chore was done. Rather than saying you are not interested in your partner's plans for the evening, make a counteroffer. Greet your partner and do not let time pass in tense silence. Speak for yourself and not for your partner. If you want to do something instead of assuring your partner of a good time, be more direct, "I would really like to go to the film downtown tonight." Couples who were counseled to follow this communication guide had a 50% lower rate of breakup than a control group (Notarius & Markman, 1993).

Interdependence theory and equity theory focus on assessing whether your relationship investments are resulting in equivalent returns. However, over the long term many relationships take on a more communal understanding of the rela-

Image © Africa Studio, 2014. Used under license from Shutterstock, Inc.

Image © wavebreakmedia, 2014. Used under license from Shutterstock, Inc.

tionship and the happiest marriages tend to follow a rule based on need, where partners simply give what the other needs without keeping track. Obviously this positive outcome occurs only when both partners adopt the need-based rule (Mikula & Schwinger, 1978).

Butzer and Kuiper (2008) examined how people used humor in their romantic relationships and found that during conflict people were more likely to use positive humor and less likely to use negative humor. Many long-term couples report humor is an important part of their relationship success (Lauer, Lauer, & Kerr, 1990). Most often humor serves to bond the couple together (Ziv, 1988), although it may also be important in managing conflict. However, hostile humor can increase a distance between partners and is more frequently used by couples who have low relationship satisfaction (Alberts, 1990).

You may have heard that you have to love yourself before anyone else can love you, and single people are often told they need to have more confidence or to improve their self-esteem if they hope to find a partner. However, the evidence is mixed. People with low self-esteem may be distrustful or have an anxious attachment style, but people with high self-esteem may be quicker to leave when things are not going their way (Rusbult, Morrow, & Johnson, 1987; Sommer et al., 2001). People who are narcissistic can be even more challenging in relationships as they are generally less committed to relationships and keenly aware of alternatives (Campbell, Foster, & Finkel,

2002). Self-acceptance may actually be related to positive relationship outcomes and lead to more positive interactions with others (Schutz, 1999). Self-verification theory also indicates that people with low self-esteem may feel more loved when their partners verify their negative thoughts about the self. They see the partner as loving them in spite of their flaws and shortcomings and this can lead to feelings of genuine and sincere love. If you have ever tried to improve others' self-esteem by telling them how great they are and how much you care about them, they may have responded by saying that if you knew who they really were, you wouldn't think they were so great.

CONFLICT AND HURT FEELINGS. Even the most loving relationships over the long run encounter conflict and result in hurt feelings. One of the ways that couples navigate conflict successfully is by making external attributions for their partner's bad behaviors and internal attributions for their partner's good behaviors. This pattern of attribution is favorable and allows one to maintain a positive view of the partner, while acknowledging bad behavior.

Loving, Le, and Crockett (2009) found that when our partners hurt our feelings we actually experience that hurt physiologically. Those closest to us are often positioned to produce the most harm with mean comments or initiating a breakup unexpectedly. Emotional or psychological abuse can result in PTSD and a variety of health consequences as a result (e.g., immune function disruption, higher T-cell counts, increased susceptibility to

Image © Stokkete, 2014. Used under license from Shutterstock, Inc.

Image © Dragon Images, 2014. Used under license from Shutterstock, Inc.

autoimmune disorders). However, even more mild hurtful behaviors such as criticizing, interrupting, and putting down the partner can increase blood pressure (Ewart et al., 1991) and stress hormones, decrease immune function, and delay wound healing (Kiecolt-Glaser et al., 2010).

Not all of our negative experiences in relationships result from the actions of our partners; sometimes it is the case that a partner withdrawing from the relationship or interaction with us that causes emotional distress. This emotional distress is also associated with elevated stress hormones (Kiecolt-Glaser et al., 2010). Conflict habits may develop within relationships such that some couples may fight frequently, but not seem to have negative emotional consequences. If the fights over time become routine, they may lose the power to really upset either partner (Fiske, 2004). People may also engage in destructive behavior during conflict by exiting the relationship or neglecting the partner (Rusbult et al., 1991). A more constructive strategy is to give voice to concerns and to maintain loyalty to the partner and the relationship.

People who can take the partner's perspective may also be more likely to engage in pro-relationship behaviors during conflict (Arriaga & Rusbult, 1998). However, other couples engage in negative tracking by focusing on negative events and attributing negative events to their partners (Holtzworth-Munroe & Jacobson, 1985). People who feel their partners care about them are more likely to seek closeness with their partner during conflict, while those who feel devalued are likely to pull away (Murray, Bellavia, Rose, & Griffin, 2003). Couples that stay close to their partner even when conflict arises are more likely to have long-term relationships. Happy couples are also more likely to tease each other in positive ways and are less aggressive and threatening when teasing their partners (Keltner, Young, Heerey, Oemig, & Monarch, 1998).

> "First best is falling in love. Second best is being in love. Least best is falling out of love. But any of it is better than never having been in love."
>
> – *Maya Angelou*

Ending Romantic Relationships

Even with the best of intentions and strategies to maintain our relationships, we often face the dissolution of our most intimate relationships. Breaking up can be mutual or one-sided, it can

be sudden or expected, and it can vary in terms of the emotions that a person might feel after the relationship ends. Interdependence theory makes it quite clear that we are likely to dissolve a relationship when our alternatives exceed our current outcomes.

Choo and colleagues (1996) found that both men and women were anxious, sad, and angry after a breakup. However, women also reported more joy and relief than men. Women may be more attuned to relationship trouble brewing and begin to take action to save the relationship. When their efforts do not result in a better relationship, it may be a relief when it is finally over. Women may be more prepared and less shocked when relationships end. When it comes to divorce, women are more likely to file (Brinig & Allen, 2000). Women are more likely to initiate breakups and men tend to be more shocked and upset when relationships end (Sprecher, 2005). Men also do not handle breakups as well as women and report more sadness, depression, and loneliness. Perhaps breakups are more devastating for men because they fall in love more quickly and are more apt to label their feelings for a partner as love (Tolhuizen, 1989).

Are there compassionate ways to end a relationship? Sprecher, Zimmerman, and Fehr (2014) have found that people who score higher on the Compassionate Love Scale are more likely to employ a more compassionate breakup strategy. Compassionate breakup strategies employ a positive tone (avoid hurting the partner's feelings as much as possible) and openness about the desire to end the relationship (telling your partner directly you would like to end the relationship). Other strategies include manipulation (attempting to get the partner to leave you by engaging in bad behavior), distant communication (broke up by email or instant messenger) or avoiding or withdrawing from the partner (avoiding the partner). Compassionate breakup strategies increase the likelihood that a friendship might be maintained after the breakup.

"If you love someone, showing them is better than telling them. If you stop loving someone telling them is better than showing them." –Ritu Ghatourey

UNREQUITED LOVE

Unrequited love occurs when a person loves another person, but these feelings are not mutual. Most people have experienced having a crush on someone who is not interested in pursuing a romantic relationship. The person experiencing the emotions and the person who is being pursued often have very different emotional experiences to the situation. The person with the crush may suffer the pain of rejection, but may also remember the hopefulness and excitement during that time positively. We are sometimes told that we should be flattered by another person's attraction, but the person who was desired may be generally uncomfortable and wish that the whole thing could have been avoided (Baumeister, Wotman, & Stillwell, 1993).

> "Let no one who loves be called unhappy. Even love unreturned has its rainbow."
>
> —*James Matthew Barrie*

MOVING ON…

Getting over a breakup can be challenging. Breakups may lead us to satiate our feelings by consuming junk food. Baumeister, DeWall, Ciarocco, and Twenge (2005) found that participants ate twice as many cookies after they were rejected from a group compared to those who had been accepted. Ending a relationship comes with a number of emotional and psychological consequences.

People may have a variety of concerns from whether they want to remain friends or how quickly they can move on. Reactions by friends and family can also become important in navigating a breakup.

Some people may want to be friends after the breakup and that can be challenging to manage. Lesbians and gay men may be especially likely to remain friends with former partners and to maintain social contact with ex-partners (Solomon et al., 2004; Weinstock, 2004). This may be because of the relatively small social networks that make up gay and lesbian communities and the benefits that may come from remaining friends within the community (Nardi 1999, Weinstock, 2004). Though it has not been studied, this may also apply to other small communities or people who are place-bound and live in rural areas.

In addition, people may engage in more rebound sex in order to cope with a breakup. Barber and Cooper (2014) found that the person who was dumped was more likely to seek other sexual partners immediately following a breakup. After a breakup many people find another partner relatively quickly. This relationship is often considered a rebound relationship. Most advice for single people is to be wary of others who are newly single as they are not likely interested in a long-term relationship and may only serve as the "rebound" partner. Certainly having sex with someone you don't know well might present higher levels of emotional, psychological, or physical risk. However, Owen, Fincham, and Moore (2011) also found that young adults who engaged in hookup sexual encounters were less depressed and lonely than those who did not. Sex may in fact be part of a healing process after a breakup (Barber & Cooper, 2014), but of course all possible safety precautions should be taken to ensure one's physical health is not sacrificed in doing so. Surprisingly, friends with benefits relationships and committed relationships are least likely to use condoms during sexual encounters because of an increased perception of trust (Mathews, 2013). Shimek and Bello (2014) reported that men were likely to adopt a ludus love style after a breakup and seek out rebound relationships more frequently than women.

> "Ultimately, who you choose to be in a relationship with and what you do in your bedroom is your business."
>
> *--Eminem*

Technology has also impacted how we manage our social lives after a breakup. LeFebvre, Blackburn, and Brody (2014) asked participants how they managed their breakup on Facebook. During the breakup, most people reduced their use of Facebook as they did not want other people involved. After the breakup, many participants engaged in impression management. Others reported decreasing their Facebook activity, engaging in virtual mourning (posting statuses grieving for the partner/relationship) or reconciliation (commenting or liking the status of the ex or re-friending the ex, sending apology messages). Some engaged in relational cleansing (purged the ex by deleting photos, removing relationship status, deleting events, and wall posts by the partner or that referenced the partner). Others sought support from their social network or found a new relationship. Still others would engage in surveillance of their ex's social network and engage in relational transgressions or withdraw the ex's access to information particularly during the breakup (defriend and deleting or blocking the ex's friends and family). Certainly these strategies have real-world correlates, but what used to be relatively private has become not only public but permanent. Barber and Cooper (2014) also found that levels of distress following a breakup leveled off about six months after the relationship ended, though we might imagine that the time period needed to recover may be dependent upon the length of the relationship. However, the work required to manage one's Facebook account after a breakup may slow down post-breakup adjustment (LeFebvre, Blackburn, & Brody, 2014).

For some people moving on might not include another relationship. While we have been told that studies indicate that married people are happier than any other people on the planet, Bella DePaulo has amassed significant counterpoints to this claim. Never-married single people are as happy as married people, though divorced and widowed people are less happy. The stereotypes about single people are largely inaccurate (DePaulo & Morris, 2006). Most Americans will spend more years of their adult life single than married (DePaulo, 2006). Married and never-married people are healthier than widowed, divorced, and cohabiting people based on data from the CDC analyzed by DePaulo. Never-married mothers and married mothers have similar mental health profiles and better health profiles than mothers who were separated or divorced (Afifi, Cox, & Enns, 2006). A study of older adults found that a lack of friendship rather than singlehood was a better predictor of loneliness (Dykstra, 1995). Never-married adults are more likely than married, divorced, or widowed adults to include siblings in their social networks and to have a higher quality contact with their siblings (Pinquart, 2003). It is clear that single people nurture a number of fulfilling relationships throughout their lives and have richer and higher quality relationships with siblings and friends.

This chapter has only briefly introduced the depth and breadth of research that social psychologists have undertaken with regard to relationships. While sexual orientation is mentioned in some sections, the research remains relatively limited to heterosexual men and women, lesbians, and gay men and to date has not thoroughly explored how asexual individuals fulfill their need to belong (Scherrer, 2008). Asexual individuals report having no sexual attraction to anyone or at least no desire to engage in sexual behavior with others.

It is important to distinguish celibacy which is a choice to not engage in sexual behavior rather than asexuality which is a lack of desire to do so in the first place. Scherrer (2008) surveyed individuals who identified as asexual and many reported close friendships or in some cases romantic companionate relationships that met their needs for social and emotional support.

Most research is focused on dyadic and monogamous relationships rather than polyamorous relationships. Klesse (2014) provides a literature review that indicates that polyamory is perhaps best understood as a label that provides a descriptor for individuals who are in a particular constellation of relationships. A less preferred term is consensual non-monogamy, but this may bring to mind open relationships which are often considered to be quite different. An open relationship often involves a primary dyadic relationship in which both partners have reached an agreement about what sexual activity would be allowed beyond the dyad. Women tend to prefer secondary relationships that are romantic (17.4%) over sexual encounters (14.5%), while men exhibit the opposite pattern preferring sexual encounters (28.2%) over romantic secondary relationships (19.2%) (Garnets & Kimmel, 2003). However, a polyamorous relationship often involves all people in the relationship having some connection and many respondents reported having two primary relationships. Historically the term polyfidelity might have been used to characterize most of today's polyamorous relationships. In these relationships three or more people agree to be faithful to one another and are expected to be romantically, emotionally, and sexually connected. Typically someone outside the group would be considered off-limits for sexual or romantic involvement. Polyamorous relationships may involve people of a variety of sexual orientations and sexes. There are often clear and communicated boundaries about who is in a relationship with whom. For these relationships to persist there are often both logistical and communication challenges. People entering into these relationships often have adopted a value system that values honesty, self-knowledge, integrity, and love over jealousy (Klesse, 2014).

Relationships are complex and dynamic. If a person wants to have close relationships, there are ways to nurture and care for others that may be more successful than others. However, few people experience a life without some heartache and disappointment. Whether you remain single, live with someone, or get married (where the law allows), the need to belong will be a motivating force for you to find others to care for and who will care about you.

"Go after her...don't sit there and wait for her to call, go after her because that's what you should do if you love someone, don't wait for them to give you a sign cause it might never come, don't let people happen to you, ... There are people I might have loved had they gotten on the airplane or run down the street after me or called me up drunk at four in the morning because they need to tell me right now ... be with her in meaningful ways because that is beautiful and that is generous and that is what loving someone is, that is raw and that is unguarded, and that is all that is worth anything, really."

– Harvey Milk

Aggression

10

Aggression: Definitions and Considerations

In social psychology aggression indicates that there must be an intent to harm another person (Anderson & Bushman, 2002). However, this definition seems to be limiting some behaviors that we refer to as aggressive. Micro-aggressions are not necessarily carried out with the intent to harm, but nevertheless cause harm. Most of the research in this chap-

Image © PathDoc, 2014. Used under license from Shutterstock, Inc.

ter aligns with the definition of aggression that indicates there must be intent to harm another person, but there are a number of dimensions worth consideration. Also, be mindful of how you think of aggression. Aggression as defined here seems negative, but certain types of behaviors that we might consider aggressive are actually viewed positively. An aggressive defense of someone may even be viewed as heroic. Therefore, we must think critically about when this definition fits and when it is too restrictive (or not narrow enough). See the aggression worksheet at the end of the chapter.

PROSOCIAL VS. ANTISOCIAL

From the definition above, it is clear that aggression is antisocial. However, it is likely that some aggression is prosocial. Prosocial aggression might include a soldier killing an enemy to defend a border

Image © shalunts, 2014. Used under license from Shutterstock, Inc.

Image © Ammentorp Photography, 2014. Used under license from Shutterstock, Inc.

or a person who hurts someone in self-defense or to save others. Prosocial aggression might also include police officers, football players, doctors, personal trainers, or others who behave aggressively in order to help. A police officer who aggressively wrestles a gun wielder to the ground is likely engaged in a prosocial act often with some intent to subdue even if the intent is not to harm. The same action if the gun wielder wrestled the officer to the ground would certainly be considered an act of aggression. Doctors who hold down patients to give painful inoculations are doing so with an attempt to provide care. Personal trainers can yell and push people to work harder but the intent is certainly to make them healthier, not to cause harm. While most of the research focuses on behavior, it is clear that intent plays a role in how we understand a particular action. Antisocial aggression is not socially sanctioned aggression and often violates some rule of law or social norm. Antisocial aggression includes everything from a fistfight to homicide.

PHYSICAL VS. VERBAL

Physical aggression can be easily understood as physical assaults with or without weapons. This may also include sexual assault which might not involve a violent altercation but nevertheless is a physically aggressive act. Verbal aggression can be characterized as an act in which others use the volume of their voice to express anger or cause harm to another person (being yelled or screamed at is often unpleasant). Verbal aggression can also refer to the content of one's speech intending to cause harm through insults, lies, or reputation assassination.

INTENTIONAL VS. UNINTENTIONAL

The definition that began the chapter focuses on the need for aggression to be intentional. However, we often experience the actions of others as harmful and aggressive even when they were unintentional. We may view an unintentional act dif-

Image © miker, 2014. Used under license from Shutterstock, Inc.

Image © Robert Nyholm, 2014. Used under license from Shutterstock, Inc.

ferently by changing how we view the person who committed the act, but this does not mean the harm is mitigated by a lack of intent. Consider a hockey or football player who plays aggressively and in doing so injures another player, perhaps so severely that he is carried off the field on a stretcher. Was this aggression? It was intentional in act and unintentional in consequence. The intent was certainly to tackle, block, or aggress against the competitor, but the degree of harm and the consequence of the aggression were likely not intentional.

On March 20, 2014, a 14-year-old male shot Angel Rojas while they were both riding a city bus in New York City (Sanchez & Assefa, 2014). The teen did not intend to shoot Rojas, but he did intend to shoot a rival gang member. Was this aggression? Was the act intentional? Did it cause harm? Does it matter that the person harmed was not the intended target?

MICRO-AGGRESSIONS. Sue and colleagues (2007) introduced a taxonomy of micro-aggressions that include micro-insults and micro-invalidations. Typically the person who is engaging in the micro-aggressions is not doing so intentionally, but nevertheless there is harm caused. However, rather than being an accident for which a person might readily apologize, people who are confronted about these micro-aggressions often defend their action by saying that because there is no intent to harm, the harm itself must not be real. Often the micro-insult (e.g., complimenting a black student by

noting he is surprisingly articulate) reveals a stereotypic expectation and surprise that the stereotype is not true, which is itself harmful. Micro-invalidations occur when people adopt a color-blind perspective that erases difference which in and of itself makes difference a negative, and at the same time erases experiences that are rooted in difference. Experiences need to be validated and can only be fully acknowledged when difference is allowed to be part of the conversation. A common nonverbal micro-aggression experienced by black people occurs when a cashier puts change or a credit card back on the counter rather than directly in the shopper's hand (Sue et al., 2008). Another example from the same study involves a white woman changing seats and sitting further away from a black woman (the participant) who reports it's not clear whether the woman was moving to be away from her or moving for some other reason.

SEXIST LANGUAGE. Another form of micro-aggression occurs when people use generic masculine pronouns (e.g., "guys") to refer to a mixed-sex group of people. If you are a person who uses this language, you may already be feeling defensive and thinking that it does not hurt anyone and you do not mean any harm. If you are a woman you may even believe that if you are not offended then in fact women as a whole are not offended. However, generic masculine language has real consequences. The pronoun *he* when used as a generic intended to include both male and females brings to mind far more male images (Gastil, 1990; Hamilton,

Just one of the "guys"?

1988). Miller and Swift (1976) provide an explanation of a study in which college students were asked to select pictures to be used in a sociology textbook. When chapters were titled using masculine generics ("Social Man" or "Political Man") students selected illustrations and photos of men and rarely chose any depictions of women. Changing the titles to ("Society" or "Political Behavior") led to a more equitable section of images. If women are not explicitly included linguistically, even when gender-neutral language is used, most people often assume that men are being discussed (Hyde, 1984).

Perhaps the harm is clearer if we discuss how female labels are used to demean men. Coaches (mostly male) of male sports teams are known for referring to their male players as "girls" or "ladies" (or female genitals) as a way to imply they are not in fact performing very well or working hard enough. Is this type of name-calling considered aggressive because it renders maleness invisible and devalues females? If your male child were to go to school every day and be bullied by someone who called him a "girl" or feminized his name, would that be aggression or not? In this case it's intentional and harmful. We return to the question, does it have to be intentional to be considered aggressive?

HUMAN VS. ANIMAL

The definition provided here focuses on intent to harm another person. This probably feels particularly challenging. Anyone who has seen someone abuse a pet probably sees this as aggressive behavior. It would be hard not to see cruelty to animals as acts of aggression. Nearly all violent crime perpetrators have a history of animal cruelty. From Jeffrey Dahmer to the Boston Strangler they all tortured small animals during their childhood. While some children may harm animals unintentionally, it is often alarming when the behavior repeats itself even after an adult has explained that a person should not be cruel to animals. People do still have some sense of what creatures should

be protected from harm (cats) and which we find expendable (insects), though this too is culturally driven. Hunting and fishing on the other hand is not about curiosity, but often about food and survival. Is hunting aggressive? What about poaching or killing animals for trophies, furs, bones, tusks, rather than food? Is fishing aggressive? Once again the definition used in most research makes it clear that aggression against humans is aggression; similar behavior directed toward non-humans is more hotly debated.

Coach Bob Knight was famous for winning 902 NCAA Division I men's college basketball games and notorious for his tantrums on the court. Among many incidents that clearly meet the definition of aggression provided at the beginning of this chapter he also exhibited aggressive behavior towards objects. In 1985, he threw a chair across the court during a game—five minutes into an IU vs. Purdue game. His behavior got him ejected from the game, but would it be considered aggressive? It was not with intent to harm another human, but rather as an expression of anger. If someone throws a chair in your house, would you think that person was being aggressive?

JUSTIFIED VS. UNJUSTIFIED

"Stand your ground" laws have been at the center of debates involving self-defense. Stand your ground laws are self-defense laws that give individuals the right to use deadly force and does not require them to evade or retreat from a dangerous situation. Since 2005 when this law was enacted in Florida, the number of deaths from shootings in self-defense have increased twofold.

Trayvon Martin was not armed. He was talking on his cell phone with a friend while walking to his relatives' home in the neighborhood. Trayvon was perceived as a threat by Zimmerman. A 911 operator told Zimmerman that police were on the way and he should not pursue Trayvon. Zimmerman shot and killed Trayvon Martin in 2012. George Zimmerman argued that he shot in self-defense

Trayvon Martin's death and Zimmerman's acquittal led to public outcry from San Diego, California, to Washington, D.C.

and was concerned about Trayvon harming him. A jury acquitted Zimmerman on the basis of his lawyers' use of the "stand your ground" defense. The killing occurred in an upscale neighborhood as Trayvon was walking home from a convenience store and George Zimmerman was surveying his neighborhood as part of the neighborhood watch.

Another case also in Florida in 2012 involved Marissa Alexander who fired a warning shot in an effort to deter her abusive husband from harming her and did not in fact harm anyone. Her attorney also used the "stand your ground" defense. The jury found Marissa guilty of aggravated assault and she was sentenced to 20 years in prison because she was overzealous (Hadad, 2012).

A third case began on November 23, 2012, when Michael Dunn parked in front of a convenience store next to an SUV full of teenagers playing loud music (Yan, 2014). Dunn asked the teens to turn down their music, as he didn't care much for that "rap crap." Dunn claims that the teens threatened him and he thought he saw the barrel of a gun sticking out of the Durango and fired 10 bullets into the SUV and drove off to stay at a bed and breakfast and then later to his own home. Jordan Davis, one of the teens in the car, was fatally wounded. The police searched the vehicle but found no evidence of a gun and no evidence that any gun had been fired from the SUV. Dunn claimed self-defense and a jury found him guilty

of three counts of attempted murder which would be 60 years in prison with minimum sentences. He was not convicted for the murder of Jordan Davis.

Even when we have laws that indicate that some types of violence might be justified, it is clear that what people view as justification for aggression can vary widely. Who was justified? Was this self-defense? Is an argument over loud music sufficient reason? An abusive husband does not present a real threat? When we consider acts of aggression that we think of as justified we often think quite differently about the aggressor and the consequences. In these cases we make external attributions for aggressive behavior (the situation made the aggressor act). When we feel that aggression is not justified we make internal attributions (the person is innately aggressive).

It is likely that you know the race of the individuals in the cases above and there is a great deal of debate about whether race played a role. Research on prejudice and discrimination make it clear that racism does exist and that subtle and implicit bias can have a real impact on our perceptions of the behavior of others.

In 2009, Oscar Grant III was fatally shot point blank in the back by a police officer Johannes Mehserle while handcuffed and seated on the ground. The whole event was captured on video via cell phone cameras of other passengers in the subway station. The video makes it clear that Grant presented no clear threat though Mehserle indicated he saw him reach towards his waistband. The officer reported that he did not intend to pull his handgun and thought he had only reached for his taser, not realizing his error until Grant says, "You shot me!" Mehserle was found guilty of involuntary manslaughter and sentenced to two years in prison. The film *Fruitvale Station* provides a look at the events that unfolded that fateful New Year's Day.

Would Mehserle acted similarly if Grant had been white? Would Grant have even been pulled off the train and handcuffed if he were white? It is hard to discount racial stereotypes as a factor in these acts of aggression, though it is clear that some people will try to do so. Is aggression against some people seen as more justified than against others? Are we more upset when a child is assaulted than an adult? Are we equally upset by sexual assault of a woman as we are by the sexual assault of a man? Do people have different reactions to learning that a gay man was raped than to hearing that a heterosexual man was raped? How is victim blame tied into perceptions of whether an assault was justified? These are just a few of the questions that remain to be answered, but are certainly worthy of consideration. What are your thoughts?

THOUGHTS VS. BEHAVIORS

Behaviors are more easily categorized as aggressive, but aggressive thoughts seem to be harder to pin down. The definition of aggression used by most social psychologists focuses on behaviors or acts of aggression. Yet, we have a legal system that punishes premeditation of a crime more severely than an aggressive act carried out without forethought. We seem to believe that having the aggressive thoughts beforehand make the act itself worthy of a harsher punishment.

Anderson and Dill (2000) found that playing violent video games increased both aggressive thoughts and feelings. Violent video games also increased aggressive behavior, but only for men who also had aggressive personalities. Aggressive thinking was measured by asking participants to read aloud words associated with aggression, anxiety, escape, or control words. Participant reaction times were measured and those who had just played a violent video game were quicker (had shorter reaction times) at reading aloud words associated with aggression compared to other words.

HOSTILE VS. INSTRUMENTAL

Hostile and instrumental aggression are two types of aggression that provide important distinctions based on motives. Hostile or emotional aggression stems from anger. Someone who is angry lashes out at another person in fury. Instrumental aggression is an aggressive act undertaken in order to achieve some goal. Certainly wars and assassinations are good examples of instrumental aggres-

How do these experiences impact our daily lives and interpretation of real-world events?

Image © Barone Firenze, 2014. Used under license from Shutterstock, Inc.

Image © Nebojsa Bobic, 2014. Used under license from Shutterstock, Inc.

sion, where violence is used as a means to an end. However, there are other examples we encounter in our everyday lives. Two toddlers are playing with some toys relatively close to one another. One of them decides he would like to have the toy the other child is holding. Reaching for the toy is not effective; crying does not seem to convince the holder of the desired toy to hand it over. It is with instrumental and toddler-like aggression that he takes a toy and hits the other child on the head with it. As the child reaches for her head and eyes fill with tears the desired toy falls to the floor and it is quickly snatched up by the aggressor. Bobby Knight's chair throwing incident is likely to be more hostile than instrumental. One assumes the coach was not throwing the chair to get evicted from the game, though that was certainly the consequence of his actions.

DIRECT VS. INDIRECT

Aggression among young men tends to be rather direct. Whether hostile or instrumental the two people in the conflict are likely to square off and have a verbal or physical altercation of some sort. Women are more likely to engage in indirect forms of aggression by spreading rumors, ruining reputations, destroying or defacing property, social ostracism, or in other ways excluding the target of aggression. Lagerspetz, Bjokqvist, and Peltonen (1988) found that adolescent girls were more like-

ly to use indirect aggression and boys more direct aggression. The tighter social networks among girls may make indirect aggression more effective than it would be for boys. However, this does not mean that women do not engage in direct physical aggression nor that men do not engage indirectly.

PHYSICAL VS. RELATIONAL AGGRESSION. Relational aggression is often indirect and intended to cause harm to someone by disrupting interpersonal relationships, breaking up friendships or romantic relationships either overtly or covertly (Archer & Coyne, 2005). Indirect aggression implies the aggression occurs "behind the back" of the target and often is social or relational aggression. Social or relational aggression is carried out by engaging in communication that is harmful to the target's relationships with others, reputation, or social standing. In some cases, social aggression can also be direct in which people say mean things directly to another person with an intent to create psychological harm.

Men are much more likely than women to engage in physical acts of aggression (Anderson & Bushman, 2002). Ostrov and Keating (2004) found that boys engaged in far more acts of physical aggression than girls and the reverse was true for relational aggression. However, the number of women who commit physically aggressive acts is on the rise, though the gender difference remains (Meyer & Oberman, 2001). These reported sex

How do these two types of aggression lead to different feelings for the targets of this aggression?

differences are moderated by a number of factors. First, men are more often likely to engage in spontaneous aggression than women, but women and men are equally alike to respond aggressively when provoked (Anderson & Bushman, 2002; Archer, 2004; Brody, 1997). Women and men may also respond similarly to strangers, but women are less likely to aggress against someone they have met (Carlo et al., 1999).

VIOLENCE IN INTIMATE RELATIONSHIPS. Intimate relationships can also involve aggression. In some cases, this type of violence is different than the types of aggression that we see in other populations or relationships. There a few general considerations. First, we spend a great deal of time interacting with our intimates (family, partners, and friends). If a person is generally aggressive and we spend most of our time around this person, chances are we will at some point be exposed to that aggression. Second, we may have learned in our family of origin how to engage in conflict and if our parents or other adults modeled violence as a way to respond in cases of conflict, we may have learned that violent arguments are just part of being in a relationship. Finally, it is important to understand the breadth of domestic violence which includes sexual assault, marital rape, and physical assault of partners and child abuse. Domestic violence over the years has become an issue in which we primarily think of battered women, rather than the broad range of people who may be experiencing intimate partner violence. The following sections explain some of the ways in which different types of relationships and aggressors engage in intimate partner violence.

PATRIARCHAL TERRORISM

Patriarchal terrorism is likely to be the sort of domestic violence that comes to mind when you first think of domestic violence. This type of violence is rooted in husbands being head of the household and wives being subservient. There is often an endorsement of traditional gender roles and men reporting they have a right to control their partners.

This often involves economic restriction (giving women an allowance and preventing her earning power), coercion, intimidation, and isolation from friends and family and controlling her behavior (Johnson, 1995). For couples in this violent situation, male batterers assault their wives on average 65 times each year. These violent altercations are exacerbated when couples are in distress (e.g., economic hardship). Violence against women by intimate partners is highest during pregnancy when paternity uncertainty may also be most prevalent (Campbell, Oliver, & Bullock, 1991; Goodwin, 2000; Waalen et al., 2000).

Not all abusive men are the same. Gottman et al. (1995) identified two types of offenders by looking at violent behavior within the relationship and physiological markers during marital discord. After establishing a baseline heart rate and then having couples engage in a conflict interaction in a lab setting two patterns of physiological response emerged (Jacobson & Gottman, 1998). One type was referred to as the pitbull type; these men had moderate levels of violence within their relationships and their heart rate increased as they became more verbally aggressive during the marital conflict interaction. The second type of men were labeled cobras. For these men their heart rate actually decreased during conflict, although violence levels tended to be much higher and severe. They were also more likely to use violence outside of the relationship, be dependent on substances, and engaged in both emotional and physical abuse. The divorce rate for pitbull batterers was 27% and for cobras 0%. Wives of cobras are less likely to leave their husbands due to fear and were more likely to be depressed. Wives of pitbull batterers were angrier and this may lead them to leave the relationships.

SITUATIONAL COUPLE VIOLENCE AND INTIMATE TERRORISTS

In contrast to patriarchal terrorism, situational couple violence is often mutual within the couple. The rate of this violence is lower with couples reporting violent interactions six times a year and

Image © Photographee.eu, 2014. Used under license from Shutterstock, Inc.

Image © wavebreakmedia, 2014. Used under license from Shutterstock, Inc.

When you think about domestic violence, are these the images that come to mind?

involving less severe forms of violence than we see with patriarchal terrorists. Situational couple violence is typically specific to a particular conflict and does not necessarily have a component of trying to gain control over the partner. Over half of all couples experiencing violence in their relationship are experiencing bidirectional violence (both partners are violent toward one another) (Langhinirichsen-Rohling et al., 2012; Straus, in press; Straus & Michel-Smith, 2013).

Archer (2000) found that within heterosexual couples women were more likely to use physical aggression and to do so more frequently. However, men were more likely to inflict injury on their partner than women. One explanation forwarded is that the norm that men should not hit women, but no converse norm deters men from aggressing against their partners, while not restricting women's violence against their male partners. While the impact of partner violence has mostly focused on female victims, men account for a third of deaths related to partner violence (Catalano, 2006). Researchers who study violence within families have proposed that domestic violence perpetrated by women is a social problem that should be addressed (Strauss, 1993).

Straus and Gozjolko (2014) analyzed data from 13,877 participants from 68 universities in 32 nations who were all in dating relationships and found that men and women were equally likely to be considered "intimate terrorists." Intimate terrorists are individuals who use violence to exert control over one's partner. Of all couples about 27% of them reported some form of intimate terrorism. The results indicate that half of all couples engaged in situational mutual violence, and about 14% of couples engaged in mutual intimate terrorism. This mutual sort of terrorism resulted in the highest rate of injuries. Males were twice as likely as females to indicate they were "pure-victims" meaning that their partners were violent and they were not.

What do women say about their reasons to aggress? Straus (1999) provided a list of rationalizations that women gave for why they would be violent toward their male partners. First, there is a norm that implies it is okay for a woman to slap a man who makes an advance, media examples abound, and surveys suggest that many people believe it is okay for a wife to slap her husband. Second, because women are smaller they believe they are not hurting the men they aggress against. Women attempt to use violence to make men pay attention to relationship conflict. Women may routinely use corporal punishment with children and hitting becomes a way to encourage correct or appropriate behavior. Women do not fear their partners will call police and if the male partner does call the police it is unlikely that she will be arrested.

Kellerman and Mercy (1992) also reported that of over 215,000 homicides studied 77% of them involved male victims with only 23% involving female victims. However, when women were killed it was much more likely that they would be killed by their husband or an intimate acquaintance. Further, when women committed the 14.7% of homicides included in the study 60% of these homicides involved killing a spouse, intimate acquaintance, or family member.

LGBT COUPLES

Much of the work on domestic violence has focused on heterosexual intimate violence. Clearly both men and women, regardless of sexual orientation, are exposed to similar socialization over the course of their lives and there is little reason to imagine that domestic violence would somehow be eliminated when a couple involved people who did not identify as heterosexual, are not cisgender, or even endorsing the binary terms gender and sex.

LGBT people general are certainly subject to hate crime, but in this section the focus will be on intimate partner violence and hate crimes will be covered later in the chapter. Physical violence between same-sex couples occurs at about the same rate as in heterosexual couples (Rohrbaugh, 2006). However, rates of domestic violence often change as relationships become more committed or over the long term begin to deteriorate. Brand and Kidd (1986) found that heterosexual college students (19–20%) reported higher rates of physical abuse and sexual assault in dating relationships compared to lesbian college students (0.05%), but once in committed relationships the rates were quite similar between the two groups (25–27%). Findings from Finnernan and Stephenson (2013) indicate that men who have sex with men (not necessarily gay men) who reported more internalized homophobia were more likely to report being violent toward male partners.

Many services related to helping individuals who are in relationships with violent or abusive partners are designed to serve the needs of heterosexual women. Women's shelters may not allow men (who may be partners of the women who are abused), but may also not provide sufficient safety for lesbian women. Men's shelters are difficult to find. The National Coalition of Anti-Violence Programs (2012) reported that few LGBTQ (Lesbian, Gay, Bisexual, Trans*, Queer) people have access to services (e.g., police, orders of protection, shelters). People of color made up a disproportionate number of intimate partner violence homicide victims (62%). Transgender survivors were more likely to face threats and intimidation within their intimate relationships and more likely to be arrested during police intervention even when they were not the abuser (NCAVP, 2012). Survivors were more likely to identify as gay men (41.7%) than lesbian (24.5%) or having other identities. The majority of survivors were youth, people of color, and transgender women. Gay men were significantly more likely to report physical injuries as a result of intimate partner violence.

There are other differences between how women in heterosexual relationships and women in lesbian relationships experience intimate partner violence. Lesbian women who are abused by partners tend to fight back and meet violence with violence (Bethea, Rexrode, Ruffo, & Washington, 2000; Marrujo & Kreger, 1996; Renzetti, 1992; Rohrbaugh, 2006). Even though there is a self-defense motive in these same-sex relationships, responders may view the situation as one of mutual batterers and the abuser and victim are treated equally by law enforcement (e.g., arrested, jailed, charged). Stereotypes about heterosexual couples and traditional gender roles make this less likely when male partners abuse female partners and the reverse is the case when female partners are abusive (males still considered to be the perpetrator of abuse). Batterers in same-sex and heterosexual relationships tend to share many characteristics (e.g., jealousy, history of mental illness, abuse in their family of origin).

Though increasingly attitudes towards gay and lesbian individuals are more positive, there are still unique threats within lesbian and gay male relationships. For those individuals who have not come out to loved ones, coworkers, or friends, the threat of being "outed" as gay or lesbian to others can be used by abusive partners as a threat that could result in loss of job, social support, or family connections (Rohrbaugh, 2006). This is a unique factor that does not impact heterosexual cisgender individuals.

Anyone who hopes to practice in the helping professions or even be someone who stands up to violence needs to have a deep understanding of the ways in which demographics and identities may impact perceptions of intimate partner violence. There are no benefits to this type of aggression, even for the abuser. Social psychologists continue to conduct research to shed light on this persistent problem in our society.

Anger and Hostility

Anger is the emotion most closely linked to aggressive behavior. Anger is more clearly tied to hostile aggression and less so to instrumental aggression. In addition to anger, people may have a hostile attribution bias in which behaviors of others are more likely to be attributed to hostile intentions (Epps & Kendall, 1995). People who have a hostile perception bias are more likely to perceive interactions as generally more hostile (Dill et al., 1997). Finally hostile expectation bias leads people to not only perceive actions of others as hostile, but to have expectations that others are going to behave aggressively in a variety of situations. People who have these biases do not believe that the actions of others could possibly be unintentional or that people may inadvertently hurt others. These biases lead people to presume that acts are both aggressive and include the intent to harm.

FRUSTRATION-AGGRESSION HYPOTHESIS

The classic scene in the movie *Office Space* when the three main characters take the fax machine into a field and stomp and bash the machine is one example of how frustration leads to aggression. However, the aggression against an inanimate object would not in fact meet the definition presented at the beginning of the chapter, but it's likely that you think taking a baseball bat to a fax machine is aggressive.

Image © Cartoonresource, 2014. Used under license from Shutterstock, Inc.

"Don't anyone say, 'That's the fax, Jack.'"

The frustration-aggression hypothesis posits that aggressive behavior "always" occurs because people are frustrated and that frustration "always" leads to aggression (Dollard et al., 1939). Road rage is a good example of frustration-aggression theory. It is typically that other drivers or traffic is preventing the achievement of a goal. The goal being arriving at your destination quickly. However, there are other situations in which the theory does not hold. Miller (1941) indicated that sometimes frustration does not actually result in aggression and people can have a variety of nonaggressive responses. In college, one of my study partners for statistics would often be very frustrated because he could not understand the material. Rather than aggress, he just dropped the course and changed his major so as not to have to experience repeated frustration. However, quitting is not always an option, and Miller (1941) also made it clear that repeated frustration would increase the chances that someone would respond aggressively.

> "Everyone gets frustrated and aggressive, and I'd sooner take my aggression out on a guitar than on a person."
>
> --*Paul Weller*

Berkowitz (1990, 1993) proposed a revision to the theory and proposed a cognitive neoassociationistic theory of aggression (also called the negative affect hypothesis). First, hostile aggression may well fit with the frustration-aggression hypothesis, but instrumental aggression does not necessarily involve frustration prior to aggression. If you are attuned to the use of the word "always," you can easily find the concerns social psychologists have about this theory. Sometimes people engage in aggression without being frustrated first. Other negative emotions besides anger may also set the stage for aggression (e.g., distress, upset) (Berkowitz 1989). Even being in pain can lead a person to aggress. When someone hurts you physically (even if unintentionally) it is likely that your first reaction is to aggress against the person causing pain. This may be one reason why dentists, nurses, and doctors warn you when something is going to hurt, so that you do not lash out at them aggressively. If you know something is going to hurt you may mentally prepare and inhibit an aggressive response, but if someone hurts you unexpectedly it may be difficult to inhibit your aggression.

Aggression does not always reduce frustration. Bullies often aggress without necessarily being frustrated, or at least not by the targets of their aggression. In addition, victims of bullying are not likely to have done anything to interfere with a bully's goal attainment. Frustration may sometimes lead to aggression, but what other factors might increase aggression?

What Factors Increase Aggression?

Aggression and violence are often framed as the source of social problems and there is a great deal of attention focused on how we might decrease aggression that is harming others. Alcohol, guns and weapons, hate crime, media exposure, and even the weather have been explored as possible factors that might influence aggression.

ALCOHOL MYOPIA

Drinking alcohol narrows a person's ability to consider situational factors that may inhibit aggressive (or other) behaviors (Steele & Josephs, 1990). Alcohol myopia can often decrease our ability to attend to our situations. People are more likely to make person attributions and less likely to make situational attributions when they are under the influence of alcohol. Bartholow and Heinz (2006) found that alcohol consumption was linked to an increase in the hostile perception bias. Imagine you are on a crowded dance floor (not a mosh pit) and a nearby dancer elbows you. If you have not been drinking you may think about how crowded it is. You may notice that the reason you were elbowed had to do with bad dance moves or an attempt to help someone who was falling. If you have been drinking, you may not take into account anything other than someone has elbowed you, immediately assume the act was hostile and intentional, and prepare to aggress against the owner of the intrusive elbow.

Giancola et al. (2010) suggest that establishments that serve alcohol might implement "fight alarms" each time there is an incident of physical aggression. This might involve turning on the lights, turning off the music, and making announcements indicating that the police would be called. Even phrases such as, "Drink, Fight, Go to Jail" might be printed on menus, staff uniforms, or signs to make it clear that there are consequences to aggression.

Gallagher and colleagues (2014) provided male participants between the ages of 21 and 35 either alcoholic or nonalcoholic beverages and then provoked them with mild electric shocks and a verbal insult delivered by a fictitious male opponent. Participants also completed a measure of thought suppression that asked them the extent to which they attempted to suppress thoughts. Participants were given the opportunity to deliver electric shocks to the male opponent. Intoxicated participants delivered higher levels of shock to the opponent if they were low in thought suppression; those who were thought suppressors did not show increases in aggression due to alcohol. Individuals who are active thought suppressors may be better able to suppress hostile thoughts even when intoxicated. However, thought suppression also involves cognitive energy and when those energy stores are depleted aggression may well return.

WEAPONS EFFECT

Men's testosterone levels increase after handling a gun. As testosterone levels rise, men become more aggressive toward others (Klinesmith et al., 2006). Early research by Berkowitz and LePage (1967) had men participate in an experiment and were told that they would be meeting another student and take turns writing down ideas for a publicity campaign. The other student then provided feedback on the men's ideas. The feedback would involve receiving one electrical shock for a good idea and up to ten shocks if the idea was very bad. Participants were randomly assigned to receive either one shock or seven shocks. Then participants were given the opportunity to retaliate and provide feedback to the partner via electric shock. Participants went to a control room to deliver the shocks. In the control room they would see either an empty table, badminton rackets, or a 12-gauge shotgun. After reading the partner's idea (which was always the same), shocks were delivered.

The findings were congruent with cognitive-neo-association theory. The unpleasant situation of receiving seven shocks increased negative feelings and when there was also a gun on the table, participants delivered six shocks to their partner. When there was no gun on the table and the participant had received seven shocks, they delivered only four or five shocks. Those who were in the room with the shotgun and had only received one shock were likely to deliver two or three shocks (the same number as when there was no gun present). Weapons do not in and of themselves increase aggressive responding. Rather the pairing of annoyance or angry feelings and weapons increases aggressive responses.

PROVOCATION

Anger is not the only cause of anger. Provocation of many sorts might lead to aggression. Having one's pride wounded might be more embarrassing or humiliating, but it still may provoke aggression. Pain can also cause direct aggression without even an opportunity to think about anger. Physiological arousal can also increase chances of aggression without necessarily increasing anger.

WOUNDED PRIDE AND NARCISSISM. People who are high in narcissism tend to respond with high levels of aggression when their egos are threatened. Prisoners who are violent tend to have higher narcissism scores (Bushman & Baumeister, 1998). Brown (1968) had male participants play a competitive game in which the participant was exploited by the confederate. Audience reponses that were positive did not lead to revenge, but if the audience told the participant he was a sucker he was more inclined to respond vengefully.

AROUSAL. Zillmann and colleagues (1972) assigned participants to exercise on a stationary bike or not to engage in exercise. Then participants were either insulted by a confederate or not insulted. At the end of the experiment participants were given an opportunity to deliver an electrical shock to the confederate. Insulted participants gave higher levels of shock to the confederate than those who were not insulted. This is congruent with anger leading to aggression. However, participants who exercised first and were then insulted and given the opportunity to deliver shocks to the confederate selected higher levels of shock for the confederate. In this case, anger increased aggressive responding, but exercise increased arousal and led to even higher levels of aggression.

Do tempers flare as temperatures climb? Yes, in part because heat also increases arousal and is paired with discomfort. The relationship between heat and aggression is not linear. As heat rises aggression increases, but only up to a certain point and then aggression drops off as heat becomes oppressive and makes people lethargic (Baron, 1972; Cohn & Rotton, 1997). Heat increases both arousal and anger and this changes not only initial actions, but also increases retaliation against the other team. Anderson and Bushman (2002) indicate that heat increases aggression through influencing affect, arousal, and cognition. Heat may

predispose people to have a hostile perception bias or hostile expectation bias in which ambiguous behaviors are more likely to be interpreted as aggressive when it is hot rather than when temperatures are cooler.

A 2011 study by Larrick and colleagues examined data from over 4.5 million batter-pitcher match ups and found that pitchers were more likely to hit batters with errant pitches on hot days. This was not just a factor of more errant pitches on hot days, but rather that batters were more likely to be hit by wayward pitches. Further, heat also increased the chances that pitchers would hit the batter if there had been a previous pitch from the other team that had hit a teammate.

MEDIA

Media violence has consistently been linked to aggressive behavior (Bushman & Anderson 2002). Huesmann and colleagues (2003) used a longitudinal study to demonstrate that childhood exposure to media violence predicted aggressive behavior in young adults. Further identification with aggressive characters and the perceived realism of TV violence was also predictive of later aggression. Britto and Noga-Styron (2014) found that support for capital punishment was related to media exposure and in particular radio and television including police and crime drama shows increased support, while newspaper and internet coverage was not related to an increase in support. Therefore, it is important to understand how particular types of media might have different impacts on perceptions of aggression.

TV, MOVIES, AND MUSIC. Early research indicated that repeated exposure to violence in film and television led viewers to become desensitized to violence (Lazarus, 1962). In 1972, Cline and colleagues as part of an NIH-funded project measured physiological arousal while boys watched the 1949 film *The Champion* which depicts a boxing champ who fights his way to the top of the game, while his personal life suffers. Children who had a history of watching a great deal of television seemed desensitized and showed low levels of arousal compared to those children who had a history of watching relatively less television.

Songs with violent lyrics also increased the accessibility of aggressive words on a reaction time task (Anderson, Carnagey, & Eubanks, 2003). In order to control for the music and the possibility that some songs increase arousal, songs were selected from the same artist and same style to compare directly based on lyrics whether this increased the accessibility of aggressive constructs.

VIOLENT VIDEO GAMES FPS. If you ask people who play video games if violent video games increase aggression, they are likely to tell you that is simply not true. However, research seems to show exactly the opposite trend. Bartholow and Anderson (2002) randomly assigned participants to play *Mortal Kombat* or *PGA Tournament Golf* for 10 minutes. They then competed with a confederate on a reaction time task that allowed for provocation and retaliation. After playing *Mortal Kombat* participants were far more likely to respond aggressively toward the confederate than after playing *PGA Tournament Golf*. This was true for both men and women, though the effect was larger for men.

Greitemeyer (2014a) posits that people who play violent video games may actually have a biased perception about aggression which leads them to see their own aggressive behaviors in real life as mild or harmless compared to the sorts of in-game aggressive acts they (or their characters) carry out. Participants in this study were randomly assigned to play *Wolfenstein* or *Tetris* for 15 minutes. They were then asked to complete a behavior inventory and asked to rate how aggressive they believe each behavior was when they do it ("I shove or push others") and when someone else does the behavior (Someone shoves or pushes others"). People who played *Wolfenstein* rated the behaviors as less aggressive when they did them compared to those who played *Tetris* or the same behaviors carried out by someone else.

Playing violent video games also leads to increases in ethnocentric beliefs and aggression against out-group members (Greitmeyer, 2014b). In one study participants played *Call of Duty 2* which is an FPS (First Person Shooter) game or *Flipper* (a pinball game). Results demonstrate that after 15 minutes of game play participants were told they would compete with an opponent on a reaction time task. They were then told that the participant was born in Austria (where all the participants were from) or in Serbia (representing an out-group). After each trial of the reaction time task participants were allowed to set a loud and uncomfortable white noise burst as "punishment" to the opponent (or no noise at all). Whomever lost the trial was blasted with the punishment set by the opponent. When the participants had played *Flipper* they chose relatively low punishing

How might anonymity also influence willingness to engage in violence during video games? What if characters actually looked like the individuals playing the game?

noises for their in-group and out-group opponent. However, when they played *Call of Duty 2* they were more likely to choose high levels and durations of noise bursts for the out-group, but not the in-group opponent.

Bushman and Anderson (2002) randomly assigned participants to play either a violent video game (*Carmageddon, Duke Nukem, Mortal Kombat, Future Cop*) or a nonviolent video game (*Glider Pro, 3D Pinball, Austin Powers, Tetra Madness*). Participants were then asked to read brief vignettes about an interpersonal interaction and complete a sentence that would determine how the interaction might proceed. Playing the violent video game led participants to report that the characters in the interaction would be more likely to have hostile feelings and thoughts and to behave aggressively. Violent video games may increase hostile expectation bias.

PORNOGRAPHY. Barker (2014) summarizes the psychological research on pornography and demonstrates that violent pornography does increase aggression (Malamuth & Donnerstein, 2000), but nudity or nonviolent pornography do not necessarily do so. However, this work has predominantly taken place in the laboratory and does not take into account the impact of internet accessibility to pornography and the role of desensitization. Indeed those who conducted the early psychological research used by the Meese Commission to define obscenity have continued to point to the fact that it was not sexuality within pornography that was problematic, but rather the violence paired with sexuality that increased aggression (Donnerstein & Linz, 1986).

Lambert and colleagues (2012) found that the more pornographic websites persons had visited the more likely they were to physically assault friends and romantic partners. These participants were also more likely to be aggressive toward a confederate and to stick a doll representing their partner with stick pins. Most sexual offenders watch pornography and of 155 men arrested for viewing child pornography, 85% of them admitted they had molested a minor (Bourke & Hernandez, 2009). On the other hand sex offenders do not seem to have as much exposure to pornography as other kinds of offenders (Allen et al., 1999). However, when sex offenders do watch pornography they show a greater response to violent pornography.

Donnerstein (1980) had participants watch either a neutral film, an erotic film, or an aggressive erotic film which involved rape. Participants were then asked to engage in a learning experiment and teach a confederate a list of nonsense syllables by delivering electric shocks to either a male or female confederate. Those watching the aggressive erotic film increased the amount of shock they delivered but only toward female targets. Lambert and others (2012) asked participants to give up either pornography or their favorite food for a month. Those who were randomly assigned to give up pornography were less aggressive after a month than those who had avoided their favorite food. In sum, the impact of pornography is related to objectification of women, but more broadly to increases in aggression when violence is sexualized.

Who Is Aggressive?

CULTURE OF HONOR

The culture of honor was investigated by Nisbett and Cohen (1996) who recognized that there was a cultural difference between the U.S. South and North. The South has had a greater number of violent activities including lynchings, sniper attacks, and homicides since the 18th century (Nisbett & Cohen, 1996). The southern states are more likely to support war, capital punishment, and corporal punishment of children (Cohen, 1996). Nisbett and Cohen (1996) propose that the raising of animals rather than growing of crops led to this higher rate of violence. It is unlikely someone can steal your crops in the middle of the night, but reasonably likely that your entire herd could be herded to another ranch. Your only choice to recover your loss would be to use violence to locate and reclaim your livestock. If people were able to develop a reputation based on honor and defense of that honor with violence, thieves may be more likely to leave your herd alone. The South is not alone in this culture; other areas where herding is a predominant occupation also develop this type of culture.

Nisbett and Cohen (1996) examined the homicide records and found that in the South there were more homicides that were argument-related. A culture of honor does not allow for senseless violence, but rather killing in defense of one's honor. Rural areas in the North where the same type of land is used to grow crops do not have as many argument-related murders. In a survey, southerners were more likely to endorse murder for trespass, defense of family, and relate the act to defense of honor. For example, 47% of southerners believed that shooting a person who sexually assaulted your 16-year-old daughter was justified compared to 23% of northerners.

One clever experiment invited white male students to the lab to participate in a study examining blood sugar levels and task performance. Upon arrival participants were instructed to walk over and get a questionnaire to complete off a table. However, there was a male confederate posing as a research assistant digging through a file drawer and blocking the path to the table. The confederate closes the drawer but is clearly frustrated by the interruption. When the participant picks up the questionnaire and attempts to return to the other side of the room, the confederate again has to close the drawer and let the participant pass. For half of the participants the confederate bumps into the participants' shoulder and says, "Asshole!" as the participant walks by. The confederate immediately goes into a room labeled photo lab and locks the door, preventing the participant from confronting him. For the control condition, the participants were not insulted by the confederate. Saliva samples were collected throughout the

In Oklahoma it is still possible to carry out a death sentence by fusillading, though this method has not been used since the national moratorium on the death penalty was lifted in 1976. Idaho banned execution by firing squad in July 2009; Utah in 2010 executed Ronnie Lee Gardner by firing squad (at his request), though anyone convicted and sentenced after 2004 does not have this option available in Utah. The most common method of execution in the United States is lethal injection as execution by electrocution was ruled as cruel and unusual punishment by many states. There are six states that still allow electrocution (Alabama, Florida, South Carolina, Kentucky, Tennessee, and Virginia)—the only places in the world where it's still possible someone could be electrocuted.

experiment to measure testosterone, though participants thought the samples would be used to measure blood sugar. The results found that participants who were from the South had an increase in testosterone after being insulted, but not so for the northerners (Cohen, 1996).

In another rendition using the same method in which participants are insulted by a confederate looking in a filing cabinet, the participants are directed to walk down a narrow hallway to a second lab room. The hallway will not easily allow two people to pass without one person yielding to another. A second confederate who played on the offensive line of a college football team and stood 6'3" tall and weight around 250 walks toward the participant. The confederate's instructions were clear, he was not to yield to the participant. The experimenters measured how far away the confederate was when the participant finally yielded the right of way. Southern participants who were insulted did not yield until they were less than 3 feet away, but otherwise southerners were more polite and stepped aside about 9 feet from the confederate. Northerners yielded right of way between 5 and 6 feet from the confederate (Cohen, 1996).

While the culture of honor has been predominantly examined in men, female offenders also are impacted by the southern culture of honor. There may also be a link to evangelical Protestant groups as communities with more of these groups also tend to have higher rates of violence (Beyerlein & Hipp, 2005; Ellison et al., 2003; Lee & Bartkowski, 2004). Doucet and colleagues (2014) examined FBI Supplementary Homicide Reports during the 1970s and church presence and memberships at the county level. The more evangelical Protestant churches and being born in the South was associated with an increase in female perpetrated homicides.

BULLYING AND CYBERBULLYING

Bullies are people who routinely and consistently use intimidation, physical aggression, and threats against victims solely to establish dominance. Cyberbullying involves threats of physical and psychological violence via the internet including use of social media and SMS (text messages). Are bullies psychopathic narcissists or do they have low self-esteem? The results from Fanti and Henrich (2014) suggests it may be both. Narcissists often have a fragile self-esteem and are prone to grandiose self-enhancement that is often not based in reality. Further narcissism is distinct from self-esteem. Self-esteem is the regard a person has for the perceived self. Narcissism does not seem to be related necessarily to one's feelings of worth, but rather toward the need to enhance and often inflate the view of the self through exploitation of others, believing oneself to be superior. A person with high self-esteem might say they are accomplished at something, a narcissist with the same level of competence might indicate they are better than anyone else at something.

Fanti and Henrich (2014) asked adolescents to complete measures of self-esteem, narcissism, and report their experiences with bullying. Some students were clearly bullies, others were victims of bullying. A third group were bully-victims, and had been victimized but also engaged in bullying behaviors toward others. Bullies were more often boys and had higher levels of narcissism and lower self-esteem. Thus, it seems that having low self-esteem does not result in more aggression toward others, unless a person also has a narcissistic personality.

Cyberbullying may also present unique harms to victims. Prior to the internet bullies had to physically wait for a victim to enter the public sphere to directly harm. Thought indirect, relational and social aggression does not require physical co-presence. However, it was at one time possible for victims to escape the bullying they experienced by going home or finding spaces where bullies were not present. However, cell phones and social media allow bullies to use text messaging, Twitter accounts, and Facebook posts to humiliate and threaten victims day and night. Further, the reach of a bully used to be limited to a small geographic area in which both the bully and victim were known to others. Now bullying can occur on a national scale or even global scale as videos, stories, and tweets can easily go viral and be viewed by hundreds of thousands of people within a short period of time. Today's victims of bullies may find that they are harmed in the present, but that the permanence of the internet includes future harms to reputation down the road.

How has the internet and smartphones changed bullying experiences?

Decreasing Aggression

Not all aggression is inherently bad; however, there remains a variety of aggressive acts that we might want to decrease. Murder, violence, bullying, and other forms of aggression often involve intervention by institutions, law, or others. Can we reduce these types of aggression? How can we use some of the theories about why people aggress to then reduce the probability that violence is the end result?

DISTRACTION

Giancola and colleagues (2010) propose a variety of ways in which distraction can decrease cognitive focus on aggression. Aggression can often stem from anger, but distraction can reduce anger by making others focus on something besides their anger. Hostile rumination is when a person continues to entertain thoughts about hostility, seeking revenge, or continuing to think about what instigated the aggressive thoughts. Distraction can also decrease hostile rumination by refocusing thoughts on something unrelated to the desire to aggress. Self-awareness might also reduce aggression, when a person has a value system that indicates that aggression is not a socially desirable response (Mann & Ward, 2007). However, self-awareness may increase aggression if the underlying value system values or encourages aggression against someone. For example, the culture of honor and self-awareness may interact to increase the chances of aggression in response to a provocation. Finally, empathy can decrease aggression. Empathy involves taking another person's perspective. If you can understand why your provocateurs behaved the way they did, you may be less likely to respond aggressively.

Mindfulness might be one way to refocus an inebriated person's attention away from an aggressive

How does mindfulness and meditation make you feel? How does being grounded or centered change your perceptions of others?

response (Kabat-Zinn, 2006). Heppner and colleagues (2008) randomly assigned participants to one of three conditions. In one condition participants were told that their co-workers wanted to work with them. The rejection condition participants were told that their co-workers did not want to work with them on the task. The third condition involved participants engaging in a mindfulness induction exercise and then told their co-workers did not want to work with them. The mindfulness induction instructed participants to eat a raisin while deeply considering the entire process. First participants were asked to think about this as if it were their first encounter with a raisin and to think about the shape, weight, color, and texture of the raisin. To think about how the raisin felt and tasted.

BIOLOGICAL APPROACHES

Wahlund and Kristiansson (2009) found that there were a number of physiological differences between the brains of aggressors and control groups. Both structural and functional differences in the brain were found. The frontal lobes, temporal lobes, corpus callosum, and amygdala differ in psychopaths and antisocial participants compared to control group participants. For example, murderers tend to have less activity in the prefrontal cortex (Raine, Buschsbaum, & Lacasse, 1997). Violent patients tend to have lower glucose metabolism, though this was truer for those who engaged in affective or hostile aggression. Predatory violent offenders were similar to healthy controls (Raine et al., 1998). Brain differences seem to largely increase impulsivity when they are correlated with violence. However, for violent offenders who are more likely to plan crimes and show less response to empathy (psychopaths) there were other differences. Intrator and colleagues (1997) found that psychopathic patients showed increased blood flow when engaging in a semantic task that involved emotion words, indicating it took more effort for psychopaths to process emotion words. However, these brain differences in and of themselves do not guarantee people will be violent, only that there may be individual differences that predispose them to respond to situations in more impulsive or less empathic ways.

Testosterone-reducing drugs subdue aggressive tendencies in men. As men age and their testosterone levels decrease, so do their levels of violent crime (Dabbs & Morris, 1990). Korui and colleagues (1995) administered testosterone doses to a small group of normal men and doubled their doses every two weeks for six weeks. Participants were also asked to work with a confederate on a game in the lab. The participants were led to believe that the confederate was punishing them by pressing a button that reduced their cash payments. Those who were given the testosterone (rather than the control group given the placebo) were more likely to retaliate against this red button pushing confederate.

Gladue (1991) found that heterosexual and gay men reported similar levels of aggression. Overall men reported more physical and verbal aggression, as well as more impulsivity and lower tolerance for frustration. Finally, heterosexual women and lesbians were similarly aggressive, though heterosexual women were more physically aggressive than lesbians. Hormonal measures indicate that testosterone and estradiol were related to higher levels of aggression for men and negatively related to aggression in women.

CATHARSIS

Catharsis theory indicates that aggressive energy can be released through venting or "letting off steam." Once the pressure of aggressive energy is released the motive to aggress is removed. However, the research is not clearly in support of catharsis. In some cases, letting off steam or venting is similar to hostile rumination and actually increases the need to aggress. On the other hand, if catharsis is done in such a way as to make a person physically exhausted then the likelihood of aggressive behavior is decreased, because the person lacks the energy to do so (Bushman, 2002).

Consider your roommate is throwing a tantrum about loud music coming from next door and keeps threatening to go next door and confront these music lovers. You suggest your roommate go out for a run to cool down and avoid confrontation. Knowing you are taking a psychology course and therefore must know something about these things, your roommate puts on running shoes and heads out the door. Your roommate returns calm and tired. The next day the neighbors come home and you say, "I'm glad they aren't playing their music loud tonight!" Your roommate is likely to be angry all over again as you recall how disturbing the music was the night before; running did not eliminate aggressive motivations. The cognitive association between the loud music and anger is not broken because a person is physically tired. On the other hand, it's possible that while out running, thoughts moved away from the neighbor's inconsiderate volume levels and to other thoughts distracting your roommate from the earlier incident. If distraction actually occurred this may in fact decrease the chances of aggression against the neighbors.

Imagine the advice of Lee (1993) to deal with anger by punching a pillow or punching bag to vent your rage. What might this behavior do? If people are mad at someone else they might imagine that the pillow is the person they are mad at as they pummel away. However, rather than decreasing aggression it is likely that this is actually

What do you do to control your desire to aggress?

a practice round for possibly later physical aggression (Bushman, 2002).

SOCIAL LEARNING

Social learning theory would predict that aggressive responding is learned through modeling. Watching others be rewarded or punished for aggression changes our own behaviors. Social learning can also be leveraged to decrease aggressive responses. Training individuals to distract themselves or engage in mindfulness may keep them from lashing out. Even apologizing for provoking aggression can resolve conflicts and decrease violence as it provides another attribution for the harm caused (Ohbuchi, Kameda, & Agarie, 1989). Hostile expectation and hostile perception biases can be corrected through teaching people to make situational attributions for the ambiguous behaviors of others (Weiner, 1986). Hudley and Graham (1993) used this sort of attributional retraining on children and found that students were less likely to respond to others aggressively after the training compared to a control group.

Aggression is a complicated area of study with many possible causes and consequences. There are a variety of ways in which aggression can be conceptualized that might drastically change our understanding of who will be most likely to be aggressive. Aggression is rarely the result of individual disposition, but rather the interaction between person and situation leads to aggressive responses.

NAME _____ DATE _____

Aggression Worksheet

Consider the following actions and decide whether you think they are aggressive or not aggressive behaviors:

- A boy kicks another boy in the sandbox.

- A girl throws a toy at her brother.

- A woman contemplates killing herself.

- A man buys a gun with the intent of defending himself.

- A man kicks a dog.

- A woman hunts and kills a deer.

- A spider eats a fly.

- A dog bites a child.

- A baby pulls his mother's hair.

- A husband hits his wife.

- A woman hits her romantic partner.

- An author writes an elaborate and violent chapter about murdering his neighbor.

- A teenager fantasizes about beating up another teen that is bullying him.

- An anonymous person posts, "You should kill yourself" on someone else's Facebook page.

- Two men get into a fight while drinking.

- A driver speeds through an intersection narrowly missing a pedestrian in the crosswalk.

- A student kicks over a trashcan after being upset by a bad grade.

- A frustrated administrative assistant bangs on a copier.

- Three football players hit an offense lineman and knock him unconscious.

- A father yells at his son and daughter in front of everyone at the mall.

NAME _____ DATE _____

Chapter Questions

1. How do you think aggression can be curbed when it is inappropriate or causes harm?

2. How would you address violence in video games and popular films? Is it a problem?

3. Why do you think we have strong responses to cruelty to animals?

4. Domestic violence is a complex issue. What advice might you give to young people who find themselves dating an abusive partner? How would your advice change for someone who is older (age 40 or 60)?

5. How does fighting between siblings (including physical altercations) inform our understanding of violence in our relationships?

Prosocial Behavior

> "When I was a boy and I would see scary things in the news, my mother would say to me, 'Look for the helpers. You will always find people who are helping.'"
>
> —*Fred Rogers*

Image © nasirkhan, 2014. Used under license from Shutterstock, Inc.

Defining Prosocial Behavior

Prosocial behavior is voluntary behavior that may include helping, sharing, or cooperating with others for any number of reasons in order to benefit the other person. Sometimes we help others because it will make us feel better about ourselves, improve our self-image, or it is practically an important thing to do. Other times we help because we care for others or tend to be oriented toward others rather than

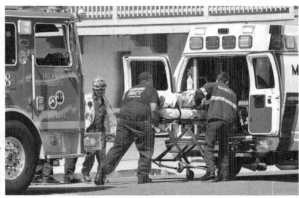

the self. This is distinct from altruism. Altruism is selfless helping and it is difficult to identify examples that would truly be considered altruistic. In almost every case there is some reward for helping even if it is intrinsic joy at knowing that we have helped someone else. Eisenberg (1991) has indicated that altruism may involve helping due to empathic concern, internalized values to assist, or a strong moral character. However, if you help to alleviate guilt or to feel good about yourself, to improve your reputation, or for an external reward (e.g., extra credit, a tax break) then that does not qualify as altruism though it is certainly prosocial behavior (Hawley, 2014).

Let's say that you see a stranded motorist on the side of the road on your way to a meeting. If you stop and help you will be late for the meeting, but you consider how bad you would feel if this stranded person made the news because a less well-meaning person happened upon them. You pull over and help, but was this altruism or prosocial behavior?

Helping and Evolution

Evolutionary theorists provide a simpler understanding of altruism: If you help another voluntarily even though it decreases your evolutionary fitness then perhaps that act is altruistic after all. If you help your own offspring, then that would not be altruistic, but if you help another person's child then perhaps it is. Although you may feel that there would be costs and risks to your reputation if you had not helped and so it may be beneficial to the self to help the other person's child. During a car pool prior to seat belt laws requiring everyone to buckle up, seatbelt use was hit or miss. A family friend would frequently insist I buckle up, while letting her own child ride unrestrained. Was this altruistic? Being a young child I inquired as it seemed unfair that my friend was not forced to buckle up. The parent told me, "Your parents would be really upset with me if I let something happen to you!" This was not so much an altruistic act as a preservation of reputation even as it

may have come at some evolutionary cost if there had been an accident.

So far we have only considered helping people, but sometimes we help animals and this clearly does not expand our evolutionary fitness. Why would we help an animal, even at our own peril? In Russia a group of men helped a female moose who had fallen through thin ice by pulling her out of the water and then warming her up. Was this altruism? What other motives or intentions might there be? A similar story unfolds in the winter of 2013 when a minivan lost control and drove off the highway landing upside down in freezing water. A man driving by pulled over, jumped in the water, and pulled all five family members out of the water, saving the three children and father, though the mother was not revived (Sinoski, 2013). The rescuer wanted to remain unnamed in the media and made it clear he did not do this for attention. Do you think he might have felt guilty if he had not tried to help? Do you think he acted the way

he would want someone to act if it had been his vehicle that went off the road? What led this man to risk his own life to help others?

KINSHIP SELECTION

Selfless helping of those who improve the propagation of our genetic material is supported by evolutionary theorists and anecdote alike. Think about the loss of a child; while we might agree that life is precious and every life deserves to be saved, we see different kinds of grieving for young children than for teenagers. Someone on the cusp of adulthood passing away seems to be much more tragic than a young child. It may be argued that a toddler has not had the opportunity to touch the lives of others in the ways that teenagers might with their friends and family. Evolutionary theorists would tell us that the closer a person is to their reproductive potential the more parental investments they represent. It's possible that peers might also see the loss of a teenager or young adult as decreasing the choice of possible mates, though same-sex peers might see a peer's death as one less person with whom you would compete for mates.

Perhaps some of the most compelling evidence that reproductive value improves chances of survival comes from analysis of adults killing children. Examinations of homicide rates in which the parent was the murderer demonstrate that the rate drops off as the child enters puberty and ages into adulthood, with the highest rates occurring before the child is one year old (Daly & Wilson, 1998). Examining the murders of minors by non-relatives, the function is essentially reversed with the highest rates occurring as the child ages out of puberty and approaches adulthood. Consider how we also see parents have quite different responses to the death of an only child compared to the death of a child who has siblings.

Badcock (1998) also posits that kinship selection leads to more altruistic behaviors shown to others who are similar to us because we perceive them as more genetically similar even if only phenotypically.

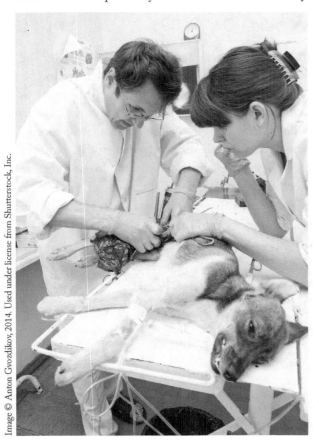

Siblings who live with their full siblings are likely to be more altruistic toward them than to half-siblings (Badcock, 1998). In some cases, one child is sacrificed for a sibling. When a child is born too close in years to a sibling that is still breastfeeding, Australian aborigines would traditionally allow the newborn baby to starve to death rather than displacing the older child who might then be at risk for death (Roheim, 1932). Indeed Burnstein, Crandall, and Kitayama (1994) had participants respond to life and death scenarios and everyday situations in which a person needed help. Participants reported they would be more likely to save close kin, younger people, healthier people, wealthy people, and pre-menopausal women from a burning building. Everyday helping such as picking up items from the store showed the cultural norm that one should help those who cannot help themselves and now participants were more likely to help the old, ill, and very young. In addition, participants were more likely to help 10 and 18 year olds, than infants and elders (75) under conditions of famine (Burnstein, Crandall, & Kitayama, 1994).

Social Learning

We might also learn to help by watching others be rewarded for helping or punished for not helping. Household chores may often be framed for children as "helping" around the house. When a child does not do chores or does not help around the house there may well be punishment. However, this type of helping is rarely voluntary and therefore may not meet the definition of helping used by most social psychologists. However, studies have shown that when we see someone else volunteer to help, we often follow suit. Rushton and Campbell (1977) found that when a model signed up to donate blood, participants were also likely to sign up and show up for blood donation appointments.

Models may not only lead to imitation, but also help others to understand how to help. For example, you may very well want to help someone in distress, but if you are not sure what to do having someone else help first can show you how to proceed. Others who help may also set up norms for whether it is appropriate to help. For example, if you are in a library with several students and one person starts helping someone with the work, it may set up a norm that in this part of the library it is appropriate to seek and offer help.

Who to Help?

In some cases we may feel overwhelmed by the number of people who might need help and so we must choose who to help or at least who to help first. Emergencies require triage systems in which those who are in the most distress receive help first. Organizations may have other patterns such that those who complain the loudest receive more benefits. Teachers often spend more time helping students who are clearly struggling rather than those who sit quietly.

We also tend to help people we think of as deserving (Betancourt, 1990). Participants were asked to either be objective or try to take the perspective of the student interviewed in the report they were about to read. In one report the student's real-life story about having missed class was beyond his or her control (having an accident that resulted in a hospital stay) or uncontrollable (going out of town with friends). After participants finished answering a survey about their perceptions, the experiment noted that they were in the same section as the student they read about. In fact the student that was interviewed had left a letter in the event someone from the same section participated. An envelope was given to the participant and the participant was left alone to read the letter. The letter asked if the participant might consider helping the student catch up in the class. If participants agreed they simply needed to leave their contact information on the back of the letter, seal the letter in the envelope, and leave it on the table. If they preferred not to they were to seal the letter in the envelope and leave it on the table. Results demonstrated that if participants felt the student had no control over missing class they were more likely to offer their contact information and extend help to the student.

> "Charity sees the need,
> not the cause."
>
> ~*German Proverb*

SIMILARITY

Fifty students were sent an email survey asking them to help by completing a questionnaire. The participants believed the email came from another student at the same university. Half of the emails were from someone with the same surname as the participant. When participants shared the same surname as the requestor they were more likely to respond and to do so quickly (Gueguen, Pichot, & Dreff, 2005).

Participants were asked to read either a first person account about Mary or the same content told in the third person (Cao, 2014). Mary's husband kept her under constant surveillance, called her names, and beat her if she went out with family or friends or even talked to someone else. When she was pregnant the abuse continued and she miscarried. She wanted to leave and he threatened to kill her and her family. One night her husband got drunk and she called a friend who took her to a shelter. She was told that she could only stay a few days because there was not enough room. She did not want to stay with friends or family because her husband might come find her to kill her and kill anyone who helped her as well. Participants were asked to complete a measure of their emotional responses and whether they were in support of helping abused women through donations, encouraging government support, and holding law enforcement accountable for helping prevent domestic violence. The results found that female participants were more likely to feel sympathy and provide support regardless of which account they read (first person or third person). However, male participants were more sympathetic when they read the first person account and sympathy was positively related to supporting efforts to stop domestic violence. It is possible we may be more willing to help those who are similar to us in part because it may be easier to have sympathy for their plight.

FAMILIARITY

Amato (1990) found that people are more likely to help familiar others. Further when we do help those who are strangers to us, we do so more spontaneously and without planning. When asked to recall four or five instances in which they engaged in helping behaviors over the past week, almost 90% of the recollections involved helping someone known to the participant, with only 10% or less involving helping strangers (Amato, 1990). The more enmeshed a person was in a social network the more likely they were to engage in planned and formal helping behaviors (e.g., helping someone move); while those with fewer social ties were less likely to have engaged in helping. Spontaneous helping was not influenced by social network (e.g., giving directions to a stranger). When we help strangers it is often without much planning and involves spur of the moment responses to requests for help.

IDENTIFIABLE INDIVIDUALS

We may also be more likely to help specific individuals that we can identify rather than unknown strangers or groups of people that we cannot identify. Work by Slovic (2007) has demonstrated that people have a greater tendency to help identifiable others. When presented with a name and a photo and a request for aid, people give more readily than when they are presented with statistics about people in need. Further, the singularity effect also suggests that we are more likely to help the single individual rather than a group of people (Kogut & Ritov, 2007). This may be in part why we will expend a great deal of energy helping neighbors find their lost dog, but feel helpless in the face of genocide. When there are so many people in need, we cannot seem to find a way to make sense of the magnitude and as a result resort to inaction.

Imagine how you might feel if someone you knew died. Think about all of the grief you might feel as that person is no longer in your life, all of their unique qualities that will be missed, and visual-ize the amount of your grief. Now imagine that 100,000 people died all of whom have rich and unique lives and people who loved them and cared for them just as you might for your friend. How much grief do you feel about the death of 100,000 people? It is likely hard to fathom, indeed it is likely that the spike in negative affect we feel when one person dies is high. A second death might increase our negative feelings. A third again might increase our grief. However, the tenth person is not likely to increase our negative feelings as much as the first. For those of you who are mathematically inclined, let's attempt to quantify this affective response. When someone close to you dies you might rate your negative feelings as -50, upon hearing of a second person's death this might go to -100, but when you think of 100,000 deaths can you imagine a feeling that is -5 million? It is psychically numbing and may be one of the reasons it can be difficult to mobilize efforts that would put an end to genocide or provide help to the hundreds of thousands of refugees who need food and clean drinking water (Slovic, 2007).

Attachment style may also play a role in who we help. Participants completed attachment style measures and were paid for their participation (Kogut & Kogut, 2013). Participants were then presented with a story about and photo of Tom (identified individual condition) who was a three-year-old boy with cancer and needed bone marrow donations to survive and many people had given

How is helping strangers different than helping family members?

blood, but there was no money to analyze the samples so there was now an effort to raise money for these tests. The other half of the participants were given the same information about a child who needed bone marrow, but there was no age, name, or photo. Donations from those who were secure in their attachment style were highest regardless of which story they read. However, those who were high in anxiety donated more money when they could identify the child, than when the child was nameless. However, there are limits to the ways in which help identifiable others. Kogut (2011) has also shown that if the person in need of help is seen as responsible for their own predicament being identifiable may decrease helping.

Commemoration ceremony held on the anniversary of the Armenian Genocide in Istanbul, Turkey on April 24, 2013.

BEAUTIFUL PEOPLE

Most research has found that we are more likely to help attractive others (Benson, Karabenick, & Le-

rner, 1976). People found a completed application form in a phone booth along with a photograph of the applicant and an addressed stamped envelope. Half of the participants saw a photo of an attractive person and the other half found a photo that was not attractive. The attractive application was much more likely to be mailed. In another study by West and Brown (1975) male participants were approached outside of a student health center by

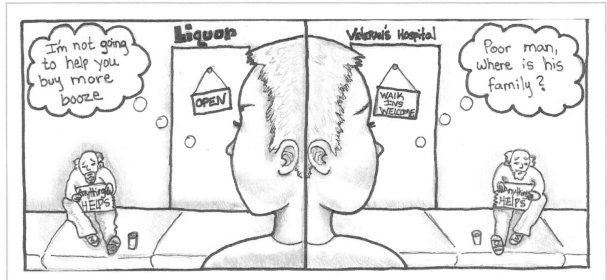

FIGURE 11.1 Your perceptions of why a person needs help may shape whether or not you think the person deserves help.

How do you think attractiveness impacts who you choose to help? How does this disadvantage people with particular needs (e.g., homeless people, disabled people)?

either an attractive or unattractive woman who needed money for a tetanus shot due to a high or low severity emergency. The more attractive woman was more likely to receive help when she was in severe distress.

Michniewicz and Vandello (2013) asked participants to read scenarios about a job applicant who is either unfairly or fairly advantaged or disadvantaged. Participants were all shown the same photos and then read that the applicant had either failed to submit a complete job application (fair disadvantage), the secretary had misplaced the list of references (unfair disadvantage), had a strong application (fair advantage), or had a friend who asked human resources to consider hiring the applicant (unfair advantage). Participants rated the fairly advantaged job applicant as more attractive. This is congruent with what is beautiful is good, such that who is good is beautiful. However, the unfairly disadvantaged applicant was also rated as more attractive. Thus, it may not be that we only help attractive others but that needing help due to unfair situations may also make us perceive others as more attractive.

We also tend to help people who seem to need our help. Therefore most research has suggested that when we have greater sympathy for a person's plight we are more likely to help. However, previous research has found that we are equally likely to help someone with a disability as we are to help an able-bodied person (Test & Bryan, 1969). Samer-

otte and Harris (1976) decided to see if disability might be linked to attractiveness. In their study a confederate had one of two types of disabilities. Either he wore an eye patch and a facial scar or he had a bandage around his forearm. The confederate either walked so closely to the participant that the participant felt they may have caused the confederate to drop the envelopes or simply dropped the envelopes in view of the participant. The participants were more likely to help the confederate with the forearm bandage and were more likely to do so when they felt they had caused the confederate to drop the envelopes.

Norms

In some cases we help because we feel it is the appropriate thing to do. Norms may guide our behaviors and often encourage cooperation with others. However, cooperation is often attenuated by whether we might also benefit from helping others. Someone who helps everyone all the time and receives no assistance in return is likely to feel like they are being exploited and others may well see them as a pushover or sucker.

RECIPROCITY

The norm of reciprocity indicates that we help others because we expect that others will help us.

In some cases this is a direct exchange with one person. You help someone mow his yard and he will give you a ride downtown next time you are late for work. In other cases, we are expecting that even if the person is not going to do something right away we might need the person to do something for us later. You help someone move and hope that in return when you move she will come help you. When the norm of reciprocity is violated we can find it very upsetting and uncomfortable. This might occur when we help someone and then the recipient never seems to return the favor. However, it can also happen when someone "over helps" us. If someone does a favor for you that you can never repay or return in kind you may have feelings of obligation and might even attempt to refuse the person's assistance.

I am reminded of a camping trip, where my family had purchased food for the week, but ended up not eating very much because it was so hot that summer. We had also bought condiments that you rarely use all of in one week (ketchup, mayonnaise, etc.). When we were getting ready to leave for a long car trip and then plane ride to another destination, we could not take the food with us or it would spoil, so we offered it to a large group that had just arrived at the campground and appeared to be having a family reunion. When I carried over the first (of several) bags of groceries they readily accepted and thanked me. However, when I brought over two more they were beginning to get uncomfortable and by the time my dad walked over with yet another bag of condiments and such they were downright insulted and become pretty hostile making it clear they did not need our charity!

Cultural norms also shape which norms might influence helping others. Miller and colleagues (2014) examined the role of communal and reciprocity norms in European American and Hindu Indian populations. Participants were provided with a scenario describing a friendship between two adult men (Rob and Mike) who both have families. Rob has a car accident and is unable to work for two months, so the other friend steps in by helping out with house-

hold chores, errands, and yard work. Participants were then asked what the injured friend might do in response to this help. Rob clearly thanks Mike, but what else might be appropriate?

In scenario 1, several years pass and when Mike's house needs a new roof, Rob invites Mike's family to stay with them during the repairs (long-term mutual responsiveness/communal). Scenario 2 involves Rob taking Mike to dinner at one of Mike's favorite restaurants (interpersonal gesture). Scenario 3 involves Rob buying Mike a bottle of Mike's favorite wine (material gesture). In scenario 4, Rob pays Mike for his labor (monetary payment). Which of these do you think is most appropriate? What do you predict each culture might prefer?

Miller and colleagues (2014) found that scenario 1 was rated as most appropriate by Hindu Indian participants. Monetary payment was rated lowest by both European American and Hindu Indian participants. European Americans were concerned about the first scenario because it seemed to them that gratitude should be shown more quickly, not three years later. Both American and Indian populations indicated that the expressive gestures were also good options and showed gratitude for the friend, but did not necessarily provide reciprocation for the friend's effort. Even though European Americans supported these gestures, they also realized that these were not sufficient repayment to the friend.

EQUITY

Equity refers to everyone receiving benefits congruent with their efforts. If people feel they are receiving less than they deserve they will likely feel distressed. Individuals who are over-benefitted also feel distress. The degree of distress about equitable distribution of benefits is likely determined by a person's equity sensitivity (Huseman, Hatfield, & Miles, 1987). When we are distressed by inequity we take action to return to balance. Consider equity-sensitive people who receive a

Is it easier to help people you do not know?

butions in an attempt to return to a state of equitable cost-benefits. In contrast, people who adopt an entitled approach to equity are distressed when they are equitably or under-benefited and are only content when being over-benefitted. Benevolent individuals are most content when they are under-benefitted and show discomfort with equity or being over-benefited. Huseman and colleagues applied their work to job satisfaction, but how might this also be tied to helping more generally? Do you think benevolent types are likely to choose certain occupations in which they would save lives and in return be paid little and work long hours? What sorts of jobs might entitled people prefer?

To (2014) examined the ways in which rural Chinese families negotiate elder care. While eldercare in Chinese culture may at first seem to be helping behavior even if there is an obligatory nature to this work, it is a far more complex negotiation. Sons and daughters-in-law often have primary responsibility for caring for the mother-in-law. However, elderly mothers-in-law provide childcare and household assistance in return for this late in life care. If the mother-in-law's services are provided for the family of one of her children and less so for the other children, then the care she receives from others will be limited by the extent to which the family feels her labor in their household will be equitable with their assistance. This is in part due to the rise of an equity norm with regard to elder care.

LABELING

People may be more inclined to help if they are told that they were helpful. Labeling someone as helpful may lead to self-fulfilling prophecy and increases in prosocial behavior. Strenta and Dejong (1981) had participants complete a series of questions that the participants believed comprised a personality test. Participants were then randomly assigned to receive results that indicated they were more kind and thoughtful than most other respondents or that they were more intelligent than other respondents. Then participants were

raise at work. If they felt they were working very hard and their efforts were previously going unnoticed, the raise may in fact restore balance. However, if they received a raise and did not previously feel underpaid they may feel guilty and redouble their efforts at work to make sure they are earning their increased benefit. Those who feel under-benefitted may also back off their efforts or contri-

sent to a waiting room to wait for another experimenter and on their way they encounter a confederate who dropped 500 used computer cards while walking behind them. People who were told they were kind and thoughtful were more likely to help than those who were labeled as intelligent. (Computer punch cards were stiff paper cards with particular patterns of punches used to program main frame computers prior to the development of the personal computers we use today.) Participants told they were kind and thoughtful responded more quickly to help the confederate, and picked up over twice as many cards as the participants in the intelligent condition.

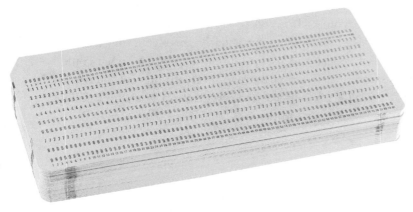

Image © Deymos Photo, 2014. Used under license from Shutterstock, Inc.

Stack of vintage unused computer punch cards used for data entry and programming in the 1960s and 1970s.

SOCIAL RESPONSIBILITY

The norm of social responsibility indicates that people are guided to behave in ways that alleviate the suffering or needs of others. De Cremer and Van Lange (2001) found that individuals who were more prosocial (rather than proself) resolved a public goods dilemma in ways that demonstrated increased cooperation for the care and concern for the common good. In groups of four, participants were told they would each begin with 30 points. They could then choose to make contributions to the common good by contributing points to the group pool. Once everyone had made their decisions the points in the common pool would be multiplied by two and divided equally among all members of the group. The best option for the common good is for each person to contribute all of their points, resulting in individuals receiving double their amount of points (60). However, the best option for individuals is to keep all of their points and have everyone else contribute to the common good (free riding produces 75 points under optimal conditions). Participants who had a greater norm of social responsibility contributed more tokens than those who were proself. Prosocials also reported feeling more social responsibility.

BYSTANDER EFFECTS

Catherine Susan "Kitty" Genovese was murdered on March 13, 1964, near her home in Queens, New York City. She was a bar manager at Ev's Eleventh Hour Sports Bar and had just finished closing up before heading home to an apartment she shared with her girlfriend, Mary Ann Zielonko. Winston Moseley approached her as she was walking from her car to her apartment building. She screamed for help as he stabbed her. A neighbor, Robert Mozer, looks out the window and yelled for Winston to "Let that girl alone!" Winston Mosely drives away and Kitty makes her way toward the rear entrance of her apartment building.

Ten minutes later Winston returns wearing a new hat and searches for her in the area, finding her in the hallway at the rear of the building. He continues the attack, stabbing her several more times while she tries to fight him off. She was near death as he raped her in the stairwell, stole less than $50 from her, and left her in the hallway to die. Neighbors come to assist and a call to the police is finally clear enough in its urgency to warrant the arrival of an ambulance which transported her to the hospital where she was declared dead on arrival. During the 30 minutes over a dozen onlookers saw or heard some part of the attack, yet they did not rush down to help. One neighbor called out to Moseley to leave her alone, others may have called the police but lacked sufficient detail to elicit a response from the police, an older woman went to assist Kitty after Winston ran off the last time, but all she could do was hold her and try to comfort her as she died. What if someone had stepped in? What if several of the neighbors came down in mass and prevented the second attack?

Winston Moseley was apprehended while committing a burglary later that week and confessed to killing and raping Kitty and two other women. In 1964, a jury found him guilty and he was sentenced to death on June 15, 1964. An appeal was filed pleading insanity and the sentence was reduced to life imprisonment in 1967. In 1968, he escaped and held a couple hostage for three days,

raping the wife, and then stealing their car and fleeing. After taking another household hostage he was recaptured and received two additional 15-year sentences. During the 1970s he obtained a BA in sociology and during parole hearings claimed his life imprisonment was more suffering than any of his victims ever endured. In December 2013 he was again denied parole; his next parole hearing will be in November 2015. You can track his record online at the New York State Department of Corrections Inmate Lookup system (http://nysdoccslookup.doccs.ny.gov).

The story of this tragedy created a media frenzy as people wondered why others had not intervened in 1964 to stop the attack. Social psychologists were particularly interested in what situational factors inhibited helping and what could be done to encourage intervention. The term "bystander effect" is derived from the research following this murder.

FIGURE 11.2 *Who will help, will you?*

There are a number of reasons the neighbors might not have assisted. Diffusion of responsibility might have led each individual to assume that someone else must have already called the police or gone down to help. The more people that are present, the less likely any one person is to help or to even feel it is their responsibility to help. Today emergency responders are trained to help and respond first. Indeed in some states the Good Samaritan laws and duty to rescue laws indicate that you have an obligation to help another person if you are capable of doing so. These laws are not without controversy. In Canada there is a protection against accusations of wrongdoing if you were trying to help a victim in distress, thus preventing you from being sued if helping might have caused some harm. We often implement laws and obligatory norms when our default reaction would be to let someone else step in.

> The first question which the priest and the Levite asked was: "If I stop to help this man, what will happen to me?" But… the good Samaritan reversed the question: "If I do not stop to help this man, what will happen to him?"
>
> ~*Martin Luther King, Jr.*

You may have heard that you should yell, "FIRE!", if you need help as people are more likely to respond. Fire is a threat that is likely to spread to others unless extinguished, therefore this particular emergency may suddenly take on new personal relevance to those in your vicinity. Another tactic is to specifically identify a person to help you, by asking them directly, "Hey, you in the red coat, can you call 911?" Also, seeking specific help may elicit more response than a general request. Helping people understand exactly what you need them to do may result in more action than waiting for them to assess the situation and then figure out what to do. Of course if you are in extreme distress it may be difficult for you to implement these strategies.

Listen to Kitty's partner share her recollections of Kitty and the evening of this tragedy at http://www.soundportraits.org/on-air/remembering_kitty_genovese/

Steps to Helping

There are five essential steps to helping in an emergency (and in other situations as well). First, you must notice that there is a need for help. My office is adjacent to three fraternity and sorority houses and on late weekend nights when I am working it can be challenging to discern which yells and screams are celebratory and which might be distress signals. A person laying on the sidewalk may be a homeless person who simply has nowhere else to go or it could be a person that has passed out or had a heart attack. How do you know?

The second step is interpreting the incident as an emergency. One cue to determining whether you should be alarmed by the person laying on the sidewalk might be how others respond. Are others walking around this person without looking as though this is normal and expected? If so, then this person must not be in need of help. Pluralistic ignorance means that everyone might well assume that if help was needed someone else would be helping and since no one is helping, then help must not be warranted. Provided you can

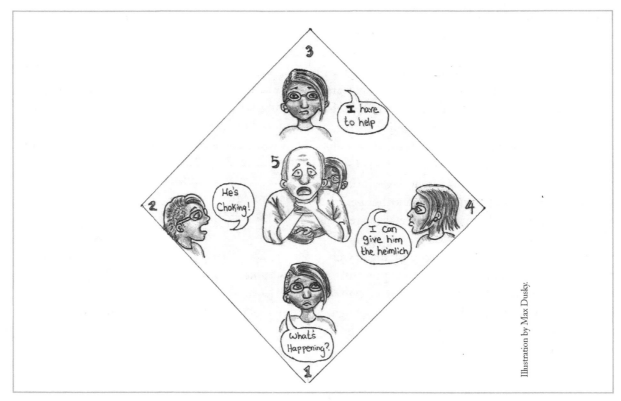

Illustration by Max Dusky.

FIGURE 11.3 *What role does training play in helping people quickly go through these steps?*

successfully identify that helping is required, the next step requires you to take responsibility for doing something about it.

The third step is accepting responsibility for helping. This is the moment when you decide it is your job to intervene. If there are others around who also witnessed the incident you may well fall prey to diffusion of responsibility and assume that it is not your place to help. Surely someone else will intervene. If no one else is around, then it increases the chances that you will feel responsible for taking action.

The fourth step is trying to determine how you are going to help and whether you are appropriately capable of carrying out the needed help. For example, it may be clear that the correct course of action is to call 911, but if you are without a phone you have to decide what to do next. Or perhaps

someone is badly injured and you have no first aid training so you are not sure how to proceed. If you are not mechanically inclined a stranded motorist might well need your help and you may feel responsible but it may take you some time to figure out how best to assist.

After 9/11, the Transportation Security Administration (TSA) began a campaign: "If you see something, say something." In an attempt to assist people through the steps quickly, they were telling people that if you notice an incident at all, proceed straight to step four and let a TSA agent or police officer know about it. Do not bother to interpret it or try to intervene, just take action and tell the authorities.

Bystander intervention was largely isolated to the social psychology classroom, but in recent times the research here has been leveraged to improve campus safety, national security, and even bullying. These

Would you step in to stop the bully? What if you were the same age as the people in the photo?

interventions include everything from helping to prevent sexual assaults to reporting bias incidents. Bystander intervention programs focus largely on helping people understand how to intervene. Providing ways to identify incidents as problematic, resources to learn how to intervene, and referrals to appropriate others help people navigate the steps to helping with relatively less effort.

There are a number of Public Service Announcements about how you can intervene to stop sexual assaults, bullying, hazing, and other harmful behaviors. The four Ds of intervention provide one way that a person might think about intervening in the fourth step. First you could directly confront the situation: "I think we have somewhere else to be" or "You might want to move on, I don't think she's interested in you." If you are skilled or trained this might be completely reasonable, but it can also be challenging for those who are not sure if this could make things worse or if it might get worse. Second, you can distract the person who is creating the harmful environment by changing the subject or turning attention away from the vulnerable person to something else that is going on: "Hey, the band is about to play again!" You can delegate by telling someone else who can take action: "My friend over there is being creeped on by that guy, can you walk over there with me and help me give her an out?" Or finally you might engage in delayed response so that if you see someone who might be in distress, simply ask, "Are you ok? Is there anything I can do to help?" to provide a safety net for the person to reach out for help.

How is rape a different sort of aggression than other types of assault? How does this change whether or not you would intervene if you thought someone was likely to be talking to a person that would coerce him or her into unwanted sexual contact? What is the rule about enthusiastic consent?

For some types of helping we may even need help with the first step. Sexual assault and sexism often go hand in hand, but because we are surrounded by examples of sexualized violence and heteronormative messages it can be difficult to know what might actually be an event requiring intervention. Finetuning your skill at knowing when someone has crossed the line from socially acceptable to potentially problematic can help in noticing moments when intervention is required. For example, if someone makes a sexualized joke at a party that portrays women as a prey or men as predators, is that okay? If it introduces into the context or primes people to see the women in the room as vulnerable and consent as unnecessary, does this set the stage for assault?

Training people to intervene has proven useful on some campuses in attempts to reduce sexual assault (Winerip, 2014). The University of New Hampshire had college men go through a bystander intervention training and found that compared to a control group they were more than twice as likely to have intervened and prevented a potential sexual assault. At Ohio University only 1.5% of men who received the training reported they had perpetrated a sexual assault compared to 6.7% of men who had not attended the training.

While you may think of domestic violence and sexual assault as a woman's issues, Katz has successfully argued in his work that in fact interventions must focus on helping the majority of men intervene and prevent the minority of men from perpetrating the majority of sexual assaults against women and men.

> "We need more men with the guts, with the courage, with the strength, with the moral integrity to break our complicit silence and challenge each other and stand with women and not against them." –Katz View his Ted Talk here: http://www.ted.com/talks/jackson_katz_violence_against_women_it_s_a_men_s_issue

Moral Hypocrisy and Overpower Moral Integrity

Moral integrity should improve helping and prosocial responses. Batson was interested in understanding how morality might influence prosocial choices. Batson and Thompson (2001) carried out several studies to understand why the goal of appearing moral by displaying moral integrity is undermined by a desire to avoid the cost of moral action and engage in moral hypocrisy. Five very clever studies explore these ideas.

In the first study, participants arrived at the lab and were told they would be going through the experiment with another participant. There were two tasks: one that would involve earning raffle tickets and one that was relatively neutral (no raffle tickets). The participant who arrived first was allowed to pick one of the two tasks, assigning the second task to the other participant. The majority of people (70–80%) chose the positive task for themselves. Was this fair or equitable? No. Batson thought perhaps that maybe it simply didn't occur to participants that they should try to be fair about this decision.

In study two, participants arrive and are given the same choice, but the concept of fairness was introduced by telling participants, "Most participants feel that giving both people an equal chance—by flipping a coin—is the fairest way to assign tasks." They were then provided a coin to flip if they wanted to do so. Half of the people did not flip the coin and simply decided outright that they will do the positive task (80–90% of the time). The other half of participants did flip the coin, which should result in half of these participants doing the positive task and half the neutral task. Surprisingly that is not what happened. Participants who flipped the coin were just as likely as non-flippers to report that the result of the coin flip was that they would be doing the positive task (85–90% of the time).

Perhaps people just forget whether they were heads or tails. In study three the coin is labeled as SELF-POS and OTHER-POS to indicate clearly who would get to do the positive task. Again, half of the participants do not even bother with the coin. The remaining participants flip the coin and still report that the result was in their favor. Perhaps the moral obligation to appear fair does not actually represent an inner value to be fair.

Raising self-awareness should help, after all seeing yourself in a mirror calls attention to the self and your inner values. In this fourth study, the coin flipping occurred in front of a mirror. Once again half of participants chose not to flip the coin, but this time those who did flip the coin abided by the flip assigning themselves to the positive task half of the time and their partner to the positive task half of the time. So it does appear that people can be moral hypocrites engaging in the appearance of fairness but circumventing fairness for self-interest in most cases. Batson refers to this as overpowered moral integrity wherein an initial motive to be fair is overwhelmed by self-interest when faced with the loss of the positive outcomes.

However, there remains concerns about the other half of the participants who could not even entertain coin flipping. What could be their rationale? In a fifth study the participants were provided the same choice dilemma as before (the mirror was not present in this study) and were told they could choose to have the experimenter flip the coin, flip the coin themselves, or just decide which task they preferred. Now 80% chose to let the experimenter flip the coin! Apparently some people in the earlier studies who chose not to flip may have been avoiding hypocrisy by just making the choice themselves rather than feigning integrity.

You may respond to all of these findings by saying that there really is no moral choice here, that it may not be fair but the other person is not harmed by having to do the neutral task. In fact, some may even go so far as to say that they felt more comfortable making the decision themselves in an unfair way because there was no harm to the other person. Two additional studies by Batson and colleagues demonstrate that this is not exactly true. In these, participants are faced with a choice between the positive task and raffle tickets and a negative task that involved uncomfortable electric shock. Now only 25% of people let the experimenter flip the coin. Another 25% flipped the coin themselves (appear to have integrity but maintain self-interest), and 91% of these assigned themselves to the positive task. The remaining half of participants did not even bother flipping the coin to appear moral and assigned themselves the positive consequences task. They also readily admitted after the fact that their choice was not morally right.

> "Just think: If personal cost is sufficient to justify setting aside moral principles, then one can set aside morality when deciding whether to stand by or intervene as the perpetrators of hate crimes pursue their victims."
>
> *—Batson & Thompson, 2001*

Forgiveness

Forgiveness requires empathy with one's transgressor (Macaskill, Maltby, & Day 2012). Witvliet and colleagues (2001) asked participants to recall hurtful memories while physiological measures of stress responses were collected. People who were thinking about grudges or who had not forgiven transgressors showed higher levels of physiological stress. Those who had forgiven others were less stressed and felt more control over the situation. Forgiving the transgressor resulted in higher ratings of empathy and control and less anger and sadness.

Strang and colleagues (2014) measured fMRI responses while participants either chose to seek forgiveness of another player after they had made a move in a decision-making game that created a negative outcome for the other and in return whether or not the other player decided to forgive. They present some evidence that areas of the brain that are involved in receiving an apology are also those most associated with empathy for others. However, the results were not as clear for forgiveness. After all not everyone who received an apology chose to forgive the transgressor.

People seem to become more forgiving as they age (Darby & Schlenker, 1982). This may be in part because as we have a wider array of life experiences we come to have empathy for a broader set of circumstances. Others have proposed a developmental model of forgiveness such that people at early developmental stages of forgiveness engage in revengeful or restitutional forgiveness. The next stage is expectational forgiveness in which forgiveness is seen as the appropriate thing to do. Those at the last stage are likely to forgive as an act of love or to maintain social harmony (Enright et al., 1989).

We are also more likely to forgive those who apologize. It may be through this process of increased empathy for the transgressor that we begin to separate the person from the behavior (Snyder & Wright, 2002). Narcissists are less likely to forgive others (Exline et al., 2008). People who are religious are more likely to forgive (Tsang, McCullough, & Hoyt, 2008). Cehajic, Brown, and Castano (2008) found that when Bosnian Muslims felt empathy for Bosnian Serbians this increased their readiness to forgive for the misdeeds during the war in the early 1990s. Empathy and trust towards the out-group also led to increased motivation to forgive.

Helping and Mood

Helping is supposed to make you feel good, but your mood may also determine when you help and why. There are three approaches to understanding the influence of mood and empathy on helping decisions: the mood as information model, the negative state relief model, and the empathy altruism model. Helping is often listed as something you can do to boost your mood, but the impact on your mood may have more to do with how you help specifically. In some cases, helping can lead to negative consequences. For example, rape victim advocates who encounter violence day in and day out with little power to stop these incidents often report high levels of burnout (Ullman & Townsend, 2007). Caregivers, doctors, nurses, psychologists, and social workers are also likely to experience burnout when they are faced with so many people needing help.

How do you deal with burnout in your work?

MOOD AS INFORMATION VS. MOOD MAINTENANCE

The mood as information model states that moods serve as information about our environment and shape how we interpret and behave in a particular situation (Schwarz & Clore, 2003). When we are in a good mood, then we are less likely to even notice that help is needed. Congruent with evolutionary theory we pay less attention when all is well. However, if we are in a bad mood we may see this as important information that we need to address the source of this negativity and may be more inclined to help others in order to do so. And the specific negative emotion may also increase helping (e.g., guilt), while other emotions such as anger might lead to less helping. For example, Regan, Williams, and Sparling (1972) had a male confederate ask females passing by if they would take his picture. When she did so the camera was rigged to break. For half of the participants, the confederate blamed her for breaking the camera; the other half were assured it was not their fault. After several minutes the woman crossed paths with another confederate who was having trouble carrying groceries that were falling out of the grocery bag. Those who felt guilty for breaking the camera were much more likely to help (55%) than those who were assured they were not to blame (15%).

Mood of course is a bit more complex than the theory implies. Research has shown that we help more frequently when we feel good (Carlson, Charlin, & Miller, 1988). When we are feeling relaxed and happy we are more likely to help someone out by completing a survey; people tip more when it is sunny which may improve our mood (Cunningham, 1979). However, if asked to complete a survey that asked us to recall topics that made us feel bad, we might decline to continue in order to maintain our positive mood. This work is congruent with the idea that we help others to maintain our good feelings. Perhaps positive moods prime positive thoughts leading to more helping (Isen, 1984).

NEGATIVE STATE RELIEF MODEL

The negative state relief model proposes that people who are sad may be motivated to help if they think it will make them feel better. Manucia, Baumann, and Cialdini (1984) gave participants a pill they were told would impact memory. Half of the participants were also told that a side effect would be that their mood would be fixed for some period of time until the drug wore off. During a memory task participants were asked to recall either happy, sad, or neutral memories from their past. As the participants left the study, they were asked whether they would be willing to help by calling to collect information related to a blood drive. Happy participants were more likely to help (over half agreed to do so). However those in the sad condition helped but only if they believed it would improve their mood (58%); and those that believed the pill had fixed their mood and they were sad were less likely to volunteer (42%). It appears that we help to alleviate our own negative mood states. However, we might also anticipate that if the opportunity to help would actually make us feel worse we might not help at all.

EMPATHY-ALTRUISM

Returning to the questions posed in the first part of this chapter, are we capable of altruism? Batson and Shaw (1991) proposed that the empathy-altruism hypothesis may provide a framework for understanding selfless acts. In this case, we believe that we have helped altruistically, not because we want a benefit for ourselves, and we also relieve the suffering of those we help. If there are unintended consequences such that we too are rewarded, then perhaps that is altruistic. Consider this example: We find a stray dog and take it to the local humane society to see if it might be reunited with its human companions. The humans are elated that we have found their beloved pet and bestow us with a monetary award. Now this example: We see a sign offering a reward for a lost dog and go look and successfully locate the lost canine; and now we call the number on the sign and expect we will be given the award. In both cases the dog is returned and there is a reward, but perhaps the motivations and intentions are different. Would one of these cases more clearly be considered altruism?

You probably are thinking the first scenario seems more altruistic and it is certainly in line with the empathy altruism model. We feel empathy for this lost pet and the owners and then seek to reduce the negative feelings we have because we empathize with their plight. A quick way to reduce our own negative feelings about the whole thing is to improve the feelings of the dog and owner. However, this reduction in negative feelings brings us back to the negative state relief model—we are helping to relieve our own emotional suffering, even if the suffering is empathic.

Batson and colleagues (1988) tested this hypothesis. Participants were put in a situation in which they first believed they could relieve the suffering of a fellow participant who was going to be receiving some electric shocks as part of the experiment. Then half of the participants (Group A) were given the opportunity to hear from the other participant who was concerned about receiving shocks. The other half of participants (Group B) did not hear from the other participant. Then just before the task was to begin each person was randomly assigned to hear either that the task they were to perform would not help the participant, or that they were still going to be performing a task that could benefit the other participant. Then another set of instructions was read to half of Group A and half of Group B, in which participants were told that in fact the other participant would not be receiving any shocks, that the other person had been assigned to a different condition (see Figure 11.4). Participants in the blue cell were quite distressed, while those with high empathy who could help or who learned the other person would not receive shocks were relieved and showed improved moods. Those who were low in empathy did not show this pattern.

Helping others may be a noble pursuit, but it is not entirely an altruistic enterprise. Indeed, the factors that determine when we will help others are largely situational and beyond our direct control. Increasing helping behaviors often requires overt disruption of how people might normally proceed. However, helping does come with a number of benefits to the self and others and when we experience empathy for the plight of others we are more likely to behave prosocially towards them.

	Low Empathy		High Empathy	
	Allowed to Help	**Not Allowed to Help**	**Allowed to Help**	**Not Allowed to Help**
Shocks	This other person I have never heard from will be receiving shocks and if I do well on my task, they might not have to receive any.	This other person I have never heard from will be receiving shocks, and there is nothing I can do.	This other person who sounded concerned about the shocks is going to get shocked, but if I do well on my task they may not have to receive any.	This other person who sounded concerned about the shocks is going to get shocked, and there is nothing I can do to help.
No Shocks	No one is going to get shocked and I am still going to be doing a task that could help the other person.	No one is going to get shocked and I am going to be doing some other task now.	The other person who sounded upset won't be shocked now and I am still going to be doing a task that could help the other person.	The other person who sounded upset won't be shocked now and I am doing another task altogether.

FIGURE 11.4 *How do you think participants in these conditions might feel?*

Data source: Batson (1988).

NAME _____ DATE _____

Chapter Questions

1. What would you want to teach people about how to intervene in violent situations?

2. How does asking for help impact people with disabilities?

3. What can helpers do to avoid burnout?

4. Think about a time when you did not help someone, what factors prevented you from helping?

5. If you won the lottery and had over $10 million to help people, who would you help and why?

6. When you help someone, does it always feel good?

7. When you have needed help, did you feel comfortable seeking help from others?

8. Are there people that you would not want to ask for help? Why is this?

9. How can you use the material in this chapter to create cultural change so that men are as likely to be helped as women?

10. Given the material in this chapter and interdependence theory, how can you help people who are in domestic violence situations?

Applying Social Psychology 12

One of the intriguing things about social psychology is that the effects and findings often have a wide range of applications. There are many areas of life that might be informed by solid understanding of person-situation interactions. Understanding why people behave in a particular way may at first lead you to think it is because of the type of person they are, but after taking this course you should recognize your first inclination as fundamental attribution error. In fact, situations often shape how people behave and can overwhelm individual differences.

The second way in which social psychology can illuminate our understanding of everyday life is by recognizing that people are often driven by competing motivations. People want to feel they are good people and also have accurate perceptions of the

Image © Alena Hovorkova, 2014. Used under license from Shutterstock, Inc.

world. In some cases this creates little conflict; you give money to charities and want to believe you are a generous person. In other cases, we might be challenged by our own behavior. You may want to believe that you are a moral person, but often act in ways that promote self-interest even at the expense of others. Accurately perceiving the world can help us survive; whether it's being accurate about how fast you can cross a street or whether someone following you on a dark night presents a danger.

Image © bikeriderlondon, 2014. Used under license from Shutterstock, Inc.

Image © Ditty_about_summer, 2014. Used under license from Shutterstock, Inc.

Image © wavebreakmedia, 2014. Used under license from Shutterstock, Inc.

Image © Andrey_Popov, 2014. Used under license from Shutterstock, Inc.

A third critical factor in understanding why people do what they do is to remember that we attempt to conserve our cognitive resources whenever possible. If there is a long and difficult way to arrive at a correct answer, but someone shows you a quicker solution, you will most likely use the quicker solution next time. The benefits are that we may be able to conserve cognitive energy for decision making that matters. So we spend little time thinking about our recent gum purchase and more energy contemplating whether we want to spend the rest of our lives with a romantic partner. This also means that we are prone to using stereotypes about others, particularly when we are not motivated by a need or value to not be biased (e.g., racist, heterosexist, sexist, ageist, ableist). Finally, we remember that perception of a situation can override any objective reality. A person who donates to an online but fraud-ridden charity is no less generous because objectively the money did not help anyone.

In this chapter we are going to apply what you have learned in the course to four areas of interest:

law, consumer behavior, environmental concerns, and health. As you read each section, think about how you might apply other social psychological effects to these areas and what other areas of application might be appropriate.

Psychology and Law

In the United States of America, we entrust our justice system to ensure that people are treated fairly in the courtroom and that investigations carried out by the police are in fact objective pursuits of truth. However, social psychologists have demonstrated a number of ways in which the justice system is imperfect and that human error is often at the root of miscarriage of justice.

Consider these three cases from the Innocence Project (www.innocenceproject.org):

In 1982, a young girl from Nampa, Idaho, was kidnapped, raped, and murdered. The young girl was walking to school and it was days later that her body was discovered near a river. Charles Irvin Fain willingly provided hair samples that the FBI indicated were similar to those found on the victim. Two "jailhouse snitches" also provided testimony indicating that Fain was guilty. Shoe print analysis was also presented as indicating that Fain was in the area. In 1983, Fain was found guilty and sentenced to death. In 2001, Fain was exonerated when DNA evidence from pubic hairs on the victims clothes were revealed not to belong to Fain.

On January 3, 1984, a white woman was raped by a black man at knifepoint in a daycare center. Four more white women were raped over the next few weeks. Thomas Haynesworth, an 18-year-old black man without a criminal record was identified by one of the women when she saw him walking down the street. His photo was shown to the other women who also identified him as their rapist. The rape victims testified that he was the rapist at trial, even though at 5'6½" he was considerably shorter than the man who was previously described as 5'10". He was ultimately convicted for two of the four assaults and sentenced to 74 years in prison. Later that same year Leon Davis was arrested for similar sexual assault crimes. Only after the governor of Virginia ordered a reexamination of cases from 1973-1984 was it determined that the semen from the rapes for which Haynesworth was serving time were matches for Leon Davis. In 2011, after 27 years in prison Haynesworth was exonerated of all charges.

Frank Sterling was accused of shooting a 74-year-old woman in the head while she was on her daily walk in 1988. He had an airtight and credible alibi. The case went cold and in 1991 a new team of investigators asked Sterling to come down to the station for questioning after he had just returned from a 36-hour trucking job. He did as requested and maintained his innocence for hours. The officers kept questioning him overnight and into the next morning. They showed him crime scene photos, provided details about the crime, used hypnosis techniques, and after 8 hours of interrogation, Frank Sterling said that he did it and he

needed help. He was convicted of the crime and sentenced in 1992. In 2010, another man by the name of Mark Christie was found to have a DNA profile consistent with a hair found on the victim; after Mark Christie confessed, Frank Sterling was exonerated after serving almost 18 years in prison.

EYEWITNESS TESTIMONY

Perhaps nothing is more convincing than others telling you what they saw with their own two eyes. Phrases such as "I'll believe it when I see it" point to our perception that our visual system and recollections of visual perceptions are infallible. However, there is much evidence we have already covered in this chapter that what you believe can impact what you perceive. Recall the waitress vs. librarian study from Chapter 3 (Cohen, 1981). Perceptions about the woman's occupation change what items participants recalled being featured in the video. The consistency effect indicates that we have better recall and recognition of items if they were consistent with our expectations. Pezdek and colleagues (1989) had participants visit either a graduate student's office or a preschool classroom. In each room there were 16 items, 8 congruent with a graduate student's office and 8 congruent with a preschool classroom. Before entering the room participants were told that they would be seeing a graduate student's office (or a preschool classroom) and that they should study the environment carefully. They were also told they would have one minute to view the room and afterwards would be asked a series of questions about the room. Participants had better recall for items that were inconsistent with their schemas about the rooms, or items that seemed out of place. Thus, we ought to be pretty good at recognizing when things are amiss, at least when explicitly instructed to do so. Another critique is that this study had an equal number of consistent and inconsistent items present, so what happens when almost everything is consistent and just a few things stand out?

Roediger, Meade, and Bergman (2001) asked participants to recall items from several household scenes collaboratively with another subject (who was really a confederate). In some conditions the confederate would offer an item that was congruent with the scene, but was not actually present. Then the participants were separated and asked to individually recall what they had viewed in the scenes. Results indicated that the confederate's mistaken recall during collaboration often resulted in participants also recalling the incorrect items individually after a bit of delay. Imagine how this might play out at the scene of a car accident or shooting. As witnesses begin to share their experiences with one another as they wait to give statements, they are likely influencing one another's recollections of what actually occurred.

Loftus and Zanni (1975) have demonstrated that eyewitness memory is quite susceptible to the influence of information from others. Participants watched a video of a car accident and were then asked to answer questions about the video. Participants were asked, "Did you see a broken headlight?" Other participants were asked, "Did you see the broken headlight?" The difference between these two questions is minimal but using "a" implies that there may or may not have been a broken headlight, while "the" implies that there was in fact a broken headlight which increases the chances someone will report having seen it (even if it wasn't in fact visually presented in the film).

Brewer and Treyens (1981) conducted a more subtle study that might have important implications for eyewitness testimony. Participants were asked to wait in an academic office/study. There were no instructions given to participants that they would be asked questions about the room later, though once they exited the room they were in fact asked to recall what they saw. Although there were no books at all in the room, many participants recalled that books had been present. If you were asked to recall a scene that had happened earlier in a restaurant, you might recall items that were consistent with the restaurant schema, even though that might not reflect reality. Further if you have not only expectations about places, but

How are eyewitness accounts of car accidents shaped by other drivers, pedestrians, and other onlookers?

also stereotypes about people, how might that impact your recollection of an altercation?

Simons and Levin (1998) conducted a clever experiment in which they explored sensitivity to change blindness in real-world settings. Change blindness is an effect whereby we do not notice changes in our environment, until they are quite obvious. In the first study an experimenter begins a conversation with a pedestrian and asks for directions. During the conversation two men walk between the pair carrying a large wood panel, and the experimenter switches places with another experimenter (one of the men carrying the panel). Pedestrians did not seem to notice any change at all and continued to provide this new man the directions that had been requested by the previous man. The two men did look similar to one another, but were not identical. If even during a relatively close face-to-face interaction people have change blindness, how can we rely on eyewitness accounts that occur at a distance and without interaction?

How do we know that eyewitness identification is not reliable? Approximately 75% of DNA exonerations were cases in which an eyewitness had mistakenly identified the innocent person as the perpetrator of a crime (Wells, 2014). According to the innocence project website there have been 314 post-conviction DNA exonerations (The Innocence Project, www.innocenceproject.org). Typically, the eyewitness is asked to identify the suspect from a lineup. A traditional simultaneous lineup (like those on TV or involving books of mug shots) leads people to compare among the individuals they are seeing to find the person who looks most like the person they saw commit the crime. Gronlund, Wixted, and Mickes (2014) have demonstrated that using a sequential lineup improves accuracy. In this case, each photo or person is seen one at a time and the question changes from, "Which of these people did you witness committing the crime?" to "Is this the person you saw committing the crime?" Wells (2014)

Image © auremar, 2014. Used under license from Shutterstock, Inc.

Image © Andy Dean Photography, 2014. Used under license from Shutterstock, Inc.

If you were not paying close attention do you think you could reliably report to someone how the people in these photos looked different from one another? Try having someone you know look at these photos briefly and then give you a verbal description of the "one on the left." As this person provides a description, examine the photos. Can the viewer describe these people in ways that differentiate the one on the left from the one on the right? Are there external cues that would likely not be present several days later as part of a lineup?

reports that at least one-third of actual eyewitnesses choose a known-innocent lineup member. The trade-off between these two types of lineups is largely one in which there are more identifications (though some inaccurate) in the simultaneous procedure and fewer identifications (but increased accuracy) in the sequential procedure. It seems that Blackstone's ratio from his work in the mid-1700s provides a foundation for our understanding of justice: "It is better that ten guilty persons escape than one innocent suffer."

Own-race bias is another effect that plagues eyewitness testimony. Not only do eyewitnesses generally have trouble accurately identifying others, when the person is of a different race eyewitnesses are only able to identify the person accurately 50% of the time (no better than chance). Meissner and Brigham (2001) published a meta-analysis and found that 80% of studies confirmed that there was an own-race bias effect. The effect is not clearly related directly to attitudes towards those of other races. However, people who have less contact with people from other races also tend to have more negative attitudes and may be more likely to demonstrate own-race bias. One possible explanation for this bias is that people are slower to think about the race of a same-race other, and quicker to use a race category when identifying someone from a different race. Quick racial cat-

egorization may also lead to decreased attention to individuating features of a person's face. For example, once a non-white person categorizes a person as white, distinctive facial features are not attended to as well as features that are congruent with typical white faces (e.g., prominent large noses, fair skin). Likewise, a white person who categorizes another person as Asian will attend to features that are typical of Asian faces (e.g., narrow eyes, dark hair), but not distinctive features that would allow for clear identification of this particular person within a lineup of Asian faces.

FALSE CONFESSIONS

There is a common saying that all prisoners proclaim their innocence. Of course we know that isn't true, as many people confess to crimes they committed. But what should we make of those who confess to crimes they later claim they did not commit? Often the public presumes that they are simply trying to escape just punishment and that no one in their right mind would ever admit to doing something they did not do. While in some cases judges give instructions to juries that a confession must be thrown out and should not be considered in deciding the case, research shows that mock-juries are not able to do so (Kassin & Kiechel, 1996; Kassin & Wrightsman, 1980, 1985). There may be up to three types of

Image © Jovan Mandic, 2014. Used under license from Shutterstock, Inc.

Image © DmitriMaruta, 2014. Used under license from Shutterstock, Inc.

When anxiety is high it is unlikely we are able to encode very many details. The woman being held up in this staged photo is looking at her attacker, but most people will keep their eyes focused on the weapon, rather than the perpetrator.

false confessions: voluntary, coerced-compliant, and coerced-internalized. Voluntary confessions are those offered without external pressure. Coerced-compliant are when people confess to avoid further punishment or pressure from authorities. Finally, is coerced-internalized whereby people are pressured and then actually come to believe that they did in fact commit the crime (Kassin & Wrightsman, 1985).

Kassin and Kiechel (1996) instructed participants that they would be participating in a task that involved entering responses on a computer keyboard. Participants reported to the lab with another participant (really a confederate) and were first asked to complete a questionnaire asking about their typing skills, speed of their reflexes, and spatial awareness. Then the participant and confederate were assigned to roles where one person would read a list of letters out loud in time with a metronome (which was either set at a slower or faster pace) and the other would type in the responses. After three minutes, the participant and confederate would switch roles. The participants were all warned not to press the ALT key because this would result in the computer crashing and the data being lost. During the participant's turn the computer would crash after about the first minute of typing. The experimenter would immediately accuse the participant of having pressed the key. All participants began by denying they had done any such thing. For half of the participants, the confederate was then asked if they had seen anything. In half of the cases the confederate would say they did see the participant hit the ALT key. The experimenter would then handwrite a confession, "I hit the ALT key and caused the program to crash. Data were lost." The confession was handed to the participant who was asked to sign it. When the confederate reported they had witnessed the key press and the task was fast paced, all participants signed the confession (see Figure 12.1). The experiment did not end there. The experimenter had the participant wait in a waiting

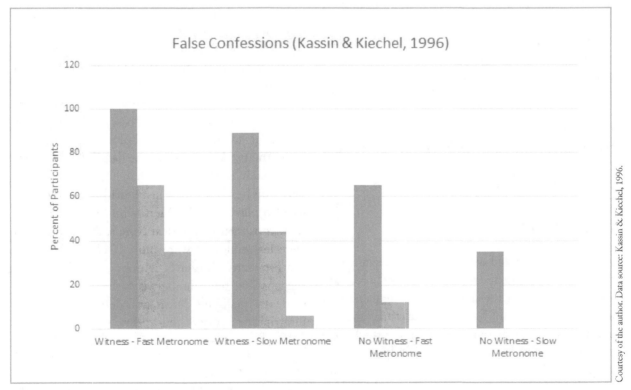

FIGURE 12.1 Your perceptions of why a person needs help may shape whether or not you think the person deserves help.

Courtesy of the author. Data source: Kassin & Kiechel, 1996.

area with another confederate while the experimenter went to retrieve a calendar to reschedule the experiment. After the experimenter was out of ear shot the confederate asked the participant what happened. Over half of those in the high speed with confederate witness condition reported to the stranger that they had in fact committed the act, "I hit the wrong button and ruined the program." However, if the participant hedged, that was not counted as internalization of guilt (e.g., I think I hit a wrong button or he said I hit a wrong button). The experimenter returns and asks the participant to come back into the lab and reread the list of letters. The experimenter asks the participant to determine when the wrong button was hit. Participants were asked to see if they could recall specific details as a measure of confabulation and some did, stating "Yes, here, I hit it with the side of my hand right after you called out the 'A'" (Kassin & Kiechel, 1996, p. 127).

If a lab setting is sufficient to get people to confess to an act they didn't commit, imagine how the additional stress of a crime against one's loved ones, or accusations that you have committed murder, set a fire, or perhaps flew into a rage you can't recall might exacerbate the situation. A police officer or detective (with far more authority than an experimenter) telling you that you must have committed a crime would likely result in rates of confession similar to those in the fast-pace conditions. If during the interrogation others indicate you did commit the crime and they have evidence or a witness, you may well infer that you must have done so!

CAPITAL PUNISHMENT

Juries are often tasked with making a determination of guilt with limited evidence. Further jurors are also aware of what the sentencing consequences of a guilty verdict might be. For most crimes there is a minimum and maximum sentence and the harshest sentences are life in prison and death. For the purposes of this section we are going to be talking about people who were in fact guilty of the crimes they committed. Rather than trying to understand

whether people are guilty, the research in this section examines the sentencing process. Is it equitable? What factors make it more likely that a person might get sentenced to death vs. life in prison?

First, you must understand how juries are selected for trials in which the defendant has been charged with a capital crime. Capital crime cases require a death-qualified jury. This means that all jurors seated on the jury for a case in which the charges include a maximum sentence of death must acknowledge during jury selection that they are comfortable sentencing someone to death if they are guilty. There are a series of questions that the judge must ask each juror.

"Will your views on the death penalty prevent or substantially impair your ability as a juror to perform your duty in accordance with your oath and the Court's instructions?"

In 1985, *Wainwright v. Witt* was decided such that a judge could excuse a juror if the judge felt the juror had a belief about the death penalty that would prevent or substantially impair the juror from carrying out the assigned duties on a capital case. Butler and Moran (2002) have demonstrated that people who are death qualified were less likely to take into account mitigating circumstances, particularly those factors that defense lawyers report are most effective in capital cases. Perhaps not surprising to the social psychology student, people with attitudes favoring the death penalty were more likely to recommend harsher sentences and had a higher belief in a just world. Demographics also played a role: Men, white people, people with conservative political beliefs, and those who were less educated were more likely to favor the death penalty (Butler & Moran 2007). What are the possible tensions between the demographics of death qualifying jurors and defendants receiving trials by a jury of their peers?

We also know that while we like to believe that attitudes predict behavior, situational factors can also influence attitudes. Haney (1984) had adults who would be eligible to be called for jury duty undergo the standard questions used to determine whether a person is qualified to sit on a jury. For half of the participants, the death qualification questions were also included in the questioning. Those who were asked the death qualification questions were much more likely to believe that the defendant was guilty than those who were not exposed to those questions prior to hearing the same case. Since that first study, the death qualification has been expanded to exclude a greater number of individuals because of their attitudes against the death penalty. It is also clear that our attitudes and interests predict our behaviors, including what news reports we watch. Butler (2007) found that individuals who met criteria to be death qualified were more likely to have read about cases and investigations that involved a defendant being charged with a capital offense.

Eberhardt and colleagues (2006) examined the ways in which individuals who were convicted of a capital crime were sentenced. Photos of 44 black male defendants who were convicted of murdering white victims were obtained from the 600 death-eligible cases in Philadelphia between 1979 and 1999. An additional 118 photos of black men who were convicted of murdering black victims were also selected for use in this study. All of these photos were presented to participants who were asked to rate each face for how "stereotypically" black the faces were. Faces that were rated as more stereotypically black were typically of men with darker skin tones, wider noses, and thicker lips. Participants were not told that the photos were of men convicted of crimes, only that they were being asked to rate the stereotypicality of black faces. The results were clear, when victims were white the more stereotypically black the convicted man was the more likely it was that he was on death row. However, when victims were black the stereotypicality ratings were not related to sentencing. Again, while we would like to perceive that the justice system is fair, there continues to be pervasive racism even in how convicted individuals are sentenced. Perhaps the intriguing thing about this work is that the comparison is not between white and black convicted people or even between guilty or not guilty findings. Though previous work has demonstrated that killing a white person results in harsher sentencing than killing a black person and that black defendants were more likely to be sentenced to death than white defendants (Baldus et al., 1997). Even if we eliminate bias when jurors provide determinations of guilt, the sentencing phase continues to be susceptible to racism.

Consumer Behavior

Social psychology is heavily used by people in marketing, product development, and direct sales. The material covered in the chapter on persuasion should give you some ideas of how social psychology informs the seller-buyer interaction. However, long before you are even considering a purchase, the marketers are already grooming you

It's hard to avoid marketing!

to buy their product. A study by Kilbourne (1999) found that children could name more brands of beer than they could name U.S. presidents!

BRAND LOYALTY

You may have a number of heuristics that you use when selecting products at the store. Some people buy the sliced bread their father always brought home from the grocery, or the brand of peanut butter that you grew up eating. It is also likely that at some point you also went down the shampoo or medicine aisle and in a quick movement selected the "familiar" product and upon arriving home realize you have the store brand product! How did that happen?

Store brands are typically packaged in ways to mimic the logo and colors of the name brand item. It is also not a coincidence that the store brand is right next to the name brand. Grocery and drug stores were not always laid out this way. As late as the 1980s, there were aisles for the generic brands of cereals, soaps, soups, and so on. Generics had perfunctory black and white labels with no colors, pictures, or real branding of any kind.

JND: JUST NOTICEABLE DIFFERENCE

You may also have noticed over the years how the branding logos change. These changes usually have a just noticeable difference; branding changes are typically not drastic as consumers may begin to think the change in packaging means the product has also changed. If you shop at a store and notice two packages of cookies, one that looks just slightly different than the other you probably do some investigating to see what might be different about these two cookies. My grandfather was a fan of Chips Ahoy chocolate chip cookies. My grandmother had gone to the store, purchased the Chips Ahoy cookies that looked to be the same, but in fact the cookies (as my grandfather made sure we all knew) were now made with even more chips. This different ratio did not suit my grandfather! Luckily the "original" formula returned shortly.

Starbucks logos have also changed, but unless you are particularly perceptive when you drink your coffee, the logo has evolved. In 1971, the brown logo included the words coffee, tea, spices; today, the green logo actually just includes an image of

Would your favorite foods be just as enticing without the label?

a woman wearing a crown that used to be at the center of earlier logos.

Most people do not even take note of a change in signage other than to recognize they have "updated," but would be hard pressed to say what exactly changed.

My grandfather was also a fan of the fudge-striped cookies made by the Keebler elves. In the 1980s, Nabisco attempted to capitalize on this by intro-ducing Striped Chips Ahoy, again my grandfather balked and so did other consumers, and you will not find these striped chocolate chips cookies on the shelf today! While some people remain true to the original, companies know that in order to keep stock prices rising, it is imperative to find a new segment of the market to entice. The most recent endeavor of the Nabisco elves are the "simply made" versions of their chocolate chip and butter cookies. In an attempt to get people who object to unpronounceable ingredients, these cookies contain wheat flour, semisweet chocolate, sugar, butter, oil, baking soda, salt, vanilla, and eggs. Compare that list to the ingredients in the more complex and traditional product: enriched flour, semisweet chocolate, dextrose, soy lecithin, high fructose corn syrup, and so on (nutritional information available at www.keebler.com).

NEEDS VS. WANTS

You likely remember Maslow's hierarchy of needs from your introductory psychology course and marketers have certainly remembered it as well. Framing products as fulfilling basic physiological needs is one clever marketing strategy. People who are experiencing the need can be persuaded to reach for a product marketed to fulfill that need. Thirsty? A 7-Up sign tells you that 7-Up is "First Against Thirst" and other ads in the late 1950s touted 7-Up was a "real thirst-quencher!" Hungry? Snickers always satisfies. Want to feel safe? Home security companies (e.g., ADT) have commercials in which these sorts of systems work to ward off burglars and home invasions. Looking for a relationship, eharmony.com and match.com will have just what you seek. What need does an iPhone serve? Depends on which market you are in what need you believe your iPhone meets. The constant production of newer versions and upgrades appeal to status and esteem needs, but commercials that demonstrate Face Time capacity are really selling a fulfillment of a social need. Adventure vacations also help people who are relatively satiated meet their needs to have experiences as self-actualizers.

Image © Diane Uhley, 2014. Used under license from Shutterstock, Inc.

Image © Robert Crum, 2014. Used under license from Shutterstock, Inc.

Everyone needs a place to live, but everything beyond a basic shelter is likely more a desire than a necessity.

Today marketers are also selling time. Time poverty is a feeling that we have fewer and fewer minutes of downtime and are increasingly engaged in activities or connected to others via social media. Products are now made that help us to do many things at once by engaging in polychronic activity (Kaufman, Lane, & Lindquist, 1991). When cell phones were recognized as a hazard when used by drivers, hands-free devices were manufactured as laws increasingly prohibited holding the phone while driving. Products are increasingly geared toward allowing people to multitask. Computer monitors were historically sold with CPUs, but now most computers have more than one (and sometimes three or more) video cards allowing a single user to have three screens to visually attend to while working (or playing). However, we are not any more capable of multitasking than the humans a generation ago. Just 30 years ago people would sit in front of the television and watch the news for an entire half hour, without reading a book or texting or monitoring the scrolling stock prices at the bottom of the screen. The busier we feel the more we try to do at once. However, this multitasking is not without a downside. Originally, working from home and flexible scheduling were thought to be ideal for workers, but increasingly workers are returning to work in an attempt to reclaim their homes as places free from workplace obligation (Kaufman-Scarborough, 2006).

What do you think would be your ideal weekday in the working world? Where and when would work happen? What would you do with your "down time"?

Time is more valuable than money; you might lose both but you will not find an extra 25 minutes laying on the sidewalk. Time evaporates, it cannot be saved only spent, making it much more valuable than money. People are likely to feel upset if they lose money, having someone waste your time is likely to cause you far more ire. Anti-wrinkle creams are sold by using slogans that refer to turn back the clock, using our time poverty to sell us what we cannot possibly retrieve. Technology is increasingly used to document our lives with people engaging in projects that allow for summative videos of seconds from an entire year. Facebook provides you with a yearend summary of your most frequent posts and "major" status updates. All of these are attempts to provide and encourage consumers to document time well spent and make people feel better about the time they spend using technology.

A recent video circulated the internet of a guitarist, Carlos Whittaker, setting up to film a music video. A homeless man comes up and spontaneously they start singing together really well. The video was filmed by a man who was talking on his cell phone the whole time narrating what was playing out in front of him. Rather than be-

Do these images stress you out? If so it's likely because you recognize time poverty as stressful. Certainly, photos of vacations often show people doing one thing at a time and not engaged with technology!

ing in the moment, or silently filming so that the documentation of the moment would capture the chemistry between these two musicians, he needed to stay connected to whomever was on the other end of the line. How do you want to spend your time? How do we connect with others without technology? What else do we consume that meets our needs for social interaction, self-esteem, and self-actualization? What do we really need?

Environmental Psychology

Environmental psychology has three primary areas: built environments, conservation, and populations. Social psychology can help to inform a variety of environmental psychology areas. Understanding how people use energy, why people litter, and what motivates them to make green (environmentally friendly or neutral) products can help environmental psychologists to address important issues related to climate change. In addition, built environments and access to nature are both situational factors that have clear influences on how people think, feel, and behave.

CONSERVATION

One predictor of whether or not someone will care for a place by preserving natural habitats or indigenous plants has to do with how attached a person feels to a particular area (Scannell & Gifford, 2013). You may care deeply about land near where you grew up or where you live now, but it may be more difficult to feel the same need for preservation of places you have never been. In some communities, the need to preserve historic buildings may be in part due to attachment to a place. However, Scanelle and Gifford (2010) found that attachment to the natural world was more likely to lead to strong attachment rather than civic attachment.

Another predictor of whether you will engage in conservation of energy, natural resources, or other pro-environment behaviors is simply whether you have done so before. A person who (for whatever reason) has always turned the lights off when leaving a room is likely to continue to do so. If your campus has numerous recycling or composting opportunities and you see other people using them, you are likely to follow this norm (Fornara et al., 2011; Matthies et al., 2012; Nolan et al., 2008). McCright and Dunlap (2013) found that conservative white males in the United States are less concerned than other people living in the United States. Religion also matters, though framing of Judeo-Christian beliefs varies. For people who frame an ethic of stewardship of nature (Judeo-Christian) or believe that humans are part of a system of life including all living things (Islam), both lead to environmental concern. However, the Judeo-Christian framing of people having dominion over nature is more likely to make them believe that the earth was provided for people to exploit for their own benefit (Gifford, 2014).

Walking to work rather than driving is one high-impact pro-environmental behavior. However, this behavior may be harder to change than lower impact behaviors (e.g., recycling). Leaving your car at home may have more costs than choosing to recycle rather than to throw away an aluminum can. The trade-off between time saved with driving and time lost by walking can certainly decrease the chances that you will keep your car in the garage (Gardner & Stern, 2002). Finally, it is important to understand how our motivations shape our behaviors. Imagine you see two people turn off the light when they exit a classroom. You may think they share a common concern about the climate, but you may be just as likely to find that they just do so out of habit or to save the school money. Some conservation efforts are not motivated by concern for the climate. A person may choose to walk to work to get more exercise rather than reduce carbon emissions. Understanding what motivates people to engage in pro-environment actions may be a first step in determining how to increase these high-impact behaviors.

IMPORTANCE OF NATURE

The forces of nature are strong. Nature provides opportunity for people to disconnect from technology and regenerate themselves through being in

When you need transportation, do you consider environmental impact?

CARPOOLS ONLY
2 OR MORE PERSONS
PER VEHICLE

Access to green space is likely to reduce stress responses and increase opportunities for exposure to nature.

nature (e.g., camping, hiking), but nature also presents us with natural disasters that destroy our built environments, cause death, and disrupt our lives.

Living near plants, grass, trees, and in green spaces reduces crime (Kuo & Sullivan, 2001), increases social activity (Sullivan et al., 2004), reduces stress, and improves mood and cognitive functioning (Berman et al., 2008). These restorative effects are particularly true when we are exposed to water (Felsten, 2009; White et al., 2010). These benefits can be derived from actually being in nature, having a plant in your room, or even in being exposed to natural scenes in 2D and virtual experiences or even photos or paintings (Raanaas et al., 2011; Kweon et al., 2007).

On the other hand, when mud slides, wildfires, heat waves, tsunamis, volcanoes, and tornados destroy our neighborhoods, we tend to experience nature quite differently. This might include mourning for a lost sense of place, the loss of life, or even feelings of safety that are no longer possible. You may think that once people experience this type of disaster they would be better prepared for the next disaster. Some people do take initial steps to rebuild and prepare for another event. Others believe it could not possibly happen a second time during their lifetime (e.g., 100-year floods). After all, people claim "lightning never strikes twice." Of course those living in tornado alley, on fault lines, or in a flood plain know bet-

ter, but that does not necessarily increase efforts to prepare for a second event.

Breezy Point, New York, on November 20, 2012, after hurricane Sandy and a six-alarm blaze. Nature cannot be controlled.

BUILT ENVIRONMENTS

Although we may be surrounded by nature, we often spend the majority of our time indoors and around other people. Noise levels are on the rise as the population increases. The increase in open-office plans where people may work around others and rarely have private offices may decrease cognitive functioning and increase workload and fatigue (Smith-Jackson & Klein, 2009). If you have forgotten how loud your day is, you might recall the last time the electricity went out in your

Image © Monkey Business Images, 2014. Used under license from Shutterstock, Inc.

Image © David Stuart Productions, 2014. Used under license from Shutterstock, Inc.

How do you use your headphones/ear buds to create distance or privacy?

Our motivations matter: When out with friends to meet new people you may seek a table near the action; but on a night out with someone special, you may prefer the corner booth. People are increasingly seeking privacy by using headphones/ear buds to create at least psychological distance from others (particularly co-commuters). People wearing headphones listening to positive music actually led people to have smaller personal spaces and allowed others to come much closer before expressing discomfort (Tajadura-Jiminez et al., 2011).

A focus on physical health has also led some communities to build walkable neighborhoods that are pedestrian friendly and include shops, amenities, and access to nature (Brown et al., 2007). Other strategies are being employed on roadways to allow for safe bike lanes that provide those forgoing driving to safely bicycle their way between work and home.

There are many ways in which our built and natural environments influence our thoughts, feelings, and behaviors. We also actively work to manipulate our environments in ways that facilitate desired behaviors and provide us with feelings of safety and comfort. Further, our sense of home is often closely tied to shelter and safety. Hadjiyanni (2014) explored the experiences of people who were undocumented and living in the United States and found that people have complex relationships with their dwellings. In some cases, they saw their current situation as temporary and that home was back in Mexico where they planned to return. For others, there was an attempt to create home in dwellings that were often in poor condition. Fear of jeopardizing their jobs often led to tolerance of substandard living conditions.

Perhaps nothing points so clearly to the comfort of home, than to consider Bender and colleagues (2014) work on homeless adolescents. Safety concerns were at the forefront of their minds and they reported using intuition to detect danger (e.g., vibes, gut-feelings). Youth also reported reading the environment by remaining aware, watching

neighborhood and the quiet you experienced as all the electrical devices stopped whirring. The difference between a normal evening and an evening without electricity is striking!

While open-office plans are becoming commonplace, we still value privacy and our personal space.

Homeless people prepare to spend the night under the bridge in a tent compound in New Orleans.

others, reading people, and attempting to predict the behaviors of others. Sense of place also provided safety. Unfamiliar territory was perceived as particularly risky, and places or situations that did not provide a clear and safe exit were also perceived as dangerous. Even without homes, built environments and the natural world intersect to create spaces in which people are striving to find a sense of place.

Health Psychology

Social psychology research addresses many of the issues and concerns that arise in health psychology. There is a significant amount of research focused on helping people to change behaviors that are related to health. For example, leveraging the theory of reasoned action or the theory of planned behavior (discussed in Chapter 5) to help people stop smoking or encouraging people to exercise or use condoms or

polyurethane gloves when they have penetrative sex. For example, it is critical not only that people have positive attitudes towards behaviors that protect or improve health, but also that they believe that others who are important to them also believe these pro-health behaviors are desirable.

Health psychologists also study the situation in which people receive health care. How are patient-doctor interactions impacting health outcomes? Consider the information in the stereotypes and prejudice chapter. How might a transman go about obtaining routine health procedures (e.g., a pap smear)? How might a transwoman complete an intake questionnaire that asks about her last menses? What prejudices are built into the health-care system and what training do physicians receive about how to work with patients who are non-heteronormative or do not fit within a gender binary? How might conversations about safer sex and sex education change to accommodate the

How does your healthcare change based on how you are perceived? If they thought you had better insurance, would you receive different treatment? What roles do sex, race, sexual orientation, and class play in your healthcare?

knowledge that even people who identify as heterosexual may be having sexual relationships with same-sex partners? Bockting and colleagues (2004) found that concerted efforts at improving friendliness and courtesy of staff in healthcare clinics improved trans* patient experiences. In some cases, sexual orientation and gender identity are not mentioned during healthcare visits and heterosexuality remains the presumption. These topics represent just a few of the issues that are currently being addressed by health psychologists.

Healthcare providers often formulate treatment plans, but it is not clear whether patients actually follow those plans. Meichenbaum and Turk (1987) estimate that on average between 30% and 60% of patients do not adhere to their doctor-prescribed treatment plans. There are a number of factors that can increase adherence to a plan. First, if patients believe that the treatment will cure the ailment they are more likely to adhere (Sackett & Snow, 1979). Patients are also more likely to adhere to short-term and simple treatment plans as opposed to drawn out plans or those that are more complicated. Patients are also more likely to follow a prescription regimen if they have symptoms (Aikens & Klinkman, 2012; Becker, Drachman, & Kirscht, 1972). There are a number of reasons why people may deviate from a prescribed health regimen (Wheeler et al., 2014). People who mis-

trust Western medicine, believing that the medicine will not be helpful, and even physical impairments (arthritis prevents opening the pill bottle) can decrease adherence (Doggrell, 2010; Gellad et al., 2011; Krueger et al., 2005).

Lacking self-efficacy to administer a medication may also decrease the chances that patients will continue with a treatment (Gellad et al., 2011). For example, diabetic persons who test their blood sugar may feel they are not adept at doing so and therefore test less frequently. Others who may have to give themselves injections find that aspect of a regiment challenging and forego the treatment. Side effects (and patients' perception that they can manage the side effects) also decrease adherence to a treatment plan. Adherence increases when patients perceive that their healthcare provider communicates well and engages in shared decision making rather than demanding compliance. A physician who seeks adherence may be more successful (Wheeler et al., 2014).

ACUTE AND CHRONIC ILLNESS

We have a norm about what it means to be sick. You may expect that if you are unwell your professor will excuse you from turning in homework on time or taking an exam. It is also likely that other household members will not expect you to do your

How is being in the hospital different than being sick at home?

daily part of the chores. The sick role provides time for you to rest and engage in self-care with the goal of improving your health. This role may function well for acute illnesses in which you are only debilitated for a short period of time, but chronic conditions require a different approach (Varul, 2010).

There are also stereotypes about illnesses. Let's say that you go to see the doctor because you feel congested. If the diagnosis is a common cold you may experience those symptoms and interpret your bodily states in ways that are congruent with a cold. If the diagnosis were flu you may interpret the same bodily states quite differently. For example, people often associate cancer with chemotherapy, even though many cancers are treated without chemotherapy or radiation. Others assume that liver disease may be directly related to one's choice to drink alcohol in excess or that HIV is a result of drug use or having unprotected sex. These stereotypes in and of themselves may take an additional psychological toll.

We often conceptualize and experience poor health and threats to health as acute and reversible. Even when diagnosed with something that requires management over the course of one's life, people resist this conceptualization and continue to adopt the sick role (Arluke, 1988). However, we increasingly experience a variety of illnesses and conditions that are chronic. Further, if we are hospitalized, we may experience a variety of other factors such as being treated as "the appendectomy in room 214" rather than as a person. Hospital patients may be expected to be passive rule followers rather than collaborative partners in their recovery. When patients return home after a prolonged hospital stay, they may find it difficult to take care of themselves because the hospital nurses and doctors were taking care of the details and now it's up to the patient to do so.

Chronically ill people must avoid the sick role in order to continue their lives. Rather than discussions around curing one's illness the language shifts to management of a condition. The focus for chronic illness is to find ways to continue to engage in one's normal life with as little disruption as possible. However, there is typically a need for people with a variety of chronic conditions to devote significant attention to self-care, diet, rest, and exercise; perhaps more so than healthy people. This may have implications for many aspects of a person's life. Time management may become a priority both at work and in relationships. Social activities may be limited by diet or even concerns that others have about your health. Even being inundated with questions about your health may present a unique burden on those who are managing a chronic condition.

Image © Monkey Business Images, 2014. Used under license from Shutterstock, Inc.

Image © Andreea Pirvu, 2014. Used under license from Shutterstock, Inc.

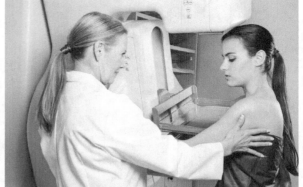

How do your perceptions of illness impact your health decisions?

Brion, Leary, and Drabkin (2014) asked 187 HIV-infected respondents to complete a self-compassion measure and a series of questions about their emotional and behavior reactions to living with HIV. When people had an orientation of self-care (rather than self-blame) and showed themselves the same compassion they would extend to others, they were better adjusted, were more likely to adhere to treatments, seek medical care, and engage in practices that would prevent partners from becoming infected. Approach to and perceptions of an illness matter, but it is also important to understand how practitioners might treat patients differently depending upon their own perceptions.

STEREOTYPES/DISCRIMINATION

In the United States, there are clear and troubling health disparities between white and black indi-viduals (Smedley, Stith, & Nelson, 2003). Native American males in southwest South Dakota had a life expectancy of 58 compared to Asian females in New Jersey who had a life expectancy of 91 years (Murray et al., 2006). There may be a number of physiological reasons why women live longer than men, but what are we to make of the role of race and class in determining health outcomes? Murray and colleagues devised eight groups within the United States that have different health outcomes driven largely by race, class, and geography. While race may play a role how are we to understand the difference between low-income white people in the North and low-income white people in the Appalachian and the Mississippi valleys? How does geography or culture within the United States impact health outcomes? Access to health-care and health insurance can certainly impact some of these life expectancy numbers, but vio-lence, poverty, and food insecurity also play a role.

8 Americas	Definitions	2001 Life Expectancy (Males)	2001 Life Expectancy (Females)
Asian	Asians living where Pacific Islanders make up less that 40% of the population	82	88
Northland low-income rural White	Whites in the northern plains/Dakotas, population density less than 100 persons/km2, per capita income below $11,755	76	82
Middle America	All other whites, Native Americans, and Asians not included in other groups	76	80
Low-income White people in Appalachia and the Mississippi Valley	Whites in Appalachia/Mississippi Valley, per capita income below $11,755	72	78
Western Native American	Native American populations in the mountain and plains areas, predominantly on reservations	69	76
Black Middle America	All other Black populations not included in other groups	69	76
Southern low-income rural Black	Black people in the Mississippi Valley or deep south, population density less than 100 persons/km2, per capital income below $7,500 and total population above 1,000	67	75
High-risk urban Black	Urban populations (more than 150,000 Black people in the county) and high-risk (cumulative probability of homicide death between 15 and 74 years olds greater than 1%)	66	75

Courtesy of the author. Adapted from Murray et al., 2006.

FIGURE 12.2 The populations at the top of the list have the highest life expectancies for children born between 1982 and 2001 (ages are approximated from image provided in original publication).

Physicians may also treat patients differently based on stereotypical assumptions about race, insurance coverage, and willingness to pay. During a recent trip to a physician where I was to be prescribed antibiotics, I was offered the cheaper option (4 doses a day for 10 days), until I specifically asked whether the 5 day (1 dose a day) option would be viable. The physician said, "They are pretty expensive for a college student," not realizing that I was a professor with good insurance happy to pay the extra money for the easier to take regimen. I suspect this is not limited to perceptions about socioeconomic status.

Ball and Elixhauser (1996) examined patient records for both black and white patients who had

Do these individuals have the same access to healthcare?

similar colorectal cancer diagnoses and presenting symptoms. They found that for the majority of patients the chance of a patient dying while in the hospital was significantly higher for black patients (98%) as compared to white patients (59%). Further, those who were not yet severely ill were provided more aggressive treatments to eradicate the cancer when they were white rather than black.

Indeed physicians who were shown videos of both black and white male patients reporting similar symptoms of a heart attack were treated quite differently (Green et al., 2007). Overall, physicians who saw a white patient in the film were more likely to decide this was a coronary artery disease (CAD) than if they saw a black patient in the film reporting the same symptoms. Physicians who did diagnose the black patient as describing CAD were less likely to offer thrombolysis than the physicians who saw a white patient they believed to be describing CAD. Physician's implicit bias against black patients was correlated less likely to diagnose CAD and less likely to prescribe the recommended thrombolysis treatment.

Participants were shown a photo of either a black or white person and asked to think about how much pain the person might feel if injured in the head or hand. Both black and white adults reported that the black person would feel less pain than the white person (Trawalter, Hoffman, & Waytz, 2012). There were no clear correlations between explicit or implicit racial bias. Dore and colleagues (2014) carried out a similar study with children asking them how much pain people might feel when they bit their tongue or hit their head. Five-year-olds did not show a significant race-based judgment, but by the age of seven there was a trend and by age ten, the difference was significant. The idea that black individuals are likely to feel less pain seems to emerge quite early!

Physicians are more likely to scrutinize pain reports by black and Hispanic patients as possibly drug-seeking behaviors (Becker et al., 2011). Even if drug seeking is not suspected, primary care pro-

viders underestimate or dismiss the pain intensity in blacks more than in other groups and therefore provide fewer prescriptions or interventions that allow for effective pain management (Tait & Chibnall, 2014). Physicians who are racially biased are less likely to engage in patient-centered conversation with black patients and in turn black patients view these physicians as less respectful

Image © Greg Epperson, 2014. Used under license from Shutterstock, Inc.

Image © bikeriderlondon, 2014. Used under license from Shutterstock, Inc.

Do you empathize with these pain experiences?

(Cooper et al., 2012). Recall that we covered mirror neurons in an earlier chapter. When we see someone else experiencing pain our anterior insula and anterior cingulate cortex show activity. Asian and white participants were asked to view videotapes of Asian and white people undergoing painful procedures and it was only when viewing someone of the same race that the mirror neurons activated in the expected ways (Xu, Zuo, Wang, & Han, 2009).

However, at other times, just seeing someone else who is unwell can result in experiencing physical symptoms. Psychogenic illness occurs when a number of people seem to fall ill at the same time, but no physiological or biological cause can be identified. Typically one person falls ill and then it seems to spread from person to person reporting similar symptoms. There are a number of reported cases over the years. In one such case, a woman who worked at the DMV fell ill, reporting headaches and respiratory distress. Her colleagues also quickly came down with similar symptoms. The first presumption was that something in the air conditioning unit must have dispersed mold or an allergen that cause these strong reactions. However, the environmental health officials could not find any organic cause.

Common symptoms include headache and nausea. If you have ever been present while a friend had the stomach flu, you probably have a pretty good sense of how your gag reflex might be motivated to mimic your friends vomiting behavior. There may be an evolutionary reason that nausea (or at least gagging) is contagious. Living in social groups often meant sharing food sources and if there was a poisonous food source and one person fell ill, the sooner your body rejected the toxin the more likely you were to live as well (Voorhees, 2008). Ditto and colleagues (2014) examined whether blood donors who were exposed to someone experiencing vasovagal symptoms (drop in blood pressure, fainting, dizziness, weakness) would increase self-reports of similar symptoms. For repeat donors, seeing someone else have vasovagal symptoms increased their own report of such symptoms.

If being sick is contagious, what about being healthy? Do healthy behaviors spread? Ball and colleagues (2010) found that social norms that promoted physical activity and healthy eating were related to increases in those behaviors for individuals. Unfortunately watching someone jog by does not actually lead us to join them. Social norms are just as important as having social support for engaging in healthy behavior. It can be difficult to avoid junk food if everyone in your family is consuming it, but social norms about what you think

Are both of these people contagious?

Image © lzf, 2014. Used under license from Shutterstock, Inc.

Image © gpointstudio, 2014. Used under license from Shutterstock, Inc.

most other people do can also influence what you do yourself (even when social support is lacking).

Social media may be just one way in which we are beginning to develop and refine our social norms. If most people in your social network post about eating healthy foods or engaging in physical activity, that may set up a social norm that endorses these behaviors. Conversely if your Facebook friends are largely posting Instagram photos of greasy fast food and updates about the latest TV show or blockbuster film, that might send a different message about what most people are eating and doing.

Summary

Social psychology is widely applicable to everyday life. People are faced with a variety of situations and understanding the ways in which person-situation interactions occur can help us to better understand how and why people think, feel, and behave as they do. In addition, having insight about how your own behaviors can be influenced by situations can provide you with an opportunity to create change. For example, knowing that eyewitness testimony is not very reliable may make you a more objective juror when asked to serve. Understanding the ways in which marketers are leveraging persuasion techniques may make you both more resistant to purchases that would not really fulfill needs and create needs that may improve the balance in your checking account. Likewise, if you go into sales and marketing you may find these techniques can increase your paycheck. Incorporating your knowledge of consumer behav-

ior with concern for the environment may allow you to fulfill real needs people have to live more sustainably while meeting a variety of their needs. Clarity about the many ways that racism, sexism, ableism, and other biases shape health behavior may also help you to increase and correct for your biases. Caring for yourself and the environment, engaging in sustainable consumer behavior, reducing bias to improve health, and ensuring that our legal system is just, are a few of the applications that can lead to a better life for you and the next generation.

Stanley Milgram was quoted as saying in 1974, "The social psychology of this century reveals a major lesson: often it is not so much the kind of person a man is as the kind of situation in which he finds himself that determines how he will act." Thirty years later, situations continue to be powerful in shaping and changing our behavior; what lies before the student of social psychology is to realize that people also have power to change the situation.

"When we can no longer change a situation, we are challenged to change ourselves."

–Viktor Frankl

NAME _____ DATE _____

Chapter Questions

1. How does death qualifying a jury impact the concept of a fair trial?

2. How can we understand racism in the justice system by examining only African American men?

3. Given what you now know about eyewitness testimony, what might you do if asked to serve on a jury or to provide a witness statement?

4. What is your favorite marketing campaign and why?

5. What role does music play in restaurants and other eating establishments?

6. What are people buying when they purchase junk food?

7. How do marketing campaigns influence your perceptions of prescription drugs?

8. Make a weekly shopping list of what you normally purchase. Then go find more sustainable products (e.g., items with less packaging, a greener manufacturing process). Is the price difference worth shifting your buying habits? (For many people, greener is also cheaper!)

9. If you were driving a car full of your friends, what would you do if one of them threw a straw wrapper out the window?

10. What strategies do you use to conserve energy or decrease your impact on the climate?

11. Most people have a strategy for dealing with illness. What is yours? Do you have remedies that you swear by? Where did you learn about them?

12. How does health coverage change how and when people seek medical treatment? What is the long-term impact of having a significant portion of the population without health insurance?

13. What do you do to stay healthy? Where did you learn to engage in those behaviors? How would you help others adopt healthier nutrition and activity habits?

14. How do these four applied areas intersect? For example, do laws about the environment change marketing strategies which also impact health? Can you give an example?

References

Afifi, T. O., Cox, B. J., & Enns, M. W. (2006). Mental health profiles among married, never-married, and separated/divorced mothers in a nationally representative sample. *Social Psychiatry and Psychiatric Epidemiology*, *41*(2), 122–129. doi:10.1007/s00127-005-0005-3

Agnew, C. R., Van Lange, P. A. M., Rusbult, C. E., & Langston, C. A. (1998). Cognitive interdependence: Commitment and the mental representation of close relationships. *Journal of Personality and Social Psychology*, *74*(4), 939–954. doi:10.1037/0022-3514.74.4.939

Aiello, J. R., & Douthitt, E. A. (2001). Social facilitation from Triplett to electronic performance monitoring. *Group Dynamics: Theory, Research, and Practice*, *5*(3), 163–180. doi:10.1037//1089-2699.5.3.163

Aikens, J. E., & Klinkman, M. S. (2012). Changes in patients' beliefs about their antidepressant during the acute phase of depression treatment. *General Hospital Psychiatry*, *34*(3), 221–226.

Ainsworth, M. S. (1989). Attachments beyond infancy. *American Psychologist*, *44*(4), 709–716. doi:10.1037/0003-066X.44.4.709

Ajzen, I., & Fishbein, M. (1972). Attitudes and normative beliefs as factors influencing behavioral intentions. *Journal of Personality and Social Psychology*, *21*(1), 1–9. doi:10.1037/h0031930

Ajzen, I., & Madden, T. J. (1986). Prediction of goal-directed behavior: Attitudes, intentions, and perceived behavioral control. *Journal of Experimental Social Psychology*, *22*(5), 453–474. doi:10.1016/0022-1031(86)90045-4

Alberts, J. K. (1990). The use of humor in managing couples' conflict interactions. In D. D. Cahn (Ed.), *Intimates in conflict: A communication perspective.* (pp. 105–120). Hillsdale, NJ: Erlbaum.

Allen, M., D'Alessio, D., & Emmers-Sommer, T. M. (1999). Reactions of criminal sexual offenders to pornography: A meta-analytic summary. *Communication Yearbook*, *22*, 139–170.

Allen, M., Emmers-Sommer, T. M., D'Alessio, D., Timmerman, L., Hanzal, A., & Korus, J. (2007). The connection between the physiological and psychological reactions to sexually explicit materials: A literature summary using meta-analysis. *Communication Monographs*, *74*(4), 541–560. doi:10.1080/03637750701578648

Alloy, L. B., & Abramson, L. Y. (1979). Judgment of contingency in depressed and nondepressed students: Sadder but wiser? *Journal of Experimental Psychology: General, 108*(4), 441–485. doi:10.1037/0096-3445.108.4.441

Allport, F. H. (1924). *Social Psychology.* Cambridge, MA: Riverside Press.

Allport, G. W. (1954). The nature of prejudice. *Reading.* MA: Addison.

Altman, I., & Taylor, D. (1973). *Social Penetration: The Development of Interpersonal Relationships.* New York: Holt.

Amabile, T. M., Hadley, C. N., & Kramer, S. J. (2002). Creativity under the gun. *Harvard Business Review, 80*(8), 52–61.

Amato, P. R. (1990). Personality and social network involvement as predictors of helping behavior in everyday life. *Social Psychology Quarterly, 53*(1), 31–43.

Amichai-Hamburger, Y., Kingsbury, M., & Schneider, B. H. (2013). Friendship: An old concept with a new meaning? *Computers in Human Behavior, 29*(1), 33–39. doi:10.1016/j.chb.2012.05.025

Amir, Y. (1969). Contact hypothesis in ethnic relations. *Psychological Bulletin, 71*(5), 319–342. doi:10.1037/h0027352

Anderson, C. A., & Bushman, B. J. (2002). Human aggression. *Annual Review of Psychology, 53*(1), 27–51. doi:10.1146/annurev.psych.53.100901.135231

Anderson, C. A., Carnagey, N. L., & Eubanks, J. (2003). Exposure to violent media: The effects of songs with violent lyrics on aggressive thoughts and feelings. *Journal of Personality and Social Psychology, 84*(5), 960–971. doi:10.1037/0022-3514.84.5.960

Anderson, C. A., & Dill, K. E. (2000). Video games and aggressive thoughts, feelings, and behavior in the laboratory and in life. *Journal of Personality and Social Psychology, 78*(4), 772–790. doi:10.1037/0022-3514.78.4.772

Anderson, V. N., Simpson-Taylor, D., & Herrmann, D. J. (2004). Gender, age, and rape-supportive rules. *Sex Roles, 50*(1/2), 77–90. doi:10.1023/B:SERS.0000011074.76248.3a

Archer, J. (2000). Sex differences in aggression between heterosexual partners: A meta-analytic review. *Psychological Bulletin, 126*(5), 651–680. doi:10.1037/0033-2909.126.5.651

Archer, J. (2004). Sex differences in aggression in real-world settings: A meta-analytic review. *Review of General Psychology, 8*(4), 291–322. doi:10.1037/1089-2680.8.4.291

Archer, J., & Coyne, S. M. (2005). An integrated review of indirect, relational, and social aggression. *Personality and Social Psychology Review, 9*(3), 212–230. doi:10.1207/s15327957pspr0903_2

Arluke, A. (1988). The sick-role concept. In D. S. Gochman (Ed.), *Health behavior: Emerging research perspectives* (pp. 169–180). New York: Plenum Press.

Armor, D. A., & Sackett, A. M. (2006). Accuracy, error, and bias in predictions for real versus hypothetical events. *Journal of Personality and Social Psychology, 91*(4), 583–600. doi:10.1037/0022-3514.91.4.583

Aron, A. (2005). Reward, Motivation, and Emotion Systems Associated With Early-Stage Intense Romantic Love. *Journal of Neurophysiology, 94*(1), 327–337. doi:10.1152/jn.00838.2004

Aron, A., Aron, E. N., & Smollan, D. (1992). Inclusion of Other in the Self Scale and the structure of interpersonal closeness. *Journal of Personality and Social Psychology, 63*(4), 596–612. doi:10.1037/0022-3514.63.4.596

Aron, A., Fisher, H., Mashek, D. J., Strong, G., Haifang, L., & Brown, L. L. (2005). Reward, motivation, and emotion systems associated with early-stage intense romantic love. *Journal of Neurophysiology, 94*(1), 327–337. doi:10.1152/jn.00838.2004

Aronson, E., & Mills, J. (1959). The effect of severity of initiation on liking for a group. *The Journal of Abnormal and Social Psychology, 59*(2), 177–181. doi:10.1037/h0047195

Arriaga, X. B., & Rusbult, C. E. (1998). Standing in my partner's shoes: Partner perspective taking and reactions to accommodative dilemmas. *Personality and Social Psychology Bulletin, 24*(9), 927–948. doi:10.1177/0146167298249002

Asch, S. E. (1951). Effects of group pressure upon the modification and distortion of judgment. In H. Guetzkow (Ed.), *Groups, leadership, and men.* (pp. 177–190). Pittsburgh, PA: Carnegie University Press.

Association of Women's Health, Obstetric, and Neonatal Nurses. (1998). *Empowering survivors of abuse: Health care for battered women and their children* (J. Campbell, Ed.). Thousand Oaks, CA: Sage Publications.

Badcock, C. R. (1998). PsychoDarwinism: The new synthesis of Darwin and Freud. In *Handbook of evolutionary psychology* (pp. 457–583). Mahwah, NJ: Erlbaum.

Baek, K., Holton, A., Harp, D., & Yaschur, C. (2011). The links that bind: Uncovering novel motivations for linking on Facebook. *Computers in Human Behavior, 27*(6), 2243–2248. doi:10.1016/j.chb.2011.07.003

Baiocco, R., Santamaria, F., Lonigro, A., Ioverno, S., Baumgartner, E., & Laghi, F. (2014). Beyond similarities: Cross-gender and cross-orientation best friendship in a sample of sexual minority and heterosexual young adults. *Sex Roles, 70*(3-4), 110–121. doi:10.1007/s11199-014-0343-2

Baldus, D. C., Woodworth, G., Zuckerman, D., & Weiner, N. A. (1997). Racial discrimination and the death penalty in the post-Furman era: An empirical and legal overview with recent findings from Philadelphia. *Cornell Law Review, 83*, 1638.

Ball, J. K., & Elixhauser, A. (1996). Treatment differences between blacks and whites with colorectal cancer. *Medical Care, 34*(9), 970–984.

Ball, K., Jeffery, R. W., Abbott, G., McNaughton, S. A., & Crawford, D. (2010). Is healthy behavior contagious: Associations of social norms with physical activity and healthy eating. *International Journal of Behavioral Nutrition and Physical Activity, 7*(1), 86. doi:10.1186/1479-5868-7-86

Bandura, A., Barbaranelli, C., Caprara, G. V., & Pastorelli, C. (1996). Mechanisms of moral disengagement in the exercise of moral agency. *Journal of Personality and Social Psychology, 71*(2), 364–374. doi:10.1037/0022-3514.71.2.364

Bandura, A. (1999). Moral disengagement in the perpetration of inhumanities. *Personality and Social Psychology Review* (Special Issue on Evil and Violence), 3, 193-209.

Bar-Tal, D. (2004). *Delegitimization.* Retrieved from http://www.beyondintractability.org/essay/delegitimization

Bar-Tal, D., & Saxe, L. (1976). Perceptions of similarly and dissimilarly attractive couples and individuals. *Journal of Personality and Social Psychology, 33*(6), 772–781. doi:10.1037/0022-3514.33.6.772

Barber, L. L., & Cooper, M. L. (2014). Rebound sex: Sexual motives and behaviors following a relationship breakup. *Archives of Sexual Behavior, 43*(2), 251–265. doi:10.1007/s10508-013-0200-3

Barker, M. (2014). Psychology and pornography: Some reflections. *Porn Studies, 1*(1-2), 120–126. doi:10.1080/23268743.2013.859468

Baron, R. A. (1972). Aggression as a function of ambient temperature and prior anger arousal. *Journal of Personality and Social Psychology, 21*(2), 183–189.

Bartholomew, K., & Horowitz, L. M. (1991). Attachment styles among young adults: A test of a four-category model. *Journal of Personality and Social Psychology, 61*(2), 226–244. doi:10.1037/0022-3514.61.2.226

Bartholow, B. D., & Anderson, C. A. (2002). Effects of violent video games on aggressive behavior: Potential sex differences. *Journal of Experimental Social Psychology, 38*(3), 283–290. doi:10.1006/jesp.2001.1502

Bartholow, B. D., & Heinz, A. (2006). Alcohol and aggression without consumption: Alcohol cues, aggressive thoughts, and hostile perception bias. *Psychological Science, 17,* 30–37.

Bass, B. M. (2008). *The Bass handbook of leadership: Theory, research, and managerial applications* (4th ed., Free Press hardcover ed.). New York: Free Press.

Batson, C. D. (2014). *The altruism question toward a social-psychological answer.* Hoboken, NJ: Taylor and Francis. Retrieved from http://public.eblib.com/EBLPublic/PublicView.do?ptiID=1588507

Batson, C. D., Dyck, J. L., Brandt, J. R., Batson, J. G., Powell, A. L., McMaster, M. R., & Griffitt, C. (1988). Five studies testing two egoistic alternatives to the empathy-altruism hypothesis. *Journal of Personality and Social Psychology, 55* (1), 52-77.

Batson, C. D., & Shaw, L. L. (1991). Evidence for altruism: Toward a pluralism of prosocial motives. *Psychological Inquiry, 2*(2), 107–122.

Batson, C. D., & Thompson, E. R. (2001). Why don't moral people act morally? Motivational considerations. *Current Directions in Psychological Science, 10*(2), 54–57. doi:10.1111/1467-8721.00114

Bauman, C. W., & Skitka, L. J. (2010). Making attributions for behaviors: The prevalence of correspondence bias in the general population. *Basic and Applied Social Psychology, 32*(3), 269–277. doi:10.1080/01973533.2010.495654

Baumeister, R. F. (1998). The self. In D. T. Gilbert, S. T. Fiske, & G. Lindzey (Eds.), *Handbook of social psychology* (4th ed., pp. 680-740). New York: McGraw-Hill.

Baumeister, R. F., DeWall, C. N., Ciarocco, N. J., & Twenge, J. M. (2005). Social exclusion impairs self-regulation. *Journal of Personality and Social Psychology, 88*(4), 589–604. doi:10.1037/0022-3514.88.4.589

Baumeister, R. F., Smart, L., & Boden, J. M. (1996). Relation of threatened egotism to violence and aggression: The dark side of high self-esteem. *Psychological Review, 103,* 5-33.

Baumeister, R. F., Wotman, S. R., & Stillwell, A. M. (1993). Unrequited love: On heartbreak, anger, guilt, scriptlessness, and humiliation. *Journal of Personality and Social Psychology, 64*(3), 377–394. doi:10.1037/0022-3514.64.3.377

Baym, N. K. (2010). *Personal connections in the digital age.* Cambridge, UK; Malden, MA: Polity.

BBC News. (2003, May 23). DR Congo pygmies appeal to UN. Retrieved from http://news.bbc.co.uk/2/hi/africa/2933524.stm

Beaman, A. L., Klentz, B., Diener, E., & Svanum, S. (1979). Self-awareness and transgression in children: Two field studies. *Journal of Personality and Social Psychology, 37*(10), 1835–1846. doi:10.1037/0022-3514.37.10.1835

Becker, M. H., Drachman, R. H., & Kirscht, J. P. (1972). Predicting mothers' compliance with pediatric regimens. *Journal of Pediatrics, 81,* 843–854.

Becker, W. C., Starrels, J. L., Heo, M., Li, X., Weiner, M. G., & Turner, B. J. (2011). Racial differences in primary care opioid risk reduction strategies. *The Annals of Family Medicine, 9*(3), 219–225. doi:10.1370/afm.1242

Beer, J. S., Chester, D. S., & Hughes, B. L. (2013). Social threat and cognitive load magnify self-enhancement and attenuate self-deprecation. *Journal of Experimental Social Psychology, 49*(4), 706–711. doi:10.1016/j.jesp.2013.02.017

Bender, K., Thompson, S., Ferguson, K., Yoder, J., & DePrince, A. (2014). Risk detection and self-protection among homeless youth. *Journal of Research on Adolescence,* n/a–n/a. doi:10.1111/jora.12123

Benson, P. L., Karabenick, S. A., & Lerner, R. M. (1976). Pretty pleases: The effects of physical attractiveness, race, and sex on receiving help. *Journal of Experimental Social Psychology, 12*(5), 409–415. doi:10.1016/0022-1031(76)90073-1

Berkowitz, L. (1989). Frustration-aggression hypothesis. *Psychological Bulletin, 106,* 59–73.

Berkowitz, L. (1990). On the formation and regulation of anger and aggression: A cognitive-neoassociationistic analysis. *American Psychologist, 45*, 494–503.

Berkowitz, L. (1993). *Aggression: Its causes, consequences, and control.* New York: McGraw Hill.

Berkowitz, L., & LePage, A. (1967). Weapons as aggression-eliciting stimuli. *Journal of Personality and Social Psychology, 7*(2, Pt.1), 202–207. doi:10.1037/h0025008

Berman, M. G., Jonides, J., & Kaplan, S. (2008). The cognitive benefits of interacting with nature. *Psychological Science, 19*(12), 1207–1212. doi:10.1111/j.1467-9280.2008.02225.x

Berscheid, E., & Walster, E. (1974). Physical attractiveness. In L. Berkowitz (Ed.), *Advances in Experimental Social Psychology* (Vol. 7, pp. 157–213). New York: Academic Press, Inc.

Berscheid, E., Walster, G. W., & Hatfield, E. (1969). *Effects of accuracy and positivity of evaluation on liking for the evaluator.* Unpublished Manuscript. Summarized in E. Berscheid and E. Hatfield (1978), Interpersonal attraction.

Betancourt, H. (1990). An attribution-empathy model of helping behavior: Behavioral intentions and judgments of help-giving. *Personality and Social Psychology Bulletin, 16*(3), 573–591. doi:10.1177/0146167290163015

Bethea, A. R., Rexrode, K. R., Ruffo, A. C., & Washington, S. D. (2000). Violence in lesbian relationships: A narrative analysis. *Perspectives: Electronic Journal of the American Association of Behavioral and Social Sciences.* Retrieved from http://www.aabss.org/journal2000/f05Bethea.jmm.html

Bettencourt, B. A., & Miller, N. (1996). Gender differences in aggression as a function of provocation: A meta-analysis. *Psychological Bulletin, 119*(3), 422–447.

Beyerlein, K., & Hipp, J. R. (2005). Social capital, too much of a good thing? American religious traditions and community trust. *Social Forces, 84*(2), 995–1013.

Blackstone, W., & William Blackstone Collection (Library of Congress). (1979). *Commentaries on the laws of England.* Chicago: University of Chicago Press.

Blaker, N. M., Rompa, I., Dessing, I. H., Vriend, A. F., Herschberg, C., & van Vugt, M. (2013). The height leadership advantage in men and women: Testing evolutionary psychology predictions about the perceptions of tall leaders. *Group Processes & Intergroup Relations, 16*(1), 17–27. doi:10.1177/1368430212437211

Blumstein, P., & Schwartz, P. (1990). Intimate relationships and the creation of sexuality. In D. P. McWhirter, S. A. Sanders, & J. M. Reinisch (Eds.), *Homosexuality/heterosexuality: Concepts of sexual orientation* (pp. 307–320). New York: Oxford University Press.

Bockting, W., Robinson, B., Benner, A., & Scheltema, K. (2004). Patient satisfaction with transgender health services. *Journal of Sex & Marital Therapy, 30*(4), 277–294. doi:10.1080/00926230490422467

Boen, F., Vanbeselaere, N., Pandelaere, M., Dewitte, S., Duriez, B., Snauwaert, B., … Van Avermaet, E. (2002). Politics and basking-in-reflected-glory: A field study in flanders. *Basic and Applied Social Psychology, 24*(3), 205–214. doi:10.1207/S15324834BASP2403_3

Bornstein, R. F., Leone, D. R., & Galley, D. J. (1987). The generalizability of subliminal mere exposure effects: Influence of stimuli perceived without awareness on social behavior. *Journal of Personality and Social Psychology, 53*(6), 1070–1079. doi:10.1037/0022-3514.53.6.1070

Bose, K. S., & Sarma, R. H. (1975). Delineation of the intimate details of the backbone conformation of pyridine nucleotide coenzymes in aqueous solution. *Biochemical and Biophysical Research Communications, 66*(4), 1173–1179.

Bosveld, W., Koomen, W., van der Pligt, J., & Plaisier, J. W. (1995). Differential construal as an explanation for false consensus and false uniqueness effects. *Journal of Experimental Social Psychology, 31*(6), 518–532. doi:10.1006/jesp.1995.1023

Bourke, M. L., & Hernandez, A. E. (2009). The "Butner study" redux: A report of the incidence of hands-on child victimization by child pornography offenders. *Journal of Family Violence*, *24*(3), 183–191. doi:10.1007/s10896-008-9219-y

Brand, P. A., & Kidd, A. H. (1986). Frequency of physical aggression in heterosexual and female homosexual dyads. *Psychological Reports*, *59*(3), 1307–1313. doi:10.2466/pr0.1986.59.3.1307

Brehm, J. W. (1966). *A theory of psychological reactance.* San Diego, CA: Academic Press.

Brewer, M. B. (1991). The social self: On being the same and different at the same time. *Personality and Social Psychology Bulletin*, *17*(5), 475–482. doi:10.1177/0146167291175001

Brewer, M. B. (1999). The psychology of prejudice: Ingroup love and outgroup hate? *Journal of Social Issues*, *55*(3), 429–444. doi:10.1111/0022-4537.00126

Brewer, M. B. (2003). Optimal distinctiveness, social identity, and the self. In M. R. Leary & J. P. Tangney (Eds.), *Handbook of self and identity* (pp. 1–16). New York: Guilford Press.

Brewer, W. F., & Treyens, J. C. (1981). Role of schemata in memory for places. *Cognitive Psychology*, *13*(2), 207–230. doi:10.1016/0010-0285(81)90008-6

Brinig, M. F. (2000). "These boots are made for walking": Why most divorce filers are women. *American Law and Economics Association*, *2*(1), 126–169. doi:10.1093/aler/2.1.126

Brion, J. M., Leary, M. R., & Drabkin, A. S. (2014). Self-compassion and reactions to serious illness: The case of HIV. *Journal of Health Psychology*, *19*(2), 218–229. doi:10.1177/1359105312467391

Britto, S., & Noga-Styron, K. E. (2014). Media consumption and support for capital punishment. *Criminal Justice Review*, *39*(1), 81–100. doi:10.1177/0734016814522645

Brockner, J. (1979). The effects of self-esteem, success-failure, and self-consciousness on task performance. *Journal of Personality and Social Psychology*, *37*(10), 1732–1741. doi:10.1037/0022-3514.37.10.1732

Brockner, J., & Swap, W. C. (1976). Effects of repeated exposure and attitudinal similarity on self-disclosure and interpersonal attraction. *Journal of Personality and Social Psychology*, *33*(5), 531–540. doi:10.1037/0022-3514.33.5.531

Brody, L. R. (1997). Gender and emotion: Beyond stereotypes. *Journal of Social Issues*, *53*(2), 369–393. doi:10.1111/j.1540-4560.1997.tb02448.x

Brophy, I. N. (1945). The luxury of anti-negro prejudice. *The Public Opinion Quarterly*, *9*(4), 456–466.

Brown, B. B., Werner, C. M., Amburgey, J. W., & Szalay, C. (2007). Walkable route perceptions and physical features: Converging evidence for en route walking experiences. *Environment and Behavior*, *39*(1), 34–61. doi:10.1177/0013916506295569

Brown, B. R. (1968). The effects of need to maintain face on interpersonal bargaining. *Journal of Experimental Social Psychology*, *4*, 107–122.

Brown, C. M., & McConnell, A. R. (2009). Effort or escape: Self-concept structure determines self-regulatory behavior. *Self and Identity*, *8*(4), 365–377. doi:10.1080/15298860802377818

Brown, R. (2000). Social identity theory: Past achievements, current problems, and future challenges. *European Journal of Social Psychology*, *30*(6), 745–778.

Bryant, W. W. (2011). Internalized racism's association with African American male youth's propensity for violence. *Journal of Black Studies*, *42*(4), 690–707. doi:10.1177/0021934710393243

Bui, N. H. (2012). False consensus in attitudes toward celebrities. *Psychology of Popular Media Culture*, *1*(4), 236–243. doi:10.1037/a0028569

Bunch, C., & Carrillo, R. (1998). Global violence against women: The challenge to human rights and development. In M. T. Klare & Y. Chandrani (Eds.), *World security: Challenges for a new century* (3rd ed.). New York: St. Martin's Press.

Burger, J. M. (2009). Replicating Milgram: Would people still obey today? *American Psychologist*, *64*(1), 1–11. doi:10.1037/a0010932

Burgess, E. W., & Wallin, P. (1953). *Engagement and Marriage*. Philadelphia, PA: J. B. Lippincott.

Burgoon, J. K., Bonito, J. A., Ramirez, A., Dunbar, N. E., Kam, K., & Fischer, J. (2002). Testing the Interactivity Principle: Effects of mediation, propinquity, and verbal and nonverbal modalities in interpersonal interaction. *Journal of Communication*, *52*(3), 657–677. doi:10.1111/j.1460-2466.2002.tb02567.x

Burnstein, E., Crandall, C., & Kitayama, S. (1994). Some neo-Darwinian decision rules for altruism: Weighing cues for inclusive fitness as a function of the biological importance of the decision. *Journal of Personality and Social Psychology*, *67*(5), 773–789. doi:10.1037/0022-3514.67.5.773

Bushman, B. J. (2002). Does venting anger feed or extinguish the flame? Catharsis, rumination, distraction, anger, and aggressive responding. *Personality and Social Psychology Bulletin*, *28*(6), 724–731. doi:10.1177/0146167202289002

Bushman, B. J., & Anderson, C. A. (2002). Violent video games and hostile expectations: A test of the general aggression model. *Personality and Social Psychology Bulletin*, *28*(12), 1679–1686. doi:10.1177/014616702237649

Bushman, B. J., & Baumeister, R. F. (1998). Threatened egotism, narcissism, self-esteem, and direct and displaced aggression: Does self-love or self-hate led to violence? *Journal of Personality and Social Psychology*, *75*, 219–229.

Butler, B. (2007). The role of death qualification in jurors' susceptibility to pretrial publicity. *Journal of Applied Social Psychology*, *37*(1), 115–123.

Butler, B. M., & Moran, G. (2002). The role of death qualification in venirepersons' evaluations of aggravating and mitigating circumstances in capital trials. *Law and Human Behavior*, *26*(2), 175–184. doi:10.1023/A:1014640025871

Butler, B., & Moran, G. (2007). The impact of death qualification, belief in a just world, legal authoritarianism, and locus of control on venirepersons' evaluations of aggravating and mitigating circumstances in capital trials. *Behavioral Sciences & the Law*, *25*(1), 57–68. doi:10.1002/bsl.734

Butler, D., & Geis, F. L. (1990). Nonverbal affect responses to male and female leaders: Implications for leadership evaluations. *Journal of Personality and Social Psychology*, *58*(1), 48–59. doi:10.1037/0022-3514.58.1.48

Butzer, B., & Kuiper, N. A. (2008). Humor use in romantic relationships: The effects of relationship satisfaction and pleasant versus conflict situations. *The Journal of Psychology*, *142*(3), 245–260. doi:10.3200/JRLP.142.3.245-260

Cacioppo, J. T., & Petty, R. E. (1982). The need for cognition. *Journal of Personality and Social Psychology*, *42*(1), 116–131. doi:10.1037/0022-3514.42.1.116

Cacioppo, J. T., Priester, J. R., & Berntson, G. G. (1993). Rudimentary determinants of attitudes: II. Arm flexion and extension have differential effects on attitudes. *Journal of Personality and Social Psychology*, *65*(1), 5–17. doi:10.1037/0022-3514.65.1.5

Camacho, L. M., & Paulus, P. B. (1995). The role of social anxiousness in group brainstorming. *Journal of Personality and Social Psychology*, *68*(6), 1071–1080. doi:10.1037/0022-3514.68.6.1071

Campbell, D. T. (1958). Common fate, similarity, and other indices of the status of aggregates of persons as social entities. *Behavioral Science*, *3*, 14-25.

Campbell, F. A. K. (2008). Exploring internalized ableism using critical race theory. *Disability & Society*, *23*(2), 151–162. doi:10.1080/09687590701841190

Campbell, J. C., Oliver, C., & Bullock, L. (1991). Why battering during pregnancy? *AWHONN's Clinical Issues in Perinatal and Women's Health Nursing*, *4*(3), 343–349.

Campbell, W. K., Foster, C. A., & Finkel, E. J. (2002). Does self-love lead to love for others? A story of narcissistic game playing. *Journal of Personality and Social Psychology, 83*(2), 340–354. doi:10.1037/0022-3514.83.2.340

Cao, X. (2014). The effects of narrative perspectives and gender similarity to a victim on sympathy and support for aid to people in need. *Studies in Media and Communication, 2*(1).

Carlo, G., Raffaelli, M., Laible, D., & Meyer, K. A. (1999). Why are girls less physically aggressive than boys? Personality and parenting mediators of physical aggression. *Sex Roles, 40*(9/10), 711–729. doi:10.1023/A:1018856601513

Carlson, M., Charlin, V., & Miller, N. (1988). Positive mood and helping behavior: A test of six hypotheses. *Journal of Personality and Social Psychology, 55*(2), 211–229. doi:10.1037/0022-3514.55.2.211

Carlyle, T. (1841). *Heroes and hero worship.* Boston: Adams.

Caruso, E. M. (2008). Use of experienced retrieval ease in self and social judgments. *Journal of Experimental Social Psychology, 44*(1), 148–155. doi:10.1016/j.jesp.2006.11.003

Catalano, S. (2006). *Intimate partner violence in the United States.* (No. BJS07007). Bureau of Justice Statistics, U.S. Department of Justice. Retrieved from http://www.ojp.usdoj.gov/bjs/intimate/ipv.htm

Cehajic, S., Brown, R., & Castano, E. (2008). Forgive and forget? Antecedents and consequences of intergroup forgiveness in Bosnia and Herzegovina. *Political Psychology, 29*(3), 351–367. doi:10.1111/j.1467-9221.2008.00634.x

Cesario, J., Plaks, J. E., & Higgins, E. T. (2006). Automatic social behavior as motivated preparation to interact. *Journal of Personality and Social Psychology, 90*(6), 893–910. doi:10.1037/0022-3514.90.6.893

Chaiken, S. (1980), "Heuristic versus Systematic Information Processing and the Use of Source versus 'Message Cues in Persuasion," *Journal of Personality and Social Psychology, 39*, 752-766.

Chan, A. W., Peelen, M. V., & Downing, P. E. (2004). The effect of viewpoint on body representation in the extrastriate body area. *Neuroreport, 15*(15), 2407-2410.

Chartrand, T. L., & Bargh, J. A. (1999). The chameleon effect: The perception–behavior link and social interaction. *Journal of personality and social psychology, 76*(6), 893.

Chen, S., Shechter, D., & Chaiken, S. (1996). Getting at the truth or getting along: Accuracy-versus impression-motivated heuristic and systematic processing. *Journal of Personality and Social Psychology, 71*(2), 262–275. doi:10.1037/0022-3514.71.2.262

Cheryan, S., & Bodenhausen, G. V. (2000). When Positive Stereotypes Threaten Intellectual Performance: The Psychological Hazards of "Model Minority" Status. *Psychological Science, 11*(5), 399–402. doi:10.1111/1467-9280.00277

Chirumbolo, A., Livi, S., Mannetti, L., Pierro, A., & Kruglanski, A. W. (2004). Effects of need for closure on creativity in small group interactions. *European Journal of Personality, 18*(4), 265–278.

Choo, P., Levine, T., & Hatfield, E. (1996). Gender, love schemas, and reactions to romantic break-ups. *Journal of Social Behavior and Personality, 11*, 143–160.

Chou, L., & Richerson, P. J. (1992). Multiple models in social transmission of food selection by Norway rats, Rattus norvegicus. *Animal Behaviour, 44*(2), 337–343. doi:10.1016/0003-3472(92)90039-C

Christie, D. J. (2006). What is peace psychology the psychology of? *Journal of Social Issues, 62*(1), 1–17. doi:10.1111/j.1540-4560.2006.00436.x

Cialdini, R. B., Borden, R. J., Thorne, A., Walker, M. R., Freeman, S., & Sloan, L. R. (1976). Basking in reflected glory: Three (football) field studies. *Journal of Personality and Social Psychology, 34*(3), 366–375.

Cialdini, R. B., Cacioppo, J. T., Bassett, R., & Miller, J. A. (1978). Low-ball procedure for producing compliance: Commitment then cost. *Journal of Personality and Social Psychology, 36*(5), 463–476. doi:10.1037/0022-3514.36.5.463

Claidiere, N., & Whiten, A. (2012). Integrating the study of conformity and culture in humans and nonhuman animals. *Psychological Bulletin, 138*(1), 126–145. doi:10.1037/a0025868

Clair, J. A., Beatty, J. E., & MacLean, T. L. (2005). Out of sight but not out of mind: Managing invisible social identities in the workplace. *Academy of Management Review, 30*(1), 78–95. doi:10.5465/AMR.2005.15281431

Clark, M. S., & Mills, J. (1993). The difference between communal and exchange relationships: What it is and is not. *Personality and Social Psychology Bulletin, 19*, 684–691.

Claypool, H. M., Housley, M. K., Hugenberg, K., Bernstein, M. J., & Mackie, D. M. (2012). Easing in: Fluent processing brings others into the in-group. *Group Processes & Intergroup Relations, 15*(4), 441–455. doi:10.1177/1368430212439115

Cline, V. B. (1972). *The desensitization of children to television violence.* National Institutes of Health.

Coan, J. A., Schaefer, H. S., & Davidson, R. J. (2006). Lending a hand: Social regulation of the neural response to threat. *Psychological Science, 17*(12), 1032–1039. doi:10.1111/j.1467-9280.2006.01832.x

Cohen, C. E. (1981). Person categories and social perception: Testing some boundaries of the processing effects of prior knowledge. *Journal of Personality and Social Psychology, 40*, 441–452.

Cohen, D. (1996). Law, social policy, and violence: The impact of regional cultures. *Journal of Personality and Social Psychology, 70*(5), 961–978. doi:10.1037/0022-3514.70.5.961

Cohen, J. (1992). A power primer. *Psychological Bulletin, 112*, 155–159.

Cohn, E. G., & Rotton, J. (1997). Assault as a function of time and temperature: A moderator-variable time-series analysis. *Journal of Personality and Social Psychology, 72*(6), 1322–1334. doi:10.1037/0022-3514.72.6.1322

Coleman, L. M., Jussim, L., & Abraham, J. (1987). Students' reactions to teachers' evaluations: The unique impact of negative feedback. *Journal of Applied Social Psychology, 17*(12), 1051–1070. doi:10.1111/j.1559-1816.1987.tb02347.x

Coleman, M. D. (2011). Emotion and the self-serving bias. *Current Psychology, 30*(4), 345–354. doi:10.1007/s12144-011-9121-2

Colen, C. G., Geronimus, A. T., Bound, J., & James, S. A. (2006). Maternal upward socioeconomic mobility and black–white disparities in infant birthweight. *American Journal of Public Health, 96*(11), 2032–2039. doi:10.2105/AJPH.2005.076547

Collins, N. L., & Feeney, B. C. (2004). Working models of attachment shape perceptions of social support: Evidence from experimental and observational studies. *Journal of Personality and Social Psychology, 87*(3), 363–383. doi:10.1037/0022-3514.87.3.363

Comas-Díaz, L., & Jacobsen, F. M. (1991). Ethnocultural transference and countertransference in the therapeutic dyad. *American Journal of Orthopsychiatry, 61*(3), 392–402. doi:10.1037/h0079267

Coogler, R. (2013). *Fruitvale station.* Biography, Dram.

Cooper, L. A., Roter, D. L., Carson, K. A., Beach, M. C., Sabin, J. A., Greenwald, A. G., & Inui, T. S. (2012). The associations of clinicians' implicit attitudes about race with medical visit communication and patient ratings of interpersonal care. *American Journal of Public Health, 102*(5), 979–987. doi:10.2105/AJPH.2011.300558

Cortina, L. M., Kabat-Farr, D., Leskinen, E. A., Huerta, M., & Magley, V. J. (2011). Selective incivility as modern discrimination in organizations: Evidence and impact. *Journal of Management, 39*(6), 1579–1605. doi:10.1177/0149206311418835

Cosmides, L., & Tooby, J. (2000). Consider the source: The evolution of adaptations for decoupling and metarepresentation. In D. Sperber (Ed.), *Metarepresentations: A multidisciplinary perspective* (pp. 53–115). Oxford; New York: Oxford University Press.

Cottrell, N. B., Wack, D. L., Sekerak, G. J., & Rittle, R. H. (1968). Social facilitation of dominant responses by the presence of an audience and the mere presence of others. *Journal of Personality and Social Psychology, 9*(3), 245–250. doi:10.1037/h0025902

Craig, T. Y., & Kelly, J. R. (1999). Group cohesiveness and creative performance. *Group Dynamics: Theory, Research, and Practice, 3*, 243-256.

Crandall, C. S. (1994). Prejudice against fat people: Ideology and self-interest. *Journal of Personality and Social Psychology, 66*(5), 882–894. doi:10.1037/0022-3514.66.5.882

Crawford, C., Krebs, D., & Badcock, C. R. (Eds.). (1998). Psychodarwinism: The new synthesis of Darwin and Freud. In *Handbook of evolutionary psychology: Ideas, issues, and applications* (pp. 457–484). Mahwah, NJ: Lawrence Erlbaum Associates.

Crocker, J., & Wolfe, C. T. (2001). Contingencies of self-worth. *Psychological Review, 108*(3), 593–623. doi:10.1037/0033-295X.108.3.593

Crowne, D. P., & Marlowe, D. (1960). A new scale of social desirability independent of psychopathology. *Journal of Consulting Psychology, 24*(4), 349–354. doi:10.1037/h0047358

Cuddy, A. J. C., Rock, M. S., & Norton, M. I. (2007). Aid in the aftermath of hurricane Katrina: Inferences of secondary emotions and intergroup helping. *Group Processes & Intergroup Relations, 10*(1), 107–118. doi:10.1177/1368430207071344

Cullum, J., O'Grady, M., Sandoval, P., Armeli, S., & Tennen, H. (2013). Ignoring norms with a little help from my friends: Social support reduces normative influence on drinking behavior. *Journal of Social and Clinical Psychology, 32*(1), 17–33. doi:10.1521/jscp.2013.32.1.17

Cunningham, M. K., Shamblen, S. R., Barbee, A. P., & Ault, L. K. (2005). Social allergies in romantic relationships: Behavioral repetition, emotional sensitization, and dissatisfaction in dating couples. *Personal Relationships, 12*(2), 273–295.

Cunningham, M. R. (1979). Weather, mood, and helping behavior: Quasi experiments with the sunshine Samaritan. *Journal of Personality and Social Psychology, 37*(11), 1947–1956. doi:10.1037/0022-3514.37.11.1947

Czopp, A. M. (2008). When is a compliment not a compliment? Evaluating expressions of positive stereotypes. *Journal of Experimental Social Psychology, 44*(2), 413–420. doi:10.1016/j.jesp.2006.12.007

Dabbs, J. M., & Morris, R. (1990). Testosterone, social class, and antisocial behavior in a sample of 4,462 men. *Psychological Science, 1*(3), 209–211. doi:10.1111/j.1467-9280.1990.tb00200.x

Daly, M., & Wilson, M. (1998). The evolutionary social psychology of family violence. In C. Crawford & D. Krebs (Eds.), *Handbook of evolutionary psychology: ideas, issues, and applications* (pp. 431–456). Mahwah, NJ: Lawrence Erlbaum Associates.

Dar-Nimrod, I., Rawn, C. D., Lehman, D. R., & Schwartz, B. (2009). The maximization paradox: The costs of seeking alternatives. *Personality and Individual Differences, 46*(5-6), 631–635. doi:10.1016/j.paid.2009.01.007

Darby, B. W., & Schlenker, B. R. (1982). Children's reactions to apologies. *Journal of Personality and Social Psychology, 43*, 742–753.

Dasgupta, N., & Asgari, S. (2004). Seeing is believing: Exposure to counterstereotypic women leaders and its effect on the malleability of automatic gender stereotyping. *Journal of Experimental Social Psychology, 40*(5), 642–658. doi:10.1016/j.jesp.2004.02.003

Dasgupta, N., & Greenwald, A. G. (2001). On the malleability of automatic attitudes: Combating automatic prejudice with images of admired and disliked individuals. *Journal of Personality and Social Psychology, 81*(5), 800–814. doi:10.1037//0022-3514.81.5.800

De Cremer, D., & Van Lange, P. A. M. (2001). Why prosocials exhibit greater cooperation than pro-selfs: The roles of social responsibility and reciprocity. *European Journal of Personality, 15*(S1), S5–S18. doi:10.1002/per.418

De Figueiredo, R. J. P., & Elkins, Z. (2003). Are patriots bigots? An inquiry into the vices of in-group pride. *American Journal of Political Science, 47*(1), 171–188. doi:10.1111/1540-5907.00012

DePaulo, B. M. (2006). *Singled out: How singles are stereotyped, stigmatized, and ignored and still live happily ever after* (1st ed.). New York: St. Martin's Press.

DePaulo, B. M., & Morris, W. L. (2006). The unrecognized stereotyping and discrimination against singles. *Current Directions in Psychological Science, 15*(5), 251–254. doi:10.1111/j.1467-8721.2006.00446.x

Deutsch, M. (1973). *The resolution of conflict.* New Haven, CT: Yale University Press.

Deutsch, M., & Krauss, R. M. (1960). The effect of threat upon interpersonal bargaining. *The Journal of Abnormal and Social Psychology, 61*(2), 181–189. doi:10.1037/h0042589

Deutsch, M., & Krauss, R. M. (1962). Studies of interpersonal bargaining. *Journal of Conflict Resolution, 6*, 52–76.

Diamond, L. M. (2003). Was it a phase? Young women's relinquishment of lesbian/bisexual identities over a 5-year period. *Journal of Personality and Social Psychology, 84*(2), 352–364. doi:10.1037/0022-3514.84.2.352

Diehl, M., & Stroebe, W. (1987). Productivity loss in brainstorming groups: Toward the solution of a riddle. *Journal of Personality and Social Psychology, 53*(3), 497–509. doi:10.1037/0022-3514.53.3.497

Dill, K. E., Anderson, C. A., Anderson, K. B., & Deuser, W. E. (1997). Effects of aggressive personality on social expectations and social perceptions. *Journal of Research in Personality, 31*, 272–292.

Dindia, K., & Allen, M. (1992). Sex differences in self-disclosure: A meta-analysis. *Psychological Bulletin, 112*(1), 106–124. doi:10.1037/0033-2909.112.1.106

Dion, K. K., Pak, A. W.-P., & Dion, K. L. (1990). Stereotyping physical attractiveness: A sociocultural perspective. *Journal of Cross-Cultural Psychology, 21*(2), 158–179. doi:10.1177/0022022190212002

Disha, I., Cavendish, J. C., & King, R. D. (2011). Historical events and spaces of hate: Hate crimes against Arabs and Muslims in post-9/11 America. *Social Problems, 58*(1), 21–46. doi:10.1525/sp.2011.58.1.21

Ditto, B., Byrne, N., Holly, C., & Balegh, S. (2014). Social contagion of vasovagal reactions in the blood collection clinic: A possible example of mass psychogenic illness. *Health Psychology.* doi:10.1037/hea0000053

Diuk, C. (2014, February 14). Facebook data science. *The formation of love.* Retrieved from https://www.facebook.com/notes/facebook-data-science/the-formation-of-love/10152064609253859

Dobyns, H. F. (1983). *Their number become thinned: Native American population dynamics in eastern North America.* Knoxville, TN; University of Tennessee Press.

Doggrell, S. A. (2010). Adherence to medicines in the older-aged with chronic conditions: Does intervention by an allied health professional help? *Drugs and Aging, 27*(3), 239–254.

Dollard, J., Miller, N. E., Doob, L. W., Mowrer, O. H., & Sears, R. R. (1939). *Frustration and aggression.* New Haven, CT: Yale University Press. Retrieved from http://content.apa.org/books/10022-000

Don't Ask Don't Tell Repeal Act of 2010, H.R. 2965, S. 4023 (2010).

Don't Ask, Don't Tell, 10 U.S. Code (1993).

Donnerstein, E. (1980). Aggressive erotica and violence against women. *Journal of Personality and Social Psychology*, *39*(2), 269–277. doi:10.1037/0022-3514.39.2.269

Donnerstein, E. I., & Linz, D. G. (1986, December). The question of pornography. *Psychology Today*, 56–59.

Dore, R. A., Hoffman, K. M., Lillard, A. S., & Trawalter, S. (2014). Children's racial bias in perceptions of others' pain. *British Journal of Developmental Psychology*, n/a–n/a. doi:10.1111/bjdp.12038

Doucet, J. M., D'Antonio-Del Rio, J. M., & Chauvin, C. D. (2014). G.R.I.T.S.: The southern subculture of violence and homicide offenses by girls raised in the south. *Journal of Interpersonal Violence*, *29*(5), 806–823. doi:10.1177/0886260513505707

Downing, P. E., Yuhong, J., Shuman, M., & Kanwisher, N. (2001). A Cortical Area Selective for Visual Processing of the Human Body. *Science*, *293*(5539), 2470–2473. doi:10.1126/science.1063414

DR Congo pygmies appeal to UN. (2003, May 23). *BBC News*. Retrieved from http://news.bbc.co.uk/2/hi/africa/2933524.stm

Duckitt, J. (1994). *The social psychology of prejudice*. New York: Praeger.

Dunton, B. C., & Fazio, R. H. (1997). An individual difference measure of motivation to control prejudiced reactions. *Personality and Social Psychology Bulletin*, *23*(3), 316–326. doi:10.1177/01461672297233009

Dykstra, P. A. (1995). Loneliness among the never and formerly married: The importance of supportive friendships and a desire for independence. *The Journals of Gerontology Series B: Psychological Sciences and Social Sciences*, *50B*(5), S321–S329. doi:10.1093/geronb/50B.5.S321

Eagly, A. H. (1987). *Sex differences in social behavior: A social-role interpretation*. Hillsdale, NJ: Lawrence Erlbaum.

Eagly, A. H., & Chaiken, S.(1993). *The psychology of attitudes*. Fort Worth, TX: Harcourt Brace Jovanovich College Publishers.

Eagly, A. H., & Karau, S. J. (2002). Role congruity theory of prejudice toward female leaders. *Psychological Review*, *109*(3), 573–598. doi:10.1037/0033-295X.109.3.573

Eastwick, P. W., Finkel, E. J., Mochon, D., & Ariely, D. (2007). Selective versus unselective romantic desire: Not all reciprocity is created equal. *Psychological Science*, *18*(4), 317–319. doi:10.1111/j.1467-9280.2007.01897.x

Eaton, A. A., & Rose, S. (2011). Has dating become more egalitarian? A 35 year review using sex roles. *Sex Roles*, *64*(11-12), 843–862. doi:10.1007/s11199-011-9957-9

Ebbesen, E. B., Kjos, G. L., & Konecni, V. J. (1976). Spatial ecology: Its effects on the choice of friends and enemies. *Journal of Experimental Psychology*, *12*, 505–518.

Eberhardt, J. L., Davies, P. G., Purdie-Vaughns, V. J., & Johnson, S. L. (2006). Looking deathworthy: Perceived stereotypicality of black defendants predicts capital-sentencing outcomes. *Psychological Science*, *17*(5), 383–386. doi:10.1111/j.1467-9280.2006.01716.x

Eisenberg, N. (1991). Values, sympathy, and individual differences: Toward a pluralism of factors influencing altruism and empathy. *Psychological Inquiry*, *2*, 128–131.

Eisenberger, N. I. (2003). Does rejection hurt? An fMRI Study of social exclusion. *Science*, *302*(5643), 290–292. doi:10.1126/science.1089134

Ellemers, N., Spears, R., & Doosje, B. (1997). Sticking together or falling apart: In-group identification as a psychological determinant of group commitment versus individual mobility. *Journal of Personality and Social Psychology*, *72*(3), 617–626. doi:10.1037/0022-3514.72.3.617

Ellison, C. G., Burr, J. A., & Mccall, P. L. (2003). The enduring puzzle of southern homicide: Is regional religious culture the missing piece? *Homicide Studies*, 7(4), 326–352. doi:10.1177/1088767903256463

Enright, R. D., Santos, M. J. D., & Al-Mabuk, R. (1989). The adolescent as forgiver. *Journal of Adolescence*, 12(1), 95–110. doi:10.1016/0140-1971(89)90092-4

Epley, N., & Gilovich, T. (2004). Are adjustments insufficient? *Personality and Social Psychology Bulletin*, 30(4), 447–460. doi:10.1177/0146167203261889

Epps, J., & Kendall, P. C. (1995). Hostile attribution bias in adults. *Cognitive Therapy and Research*, 19, 159–178.

Espenshade, T. J., & Hempstead, K. (1996). Contemporary American attitudes toward US immigration. *International Migration Review, 30*, 535-570.

Esses, V. M., Jackson, L. M., & Armstrong, T. L. (1998). Intergroup competition and attitudes toward immigrants and immigration: An instrumental model of group conflict. *Journal of Social Issues*, 54(4), 699–724. doi:10.1111/j.1540-4560.1998.tb01244.x

Ethier, K. A., & Deaux, K. (1994). Negotiating social identity when contexts change: Maintaining identification and responding to threat. *Journal of Personality and Social Psychology*, 67(2), 243–251. doi:10.1037/0022-3514.67.2.243

Ewart, C. K., Taylor, C. B., Kraemer, H. C., & Agras, W. S. (1991). High blood pressure and marital discord: Not being nasty matters more than being nice. *Health Psychology*, 10(3), 155–163. doi:10.1037/0278-6133.10.3.155

Exline, J. J., Baumeister, R. F., Zell, A. L., Kraft, A. J., & Witvliet, C. V. O. (2008). Not so innocent: Does seeing one's own capability for wrongdoing predict forgiveness? *Journal of Personality and Social Psychology*, 94(3), 495–515. doi:10.1037/0022-3514.94.3.495

Fanti, K. A., & Henrich, C. C. (2014). Effects of self-esteem and narcissism on bullying and victimization during early adolescence. *The Journal of Early Adolescence*. doi:10.1177/0272431613519498

Fay, A. J., & Maner, J. K. (2012). Warmth, spatial proximity, and social attachment: The embodied perception of a social metaphor. *Journal of Experimental Social Psychology*, 48(6), 1369–1372. doi:10.1016/j.jesp.2012.05.017

Feeley, T. H., Anker, A. E., & Aloe, A. M. (2012). The door-in-the-face persuasive message strategy: A Meta-analysis of the first 35 years. *Communication Monographs*, 79(3), 316–343. doi:10.1080/03637751.2012.697631

Feingold, A. (1988). Matching for attractiveness in romantic partners and same-sex friends: A meta-analysis and theoretical critique. *Psychological Bulletin*, 104(2), 226–235. doi:10.1037/0033-2909.104.2.226

Feingold, A. (1992). Good-looking people are not what we think. *Psychological Bulletin*, 111(2), 304–341. doi:10.1037/0033-2909.111.2.304

Felsten, G. (2009). Where to take a study break on the college campus: An attention restoration theory perspective. *Journal of Environmental Psychology*, 29(1), 160–167. doi:10.1016/j.jenvp.2008.11.006

Fere, C. (1887). *Sensation and movement: Experimental lessons of psychomechanics*. Paris, France: Alcan.

Ferrer, E., & Helm, J. L. (2013). Dynamical systems modeling of physiological coregulation in dyadic interactions. *International Journal of Psychophysiology*, 88(3), 296–308. doi:10.1016/j.ijpsycho.2012.10.013

Feschbach, S. (1994). Aggressive behavior: Nationalsim, patriotism, and aggression. In L. R. Huesmann (Ed.), *Aggressive Behavior*. Boston, MA: Springer US. Retrieved from http://link.springer.com/10.1007/978-1-4757-9116-7

Festinger, L. *A theory of cognitive dissonance*. Evanston, Ill: Row Peterson, 1957.

Festinger, L., & Carlsmith, J. M. (1959). Cognitive consequences of forced compliance. *The Journal of Abnormal and Social Psychology, 58*(2), 203–210. doi:10.1037/h0041593

Festinger, L., Schacter, S., & Back, K. (1970). *Social pressures in informal groups: A study of human factors in housing.* Stanford University Press.

Fiedler, F. E. (1978). The contingency model and the dynamics of the leadership process. In *Advances in Experimental Social Psychology* (Vol. 11, pp. 59–112). Elsevier. Retrieved from http://linkinghub. elsevier.com/retrieve/pii/S0065260108600052

Finneran, C., & Stephenson, R. (2013). Intimate partner violence, minority stress, and sexual risk-taking among US MSM. *Journal of Homosexuality*, 131118115540005. doi:10.1080/00918369.20 14.865450

Fischer-Lokou, J., Martin, A., GuéGuen, N., & Lamy, L. (2011). Mimicry and propagation of prosocial behavior in a natural setting. *Psychological Reports, 108*(2), 599–605. doi:10.2466/07.17.21. PR0.108.2.599-605

Fiske, S. T. (2004). *Social beings: A core motives approach to social psychology.* Hoboken, NJ: J. Wiley.

Fitzsimons, G. M., & Kay, A. C. (2004). Language and interpersonal cognition: Causal effects of variations in pronoun usage on perceptions of closeness. *Personality and Social Psychology Bulletin, 30*(5), 547–557. doi:10.1177/0146167203262852

Forgas, J. P. (2011). Can negative affect eliminate the power of first impressions? Affective influences on primacy and recency effects in impression formation. *Journal of Experimental Social Psychology, 47*(2), 425–429. doi:10.1016/j.jesp.2010.11.005

Fornara, F., Carrus, G., Passafaro, P., & Bonnes, M. (2011). Distinguishing the sources of normative influence on proenvironmental behaviors: The role of local norms in household waste recycling. *Group Processes & Intergroup Relations, 14*(5), 623–635. doi:10.1177/1368430211408149

Forsyth, D. R. (2006). *Group dynamics* (4th ed.). Belmont, CA: Thomson/Wadsworth.

Fox, C. (2006). The availability heuristic in the classroom: How soliciting more criticism can boost your course ratings. *Judgment and Decision Making, 1*(1), 86–90.

Fox, R., & McDaniel, C. (1982). The perception of biological motion by human infants. *Science, 218*, 486–187.

Fox, J., & Warber, K. M. (2013). Romantic relationship development in the age of Facebook: An exploratory study of emerging adults' perceptions, motives, and behaviors. *Cyberpsychology, Behavior, and Social Networking, 16*(1), 3–7. doi:10.1089/cyber.2012.0288

Frenda, S. J., Knowles, E. D., Saletan, W., & Loftus, E. F. (2013). False memories of fabricated political events. *Journal of Experimental Social Psychology, 49*(2), 280–286. doi:10.1016/j.jesp.2012.10.013

Gaertner, S. L., Mann, J. A., Dovidio, J. F., Murrell, A. J., & et al. (1990). How does cooperation reduce intergroup bias? *Journal of Personality and Social Psychology, 59*(4), 692–704. doi:10.1037/0022-3514.59.4.692

Galanaki, E. (2004). Are children able to distinguish among the concepts of aloneness, loneliness, and solitude? *International Journal of Behavioral Development, 28*(5), 435–443. doi:10.1080/01650250444000153

Gallagher, K. E., Lisco, C. G., Parrott, D. J., & Giancola, P. R. (2014). Effects of thought suppression on provoked men's alcohol-related physical aggression in the laboratory. *Psychology of Violence, 4*(1), 78–89. doi:10.1037/a0032304

Gallupe, R. B., Dennis, A. R., Cooper, W. H., Valacich, J. S., Bastianutti, L. M., & Bybanajer, J. F. (1992). Electronic brainstorming and group size. *The Academy of Management Journal, 35*(2), 350–369.

Galupo, M. P., & Gonzalez, K. A. (2013). Friendship values and cross-category friendships: Understanding adult friendship patterns across gender, sexual orientation and race. *Sex Roles*, *68*(11-12), 779–790. doi:10.1007/s11199-012-0211-x

Gardner, G. T., & Stern, P. C. (2002). *Environmental problems and human behavior* (2nd ed.). Pearson Learning Solutions.

Garnets, L., & Kimmel, D. C. (Eds.). (2003). *Psychological perspectives on lesbian, gay, and bisexual experiences* (2nd ed.). New York: Columbia University Press.

Gastil, J. (1990). Generic pronouns and sexist language: The oxymoronic character of masculine generics. *Sex Roles*, *23*(11/12), 629–643.

Gauthier, I. W., Skudlarski, P., Gore, J. C., & Anderson, A. W. (2000). Expertise for cars and birds recruits brain areas involved in face recognition. *Nature Neuroscience*, *3*(2), 191.

Gawronski, B. (2012). Back to the future of dissonance theory: Cognitive consistency as a core motive. *Social Cognition*, *30*(6), 652–668. doi:10.1521/soco.2012.30.6.652

Gawronski, B., Walther, E., & Blank, H. (2005). Cognitive consistency and the formation of interpersonal attitudes: Cognitive balance affects the encoding of social information. *Journal of Experimental Social Psychology*, *41*(6), 618–626. doi:10.1016/j.jesp.2004.10.005

Gelfand, M. J., Higgins, M., Nishii, L. H., Raver, J. L., Dominguez, A., Murakami, F., … Toyama, M. (2002). Culture and egocentric perceptions of fairness in conflict and negotiation. *Journal of Applied Psychology*, *87*(5), 833–845. doi:10.1037/0021-9010.87.5.833

Gellad, W. F., Grenard, J. L., & Marcum, Z. A. (2011). A systematic review of barriers to medication adherence in the elderly: Looking beyond cost and regimen complexity. *American Journal of Geriatric Pharmacotherapy*, *9*(1), 11–23.

Gentry, M. (1998). The sexual double standard. The influence of number of relationships and level of sexual activity on judgments of women and men. *Psychology of Women Quarterly, 22*, 505-511.

Giancola, P. R., Josephs, R. A., Parrott, D. J., & Duke, A. A. (2010). Alcohol myopia revisited: Clarifying aggression and other acts of disinhibition through a distorted lens. *Perspectives on Psychological Science*, *5*(3), 265–278. doi:10.1177/1745691610369467

Gibson, S. (2013). "The last possible resort": A forgotten prod and the in situ standardization of Stanley Milgram's voice-feedback condition. *History of Psychology*, *16*(3), 177–194. doi:10.1037/a0032430

Gifford, R. (2014). Environmental psychology matters. *Annual Review of Psychology*, *65*(1), 541–579. doi:10.1146/annurev-psych-010213-115048

Gilovich, T., Medvec, V. H., & Savitsky, K. (2000). The spotlight effect in social judgment: An egocentric bias in estimates of the salience of one's own actions and appearance. *Journal of Personality and Social Psychology*, *78*(2), 211–222. doi:10.1037/0022-3514.78.2.211

Gladue, B. A. (1991). Aggressive behavioral characteristics, hormones, and sexual orientation in men and women. *Aggressive Behavior*, *17*(6), 313–326. doi:10.1002/1098-2337(1991)17:6<313::AID-AB2480170603>3.0.CO;2-Z

Goldenberg, O., Larson, J. R., & Wiley, J. (2013). Goal instructions, response format, and idea generation in groups. *Small Group Research*, *44*(3), 227–256. doi:10.1177/1046496413486701

Gonsalkorale, K., & Williams, K. D. (2007). The KKK won't let me play: Ostracism even by a despised outgroup hurts. *European Journal of Social Psychology*, *37*(6), 1176–1186. doi:10.1002/ejsp.392

Goodfriend, W., & Agnew, C. R. (2008). Sunken costs and desired plans: Examining different types of investments in close relationships. *Personality and Social Psychology Bulletin*, *34*(12), 1639–1652. doi:10.1177/0146167208323743

Goodwin. (2000). Pregnancy intendedness and physical abuse around the time of pregnancy: Findings from the pregnancy risk assessment monitoring system. 1996-1997. *Maternal and Child Health Journal.*, *4*(2), 85.

Gottman, J. M., Jacobson, N. S., Rushe, R. H., & Shortt, J. W. (1995). The relationship between heart rate reactivity, emotionally aggressive behavior, and general violence in batterers. *Journal of Family Psychology, 9*(3), 227–248. doi:10.1037/0893-3200.9.3.227

Gray, K., Ward, A. F., & Norton, M. I. (2012). Paying it forward: Generalized reciprocity and the limits of generosity. *Journal of Experimental Psychology: General.* doi:10.1037/a0031047

Graziano, W., Brothen, T., & Berscheid, E. (1978). Height and attraction: Do men and women see eye-to-eye? *Journal of Personality, 46*(1), 128–145. doi:10.1111/j.1467-6494.1978.tb00606.x

Green, A. R., Carney, D. R., Pallin, D. J., Ngo, L. H., Raymond, K. L., Iezzoni, L. I., & Banaji, M. R. (2007). Implicit bias among physicians and its prediction of thrombolysis decisions for black and white patients. *Journal of General Internal Medicine, 22*(9), 1231–1238. doi:10.1007/s11606-007-0258-5

Greitemeyer, T. (2014a). Intense acts of violence during video game play make daily life aggression appear innocuous: A new mechanism why violent video games increase aggression. *Journal of Experimental Social Psychology, 50*, 52–56. doi:10.1016/j.jesp.2013.09.004

Greitemeyer, T. (2014b). Playing violent video games increases intergroup bias. *Personality and Social Psychology Bulletin, 40*(1), 70–78. doi:10.1177/0146167213505872

Gronlund, S. D., Wixted, J. T., & Mickes, L. (2014). Evaluating eyewitness identification procedures using receiver operating characteristic analysis. *Current Directions in Psychological Science, 23*(1), 3–10. doi:10.1177/0963721413498891

Guéguen, N., Joule, R.-V., Courbet, D., Halimi-Falkowicz, S., & Archand, A. A. (2013). Repeating "yes" in a first request and compliance with a later request: The four walls technique. *Social Behavior and Personality: An International Journal, 41*(2), 199–202. doi:10.2224/sbp.2013.41.2.199

Gueguen, N., Pichot, N., & Dreff, G. (2005). Similarity and helping behavior on the web: The impact of the convergence of surnames between a solicitor and a subject in a request made by e-mail. *Journal of Applied Social Psychology, 35*(2), 423–429. doi:10.1111/j.1559-1816.2005.tb02128.x

Hadad, C. (2012, May 3). "Stand your ground" denied in domestic violence case. *CNN Justice.* Retrieved from http://www.cnn.com/2012/04/24/justice/ac360-stand-your-ground-law/

Hadjiyanni, T. (2014). Transbodied spaces: The home experiences of undocumented Mexicans in Minnesota. *Space and Culture.* doi:10.1177/1206331213510446

Hafner, R. J., White, M. P., & Handley, S. J. (2012). Spoilt for choice: The role of counterfactual thinking in the excess choice and reversibility paradoxes. *Journal of Experimental Social Psychology, 48*(1), 28–36. doi:10.1016/j.jesp.2011.06.022

Halevy, N., Bornstein, G., & Sagiv, L. (2008). "In-group love" and "out-group hate" as motives for individual participation in intergroup conflict: A new game paradigm. *Psychological Science, 19*(4), 405–411. doi:10.1111/j.1467-9280.2008.02100.x

Hamann, S. B., Ely, T. D., Hoffman, J. M., & Kilts, C. D. (2002). Ecstasy and agony: activation of the human amygdala in positive and negative emotion. *Psychological Science, 13*(2), 135–141.

Hamilton, M. C. (1988). Using masculine generics: Does generic he increase male bias in the user's imagery? *Sex Roles, 19*(11/12), 785–799.

Haney, C. (1984). On the selection of capital juries: The biasing effects of the death-qualification process. *Law and Human Behavior, 8*(1-2), 121–132. doi:10.1007/BF01044355

Haney, C., Banks, W. C., & Zimbardo, P. (1973). Interpersonal dynamics in a simulated prison. *International Journal of Criminology and Penology, 1*, 69–97.

Haney, C., Hurtado, A., & Vega, L. (1994). "Modern" death qualification: New data on its biasing effects. *Law and Human Behavior, 18*(6), 619–633. doi:10.1007/BF01499328

Harris, L. T., & Fiske, S. T. (2006). Dehumanizing the Lowest of the Low: Neuroimaging Responses to Extreme Out-Groups. *Psychological Science*, *17*(10), 847–853. doi:10.1111/j.1467-9280.2006.01793.x

Harrison, D. A., Price, K. H., Gavin, J. H., & Florey, A. T. (2002). Time, teams, and task performance: Changing effects of surface- and deep-level diversity on group functioning. *The Acade*, *45*(5), 1029–1045.

Haselton, M. G., & Gangestad, S. W. (2006). Conditional expression of women's desires and men's mate guarding across the ovulatory cycle. *Hormones and Behavior*, *49*(4), 509–518. doi:10.1016/j.yhbeh.2005.10.006

Haslam, N. (2006). Dehumanization: An integrative review. *Personality and Social Psychology Review*, *10*(3), 252–264. doi:10.1207/s15327957pspr1003_4

Haslam, N., Bastian, B., & Loughnan, S. (2010). Dehumanization/infrahumanization. In J. M. Levine & M. A. Hogg (Eds.), *Encyclopedia of group processes & intergroup relations* (pp. 189–191). Thousand Oaks, CA: Sage Publications.

Haslam, N., Bastian, B., & Loughnan, S. (2010). Dehumanization/infrahumanization. In J. M. Levine & M. A. Hogg (Eds.), *Encyclopedia of group processes & intergroup relations* (pp. 189–191). Thousand Oaks, CA: Sage Publications.

Haslam, N., & Loughnan, S. (2014). Dehumanization and infrahumanization. *Annual Review of Psychology*, *65*(1), 399–423. doi:10.1146/annurev-psych-010213-115045

Haslam, S. A., & Ryan, M. K. (2008). The road to the glass cliff: Differences in the perceived suitability of men and women for leadership positions in succeeding and failing organizations. *The Leadership Quarterly*, *19*(5), 530–546. doi:10.1016/j.leaqua.2008.07.011

Hastorf, A. H., & Cantril, H. (1954). They saw a game; a case study. *The Journal of Abnormal and Social Psychology*, *49*(1), 129–134. doi:10.1037/h0057880

Hatfield, E., Bensman, L., & Rapson, R. L. (2012). A brief history of social scientists' attempts to measure passionate love. *Journal of Social and Personal Relationships*, *29*(2), 143–164. doi:10.1177/0265407511431055

Haun, D. B. M., & Tomasello, M. (2011). Conformity to peer pressure in preschool children. *Child Development*, *82*(6), 1759–1767. doi:10.1111/j.1467-8624.2011.01666.x

Hawley, P. H. (2014). Evolution, prosocial behavior, and altruism: A roadmap for understanding where the proximate meets the ultimate. In L. M. Padilla-Walker & G. Carlo (Eds.), *Prosocial development: A multidimensional approach* (pp. 43–69). Oxford: Oxford University Press.

Hedges, C. (2003). *War is a force that gives us meaning*. New York: Anchor Books.

Heider, F. (1946). Attitudes and Cognitive Organization. *The Journal of Psychology*, *21*(1), 107–112. doi:10.1080/00223980.1946.9917275

Heilman, M. E., Block, C. J., & Martell, R. F. (1995). Sex stereotypes: Do they influence perceptions of managers? *Journal of Social Behavior and Personality*, *10*(6), 237–252.

Heilman, M. E., Wallen, A. S., Fuchs, D., & Tamkins, M. M. (2004a). Penalties for success: Reactions to women who succeed at male gender-typed tasks. *Journal of Applied Psychology*, *89*(3), 416–427. doi:10.1037/0021-9010.89.3.416

Heilman, M. E., Wallen, A. S., Fuchs, D., & Tamkins, M. M. (2004b). Penalties for success: Reactions to women who succeed at male gender-typed tasks. *Journal of Applied Psychology*, *89*(3), 416–427. doi:10.1037/0021-9010.89.3.416

Henningsen, D. D., & Henningsen, M. L. M. (2013). Generating ideas about the uses of brainstorming: Reconsidering the losses and gains of brainstorming groups relative to nominal groups. *Southern Communication Journal*, *78*(1), 42–55. doi:10.1080/1041794X.2012.717684

Henry, R. A. (1995). Improving group judgment accuracy: Information sharing and determining the best member. *Organizational Behavior and Human Decision Processes*, *62*(2), 190–197. doi:10.1006/obhd.1995.1042

Heppner, W. L., Kernis, M. H., Lakey, C. E., Campbell, W. K., Goldman, B. M., Davis, P. J., & Cascio, E. V. (2008). Mindfulness as a means of reducing aggressive behavior: Dispositional and situational evidence. *Aggressive Behavior*, *34*(5), 486–496. doi:10.1002/ab.20258

Hernandez, I., & Preston, J. L. (2013). Disfluency disrupts the confirmation bias. *Journal of Experimental Social Psychology*, *49*(1), 178–182. doi:10.1016/j.jesp.2012.08.010

Herrera, P., Bourgeois, P., & Hess, U. (1998). *Counter mimicry effects as a function of racial attitudes*. In Poster presented at the 38th Annual Meeting of the Society for Psychophysiological Research, Denver, Colorado, USA.

Hess, U., Blairy, S., & Kleck, R. E. (2000). The influence of expression intensity, gender, and ethnicity on judgments of dominance and affiliation. *Journal of Nonverbal Behavior*, *24*, 265-283.

Hess, U., & Fischer, A. (2013). Emotional mimicry as social regulation. *Personality and Social Psychology Review*, *17*(2), 142–157. doi:10.1177/1088868312472607

Hill, C. V., Neighbors, H. W., & Gayle, H. D. (2004). The relationship between racial discrimination and health for black Americans: Measurement challenges and the realities of coping. *African American Research Perspectives*, *10*(1), 89–98.

Hinsz, V. B., & Tomhave, J. A. (1991). Smile and (Half) the World Smiles with You, Frown and You Frown Alone. *Personality and Social Psychology Bulletin*, *17*(5), 586–592. doi:10.1177/0146167291175014

Hollenbaugh, E. E., & Ferris, A. L. (2014). Facebook self-disclosure: Examining the role of traits, social cohesion, and motives. *Computers in Human Behavior*, *30*, 50–58. doi:10.1016/j.chb.2013.07.055

Hollingshead, A. B., & Fraidin, S. N. (2003). Gender stereotypes and assumptions about expertise in transactive memory. *Journal of Experimental Social Psychology*, *39*(4), 355–363. doi:10.1016/S0022-1031(02)00549-8

Holoien, D. S., & Shelton, J. N. (2012). You deplete me: The cognitive costs of colorblindness on ethnic minorities. *Journal of Experimental Social Psychology*, *48*(2), 562–565. doi:10.1016/j.jesp.2011.09.010

Holtzworth-Munroe, A., & Jacobson, N. S. (1985). Causal attributions of married couples: When do they search for causes? What do they conclude when they do? *Journal of Personality and Social Psychology*, *48*(6), 1398–1412. doi:10.1037/0022-3514.48.6.1398

Hudley, C., & Graham, S. (1993). An attributional intervention to reduce peer-directed aggression among African-American boys. *Child Development*, *64*(1), 124–138. doi:10.1111/j.1467-8624.1993.tb02899.x

Huesmann, L. R., Moise-Titus, J., Podolski, C.-L., & Eron, L. D. (2003). Longitudinal relations between children's exposure to TV violence and their aggressive and violent behavior in young adulthood: 1977-1992. *Developmental Psychology*, *39*(2), 201–221. doi:10.1037/0012-1649.39.2.201

Huseman, R. C., Hatfield, J. D., & Miles, E. W. (1987). A new perspective on equity theory: The equity sensitivity construct. *The Academy of Management Review*, *12*(2), 222–234.

Hyde, J. S. (1984). Children's understanding of sexist language. *Developmental Psychology*, *20*(4), 697–706. doi:10.1037/0012-1649.20.4.697

IJzerman, H., Gallucci, M., Pouw, W. T. J. L., Weibgerber, S. C., Van Doesum, N. J., & Williams, K. D. (2012). Cold-blooded loneliness: Social exclusion leads to lower skin temperatures. *Acta Psychologica*, *140*(3), 283–288. doi:10.1016/j.actpsy.2012.05.002

IJzerman, H., & Semin, G. R. (2010). Temperature perceptions as a ground for social proximity. *Journal of Experimental Social Psychology*, *46*(6), 867–873. doi:10.1016/j.jesp.2010.07.015

Intrator, J., Hare, R., Stritzke, P., Brichtswein, K., Dorfman, D., Harpur, T., … Machac, J. (1997). A brain imaging (single photon emission computerized tomography) study of semantic and affective processing in psychopaths. *Biological Psychiatry*, *42*(2), 96–103. doi:10.1016/S0006-3223(96)00290-9

Isaac, R. M., Walker, J. M., & Williams, A. W. (1994). Group size and the voluntary provision of public goods: Experimental evidence utilizing large groups. *Journal of Public Economics*, *54*, 1–36.

Isen, A. (1984). Toward understanding the role of affect in cognition. In R. S. Wyer & T. K. Srull (Eds.), *Handbook of social cognition* (Vol. 3, pp. 179–236). Hillsdale, NJ: Erlbaum.

Iyengar, S. S., & Lepper, M. R. (2000). When choice is demotivating: Can one desire too much of a good thing? *Journal of Personality and Social Psychology*, *79*(6), 995–1006. doi:10.1037/0022-3514.79.6.995

Jacobson, N. S., & Gottman, J. M. (1998). *When men batter women: New insights into ending abusive relationships*. New York: Simon & Schuster.

Janis, I. L. (1972). *Victims of groupthink: A psychological study of foreign-policy decisions and fiascoes*. Osford, England: Houghton Mifflin.

Janoff-Bulman, R., & Werther, A. (2008). The social psychology of respect: Implications for delegitimization and reconciliation. In A. Nadler, T. E. Malloy, & J. D. Fisher (Eds.), *The social psychology of intergroup reconciliation* (pp. 145–170). Oxford ; New York: Oxford University Press.

Johnson, M. P. (1995). Patriarchal terrorism and common couple violence: Two forms of violence against women. *Journal of Marriage and the Family*, *57*(2), 283. doi:10.2307/353683

Jones, E. E., Carter-Sowell, A. R., Kelly, J. R., & Williams, K. D. (2009). `I'm out of the loop': Ostracism through information exclusion. *Group Processes & Intergroup Relations*, *12*(2), 157–174. doi:10.1177/1368430208101054

Jones, E. E., & Harris, V. A. (1967). The attribution of attitudes. *Journal of Experimental Social Psychology*, *3*, 1-24

Jost, J. T., (1995). Negative illusions: Conceptual clarification and psychological evidence concerning false consciousness. *Political Psychology*, *16*, 397-424.

Judd, C. M., Park, B., Yzerbyt, V., Gordijn, E. H., & Muller, D. (2005). Attributions of intergroup bias and outgroup homogeneity to ingroup and outgroup others. *European Journal of Social Psychology*, *35*(6), 677–704. doi:10.1002/ejsp.281

Judge, T. A., & Cable, D. M. (2004). The Effect of Physical Height on Workplace Success and Income: Preliminary Test of a Theoretical Model. *Journal of Applied Psychology*, *89*(3), 428–441. doi:10.1037/0021-9010.89.3.428

Jump, P. (2011, November 28). A star's collapse. *The Times Higher Education*. Retrieved from http://www.insidehighered.com/news/2011/11/28/scholars-analyze-case-massive-research-fraud

Kabat-Zinn, J. (2006). Mindfulness-based interventions in context: Past, present, and future. *Clinical Psychology: Science and Practice*, *10*(2), 144–156. doi:10.1093/clipsy.bpg016

Kahneman, D., Knetsch, J. L., & Thaler, R. H. (1991). Anomalies: The Endowment Effect, Loss Aversion, and Status Quo Bias. *Journal of Economic Perspectives*, *5*(1), 193–206. doi:10.1257/jep.5.1.193

Kanter, R. M. (1977). Some effects of proportions on group life: Skewed sex ratios and responses to token women. *American Journal of Sociology*, *82*(5), 965. doi:10.1086/226425

Kassin, S. M., & Kiechel, K. L. (1996). The social psychology of false confessions: Compliance, internalization, and confabulation. *Psychological Science*, *7*(3), 125–128. doi:10.1111/j.1467-9280.1996.tb00344.x

Kassin, S. M., & Wrightsman, L. S. (1980). Prior confessions and mock juror verdicts. *Journal of Applied Social Psychology*, *10*(2), 133–146. doi:10.1111/j.1559-1816.1980.tb00698.x

Kassin, S. M., & Wrightsman, L. S. (1985). Confession evidence. In S. Kassin & L. Wrightsman (Eds.), *The psychology of evidence and trial procedure* (pp. 67–94). Beverly Hills, CA: Sage Publications.

Kaufman, C. F., Lane, P. M., & Lindquist, J. D. (1991). Exploring more than 24 hours a day: A preliminary investigation of polychronic time use. *Journal of Consumer Research*, *18*(3), 392. doi:10.1086/209268

Kaufman-Scarborough, C. (2006). Time use and the impact of technology: Examining workspaces in the home. *Time & Society*, *15*(1), 57–80. doi:10.1177/0961463X06061782

Kay, A. C., Day, M. V., Zanna, M. P., & Nussbaum, A. D. (2013). The insidious (and ironic) effects of positive stereotypes. *Journal of Experimental Social Psychology*, *49*(2), 287–291. doi:10.1016/j.jesp.2012.11.003

Kellerman, A., & Mercy, J. (1992). Men, women, and murder: Gender-specific differences in rates of fatal violence and victimization. *Journal of Trauma-Injury Infection & Critical Care*, *33*(1).

Kelley, H. H. (1950). The warm cold variable in first impressions of persons. *Journal of Personality*, *18*(4), 431–439. doi:10.1111/j.1467-6494.1950.tb01260.x

Kelley, H. H. (1973). The processes of causal attribution. *American Psychologist*, *28*(2), 107–128. doi:10.1037/h0034225

Kelley, H. H. (1978). *Interpersonal relations: A theory of interdependence*. New York: Wiley.

Kelley, H. H., & Thibaut, J. W. (1978). *Interpersonal relations: A theory of interdependence* (p. 341). New York: Wiley.

Kelly, J. R., & Karau, S. J. (1999). Group decision making: The effects of initial preferences and time pressure. *Personality and Social Psychology Bulletin*, *25*(11), 1342–1354. doi:10.1177/0146167299259002

Kelman. (2008). Reconciliation from a social-psychological perspective. In A. Nadler, T. E. Malloy, & J. D. Fisher (Eds.), *The social psychology of intergroup reconciliation* (pp. 15–36). Oxford ; New York: Oxford University Press.

Kelman, H. G., (1973). Violence without moral restraint: Reflections on the dehumanization of victims and victimizers. *Journal of Social Issues, 29* (4), 25-61.

Keltner, D., Young, R. C., Heerey, E. A., Oemig, C., & Monarch, N. D. (1998). Teasing in hierarchical and intimate relations. *Journal of Personality and Social Psychology*, *75*(5), 1231–1247. doi:10.1037/0022-3514.75.5.1231

Kiecolt-Glaser, J. K., Gouin, J.-P., & Hantsoo, L. (2010). Close relationships, inflammation, and health. *Neuroscience & Biobehavioral Reviews*, *35*(1), 33–38. doi:10.1016/j.neubiorev.2009.09.003

Kilbourne, W. (1999). *Deadly persuasion: Why women and girls must fight the addictive power of advertising*. New York: Free Press.

Klesse, C. (2014). Polyamory: Intimate practice, identity or sexual orientation? *Sexualities*, *17*(1-2), 81–99. doi:10.1177/1363460713511096

Klimas, L. (2012, April 5). How long could you last in the world's quietest room? The record is only 45 minutes. *The Blaze*. Retrieved from http://www.theblaze.com/stories/2012/04/05/how-long-could-you-last-in-the-worlds-quietest-room-the-record-is-only-45-minutes/

Klinesmith, J., Kasser, T., & McAndrew, F. T. (2006). Guns, testosterone, and aggression: An experimental test of a mediational hypothesis. *Psychological Science*, *17*(7), 568–571. doi:10.1111/j.1467-9280.2006.01745.x

Klinkenberg, D., & Rose, S. (1994). Dating scripts of gay men and lesbians. *Journal of Homosexuality*, *26*(4), 23–35. doi:10.1300/J082v26n04_02

Kogut, T. (2011). Someone to blame: When identifying a victim decreases helping. *Journal of Experimental Social Psychology*, *47*(4), 748–755. doi:10.1016/j.jesp.2011.02.011

Kogut, T., & Kogut, E. (2013). Exploring the relationship between adult attachment style and the identifiable victim effect in helping behavior. *Journal of Experimental Social Psychology*, *49*(4), 651–660. doi:10.1016/j.jesp.2013.02.011

Kogut, T., & Ritov, I. (2007). "One of us": Outstanding willingness to help save a single identified compatriot. *Organizational Behavior and Human Decision Processes*, *104*(2), 150–157. doi:10.1016/j.obhdp.2007.04.006

Kouri, E., Lukas, S., Pope, H., & Olivia, P. (1995). Increased aggressive responding in male volunteers following the administration of gradually increasing doses of testosterone cypionate. *Drug and Alcohol Dependence*, *40*, 73–79.

Krause, S., Back, M. D., Egloff, B., & Schmukle, S. C. (2014). Implicit interpersonal attraction in small groups: Automatically activated evaluations predict actual behavior toward social partners. *Social Psychological and Personality Science*. doi:10.1177/1948550613517723

Krauss, R. M., & Deutsch, M. (1966). Communication in interpersonal bargaining. *Journal of Personality and Social Psychology*, *4*(5), 572–577. doi:10.1037/h0023899

Kriss, P. H., Loewenstein, G., Wang, X., & Weber, R. A. (2011). Behind the veil of ignorance: Self-serving bias in climate change negotiations. *Judgment and Decision Making*, *6*(7), 602–615.

Krueger, J., & Zeiger, J. S. (1993). Social categorization and the truly false consensus effect. *Journal of Personality and Social Psychology*, *65*(4), 670–680. doi:10.1037/0022-3514.65.4.670

Krueger, K. P., Berger, B. A., & Felkey, B. (2005). Medication adherence and persistence: A comprehensive review. *Advances in Therapy*, *22*(4), 313–356.

Krusemark, E. A., Campbell, W. K., & Clementz, B. A. (2008). Attributions, deception, and event related potentials: An investigation of the self-serving bias. *Psychophysiology*, *45*(4), 511–515. doi:10.1111/j.1469-8986.2008.00659.x

Kuo, F. E., & Sullivan, W. C. (2001). Environment and crime in the inner city: Does vegetation reduce crime? *Environment and Behavior*, *33*(3), 343–367. doi:10.1177/0013916501333002

Kweon, B.-S., Ulrich, R. S., Walker, V. D., & Tassinary, L. G. (2007). Anger and stress: The role of landscape posters in an office setting. *Environment and Behavior*, *40*(3), 355–381. doi:10.1177/0013916506298797

Lagerspetz, K. M. J., Bjorkqvist, K., & Peltonen, T. (1988). Is indirect aggression typical of females? Gender differences in aggressiveness in 11 to 12 year old children. *Aggressive Behavior*, *14*, 403–414.

Lambert, N. M., Negash, S., Stillman, T. F., Olmstead, S. B., & Fincham, F. D. (2012). A love that doesn't last: Pornography consumption and weakened commitment to one's romantic partner. *Journal of Social and Clinical Psychology*, *31*(4), 410–438. doi:10.1521/jscp.2012.31.4.410

Lamm, C., Nusbaum, H. C., Meltzoff, A. N., & Decety, J. (2007). What are you feeling? Using functional magnetic resonance imaging to assess the modulation of sensory and affective responses during empathy for pain. *PLoS ONE*, *2*(12), e1292. doi:10.1371/journal.pone.0001292

Lammers, J., & Stapel, D. A. (2009). How power influences moral thinking. *Journal of Personality and Social Psychology*, *97*(2), 279–289. doi:10.1037/a0015437

Lammers, J., & Stapel, D. A. (2011). Power increases dehumanization. *Group Processes & Intergroup Relations*, *14*(1), 113–126. doi:10.1177/1368430210370042

Landau, J. (1995). The relationship of race and gender to managers' ratings of promotion potential. *Journal of Organizational Behavior*, *16*(4), 391–400. doi:10.1002/job.4030160409

Landrine, H., & Klonoff, E. A. (1996). The schedule of racist events: A measure of racial discrimination and a study of its negative physical and mental health consequences. *Journal of Black Psychology*, *22*(2), 144–168. doi:10.1177/00957984960222002

Langer, T., Walther, E., Gawronski, B., & Blank, H. (2009). When linking is stronger than thinking: Associative transfer of valence disrupts the emergence of cognitive balance after attitude change. *Journal of Experimental Social Psychology*, *45*(6), 1232–1237. doi:10.1016/j.jesp.2009.07.005

Langhinrichsen-Rohling, J., Selwyn, C., & Rohling, M. L. (2012). Rates of bidirectional versus unidirectional intimate partner violence across samples, sexual orientations, and race/ethnicities: A comprehensive review. *Partner Abuse, 3*(2), 199–230. doi:10.1891/1946-6560.3.2.199

Larrick, R. P., Timmerman, T. A., Carton, A. M., & Abrevaya, J. (2011). Temper, temperature, and temptation: Heat-related retaliation in baseball. *Psychological Science, 22*(4), 423–428. doi:10.1177/0956797611399292

Larson, J. R., Christensen, C., Abbott, A. S., & Franz, T. M. (1996). Diagnosing groups: Charting the flow of information in medical decision-making teams. *Journal of Personality and Social Psychology, 71*(2), 315–330. doi:10.1037/0022-3514.71.2.315

Larson, R. W. (1990). The solitary side of life: An examination of the time people spend alone from childhood to old age. *Developmental Review, 10*(2), 155–183. doi:10.1016/0273-2297(90)90008-R

Lassiter, G. D., Geers, A. L., Handley, I. M., Weiland, P. E., & Munhall, P. J. (2002). Videotaped interrogations and confessions: A simple change in camera perspective alters verdicts in simulated trials. *Journal of Applied Psychology, 87*(5), 867–874. doi:10.1037/0021-9010.87.5.867

Latane, B., & Darley, J. M. (1968). Group inhibition of bystander intervention in emergencies. *Journal of Personality and Social Psychology, 10*(3), 215–221. doi:10.1037/h0026570

Lau, D. C., & Murnighan, J. K. (1998). Demographic diversity and faultlines: The compositional dynamics of organizational groups. *The Academy of Management Review, 23*(2), 325–340.

Lauer, R. H., Lauer, J. C., & Kerr, S. T. (1990). The long-term marriage: Perceptions of stability and satisfaction. *The International Journal of Aging and Human Development, 31*(3), 189–195. doi:10.2190/H4X7-9DVX-W2N1-D3BF

Lazarus, R., Speisman, J., Mordkoff, A., & Davison, L. (1962). A laboratory study of psychological stress produced by a motion picture film. *Psychological Monographs, 76*(34), 553.

Lee, J. A. (1973). *Colours of love: An exploration of the ways of loving.* Toronto, CA: New Press.

Lee, J. A. (1988). Love-styles. In R. J. Sternberg & M. L. Barnes (Eds.), *The psychology of love.* (pp. 38–67). New Haven, CT: Yale University Press.

Lee, J. H. (1993). *Facing the fire: Experiencing and expressing anger appropriately.* New York: Bantam Books.

Lee, M. R., & Bartkowski, J. P. (2004). Love thy neighbor? Moral communities, civic engagement, and juvenile homicide in rural areas. *Social Forces, 82*(3), 1001–1035. doi:10.1353/sof.2004.0044

Lee, S., Adair, W. L., Mannix, E. A., & Kim, J. (2012). The relational versus collective "We" and intergroup allocation: The role of nested group categorization. *Journal of Experimental Social Psychology, 48*(5), 1132–1138. doi:10.1016/j.jesp.2012.04.008

LeFebvre, L., Blackburn, K., & Brody, N. (2014). Navigating romantic relationships on Facebook: Extending the relationship dissolution model to social networking environments. *Journal of Social and Personal Relationships.* doi:10.1177/0265407514524848

Legault, L., & Inzlicht, M. (2013). Self-determination, self-regulation, and the brain: Autonomy improves performance by enhancing neuroaffective responsiveness to self-regulation failure. *Journal of Personality and Social Psychology, 105*(1), 123–138. doi:10.1037/a0030426

Legenbauer, T., Vocks, S., Schäfer, C., Schütt-Strömel, S., Hiller, W., Wagner, C., & Vögele, C. (2009). Preference for attractiveness and thinness in a partner: Influence of internalization of the thin ideal and shape/weight dissatisfaction in heterosexual women, heterosexual men, lesbians, and gay men. *Body Image, 6*(3), 228–234. doi:10.1016/j.bodyim.2009.04.002

Lemyre, L., & Smith, P. M. (1985). Intergroup discrimination and self-esteem in the minimal group paradigm. *Journal of Personality and Social Psychology, 49*(3), 660–670. doi:10.1037/0022-3514.49.3.660

Lerner, M. J. (1980). *The belief in a just world: A fundamental delusion.* New York: Plenum Press.

Levine, J. M., & Hogg, M. A. (Eds.). (2010). *Encyclopedia of group processes & intergroup relations.* Thousand Oaks, CA: Sage Publications.

Levine, J. M., Hogg, M. A., Smith, E. R., & Mackie, D. M. (Eds.). (2010). Intergroup emotions theory. In *Encyclopedia of group processes & intergroup relations* (pp. 474–476). Thousand Oaks, CA: Sage Publications.

LeVine, R. A., & Campbell, D. T. (1972). *Ethnocentrism: Theories of conflict, ethnic attitudes, and group behavior.* Oxford, England: John Wiley & Sons.

Lewin, K. (1948). *Resolving social conflicts.* New York: Harper.

Lewinsohn, P. M., Mischel, W., Chaplin, W., & Barton, R. (1980). Social competence and depression: The role of illusory self-perceptions. *Journal of Abnormal Psychology, 89*(2), 203–212. doi:10.1037/0021-843X.89.2.203

Leyens, J.-P., Paladino, P. M., Rodriguez-Torres, R., Vaes, J., Demoulin, S., Rodriguez-Perez, A., & Gaunt, R. (2000). The emotional side of prejudice: The attribution of secondary emotions to ingroups and outgroups. *Personality and Social Psychology Review, 4*(2), 186–197. doi:10.1207/S15327957PSPR0402_06

Li, Q., & Brewer, M. B. (2004). What does it mean to be an American? Patriotism, nationalism, and American identity after 9/11. *Political Psychology, 25*(5), 727–739. doi:10.1111/j.1467-9221.2004.00395.x

Lickel, B., Hamilton, D. L., & Sherman, S. J. (2001). Elements of a Lay Theory of Groups: Types of Groups, Relational Styles, and the Perception of Group Entitativity. *Personality and Social Psychology Review, 5*(2), 129–140. doi:10.1207/S15327957PSPR0502_4

Lickerman, A. (2013, December 15). The true meaning of friendship. *Psychology Today: Happiness in this World.* Retrieved March 20, 2013, from http://www.psychologytoday.com/blog/happiness-in-world/201312/the-true-meaning-friendship

Lieberman, M. D. (2010). Social cognitive neuroscience. In S. T. Fiske, D. T. Gilbert, G. Lindzey, & A. E. Jongsma (Eds.), *Handbook of social psychology* (5th ed.). Hoboken, N.J: Wiley.

Likowski, K. U., Weyers, P., Seibt, B., Stöhr, C., Pauli, P., & Mühlberger, A. (2011). Sad and lonely? Sad mood suppresses facial mimicry. *Journal of Nonverbal Behavior, 35*(2), 101–117. doi:10.1007/s10919-011-0107-4

Lindau, S. T., Schumm, L. P., Laumann, E. O., Levinson, W., O'Muircheartaigh, C. A., & Waite, L. J. (2007). A study of sexuality and health among older adults in the United States. *New England Journal of Medicine, 357*(8), 762–774. doi:10.1056/NEJMoa067423

Lindeman, M., & Sundvik, L. (1994). Impact of height on assessments of Finnish female job applicants' managerial abilities. *The Journal of Social Psychology, 134*(2), 169–174.

Lindenberg, S., Joly, J. F., & Stapel, D. A. (2011). The norm-activating power of celebrity: The dynamics of success and influence. *Social Psychology Quarterly, 74*(1), 98–120. doi:10.1177/0190272511398208

Linville, P. W. (1985). Self-complexity and affective extremity: Don't put all of your eggs in one cognitive basket. *Social Cognition, 3*(1), 94–120. doi:10.1521/soco.1985.3.1.94

Lodewijkx, H. F. M., Wildschut, T., Syroit, J. E. E. M., Visser, L., & Rabbie, J. M. (1999). Competition between individuals and groups: Do incentives matter? A group adaptiveness perspective. *Small Group Research, 30*(4), 387–404. doi:10.1177/104649649903000401

Loftus, E. F., & Palmer, J. C. (1974). Reconstruction of auto-mobile destruction: An example of the interaction between language and memory. *Journal of Verbal Learning and Verbal Behaviour, 13,* 585–589.

Loftus, E. F., & Zanni, G. (1975). Eyewitness testimony: The influence of the wording of a question. *Bulletin of the Psychonomic Society, 5*(1), 86–88. doi:10.3758/BF03336715

Long, C. R., & Averill, J. R. (2003). Solitude: An exploration of benefits of being alone. *Journal for the Theory of Social Behavior, 33*(1), 21–44.

Lonsdale, A. J., & North, A. C. (2011). Musical taste and the representativeness heuristic. *Psychology of Music, 40*(2), 131–142. doi:10.1177/0305735611425901

Lord, R., & Maher, K. J. (2002). *Leadership and information processing: Linking perceptions and performance.* Routledge.

Lorenzo, G. L., Biesanz, J. C., & Human, L. J. (2010). What is beautiful is good and more accurately understood: Physical attractiveness and accuracy in first impressions of personality. *Psychological Science, 21*(12), 1777–1782. doi:10.1177/0956797610388048

Loughnan, S., Haslam, N., Sutton, R. M., & Spencer, B. (2014). Dehumanization and social class: Animality in the stereotypes of "White Trash," "Chavs," and "Bogans." *Social Psychology, 45*(1), 54–61. doi:10.1027/1864-9335/a000159

Loving, T. J., Le, B., & Crockett, E. E. (2009). The physiology of feeling hurt. In A. L. Vangelisti (Ed.), *Feeling hurt in close relationships* (pp. 359–375). Cambridge University Press.

Macaskill, A., Maltby, J., & Day, L. (2002). Forgiveness of self and others and emotional empathy. *The Journal of Social Psychology, 142*(5), 663–665. doi:10.1080/00224540209603925

Macrae, C. N., Bodenhausen, G. V., Milne, A. B., & Jetten, J. (1994). Out of mind but back in sight: Stereotypes on the rebound. *Journal of Personality and Social Psychology, 67*(5), 808–817. doi:10.1037/0022-3514.67.5.808

Madey, S. F., & Gilovich, T. (1993). Effect of temporal focus on the recall of expectancy-consistent and expectancy-inconsistent information. *Journal of Personality and Social Psychology, 65*, 458–468.

Malamuth, N. M., & Donnerstein, E. I. (2000). Pornography and sexual aggression. *Annual Review of Sex Research, 11*, 26–91.

Malle, B. F., & Holbrook, J. (2012). Is there a hierarchy of social inferences? The likelihood and speed of inferring intentionality, mind, and personality. *Journal of Personality and Social Psychology, 102*(4), 661–684. doi:10.1037/a0026790

Mandel, M. (2014, January 10). York U prof won't let male student opt out of working with female classmates. *Toronto Sun.* Retrieved from http://www.torontosun.com/2014/01/09/york-u-prof-wont-let-male-student-opt-out-of-working-with-female-classmates

Mann, T., & Ward, A. (2007). Attention, self-control, and health behaviors. *Current Directions in Psychological Science, 16*(5), 280–283. doi:10.1111/j.1467-8721.2007.00520.x

Manucia, G. K., Baumann, D. J., & Cialdini, R. B. (1984). Mood influences on helping: Direct effects or side effects? *Journal of Personality and Social Psychology, 46*(2), 357–364. doi:10.1037/0022-3514.46.2.357

Marazziti, D., & Canale, D. (2004). Hormonal changes when falling in love. *Psychoneuroendocrinology, 29*(7), 931–936. doi:10.1016/j.psyneuen.2003.08.006

Marks, M. J. (2002). [Internet survey of attitudes of sexual freedom.] Unpublished raw data. As cited in Marks & Fraley (2006).

Marks, M. J., & Fraley, R. C. (2006). Confirmation bias and the sexual double standard. *Sex Roles, 54*(1-2), 19–26. doi:10.1007/s11199-006-8866-9

Marrujo, B., & Kreger, M. (1996). Definition of roles in abusive lesbian relationships. *Journal of Gay & Lesbian Social Services, 4*(1), 23–34. doi:10.1300/J041v04n01_03

Martinez, A. G., Piff, P. K., Mendoza-Denton, R., & Hinshaw, S. P. (2011). The power of a label: Mental illness diagnoses, ascribed humanity, and social rejection. *Journal of Social and Clinical Psychology, 30*(1), 1–23. doi:10.1521/jscp.2011.30.1.1

Martyna, W. (1980). Beyond the "he/man" approach: The case for nonsexist language. *Signs, 5*(3), 482–493.

Mathews, J. F. (2013). *Condom use and trust differences by relationship type: Friends with benefits, committed relationships, and casual sex.* (Dissertation). Walden University.

Matthies, E., Selge, S., & Klöckner, C. A. (2012). The role of parental behaviour for the development of behaviour specific environmental norms – The example of recycling and re-use behaviour. *Journal of Environmental Psychology, 32*(3), 277–284. doi:10.1016/j.jenvp.2012.04.003

McConahay, J. B. (1986). Modern racism, ambivalence, and the Modern Racism Scale. In J. F. Dovidio & S. L. Gaertner (Eds.), *Prejudice, discrimination, and racism* (pp. 99–125). New York: Academic Press.

McConnell, A. R., & Leibold, J. M. (2001). Relations among the implicit association test, discriminatory behavior, and explicit measures of racial attitudes. *Journal of Experimental Social Psychology, 37*(5), 435–442. doi:10.1006/jesp.2000.1470

McCrea, S. M., Hirt, E. R., & Milner, B. J. (2008). She works hard for the money: Valuing effort underlies gender differences in behavioral self-handicapping. *Journal of Experimental Social Psychology, 44*(2), 292–311. doi:10.1016/j.jesp.2007.05.006

McCright, A. M., & Dunlap, R. E. (2013). Bringing ideology in: the conservative white male effect on worry about environmental problems in the USA. *Journal of Risk Research, 16*(2), 211–226. doi:10.1080/13669877.2012.726242

McCullough, M. E., & Witvliet, C. V. (2002). The psychology of forgiveness. In C. R. Snyder & S. J. Lopez (Eds.), *Handbook of positive psychology*. Oxford [England]; New York: Oxford University Press. Retrieved from http://public.eblib.com/EBLPublic/PublicView.do?ptiID=271581

McGrew, J. F., Bilotta, J. G., & Deeney, J. M. (1999). Software team formation and decay: Extending the standard model for small groups. *Small Group Research, 30*(2), 209–234. doi:10.1177/104649649903000204

McKenna, K. Y. A., & Bargh, J. A. (1999). Causes and consequences of social interaction on the internet: A conceptual framework. *Media Psychology, 1*(3), 249–269. doi:10.1207/s1532785x-mep0103_4

Meertens, R. W., & Pettigrew, T. F. (1997). Is subtle prejudice really prejudice? *Public Opinion Quarterly, 61*(1, Special Issue on Race), 54. doi:10.1086/297786

Mehl, M. R., Vazire, S., Ramirez-Esparza, N., Slatcher, R. B., & Pennebaker, J. W. (2007). Are women really more talkative than men? *Science, 317*(5834), 82–82. doi:10.1126/science.1139940

Meichenbaum, D., & Turk, D. C. (1987). *Facilitating treatment adherence: A practitioner's guidebook.* New York: Plenum Press.

Meindl, J., Ehrlich, S., & Durkerich, J. (1985). The romance of leadership. *Administrative Science Quarterly, 30*(1), 78–102.

Meissner, C. A., & Brigham, J. C. (2001). Thirty years of investigating the own-race bias in memory for faces: A meta-analytic review. *Psychology, Public Policy, and Law, 7*(1), 3–35. doi:10.1037//1076-8971.7.1.3

Meyer, C. L., & Oberman, M. (2001). *Mothers who kill their children: understanding the acts of moms from Susan Smith to the "Prom Mom."* New York: New York University Press.

Meyer v. Mitnick (Michigan Court of Appeals February 20, 2001).

Meyer v. Mitnick, 625 N. W. 2d (Mich. App. 2011).

Michniewicz, K. S., & Vandello, J. A. (2013). The attractive underdog: When disadvantage bolsters attractiveness. *Journal of Social and Personal Relationships, 30*(7), 942–952. doi:10.1177/0265407513477629

Mikula, G., & Schwinger, T. (1978). Intermember relations and reward allocations. In *Dynamics of group decisions.*

Milgram, S. (1963). Behavioral study of obedience. *The Journal of Abnormal and Social Psychology, 67*(4), 371–378. doi:10.1037/h0040525

Milgram, S. (1974). *Obedience to authority: An experimental view.* New York: Harper & Row.

Milgram, S. (1983). Reflections on Morelli's "dilemma of obedience." *Metaphilosophy, 14,* 190–194.

Milgram, S., & Sabini, J. (1978). On maintaining urban norms: A field experiment in the subway. In *Advances in environmental psychology: The urban environment* (Vol. 1, pp. 31–40). Hillsdale, NJ: Erlbaum.

Miller, C., & Swift, K. (1976). *Words and women.* San Jose, CA: IUniverse.com.

Miller, J. G., Bland, C., Källberg-Shroff, M., Tseng, C.-Y., Montes-George, J., Ryan, K., … Chakravarthy, S. (2014). Culture and the role of exchange vs. communal norms in friendship. *Journal of Experimental Social Psychology, 53,* 79–93. doi:10.1016/j.jesp.2014.02.006

Miller, M. M., & James, L. E. (2009). Is the generic pronoun he still comprehended as excluding women? *American Journal of Psychology, 122*(4), 483–496.

Miller, N. E. (1941). I. The frustration-aggression hypothesis. *Psychological Review, 48*(4), 337–342. doi:10.1037/h0055861

Miller, R. L., Seligman, C., Clark, N. T., & Bush, M. (1976). Perceptual contrast versus reciprocal concession as mediators of induced compliance. *Canadian Journal of Behavioural Science/Revue Canadienne Des Sciences Du Comportement, 8*(4), 401–409. doi:10.1037/h0081965

Miller, S. L., & Maner, J. K. (2010). Evolution and relationship maintenance: Fertility cues lead committed men to devalue relationship alternatives. *Journal of Experimental Social Psychology, 46*(6), 1081–1084. doi:10.1016/j.jesp.2010.07.004

Mishra, S., Mazumdar, S., & Suar, D. (2010). Place attachment and flood preparedness. *Journal of Environmental Psychology, 30*(2), 187–197. doi:10.1016/j.jenvp.2009.11.005

Mita, T. H., Dermer, M., & Knight, J. (1977). Reversed facial images and the mere-exposure hypothesis. *Journal of Personality and Social Psychology, 35*(8), 597–601. doi:10.1037/0022-3514.35.8.597

Moreland, R. L., & Beach, S. R. (1992). Exposure effects in the classroom: The development of affinity among students. *Journal of Experimental Social Psychology, 28*(3), 255–276. doi:10.1016/0022-1031(92)90055-O

Morrison, M. A., Morrison, T. G., & Sager, C.-L. (2004). Does body satisfaction differ between gay men and lesbian women and heterosexual men and women? *Body Image, 1*(2), 127–138. doi:10.1016/j.bodyim.2004.01.002

Mosbacher, D., & Yacker, F. (2009). *Training rules.* USA: Woman Vision.

Mullen, B., Johnson, C., & Salas, E. (1991). Productivity loss in brainstorming groups: A meta-analytic integration. *Basic and Applied Social Psychology, 12*(1), 3–23.

Mullen, B., Salas, E., & Driskell, J. E. (1989). Salience, motivation, and artifact as contributions to the relation between participation rate and leadership. *Journal of Experimental Social Psychology, 25*(6), 545–559. doi:10.1016/0022-1031(89)90005-X

Mummendey, A., Simon, B., Dietze, C., Grünert, M., Haeger, G., Kessler, S., … Schäferhoff, S. (1992). Categorization is not enough: Intergroup discrimination in negative outcome allocation. *Journal of Experimental Social Psychology, 28*(2), 125–144. doi:10.1016/0022-1031(92)90035-I

Murphy, M. C., Richeson, J. A., Shelton, J. N., Rheinschmidt, M. L., & Bergsieker, H. B. (2012). Cognitive costs of contemporary prejudice. *Group Processes & Intergroup Relations, 16*(5), 560–571. doi:10.1177/1368430212468170

Murray, C. J. L., Kulkarni, S. C., Michaud, C., Tomijima, N., Bulzacchelli, M. T., Iandiorio, T. J., & Ezzati, M. (2006). Eight Americas: Investigating mortality disparities across races, counties, and race-counties in the United States. *PLoS Medicine, 3*(9), e260. doi:10.1371/journal.pmed.0030260

Murray, S. L., Bellavia, G. M., Rose, P., & Griffin, D. W. (2003). Once hurt, twice hurtful: How perceived regard regulates daily marital interactions. *Journal of Personality and Social Psychology, 84*(1), 126–147. doi:10.1037/0022-3514.84.1.126

Murray, S. L., & Holmes, J. G. (1997). A leap of faith? Positive illusions in romantic relationships. *Personality and Social Psychology Bulletin*, *23*(6), 586–604. doi:10.1177/0146167297236003

Nadler, A. (2002). Postresolution processes: Instrumental and socioemotional routes to reconciliation. In G. Salomon & B. Nevo (Eds.), *Peace education: The concept, principles, and practices around the world* (pp. 127–141). Mahwah, NJ: Lawrence Erlbaum Associates.

Nardi, P. M. (1999). *Gay men's friendships: Invincible communities.* Chicago: University of Chicago Press.

Nasroen, R. A., & Suwartono, C. (2014). *Mirror imagery and conflict styles in post-crisis phase of intergroup conflict.* Gadjah Mada University. Retrieved from https://www.academia.edu/311372/Mirror_Imagery_and_Conflict_Styles_in_Post-Crisis_Phase_of_Intergroup_Conflict

National Center for Victims of Crime and NCAVP. (n.d.). *Why it matters: Rethinking victim assistance for lesbian, gay, bisexual, transgender, and queer victims of hate violence & intimate partner violence.* Retrieved from http://www.avp.org/documents/WhyItMatters.pdf

National Coalition of Anti-Violence Programs. (2013). *Lesbian, gay, bisexual, transgender, queer and HIV-infected intimate partner violence in 2012.* New York: National Coalition of Anti-Violence Programs. Retrieved from http://avp.org/storage/documents/ncavp_2012_ipvreport.final.pdf

Neville, H. A. (2009). Rationalizing the racial order: Racial color-blindness as a legitimizing ideology. In T. Koditschek, S. K. Cha-Jua, & H. A. Neville (Eds.), *Race struggles* (pp. 115–137). Urbana, IL: University of Illinois Press.

Newcomb, T. M. (1960). Varieties of interpersonal attraction. In D. Cartwright & A. Zander (Eds.), *Group dynamics: Research and theory* (2nd ed., pp. 104–119). New York: Harper & Row, Publishers.

Newsom, J. S., & Acquaro, K. (2011). *Miss representation.* USA: Girl's Club Entertainment.

Ng, S. H., & Chan, K. K. (1996). Biases in the description of various age groups: A linguistic category model analysis. *Bulletin of the Hong Kong Psychological Society*, *36-37*, 5–20.

Nichols, A. L., & Maner, J. K. (2008). The good-subject effect: Investigating participant demand characteristics. *The Journal of General Psychology*, *135*(2), 151–165.

Nickerson, R. S. (1999). How we know—and sometimes misjudge—what others know: Imputing one's own knowledge to others. *Psychological Bulletin*, *125*(6), 737–759. doi:10.1037/0033-2909.125.6.737

Nicolas, G., & Skinner, A. L. (2012). "That's so gay!" Priming the general negative usage of the word 'gay' increases implicit anti-gay bias. *The Journal of Social Psychology*, *152*(5), 654–658. doi:10.1080/00224545.2012.661803

Nier, J. A., Gaertner, S. L., Dovidio, J. F., Banker, B. S., Ward, C. M., & Rust, M. C. (2001). Changing interracial evaluations and behavior: The effects of a common group identity. *Group Processes & Intergroup Relations*, *4*(4), 299–316. doi:10.1177/1368430201004004001

Nisbett, R. E., & Cohen, D. (1996). *Culture of honor: The psychology of violence in the South.* Boulder, CO: Westview Press.

Nolan, J. M., Schultz, P. W., Cialdini, R. B., Goldstein, N. J., & Griskevicius, V. (2008). Normative social influence is underdetected. *Personality and Social Psychology Bulletin*, *34*(7), 913–923. doi:10.1177/0146167208316691

Notarius, C., & Markman, H. (1993). *We can work it out: Making sense of marital conflict.* New York: Putnam.

Nye, J. L., & Forsyth, D. R. (1991). The effects of prototype-based biases on leadership appraisals: A test of leadership categorization theory. *Small Group Research*, *22*(3), 360–379. doi:10.1177/1046496491223005

O'Boyle, E. H., Forsyth, D. R., Banks, G. C., & McDaniel, M. A. (2012). A meta-analysis of the dark triad and work behavior: A social exchange perspective. *Journal of Applied Psychology*, *97*(3), 557–579. doi:10.1037/a0025679

O'Brien, L., Albert, D., Chein, J., & Steinberg, L. (2011). Adolescents prefer more immediate rewards when in the presence of their peers. *Journal of Research on Adolescence, 21*(4), 747–753. doi:10.1111/j.1532-7795.2011.00738.x

O'Keefe, D. J., & Figge, M. (1997). A guilt-based explanation of the door-in-the-face influence strategy. *Human Communication Research, 24,* 64–81.

Obermann, M.-L. (2011). Moral disengagement in self-reported and peer-nominated school bullying. *Aggressive Behavior, 37*(2), 133–144. doi:10.1002/ab.20378

Ohbuchi, K., Kameda, M., & Agarie, N. (1989). Apology as aggression control: Its role in mediating appraisal of and response to harm. *Journal of Personality and Social Psychology, 56*(2), 219–227. doi:10.1037/0022-3514.56.2.219

Onuigbo, W. I. (1976). Tubal pregnancy in Nigerian Igbos. *International Journal of Fertility, 21*(3), 186–188.

Opotow, S. (1990). Moral exclusion and injustice: An introduction. *Journal of Social Issues, 46*(1), 1–20. doi:10.1111/j.1540-4560.1990.tb00268.x

Osgood, C. E. (1970). *An alternative to war or surrender.* Urbana: University of Illinois.

Ostrov, J. M., & Keating, C. F. (2004). Gender differences in preschool aggression during free play and structured interactions: An observational study. *Social Development, 13*(2), 255–277. doi:10.1111/j.1467-9507.2004.000266.x

Owen, J., Fincham, F. D., & Moore, J. (2011). Short-term prospective study of hooking up among college students. *Archives of Sexual Behavior, 40*(2), 331–341. doi:10.1007/s10508-010-9697-x

Padilla-Walker, L. M., & Carlo, G. (Eds.). (2014). *Prosocial development: A multidimensional approach.* Oxford: Oxford University Press.

Pahuja, N. (2012). *The world before her.* Canada: Storyline Entertainment.

Panksepp, J. (2003). Neuroscience: Feeling the pain of social loss. *Science, 302*(5643), 237–239. doi:10.1126/science.1091062

Papp, L. M., Danielewicz, J., & Cayemberg, C. (2012). "Are we Facebook official?" Implications of dating partners' Facebook use and profiles for intimate relationship satisfaction. *Cyberpsychology, Behavior, and Social Networking, 15*(2), 85–90. doi:10.1089/cyber.2011.0291

Pariser, E. (2011). *The filter bubble what the internet is hiding from you.* New York: Penguin Press. Retrieved from http://www.contentreserve.com/TitleInfo.asp?ID={DA99F154-C694-44E2-9EAB-62A78D73A2F2}&Format=50

Park, Y. (2008). Facilitating injustice: Tracing the role of social workers in the World War II internment of Japanese Americans. *Social Service Review, 82*(3), 447–483. doi:10.1086/592361

Parkhurst, J. T., & Hopmeyer, A. (1999). Developmental change in sources of loneliness in childhood and adolescence: Constructing a theoretical model. In K. J. Rotenberg & S. Hymel (Eds.), *Loneliness in childhood and adolescence* (pp. 56–79). Cambridge; New York: Cambridge University Press.

Parks, C. D. (2010). Graduated reciprocation in tension reduction (GRIT). In J. M. Levine & M. A. Hogg (Eds.), *Encyclopedia of group processes & intergroup relations* (pp. 310–312). Thousand Oaks, CA: Sage Publications.

Parks, M. R., & Roberts, L. D. (1998). `Making moosic': The development of personal relationships on line and a comparison to their off-line counterparts. *Journal of Social and Personal Relationships, 15*(4), 517–537. doi:10.1177/0265407598154005

Pascoe, E. A., & Smart Richman, L. (2009). Perceived discrimination and health: A meta-analytic review. *Psychological Bulletin, 135*(4), 531–554. doi:10.1037/a0016059

Patrick, D. L., Bell, J. F., Huang, J. Y., Lazarakis, N. C., & Edwards, T. C. (2013). Bullying and quality of life in youths perceived as gay, lesbian, or bisexual in Washington State, 2010. *American Journal of Public Health, 103*(7), 1255–1261. doi:10.2105/AJPH.2012.301101

Pavitt, C. (1999). Theorizing about the group communication-leadership relationship: Input-process-output and functional models. In L. R. Frey, D. S. Gouran, & M. S. Poole (Eds.), *The handbook of group communication theory and research* (pp. 313–334). Thousand Oaks, CA: Sage Publications, Inc.

Pearce, C. L., & Conger, J. A. (Eds.). (2003). *Shared leadership: Reframing the hows and whys of leadership*. Thousand Oaks, CA: Sage Publications.

Pennington, N. (2008). Will you be my friend: Facebook as a model for the evolution of the social penetration theory. In *Conference Papers*.

Peters, W. (1986). *A class divided*. Yale University Films.

Pettigrew, T. F. (1979). The ultimate attribution error: Extending Allport's cognitive analysis of prejudice. *Personality and Social Psychology Bulletin, 5*(4), 461–476. doi:10.1177/014616727900500407

Pettigrew, T. F., & Tropp, L. R. (2006). A meta-analytic test of intergroup contact theory. *Journal of Personality and Social Psychology, 90*(5), 751–783. doi:10.1037/0022-3514.90.5.751

Petty, R. E., & Cacioppo, J. T. (1981), *Attitudes and persuasion: Classic and contemporary approaches*. Dubuque, IA: Wm. C. Brown.

Pezdek, K., Whetstone, T., Reynolds, K., Askari, N., & et al. (1989). Memory for real-world scenes: The role of consistency with schema expectation. *Journal of Experimental Psychology: Learning, Memory, and Cognition, 15*(4), 587–595. doi:10.1037/0278-7393.15.4.587

Phinney, J. S. (1989). Stages of ethnic identity development in minority group adolescents. *The Journal of Early Adolescence, 9*(1-2), 34–49. doi:10.1177/0272431689091004

Pinquart, M. (2003). Loneliness in married, widowed, divorced, and never-married older adults. *Journal of Social and Personal Relationships, 20*(1), 31–53. doi:10.1177/02654075030201002

Poirier, P. (1997). *Pride divide*. USA.

Pratto, F., Sidanius, J., Stallworth, L. M., & Malle, B. F. (1994). Social dominance orientation: A personality variable predicting social and political attitudes. *Journal of Personality and Social Psychology, 67*(4), 741–763. doi:10.1037/0022-3514.67.4.741

Pyke, K., & Dang, T. (2003). "FOB" and "whitewashed": Idenitty and internalized racism among second generation Asian Americans. *Qualitative Sociology, 26*, 147–172.

Raanaas, R. K., Evensen, K. H., Rich, D., Sjøstrøm, G., & Patil, G. (2011). Benefits of indoor plants on attention capacity in an office setting. *Journal of Environmental Psychology, 31*(1), 99–105. doi:10.1016/j.jenvp.2010.11.005

Raanaas, R. K., Patil, G. G., & Hartig, T. (2012). Health benefits of a view of nature through the window: A quasi-experimental study of patients in a residential rehabilitation center. *Clinical Rehabilitation, 26*(1), 21–32. doi:10.1177/0269215511412800

Raine, A., Buchsbaum, M., & Lacasse, L. (1997). Brain abnormalities in murderers indicated by positron emission tomography. *Biological Psychiatry, 42*(6), 495–508. doi:10.1016/S0006-3223(96)00362-9

Raine, A., Meloy, J. R., Bihrle, S., Stoddard, J., LaCasse, L., & Buchsbaum, M. S. (1998). Reduced prefrontal and increased subcortical brain functioning assessed using positron emission tomography in predatory and affective murderers. *Behavioral Sciences & The Law, 16*(3), 319–332.

Ramsey, R., & Hamilton, A. F. d. C. (2010). How does your own knowledge influence the perception of another person's action in the human brain? *Social Cognitive and Affective Neuroscience, 7*(2), 242–251. doi:10.1093/scan/nsq102

Regan, D. T., Williams, M., & Sparling, S. (1972). Voluntary expiation of guilt: A field experiment. *Journal of Personality and Social Psychology, 24*(1), 42–45. doi:10.1037/h0033553

Reifman, A. S., Larrick, R. P., & Fein, S. (1991). Temper and temperature on the diamond: The heat-aggression relationship in Major League Baseball. *Personality and Social Psychology Bulletin, 17,* 580–585.

Reimann, R. (2001). Lesbian mothers at work. In *Queer families, queer politics: Challenging culture and the state* (pp. 254–271). New York: Columbia University Press.

Reis, H. T., & Shaver, P. (1988). Intimacy as an interpersonal process. In S. Duck (Ed.), *Handbook of personal relationships* (pp. 367–389). Chichester, England: Wiley.

Rempala, D. M., & Geers, A. L. (2009). The effect of victim information on causality judgments in a rape trial scenario. *The Journal of Social Psychology, 149*(4), 495–512.

Renzetti, C. M. (1992). *Violent betrayal: Partner abuse in lesbian relationships.* Thousand Oaks, CA: Sage Publications, Inc.

Rescuers save 600-kilogram moose trapped in frozen lake. (2013, March 8). *The Moscow Times.* Moscow, Russia. Retrieved from http://www.themoscowtimes.com/news/article/rescuers-save-600-kilogram-moose-trapped-in-frozen-lake-video/476641.html

Reyniers, D., & Bhalla, R. (2013). Reluctant altruism and peer pressure in charitable giving. *Judgment and Decision Making, 8*(1), 7–15.

Rhodes, G., Chan, J., Zebrowitz, L. A., & Simmons, L. W. (2003). Does sexual dimorphism in human faces signal health? *Proceedings of the Royal Society B: Biological Sciences, 270*(Suppl 1), S93–S95. doi:10.1098/rsbl.2003.0023

Rhodes, G., Geddes, K., Jeffery, L., Dziurawiec, S., & Clark, A. (2002). Are average and symmetric faces attractive to infants? Discrimination and looking preferences. *Perception, 31*(3), 315–321. doi:10.1068/p3129

Rhodes, G., Yoshikawa, S., Clark, A., Lee, K., McKay, R., & Akamatsu, S. (2001). Attractiveness of facial averageness and symmetry in non-Western cultures: In search of biologically based standards of beauty. *Perception, 30*(5), 611–625. doi:10.1068/p3123

Rhodes, G., Zebrowitz, L. A., Clark, A., Kalick, S. M., Hightower, A., & McKay, R. (2001). Do facial averageness and symmetry signal health? *Evolution and Human Behavior, 22*(1), 31–46. doi:10.1016/S1090-5138(00)00060-X

Richard, F. D., Bond, C. F., & Stokes-Zoota, J. J. (2003). One hundred years of social psychology quantitatively described. *Review of General Psychology, 7*(4), 331–363. doi:10.1037/1089-2680.7.4.331

Richman, J. A., Rospenda, K. M., Nawyn, S. J., Flaherty, J. A., Fendrich, M., Drum, M. L., & Johnson, T. P. (1999). Sexual harassment and generalized workplace abuse among university employees: Prevalence and mental health correlates. *American Journal of Public Health, 89,* 358-363.

Rieber, R. W., & Robinson, D. K. (Eds.). (2001). *Wilhelm Wundt in History.* Boston, MA: Springer US. Retrieved from http://www.springerlink.com/index/10.1007/978-1-4615-0665-2

Risen, J. L., & Critcher, C. R. (2011). Visceral fit: While in a visceral state, associated states of the world seem more likely. *Journal of Personality and Social Psychology, 100*(5), 777–793. doi:10.1037/a0022460

Rodin, M. J. (1987). Who is memorable to whom: A study of cognitive disregard. *Social Cognition, 5*(2), 144–165. doi:10.1521/soco.1987.5.2.144

Roediger, H. L., Meade, M. L., & Bergman, E. T. (2001). Social contagion of memory. *Psychonomic Bulletin and Review, 8*(2), 365–371.

Rogers, T. B., Kuiper, N. A., & Kirker, W. S. (1977). Self-reference and the encoding of personal information. *Journal of Personality and Social Psychology, 35*(9), 677–688. doi:10.1037/0022-3514.35.9.677

Roheim, G. (1932). Psycho-analysis of primitive cultural types. *Psycho-Analysis, 13,* 1–221.

Rohrbaugh, J. B. (2006). Domestic violence in same-gender relationships. *Family Court Review*, *44*(2), 287–299.

Roll, S., McClelland, G., & Abel, T. (1996). Differences in susceptibility to influence in Mexican American and Anglo females. *Hispanic Journal of Behavioral Sciences*, *18*(1), 13–20. doi:10.1177/07399863960181002

Rosenthal, R., & Jacobsen, L. (1968). *Pygmalion in the classroom: Teacher expectation and pupils' intellectual development.* New York: Holt, Rinhart, and Winston.

Rosenthal, R., & Rosnow, R. L. (1975). *The volunteer subject.* New York: Wiley.

Rosentiel, T., Mitchell, A., & Jurkowitz, M. (2012). *Winning the media campaign 2012.* Washington, DC: Pew Research Center. Retrieved from http://www.journalism.org/files/legacy/Winningthemediacampaign2012.pdf

Ross, L., Lepper, M. R., & Hubbard, M. (1975). Perseverance in self-perception and social perception: Biased attributional processes in the debriefing paradigm. *Journal of Personality and Social Psychology*, *32*(5), 880–892. doi:10.1037/0022-3514.32.5.880

Rouhana, N. N., & Fiske, S. T. (1995). Perception of power, threat and conflict intensity in asymmetric intergroup conflict: Arab and Jewish citizens of Israel. *Journal of Conflict Resolution*, *39*(1), 49–81. doi:10.1177/0022002795039001003

Ruback, R. B., & Juieng, D. (1997). Territorial defense in parking lots: Retaliation against waiting drivers. *Journal of Applied Social Psychology*, *27*, 821–834.

Rubin, Z., & Peplau, L. A. (1975). Who believes in a just world? *Journal of Social Issues*, *31*(3), 65–89. doi:10.1111/j.1540-4560.1975.tb00997.x

Rudman, L. A., & Glick, P. (2001). Prescriptive gender stereotypes and backlash toward agentic women. *Journal of Social Issues*, *57*(4), 743–762. doi:10.1111/0022-4537.00239

Rudman, L. A., & Mescher, K. (2012). Of animals and objects: Men's implicit dehumanization of women and likelihood of sexual aggression. *Personality and Social Psychology Bulletin*, *38*(6), 734–746. doi:10.1177/0146167212436401

Rueger, S. Y., Malecki, C. K., & Demaray, M. K. (2008). Gender differences in the relationship between perceived social support and student adjustment during early adolescence. *School Psychology Quarterly*, *23*, 496–514.

Rusbult, C. E., & Buunk, B. P. (1993). Commitment processes in close relationships: An interdependence analysis. *Journal of Social and Personal Relationships*, *10*(2), 175–204. doi:10.1177/026540759301000202

Rusbult, C. E., & Martz, J. M. (1995). Remaining in an abusive relationship: An investment model analysis of nonvoluntary dependence. *Personality and Social Psychology Bulletin*, *21*(6), 558–571. doi:10.1177/0146167295216002

Rusbult, C. E., Morrow, G. D., & Johnson, D. J. (1987). Self-esteem and problem-solving behaviour in close relationships. *British Journal of Social Psychology*, *26*(4), 293–303. doi:10.1111/j.2044-8309.1987.tb00792.x

Rusbult, C. E., Verette, J., Whitney, G. A., Slovik, L. F., & et al. (1991). Accommodation processes in close relationships: Theory and preliminary empirical evidence. *Journal of Personality and Social Psychology*, *60*(1), 53–78. doi:10.1037/0022-3514.60.1.53

Rushton, J., & Campbell, A. C. (1977). Modeling, vicarious reinforcement and extraversion on blood donating in adults: Immediate and long-term effects. *European Journal of Social Psychology*, *7*, 297–306.

Ryan, M. K., & Haslam, S. A. (2005). The glass cliff: Evidence that women are over-represented in precarious leadership positions. *British Journal of Management*, *16*(2), 81–90. doi:10.1111/j.1467-8551.2005.00433.x

Ryan, R., LaGuardia, J. G., & Rawsthorne, L. J. (2005). Self-complexity and the authenticity of self-aspects: Effects on well-being and resilience to stressful events. *North American Journal of Psychology*, *7*(3), 431–447.

Rydell, R. J., & McConnell, A. R. (2006). Understanding implicit and explicit attitude change: A systems of reasoning analysis. *Journal of Personality and Social Psychology*, *91*(6), 995–1008. doi:10.1037/0022-3514.91.6.995

Saarela, M. V., & Hari, R. (2008). Listening to humans walking together activates the social brain circuitry. *Social Neuroscience*, *3*(3-4), 401–409. doi:10.1080/17470910801897633

Sabini, J., Cosmas, K., Siepmann, M., & Stein, J. (1999). Underestimates and truly false consensus effects in estimates of embarrassment and other emotions. *Basic and Applied Social Psychology*, *21*(3), 223–241. doi:10.1207/S15324834BASP2103_6

Sackett, D. L., & Snow, J. C. (1979). The magnitude of compliance and noncompliance. In R. B. Haynes, D. W. Taylor, & D. L. Sackett (Eds.), *Compliance in health care.* (pp. 11–22). Baltimore: Johns Hopkins University Press.

Sacks, O. W. (1998). *The man who mistook his wife for a hat and other clinical tales* (1st Touchstone ed.). New York, NY: Simon & Schuster.

Salganik, M. J., Dodds, P. S., & Watts, D. J. (2006). Experimental study of inequality and unpredictability in an artificial cultural market. *Science*, *311*(5762), 854–856. doi:10.1126/science.1121066

Samerotte, G. C., & Harris, M. B. (1976). Some factors influencing helping: The effects of a handicap, responsibility and requesting help. *The Journal of Social Psychology*, *98*, 39–45.

Sanchez, R., & Assefa, H. (2014, March 22). Teenager charged with killing NY bus rider who was not target. CNN.com. Retrieved from http://www.cnn.com/2014/03/22/justice/new-york-bus-shooting-death

Sandberg, S. (2013). *Lean in: Women, work, and the will to lead.* Knopf.

Scannell, L., & Gifford, R. (2010). The relations between natural and civic place attachment and pro-environmental behavior. *Journal of Environmental Psychology*, *30*(3), 289–297. doi:10.1016/j.jenvp.2010.01.010

Scannell, L., & Gifford, R. (2013). Personally relevant climate change: The role of place attachment and local versus global message framing in engagement. *Environment and Behavior*, *45*(1), 60–85. doi:10.1177/0013916511421196

Schade, L. C., Sandberg, J., Bean, R., Busby, D., & Coyne, S. (2013). Using technology to connect in romantic relationships: Effects on attachment, relationship satisfaction, and stability in emerging adults. *Journal of Couple & Relationship Therapy*, *12*(4), 314–338. doi:10.1080/15332691.2013.836051

Scherrer, K. S. (2008). Coming to an asexual identity: Negotiating identity, negotiating desire. *Sexualities*, *11*(5), 621–641. doi:10.1177/1363460708094269

Schmitt, D. P., & Buss, D. M. (1996). Strategic self-promotion and competitor derogation: Sex and context effects on the perceived effectiveness of mate attraction tactics. *Journal of Personality and Social Psychology*, *70*(6), 1185–1204. doi:10.1037/0022-3514.70.6.1185

Schopler, J., & Insko, C. A. (1992). The discontinuity effect in interpersonal and intergroup relations: Generality and mediation. *European Review of Social Psychology, 3*(1), 121-151.

Schutz, A. (2003). Self-esteem and interpersonal strategies. In J. P. Forgas, K. D. Williams, & L. Wheeler (Eds.), *The social mind: Cognitive and motivational aspects of interpersonal behavior* (pp. 157–176). Cambridge: Cambridge University Press.

Schwartz, C.E., Wright, C.I., Shin, L.M., Kagan, J., Whalen, P.J., McMullin, K.G., Rauch, S.L., (2003). Differential amygdalar response to novel versus newly familiar neutral faces: a functional MRI probe developed for studying inhibited temperament. *Biol. Psychiatry, 53*, 854–862.

Schwarz, N., & Clore, G. L. (2003). Mood as information: 20 years later. Psychological Inquiry, *14*(3-4), 296–303. doi:10.1080/1047840X.2003.9682896

Semin, G. R., & Fiedler, K. (1991). The linguistic category model, its bases, applications and range. *European Review of Social Psychology*, *2*(1), 1–30. doi:10.1080/14792779143000006

Shamir, J., & Shikaki, K. (2002). Self-Serving perceptions of terrorism among Israelis and Palestinians. *Political Psychology*, *23*(3), 537–557. doi:10.1111/0162-895X.00297

Shen, H., Wan, F., & Wyer, R. S. (2011). Cross-cultural differences in the refusal to accept a small gift: The differential influence of reciprocity norms on Asians and North Americans. *Journal of Personality and Social Psychology*, *100*(2), 271–281. doi:10.1037/a0021201

Sherif, M. (1935). A study of some social factors in perception. *Archives of Psychology*, *187*, 60.

Sherif, M., & Sherif, C. W. (1953). *Groups in harmony and tension*. Harper & Brothers.

Shimek, C., & Bello, R. (2014). Coping with break-ups: Rebound relationships and gender socialization. *Social Sciences*, *3*(1), 24–43. doi:10.3390/socsci3010024

Sigelman, C. K. (1991). Social distance from stigmatized groups: False consensus and false uniqueness effects on responding. *Rehabilitation Psychology*, *36*(3), 139–151. doi:10.1037/h0079081

Simons, D. J., & Levin, D. T. (1998). Failure to detect changes to people during a real-world interaction. *Psychonomic Bulletin & Review*, *5*(4), 644–649. doi:10.3758/BF03208840

Simpson, J. A. (1990). Influence of attachment styles on romantic relationships. *Journal of Personality and Social Psychology*, *59*(5), 971–980. doi:10.1037/0022-3514.59.5.971

Sims, T. B., Van Reekum, C. M., Johnstone, T., & Chakrabarti, B. (2012). How reward modulates mimicry: EMG evidence of greater facial mimicry of more rewarding happy faces. *Psychophysiology*, *49*(7), 998–1004. doi:10.1111/j.1469-8986.2012.01377.x

Sims, V. M., & Patrick, J. R. (1936). Attitude toward the Negro of northern and southern college students. *Journal of Social Psychology*, *7*, 192–204.

Sindic, D., & Reicher, S. D. (2009). "Our way of life is worth defending": Testing a model of attitudes towards superordinate group membership through a study of Scots' attitudes towards Britain. *European Journal of Social Psychology*, *39*(1), 114–129. doi:10.1002/ejsp.503

Singh, D. (1995). Female judgment of male attractiveness and desirability for relationships: Role of waist-to-hip ratio and financial status. *Journal of Personality and Social Psychology*, *69*(6), 1089–1101. doi:10.1037/0022-3514.69.6.1089

Singh, D., & Singh, D. (2006). Role of body fat and body shape on judgment of female health and attractiveness: An evolutionary perspective. *Psychological Topics*, *2*, 331–350.

Sinoski, K. (2013, December 2). "Hero" jumps into freezing river to save members of Alberta family in Fernie crash: RCMP. *Vancouver Sun*. Vancouver, Canada. Retrieved from http://www.vancouversun.com/Hero+jumps+into+freezing+river+save+members+Alberta+family+Fernie+crash+RCMP/9234653/story.html

Slotter, E. B., Duffy, C. W., & Gardner, W. L. (2014). Balancing the need to be "me" with the need to be "we": Applying optimal distinctiveness theory to the understanding of multiple motives within romantic relationships. *Journal of Experimental Social Psychology*, *52*, 71–81. doi:10.1016/j.jesp.2014.01.001

Slovic, P. (2007). If I look at the mass I will never act: Psychic numbing and genocide. *Judgment and Decision Making*, *2*(2), 79–95.

Smedley, B. D., Stith, A. Y., & Nelson, A. R. (2003). Committee on understanding and eliminating racial and ethnic disparities in health care, Board on Health Sciences Policy, Institute of Medicine. *Unequal Treatment Confronting Racial and Ethnic Disparities in Health Care*, 160–179.

Smith, A., & Williams, K. D. (2004). R U there? Ostracism by cell phone text messages. *Group Dynamics: Theory, Research, and Practice*, *8*(4), 291–301. doi:10.1037/1089-2699.8.4.291

Smith, C. A., & Stillman, S. (2002). What do women want? The effects of gender and sexual orientation on the desirability of physical attributes in the personal ads of women. *Sex Roles*, *46*(9/10), 337–342.

Smith, E. R., & Mackie, D. M. (2008). Intergroup emotions. In M. Lewis, J. M. Haviland-Jones, & L. F. Barrett (Eds.), *Handbook of emotions* (3rd ed., pp. 728-439). New York, NY: Guilford.

Smith-Jackson, T. L., & Klein, K. W. (2009). Open-plan offices: Task performance and mental workload. *Journal of Environmental Psychology*, *29*(2), 279–289. doi:10.1016/j.jenvp.2008.09.002

Snyder, C. R., & Lopez, S. J. (2002). *Handbook of positive psychology*. Oxford [England]; New York: Oxford University Press. Retrieved from http://public.eblib.com/EBLPublic/PublicView.do?ptiID=271581

Snyder, C. R., & Wright, E. (2002). *Handbook of Positive Psychology*. New York: Oxford University Press.

Snyder, M., Tanke, E. D., & Berscheid, E. (1977). Social perception and interpersonal behavior: On the self-fulfilling nature of social stereotypes. *Journal of Personality and Social Psychology*, *35*(9), 656–666. doi:10.1037/0022-3514.35.9.656

Solomon, S. E., Rothblum, E. D., & Balsam, K. F. (2004). Pioneers in partnership: Lesbian and gay male couples in civil unions compared with those not in civil unions and married heterosexual siblings. *Journal of Family Psychology*, *18*(2), 275–286. doi:10.1037/0893-3200.18.2.275

Sommer, K. L., Williams, K. D., Ciarocco, N. J., & Baumeister, R. F. (2001). When silence speaks louder than words: Explorations into the intrapsychic consequences of social ostracism. *Basic and Applied Social Psychology*, *23*(4), 225–243. doi:10.1207/S15324834BASP2304_1

Spellman, B. A. (2012). Introduction to the Special Section: Data, Data, Everywhere... Especially in My File Drawer. *Perspectives on Psychological Science*, *7*(1), 58–59. doi:10.1177/1745691611432124

Spender, D. (1990). *Man made language* (2nd ed.). Pandora Press.

Spindel, J. (2007). *How to date men: Dating secrets from America's top matchmaker*. New York: Plume.

Spoor, J. R., & Kelly, J. R. (2004). The evolutionary significance of affect in groups: Communication and group bonding. *Group Processes & Intergroup Relations*, *7*(4), 398–412. doi:10.1177/1368430204046145

Sprecher, S. (1994). Two sides to the breakup of dating relationships. *Personal Relationships*, *1*(3), 199–222. doi:10.1111/j.1475-6811.1994.tb00062.x

Sprecher, S., Zimmerman, C., & Fehr, B. (2014). The influence of compassionate love on strategies used to end a relationship. *Journal of Social and Personal Relationships*. doi:10.1177/0265407513517958

Srivastava, S., McGonigal, K. M., Richards, J. M., Butler, E. A., & Gross, J. J. (2006). Optimism in close relationships: How seeing things in a positive light makes them so. *Journal of Personality and Social Psychology*, *91*(1), 143–153. doi:10.1037/0022-3514.91.1.143

Srull, T. K. (1981). Person memory: Some tests of associative storage and retrieval models. *Journal of Experimental Psychology: Human Learning and Memory*, *7*, 440-463.

Staff. (2012, May 11). Florida woman sentenced to 20 years in controversial warning shot case. CNN. com. Retrieved from http://www.cnn.com/2012/05/11/justice/florida-stand-ground-sentencing/

Stapel, D. A., & Lindenberg, S. (2011). Coping with chaos: How disordered contexts promote stereotyping and cscrimination. *Science*, *332*(6026), 251–253. doi:10.1126/science.1201068

Stasser, G., & Titus, W. (2003). Hidden profiles: A brief history. *Psychological Inquiry*, *14*(3/4), 304–313.

Staub, E. (2008). Promoting reconciliation after genocide and mass killing in Rwanda—and other post-conflict settings: Understanding the roots of violence, healing, shared history, and general principles. In A. Nadler, T. Malloy, & J. D. Fisher (Eds.), *The Social Psychology of Intergroup Recon-

ciliation (pp. 395–422). Oxford University Press. Retrieved from http://www.oxfordscholarship. com/view/10.1093/acprof:oso/9780195300314.001.0001/acprof-9780195300314-chapter-18

Staub, E., (1989). *The roots of evil: The origins of genocide and other group violence.* New York: Cambridge University Press.

Staub, E. (1999). The origins and prevention of genocide, mass killing and other collective violence. *Peace and Conflict: Journal of Peace Psychology, 5,* 303-337.

Steele, C. M., & Josephs, R. A. (1990). Alcohol myopia: Its prized and dangerous effects. *American Psychologist, 45*(8), 921–933.

Steenbergen, H., Langeslag, S. J. E., Band, G. P. H., & Hommel, B. (2013). Reduced cognitive control in passionate lovers. *Motivation and Emotion.* doi:10.1007/s11031-013-9380-3

Stephan, C. W., & Langlois, J. H. (1984). Baby beautiful: Adult attributions of infant competence as a function of infant attractiveness. *Child Development, 55*(2), 576. doi:10.2307/1129969

Stephan, W. G., & Stephan, C. W. (1985). Intergroup anxiety. *Journal of Social Issues, 41,* 157–176.

Stephan, W. G., & Stephan, C. W. (1992). Reducing intercultural anxiety through intercultural contact. *International Journal of Intercultural Relations, 16,* 96–106.

Sternberg, R. J. (1986). A triangular theory of love. *Psychological Review, 93*(2), 119–135. doi:10.1037/0033-295X.93.2.119

Stogdill, R. M. (1948). Personal factors associated with leadership: A survey of the literature. *The Journal of Psychology, 25*(1), 35–71. doi:10.1080/00223980.1948.9917362

Stogdill, R. M. (1974). *Handbook of leadership; a survey of theory and research.* New York: Free Press.

Stoner, J. A. (1961). *A comparison of individual and group decision involving risk.* Massachusetts Institute of Technology.

Strang, S., Utikal, V., Fischbacher, U., Weber, B., & Falk, A. (2014). Neural correlates of receiving an apology and active forgiveness: An fMRI Study. *PLoS ONE, 9*(2), e87654. doi:10.1371/journal. pone.0087654

Straus, M. A. (in press). Addressing violence by female partners is vital to prevent or stop violence against women: Evidence from the multisite batterer intervention evaluation. *Violence Against Women.* Retrieved from http://gauss.unh.edu/~mas2/V86%20Gondolf%20rejoinder%20Revised%20R6.pdf

Straus, M. A. (1993). Identifying offenders in criminal justice research on domestic assault. *American Behavioral Scientist, 36*(5), 587–600. doi:10.1177/0002764293036005004

Straus, M. A. (1999). The controversy over domestic violence by women: A methodological, theoretical, and sociology of science analysis. In X. B. Arriaga & S. Oskamp (Eds.), *Violence in intimate relationships.* Thousand Oaks, CA: Sage Publications.

Straus, M. A. (2010). Thirty years of denying the evidence on gender symmetry in partner violence: Implications for prevention and treatment. *Partner Abuse, 1*(3), 332–362. doi:10.1891/1946-6560.1.3.332

Straus, M. A., & Gozjolko, K. L. (2014). "Intimate terrorism" and gender differences in injury of dating partners by male and female university students. *Journal of Family Violence, 29*(1), 51–65. doi:10.1007/s10896-013-9560-7

Straus, M. A., & Michel-Smith, Y. (2013). Mutuality, severity, and chronicity of violence by father-only, mother-only, and mutually violent parents as reported by university students in 15 nations. *Child Abuse & Neglect.* doi:10.1016/j.chiabu.2013.10.004

Strauss, M. A. (1993). Identifying offenders in criminal justice research on domestic assault. *36,* 587–600.

Strenta, A., & Dejong, W. (1981). The effect of a prosocial label on helping behavior. *Social Psychology Quarterly, 44*(2), 142–147.

Stroebe, W. (2012). The truth about Triplett (1898), but nobody seems to care. *Perspectives on Psychological Science, 7*(1), 54–57. doi:10.1177/1745691611427306

Strube, M. J. (2005). What did Triplett really find? A contemporary analysis of the first experiment in social psychology. *American Journal of Psychology, 118*, 271–286.

Sue, D. W., Capodilupo, C. M., & Holder, A. M. B. (2008). Racial microaggressions in the life experience of black Americans. *Professional Psychology: Research and Practice, 39*(3), 329–336. doi:10.1037/0735-7028.39.3.329

Sue, D. W., Capodilupo, C. M., Torino, G. C., Bucceri, J. M., Holder, A. M. B., Nadal, K. L., & Esquilin, M. (2007). Racial microaggressions in everyday life: Implications for clinical practice. *American Psychologist, 62*(4), 271–286. doi:10.1037/0003-066X.62.4.271

Sullivan, P. (1998). Sexual identity development: The importance of target or dominant group membership. In R. L. Sanlo (Ed.), *Working with lesbian, gay, bisexual, and transgender college students: A handbook for faculty and administrators.* (pp. 3–12). Westport, CT: Greenwood.

Sullivan, W. C. (2004). The fruit of urban nature: Vital neighborhood spaces. *Environment and Behavior, 36*(5), 678–700. doi:10.1177/0193841X04264945

Swim, J. K., Aikin, K. J., Hall, W. S., & Hunter, B. A. (1995). Sexism and racism: Old-fashioned and modern prejudices. *Journal of Personality and Social Psychology, 68*(2), 199–214. doi:10.1037/0022-3514.68.2.199

Symons, D. (1979). *The evolution of human sexuality*. USA: Oxford University Press.

Szymanski, D. M., Gupta, A., Carr, E. R., & Stewart, D. (2009). Internalized misogyny as a moderator of the link between sexist events and women's psychological distress. *Sex Roles, 61*(1-2), 101–109. doi:10.1007/s11199-009-9611-y

Tait, R. C., & Chibnall, J. T. (2014). Racial/ethnic disparities in the assessment and treatment of pain: Psychosocial perspectives. *American Psychologist, 69*(2), 131–141. doi:10.1037/a0035204

Tajadura-Jiménez, A., Pantelidou, G., Rebacz, P., Västfjäll, D., & Tsakiris, M. (2011). I-Space: The effects of emotional valence and source of music on interpersonal distance. *PLoS ONE, 6*(10), e26083. doi:10.1371/journal.pone.0026083

Tajfel, H., Billig, M. G., Bundy, R. P., & Flament, C. (1971). Social categorization and intergroup behaviour. *European Journal of Social Psychology, 1*(2), 149–178. doi:10.1002/ejsp.2420010202

Taylor, S. E., & Fiske, S. T. (1975). Point of view and perception so causality. *Journal of Personality and Social Psychology, 32*, 439-445.

Test, M. A., & Bryan, J. H. (1969). The effects of dependency, models, and reciprocity upon subsequent helping behavior. *Journal of Social Psychology, 78*, 205–212.

The Wilderness Act, US (1964).

Thornton, R. (1990). *American Indian holocaust and survival: A population history since 1492*. Oklahoma City: University of Oklahoma Press.

Tiedens, L. Z. (2001). Anger and advancement versus sadness and subjugation: The effect of negative emotion expressions on social status conferral. *Journal of Personality and Social Psychology, 80*(1), 86–94. doi:10.1037/0022-3514.80.1.86

Tiedens, L. Z., Ellsworth, P. C., & Mesquita, B. (2000). Sentimental stereotypes: Emotional expectations for high-and low-status group members. *Personality and Social Psychology Bulletin, 26*(5), 560–575. doi:10.1177/0146167200267004

To, C. W. (2014). Domestic labor, gendered intergenerational contract, and shared elderly care in rural South China. In Z. Hao & S. Chen (Eds.), *Social issues in China* (pp. 67–84). New York: Springer New York. Retrieved from http://link.springer.com/10.1007/978-1-4614-2224-2_4

Tolhuizen, J. H. (1989). Communication strategies for intensifying dating relationships: Identification, use and structure. *Journal of Social and Personal Relationships*, *6*(4), 413–434. doi:10.1177/0265407589064002

Trampe, D., Stapel, D. A., & Siero, F. W. (2007). On models and vases: Body dissatisfaction and proneness to social comparison effects. *Journal of Personality and Social Psychology*, *92*(1), 106–118. doi:10.1037/0022-3514.92.1.106

Trawalter, S., Hoffman, K. M., & Waytz, A. (2012). Racial bias in perceptions of others' pain. *PLoS ONE*, *7*(11), e48546. doi:10.1371/journal.pone.0048546

Triplett, N. (1898). The dynamogenic factors in pacemaking and competition. *American Journal of Psychology*, *9*, 507–533.

Trzesniewski, K. H., Donnellan, M. B., Moffitt, T. E., Robins, R. W., Poulton, R., & Caspi, A. (2006). Low self-esteem during adolescence predicts poor health, criminal behavior, and limited economic prospects during adulthood. *Developmental Psychology*, *42*(2), 381–390. doi:10.1037/0012-1649.42.2.381

Tsang, J.-A., McCullough, M. E., & Hoyt, W. T. (2005). Psychometric and rationalization accounts of the religion-forgiveness discrepancy. *Journal of Social Issues*, *61*(4), 785–805. doi:10.1111/j.1540-4560.2005.00432.x

Tsui, A. S., & Gutek, B. A. (1999). *Demographic differences in organizations: Current research and future directions*. Lexington Books.

Ullman, S. E., & Townsend, S. M. (2007). Barriers to working with sexual assault survivors: A qualitative study of rape crisis center workers. *Violence Against Women*, *13*(4), 412–443. doi:10.1177/1077801207299191

University of South Africa. (1996). *Beyond the man approach: Guidelines for gender-inclusive language*. Muckleneuk, Pretoria: University of South Africa.

Vaes, J., & Muratore, M. (2013). Defensive dehumanization in the medical practice: A cross-sectional study from a health care worker's perspective. *British Journal of Social Psychology*, *52*(1), 180–190. doi:10.1111/bjso.12008

Vaes, J., Paladino, M. P., Castelli, L., Leyens, J.-P., & Giovanazzi, A. (2003). On the behavioral consequences of infrahumanization: The implicit role of uniquely human emotions in intergroup relations. *Journal of Personality and Social Psychology*, *85*(6), 1016–1034. doi:10.1037/0022-3514.85.6.1016

Vaes, J., Paladino, M.-P., & Leyens, J.-P. (2002). The lost e-mail: Prosocial reactions induced by uniquely human emotions. *British Journal of Social Psychology*, *41*(4), 521–534. doi:10.1348/014466602321149867

Vaes, J., Paladino, P., & Puvia, E. (2011). Are sexualized women complete human beings? Why men and women dehumanize sexually objectified women: Dehumanization of sexually objectified women. *European Journal of Social Psychology*, *41*(6), 774–785. doi:10.1002/ejsp.824

Vallone, R. P., Ross, L., & Lepper, M. R. (1985). The hostile media phenomena: Biased perception and perceptions of media bias in coverage of the Beirut Massacre. *Journal of Personality and Social Psychology*, *49*(3), 577–585.

Van der Schalk, J., Hawk, S. T., Fischer, A. H., & Doosje, B. (2011). Moving faces, looking places: Validation of the Amsterdam Dynamic Facial Expression Set (ADFES). *Emotion*, *11*(4), 907–920. doi:10.1037/a0023853

Van Vugt, M., & Ahuja, A. (2011). *Naturally selected: Why some people lead, why others follow, and why it matters*. HarperCollins Publishers.

vanOyen Witvliet, C., Ludwig, T. E., & Vander Laan, K. L. (2001). Granting forgiveness or harboring grudges: Implications for emotion, physiology, and health. *Psychological Science, 12*(2), 117–123.

Varul, M. Z. (2010). Talcott Parsons, the sick role and chronic illness. *Body & Society, 16*(2), 72–94. doi:10.1177/1357034X10364766

Vogel, G. (2011). Psychologist accused of fraud on "Astonishing Scale." *Science, 334,* 579.

Voorhees, D. (2008). *Disgusting things: A miscellany.* New York: Perigee.

Vrig, A., Edward, K., Roberts, K. P., & Bull, R. (2000). Detecting deceit via analysis of verbal and non-verbal behavior. *Journal of Nonverbal Behavior, 24,* 239–263.

Waalen, J., Goodwin, M. M., Spitz, A. M., Petersen, R., & Saltzman, L. E. (2000). Screening for intimate partner violence by health care providers: barriers and interventions. *American Journal of Preventive Medicine, 19*(4), 230–237. doi:10.1016/S0749-3797(00)00229-4

Wade-Benzoni, K. A., Okumura, T., Brett, J. M., Moore, D. A., Tenbrunsel, A. E., & Bazerman, M. H. (2002). Cognitions and behavior in asymmetric social dilemmas: A comparison of two cultures. *Journal of Applied Psychology, 87*(1), 87–95. doi:10.1037/0021-9010.87.1.87

Wahlund, K., & Kristiansson, M. (2009). Aggression, psychopathy and brain imaging — Review and future recommendations. *International Journal of Law and Psychiatry, 32*(4), 266–271. doi:10.1016/j.ijlp.2009.04.007

Wainright v. Witt, No. 412 (US 1985).

Wallach, M. A., & Kogan, N. (1961). Aspects of judgment and decision making: interrelationships and changes with age. *Behavioral Science, 6,* 23-36.

Waller, J. (2002). *Becoming evil: How ordinary people commit genocide and mass killing.* New York: Oxford University Press.

Walster, E., Walster, G. W., & Berscheid, E. (1978). *Equity: Theory and research.* Boston, MA: Allyn & Bacon.

Walster, E., Walster, G. W., & Traupmann, J. (1978). Equity and premarital sex. *Journal of Personality and Social Psychology, 36,* 82–92.

Wann, D. L., & Branscombe, N. R. (1990). Die-hard and fair-weather fans: Effects of identification on BIRGing and CORFing tendencies. *Journal of Sport & Social Issues, 14*(2), 103–117. doi:10.1177/019372359001400203

Warshaw, P. R., & Davis, F. D. (1985). Disentangling behavioral intention and behavioral expectation. *Journal of Experimental Social Psychology, 21*(3), 213–228. doi:10.1016/0022-1031(85)90017-4

Watson, B., & Gallois, C. (2002). Patients' interactions with health providers: A linguistic category model approach. *Journal of Language and Social Psychology, 21*(1), 32–52. doi:10.1177/0261927X02021001003

Watt, S. E., & Larkin, C. (2010). Prejudiced people perceive more community support for their views: The role of own, media, and peer attitudes in perceived consensus. *Journal of Applied Social Psychology, 40*(3), 710–731. doi:10.1111/j.1559-1816.2010.00594.x

Wegner, D. M., Erber, R., & Raymond, P. (1991). Transactive memory in close relationships. *Journal of Personality and Social Psychology, 61*(6), 923–929.

Weiner, B. (1986). *An attributional theory of motivation and emotion.* New York: Springer-Verlag.

Weinstock, J. S. (2004). Lesbian FLEX-ibility: Friend and/or family connections among lesbian ex-lovers. *Journal of Lesbian Studies, 8*(3-4), 193–238. doi:10.1300/J155v08n03_30

Wells, G. L. (2014). Eyewitness identification: Probative value, criterion shifts, and policy regarding the sequential lineup. *Current Directions in Psychological Science, 23*(1), 11–16. doi:10.1177/0963721413504781

Wesselmann, E. D., Bagg, D., & Williams, K. D. (2009). "I Feel Your Pain": The effects of observing ostracism on the ostracism detection system. *Journal of Experimental Social Psychology*, *45*(6), 1308–1311. doi:10.1016/j.jesp.2009.08.003

West, S. G., & Brown, J. T. (1975). Physical attractiveness, the severity of the emergency and helping: A field experiment and interpersonal simulation. *Journal of Experimental Social Psychology*, *11*(6), 531–538. doi:10.1016/0022-1031(75)90004-9

Weyers, P., Mühlberger, A., Kund, A., Hess, U., & Pauli, P. (2009). Modulation of facial reactions to avatar emotional faces by nonconscious competition priming. *Psychophysiology*, *46*(2), 328–335. doi:10.1111/j.1469-8986.2008.00771.x

Wheelan, S. A. (2003). An initial exploration of the internal dynamics of leadership teams. *Consulting Psychology Journal: Practice and Research*, *55*(3), 179–188. doi:10.1037/1061-4087.55.3.179

Wheeler, K. J., Roberts, M. E., & Neiheisel, M. B. (2014). Medication adherence part two: Predictors of nonadherence and adherence: Medication adherence part 2. *Journal of the American Association of Nurse Practitioners*, *26*(4), 225–232. doi:10.1002/2327-6924.12105

Wheeler, L., & Kim, Y. (1997). What is beautiful is culturally good: The physical attractiveness stereotype has different content in collectivistic cultures. *Personality and Social Psychology Bulletin*, *23*(8), 795–800. doi:10.1177/0146167297238001

White, M., Smith, A., Humphryes, K., Pahl, S., Snelling, D., & Depledge, M. (2010). Blue space: The importance of water for preference, affect, and restorativeness ratings of natural and built scenes. *Journal of Environmental Psychology*, *30*(4), 482–493. doi:10.1016/j.jenvp.2010.04.004

Wiley, M. G., & Eskilson, A. (1985). Speech style, gender stereotypes, and corporate success: What if women talk more like men? *Sex Roles*, *12*(9-10), 993–1007. doi:10.1007/BF00288100

Williams, C. L. (1992). The glass escalator: Hidden advantages for men in the "female" professions. *Social Problems*, *39*(3), 253–267. doi:10.2307/3096961

Williams, E. F., & Gilovich, T. (2008). Do people really believe they are above average? *Journal of Experimental Social Psychology*, *44*(4), 1121–1128. doi:10.1016/j.jesp.2008.01.002

Williams, K. D., Forgas, J. P., & von Hipple, W. (2005). *The social outcast: Ostracism, social exclusion, rejection, and bullying*. New York: Taylor and Francis Group.

Williams, K. D., & Sommer, K. L. (1997). Social ostracism by coworkers: Does rejection lead to loafing or compensation? *Personality and Social Psychology Bulletin*, *23*(7), 693–706. doi:10.1177/0146167297237003

Willis, J., & Todorov, A. (2006). First Impressions: Making Up Your Mind After a 100-Ms Exposure to a Face. *Psychological Science*, *17*(7), 592–598. doi:10.1111/j.1467-9280.2006.01750.x

Wimmer, H., & Perner, J. (1983). Beliefs about beliefs: Representation and constraining function of wrong beliefs in young children's understanding of deception. *Cognition*, *13*, 103–128.

Winerip, M. (2014, February 7). Steppin up to stop sexual assault. *The New York Times*. Retrieved from http://www.nytimes.com/2014/02/09/education/edlife/stepping-up-to-stop-sexual-assault.html?_r=0

Wise, T. J. (2010). *Colorblind: The rise of post-racial politics and the retreat from racial equity*. San Francisco: City Lights Books.

Xu, X., Zuo, X., Wang, X., & Han, S. (2009). Do you feel my pain? Racial group membership modulates empathic neural responses. *Journal of Neuroscience*, *29*(26), 8525–8529. doi:10.1523/JNEUROSCI.2418-09.2009

Yan, H. (2014, February 17). Florida loud music trial: After convictions, both sides not giving up. CNN.com. Retrieved from http://www.cnn.com/2014/02/17/justice/florida-loud-music-trial

Yang, C. -c., Brown, B. B., & Braun, M. T. (2014). From Facebook to cell calls: Layers of electronic intimacy in college students' interpersonal relationships. *New Media & Society*, *16*(1), 5–23. doi:10.1177/1461444812472486

Yardi, S., & Boyd, D. (2010). Dynamic debates: An analysis of group polarization over time on twitter. *Bulletin of Science, Technology & Society*, *30*(5), 316–327. doi:10.1177/0270467610380011

Yelland, C., & Tiggemann, M. (2003). Muscularity and the gay ideal: Body dissatisfaction and disordered eating in homosexual men. *Eating Behaviors*, *4*(2), 107–116. doi:10.1016/S1471-0153(03)00014-X

Yukl, G. A. (2013). *Leadership in organizations* (8th ed.). Boston: Pearson.

Yzerbyt, V. Y., & Leyens, J.-P. (1991). Requesting information to form an impression: The influence of valence and confirmatory status. *Journal of Experimental Social Psychology*, *27*(4), 337–356. doi:10.1016/0022-1031(91)90030-A

Zaccaro, S. J., & Lowe, C. A. (1988). Cohesiveness and performance on an additive task: Evidence for multidimensionality. *The Journal of Social Psychology*, *128*(4), 547–558.

Zaccaro, S. J., & McCoy, M. C. (1988). The effects of task and interpersonal cohesiveness on performance of a disjunctive group task. *Journal of Applied Social Psychology*, *18*(10), 837–851.

Zadro, L., Williams, K. D., & Richardson, R. (2004). How low can you go? Ostracism by a computer is sufficient to lower self-reported levels of belonging, control, self-esteem, and meaningful existence. *Journal of Experimental Social Psychology*, *40*(4), 560–567. doi:10.1016/j.jesp.2003.11.006

Zajonc, R. B. (1965). Social facilitation. *Science*, *149*(3681), 269–274.

Zhong, C.-B., & Leonardelli, G. J. (2008). Cold and Lonely: Does Social Exclusion Literally Feel Cold? *Psychological Science*, *19*(9), 838–842. doi:10.1111/j.1467-9280.2008.02165.x

Zillmann, D., Katcher, A. H., & Milavsky, B. (1972). Excitation transfer from physical exercise to subsequent aggressive behavior. *Journal of Experimental Social Psychology*, *8*(3), 247–259. doi:10.1016/S0022-1031(72)80005-2

Ziv, A. (1988). Teaching and learning with humor: Experiment and replication. *Journal of Experimental Education*, *57*(1), 5–15.

Zuckerman, M., & Driver, R. E. (1988). What sounds beautiful is good: The vocal attractiveness stereotype. *Journal of Nonverbal Behavior*, *13*(2), 67–82. doi:10.1007/BF00990791

Index